ISBN 978-1-332-54115-7
PIBN 10120495

1 MONTH OF
FREE
READING

at

www.ForgottenBooks.com

By purchasing this book you are eligible for one month membership to ForgottenBooks.com, giving you unlimited access to our entire collection of over 700,000 titles via our web site and mobile apps.

To claim your free month visit:

www.forgottenbooks.com/free120495

English
Français
Deutsche
Italiano
Español
Português

www.forgottenbooks.com

Mythology Photography **Fiction**
Fishing Christianity **Art** Cooking
Essays Buddhism Freemasonry
Medicine **Biology** Music **Ancient**
Egypt Evolution Carpentry Physics
Dance Geology **Mathematics** Fitness
Shakespeare **Folklore** Yoga Marketing
Confidence Immortality Biographies
Poetry **Psychology** Witchcraft
Electronics Chemistry History **Law**
Accounting **Philosophy** Anthropology
Alchemy Drama Quantum Mechanics
Atheism Sexual Health **Ancient History**
Entrepreneurship Languages Sport
Paleontology Needlework Islam
Metaphysics Investment Archaeology
Parenting Statistics Criminology
Motivational

CARDIPHONIA:

OR,

THE UTTERANCE OF THE HEART

June 2, 2017

Dr. Edwards,

Despite my increased cynicism pointed out by my wife, you have positively impacted me in ways that I hope will reach to my children's children and beyond, all for the ultimate cause of Christ in this fallen world. My family and I are indebted to you, and though this book is wonderful, I doubt it will repay that debt. Accept this book as a token of gratitude, nevertheless, and may it somehow prove useful in your own walk with the Lord.

Sincerely,

Drew Santa

CARDIPHONIA:

OR,

THE UTTERANCE OF THE HEART;

IN THE COURSE OF

A REAL CORRESPONDENCE

BY

THE REV. JOHN NEWTON

RECTOR OF ST. MARY WOOLNOTH, LONDON

WITH AN APPRECIATION BY

REV. DR. ALEXANDER WHYTE

PRINCIPAL OF NEW COLLEGE, EDINBURGH

AUTHOR OF "BIBLE CHARACTERS," "BUNYAN CHARACTERS," ETC

Hæc res et jungit, junctos et servat amicos.
Hor. Lib. i. Sat. 3.

As in water face answereth to face, so the
heart of man to man.   Prov. xxvii. 19.

LONDON

MORGAN & SCOTT LD.

12, PATERNOSTER BUILDINGS, E.C.

MCMXI

AN APPRECIATION BY
REV. DR. ALEXANDER WHYTE

"My Cardiphonia," as William Cowper baptized this book, is an English classic of rare excellence and of very high value. Very much what Cowper's own letters are in pure literature, that his friend's letters are in the literature of personal and evangelical religion.

"Newton's most distinctive office in the great Evangelical Revival was to be a writer of spiritual letters." And "the letters are full of passages hardly surpassed for their genuine beauty." The truth is the whole Cardiphonia is a volume of the purest apostolical and evangelical truth, written in a strong, clear, level, and idiomatic English style. For myself, I keep John Newton on my selectest shelf of spiritual books : by far the best kind of books in the whole world of books. In my opinion you are doing your publishing what appears under his name, that circumstance has some-times given occasion to an indiscriminate and injudicious publication of letters collected from all quarters, in which more attention is paid to the bulk than the value. For amongst a number of letters written to intimate friends, some will be too trivial to deserve notice, and others may be so intermingled with details of private or domestic concerns, as perhaps to give pain to those who are interested in them, when they see them in print. The writer of the following Letters thought himself more competent to decide at present, which and how much of the papers before him might be not utterly unworthy of being preserved, than a stranger could be after his decease.

Farther, he finds, that between an increase of engagements on the one hand, and the unavoidable effects of advancing years on the other, he can expect but little leisure or ability for writing letters in future, except upon necessary business. By this method of sending to each of his correspondents many letters at once, he takes leave of them with the less regret, persuaded that he thus communicates the substance of all he could offer, if he was able to write to them severally as often and as much at large as in times past.

Though some attention has been paid to variety, it was not practicable wholly to avoid what may be thought repetition, without destroying the texture and connexion of many letters ; particularly in those which treat of afflic-tion. But where the same subject recurs, it is usually placed in something of a different point of view, or illustrated in a different manner.

Thus much to bespeak the reader's favourable and candid perusal of what is now put into his hands. But the writer stands before a higher tribunal, and would be much to be pitied if he were not conscious, that in this publication he has no allowed aims, but to be subservient to the gracious designs of God by the Gospel, and to promote the good of his fellow-creatures.

Nov. 19, 1780.

LETTERS TO A NOBLEMAN

LETTER I

My Lord,   *March — 1765.*

I REMEMBER, when I once had the pleasure of waiting on you, you were pleased to begin an interesting conversation, which, to my concern, was soon interrupted. The subject was concerning the causes, nature, and marks of a decline in grace ; how it happens that we lose that warm impression of divine things, which in some favoured moments we think it almost impossible to forget ; how far this change of frame is consistent with a spiritual growth in other respects ; how to form a comparative judgment of our proficiency upon the whole ; and by what steps the losses we sustain from our necessary connexions with a sinful nature and a sinful world may be retrieved from time to time. I beg your Lordship's permission to fill up the paper with a view to these inquiries. I do not mean to offer a 'aboured essay on them, but such thoughts as shall occur while the pen is in my hand.

The awakened soul (especially when, after a season of distress and terror, it begins to taste that the Lord is gracious) finds itself as in a new world. No change in outward life can be so sensible, so affecting. No wonder, then, that at such a time little else can be thought of ; the transition from darkness to light, from a sense of wrath to a hope of glory, is the greatest that can be imagined, and is oftentimes as sudden as wonderful. Hence the general characteristics of young converts are zeal and love. Like Israel at the Red Sea, they have just seen the wonderful works of the Lord, and they cannot but sing His praise ; they are deeply affected with the danger they have lately escaped, and with the case of multitudes around them, who are secure and careless in the same alarming situation ; and a sense of their own mercies, and a compassion for the souls of others, is so transporting, that they can hardly forbear preaching to every one they meet.

This emotion is highly just and reasonable, with respect to the causes from whence it springs ; and it is doubtless a proof, not only of the imperfection, but the depravity of our nature, that we are not always thus affected ;—yet it is not entirely genuine. If we examine this character closely, which seems at first sight a pattern and a reproof to Christians of longer standing, we shall for the most part find it attended with considerable defects.

1. Such persons are very weak in faith. Their confidence arises rather from the lively impressions of joy within, than from a distinct and clear apprehension of the work of God in Christ. The comforts which are intended as cordials to animate them against the opposition of an unbelieving world, they mistake and rest in as the proper evidences of their hope. And hence it comes to pass, that when the Lord varies His dispensations, and hides His face, they are soon troubled and at their wits' end.

2. They who are in this state of their first love are seldom free from something of a censorious spirit. They have not yet felt all the deceitfulness of their own hearts ; they are not well acquainted with the devices or temptations of Satan ; and therefore know not how to sympathize or make allowances, where allowances are necessary and due, and can hardly bear with any who do not discover the same earnestness as themselves.

3. They are likewise more or less under the influence of self-righteousness and self-will. They mean well ; but not being as yet well acquainted with the spiritual meaning and proper use of the law, nor established in the life of faith, a part (oftentimes a very considerable part) of their zeal spends itself in externals and non-essentials, prompts them to practise what is not commanded, to refrain from what is lawful, and to observe various and needless austerities and singularities, as their tempers and circumstances differ.

However, with all their faults, methinks there is something very beautiful and engaging in the honest vehemence of a young convert. Some cold and rigid judges are ready to reject these promising appearances, on account of incidental blemishes. But would a gardener throw away a fine nectarine, because it is green, and has not yet attained all that beauty and flavour which a few more showers and suns will impart ? Perhaps it will hold for the most part in grace as in nature (some exceptions there are), if there is not some fire in youth, we can hardly expect a proper warmth in old age.

But the great and good Husbandman watches over what His own hand has planted, and carries on His work by a variety of different, and even contrary dispensations. While their mountain stands thus strong, they think they shall never be moved ; but at length they find a change. Sometimes it comes on by insensible degrees. That part of their affection which was purely natural, will abate of course when the power of novelty ceases ; they will begin, in some instances, to perceive their own indiscretions, and an endeavour to correct the excesses of imprudent zeal will often draw them towards the contrary extreme of remissness ; the evils of their hearts, which, though overpowered, were not eradicated, will revive again : the enemy will watch his occasions to meet them with suitable temptations ; and as it is the Lord's design that they should experimentally learn and feel their own weakness, he will, in some instances, be permitted to succeed. When guilt is thus brought upon the conscience, the heart grows hard, the hands feeble, and the knees weak ; then confidence is shaken, the spirit of prayer interrupted, the armour gone, and thus things grow worse and worse, till the Lord is pleased to interpose : for though we can fall of ourselves, we cannot rise without His help. Indeed, every sin, in its own nature, has a tendency towards a final apostacy ; but there is a provision in the covenant of grace, and the Lord, in His own time, returns to convince, humble, pardon, comfort, and renew the soul. He touches the rock, and the waters flow. By repeated experiments and exercises of this sort (for this wisdom is seldom acquired by one or a few lessons), we begin at length to learn that we are nothing, have nothing, can do nothing, but sin. And thus we are gradually prepared to live more out of ourselves, and to derive all our sufficiency of every kind from Jesus, the fountain of grace. We learn to tread more warily, to trust less to our own strength, to have lower thoughts of ourselves, and higher thoughts of *Him;* in which two last particulars I apprehend what the Scripture means by a growth of grace does properly consist. Both are increasing in the lively Christian :—every day shows him more of his own heart, and more of the power, sufficiency, compassion, and grace of his adorable Redeemer; but neither will be complete till we get to Heaven.

I apprehend, therefore, that though we find an abatement of that sensible warmth of affection which we felt at first setting out ;—yet if our views are more evangelical, our judgment more ripened, our hearts more habitually humbled under a sense of inward depravity, our tempers more softened into sympathy and tenderness ; if our prevailing desires are spiritual, and we practically esteem the precepts, ordinances, and people of God ; we may warrantably con-clude, that His good work of grace in us is, upon the whole, on an increase.

But still it is to be lamented, that an increase of know-ledge and experience should be so generally attended with a decline of fervour. If it was not for what has passed in my own heart, I should be ready to think it impossible. But this very circumstance gives me a still more emphatical conviction of my own vileness and depravity. The want of humiliation humbles me, and my very indifference rouses and awakens me to earnestness. There are, however, sea-sons of refreshment, ineffable glances of light and power upon the soul, which, as they are derived from clearer displays of divine grace, if not so tumultuous as the first joys, are more penetrating, transforming, and animating. A glance of these, when compared with our sluggish stupidity when they are withheld, weans the heart from this wretched state of sin and temptation, and makes the thoughts of death and eternity desirable. Then this conflict shall cease ;—I shall sin and wander no more, see Him as He is, and be like Him for ever.

If the question is, How are these bright moments to be prolonged, renewed, or retrieved ? we are directed to faith and diligence. A careful use of the appointed means of grace, a watchful endeavour to avoid the occasions and appearances of evil, and especially assiduity in secret prayer, will bring us as much of them as the Lord sees good for us. He knows best why we are not to be trusted with them continually. Here we are to walk by faith, to be exercised and tried ; by and by we shall be crowned, and the desires He has given shall be abundantly satisfied.

I am, &c.

LETTER II

MY LORD,   *April* — 1766.

I SHALL embrace your permission to fill my paper.— As to subject, that which has been a frequent theme of my heart of late, I shall venture to lay before your Lordship. —I mean the remarkable and humbling difference, which I suppose all who know themselves may observe, between their acquired and their experimental knowledge, or, in other words, between their judgment and their practice. To hear a believer speak his apprehensions of the evil of sin, the vanity of the world, the love of Christ, the beauty of holiness, or the importance of eternity, who would not suppose him proof against temptation ? To hear with what strong arguments he can recommend watchfulness, prayer, forbearance, and submission, when he is teaching or advising others, who would not suppose but he could also teach himself, and influence his own conduct ? Yet, alas ! *Quam dispar sibi !* The person who rose from his knees, before he left his chamber, a poor indigent, fallible, dependent creature, who saw and acknowledged that he was unworthy to breathe the air or to see the light, may meet with many occasions, before the day is closed, to discover the corruptions of his heart, and to show how weak and faint his best principles and clearest convictions are in their actual exercise. And in this view, how vain is man ! what a contradiction is a believer to himself ! He is called a *believer* emphatically, because he cordially assents to the word of God ; but, alas ! how often unworthy of the name !

If I was to describe him from the Scripture-character, I should say, he is one whose heart is athirst for God, for His glory, His image, His presence : his affections are fixed upon an unseen Saviour : his treasures, and consequently his thoughts, are on high, beyond the bounds of sense. Having experienced much forgiveness, he is full of bowels of mercy to all around ; and having been often deceived by his own heart, he dares trust it no more, but alive by faith in the Son of God, for wisdom, righteousness, and sanctification, and derives from Him grace for grace ; sensible that without Him he has not sufficiency even to think a good thought. In short, he is dead to the world, to sin, to self, but alive to God, and lively in His service. Prayer is his breath, the word of God his food, and the ordinances more precious to him than the light of the sun. Such is a believer—in his judgment and prevailing desires.

But was I to describe him from experience, especially at some times, how different would the picture be ! Though he knows that communion with God is his highest privilege, he too seldom finds it so ; on the contrary, if duty, con- science, and necessity did not compel, he would leave the throne of grace unvisited from day to day. He takes up the Bible, conscious that it is the fountain of life and true comfort ; yet, perhaps, while he is making the reflection, he feels a secret distaste which prompts him to lay it down, and give his preference to a newspaper. He needs not to be told of the vanity and uncertainty of all beneath the sun ; and yet is almost as much elated or cast down by a trifle, as those who have their portion in this world. He believes that all things shall work together for his good, and that the most high God appoints, adjusts, and over-rules all his concerns ; yet he feels the risings of fear, anxiety, and displeasure, as though the contrary was true. He owns himself ignorant, and liable to be deceived by a thousand fallacies ; yet is easily betrayed into positiveness and self- conceit. He feels himself an unprofitable, unfaithful, un- thankful servant, and therefore blushes to harbour a thought of desiring the esteem and commendations of men, yet he cannot suppress it. Finally, (for I must observe some bounds,) on account of these and many other inconsist- encies, he is struck dumb before the Lord, stripped of every hope and plea, but what is provided in the free grace of God, and yet his heart is continually leaning and returning to a covenant of works.

Two questions naturally arise from such a view of ourselves. First,—How can these things be, or why are they permitted ? Since the Lord hates sin, teaches His people to hate it and cry against it, and has promised to hear their prayers, how is it that they go thus burthened ? Surely if He could not or would not overrule evil for good, He would not permit it to continue. By these exercises He teaches us more truly to know and feel the utter depravity and corruption of our whole nature, that we are indeed defiled in every part. His method of salvation is likewise hereby exceedingly endeared to us ; we see that it is and must be of grace, wholly of grace ; and that the Lord Jesus Christ, and His perfect righteousness, is and must be our all in all. His power likewise in maintaining His own work, notwithstanding our infirmities, temptations, and enemies, is hereby displayed in the clearest light,—his strength is manifested in our weakness. Satan likewise is more remarkably disappointed and put to shame, when he finds bounds set to his rage and policy, beyond which he cannot pass ; and that those in whom he finds so much to work upon, and over whom he so often prevails for a season, escape at last out of his hands. He casts them down, but they are raised again ; he wounds them, but they are healed ; he obtains his desire to sift them as wheat, but the prayer of their great Advocate prevails for the maintenance of their faith. Farther, by what believers feel in themselves, they learn by degrees how to warn, pity, and bear with others. A soft, patient, and compassionate spirit, and a readiness and skill in comforting those who are cast down, is not perhaps attainable in any other way. And lastly, I believe nothing more habitually reconciles a child of God to the thought of death, than the wearisomeness of this warfare. Death is unwelcome to nature ;—but then, and not till then, the conflict will cease. Then we shall sin no more. The flesh, with all its attendant evils, will be laid in the grave ;—then the soul, which has been partaker of a new and heavenly birth, shall be freed from every incumbrance, and stand perfect in the Redeemer's righteousness before God in glory.

C. B

But though these evils cannot be wholly removed, it is worth while to inquire, Secondly, How they may be mitigated ? This we are encouraged to hope for. The word of God directs and animates to a growth in grace. And though we can do nothing spiritually of ourselves, yet there is a part assigned us. We cannot conquer the obstacles in our way by our own strength ; yet we can give way to them ; and if we do, it is our sin, and will be our sorrow. The disputes concerning inherent power in the creature, have been carried to inconvenient lengths : for my own part, I think it safe to use Scriptural language.—The apostles exhort us· to give all diligence to resist the devil, to purge ourselves from all filthiness of flesh and spirit, to give ourselves to reading, meditation, and prayer, to watch, to put on the whole armour of God, and to abstain from all appearance of evil. Faithfulness to light received, and a sincere endeavour to conform to the means prescribed in the word of God, with a humble application to the blood of sprinkling, and the promised Spirit, will undoubtedly be answered by increasing measures of light, faith, strength, and comfort ; and we shall know, if we follow on to know the Lord.

I need not tell your Lordship that I am an extempore writer. I dropt the consideration of whom I was addressing from the first paragraph : but I now return, and subscribe myself with the greatest deference, &c.

LETTER III

My Lord,   *April* — 1770.

I HAVE a desire to fill the paper, and must therefore betake myself to the expedient I lately mentioned. Glorious things are spoken of the city of God, or (as I suppose) the state of glory, in Rev. xxi. from verse 10 *ad finem*. The description is doubtless mystical, and perhaps nothing short of a happy experience and participation will furnish an adequate exposition. One expression, in particular, has, I believe, puzzled wiser heads than mine to explain. *The street of the city was pure gold, as it were transparent glass.* The construction likewise in the Greek is difficult. Some render it *pure gold transparent as glass :* this is the sense, but then it should be neuter διαφανες to agree with χρυσιον. If our reading is right, we must understand it either of *gold, pure,* bright, and perspicuous as the finest transparent glass, (for all glass is not transparent,) or else, as two distinct comparisons, splendid and durable as the purest gold, clear and transparent as the finest glass. In that happy world, the beauties and advantages which here are divided and incompatible, will unite and agree. Our glass is clear, but brittle ; our gold is shining and solid, but it is opaque, and discovers only a surface. And thus it is with our minds. The powers of the imagination are lively and extensive, but transient and uncertain. The powers of the understanding are more solid and regular, but at the same time more slow and limited, and confined to the outside properties of the few objects around us. But when we arrive within the vail, the perfections of the glass and the gold will be combined, and the imperfections of each will entirely cease. Then we shall *know* more than we can imagine. *The glass will be all gold.* And then we shall apprehend truth in its relations and consequences ; not (as at present) by that tedious and fallible process which we call *reasoning,* but by a single glance of thought, as the sight pierces in an instant through the largest transparent body. *The gold will be all glass.*

I do not offer this as the sense of the passage, but as a thought which once occurred to me while reading it. I daily groan under a desultory ungovernable imagination, and a palpable darkness of understanding, which greatly impede me in my attempts to contemplate the truths of God. Perhaps these complaints, in a greater or less degree, are common to all our fallen race, and exhibit mournful proofs that our nature is essentially depraved. The grace of God affords some assistance for correcting the wildness of the fancy, and enlarging the capacity of the mind : yet the cure at present is but palliative ; but ere long it shall be perfect, and our complaints shall cease for ever. Now it costs us much pains to acquire a *pittance* of solid and useful knowledge ; and the ideas we have collected are far from being at the disposal of judgment, and, like men in a crowd, are perpetually clashing and interfering with each other. But it will not be so when we are completely freed from the effects of sin. Confusion and darkness will not follow us into the world where light and order reign. Then, and not till then, our knowledge will be perfect, and our possession of it uninterrupted and secure.

Since the radical powers of the soul are thus enfeebled and disordered, it is not to be wondered at that the best of men, and under their highest attainments, have found cause to make the acknowledgment of the apostle, " When I would do good, evil is present with me." But, blessed be God, though we must feel hourly cause for shame and humiliation for what we are in ourselves, we have cause to rejoice continually in Christ Jesus, who, as He is revealed unto us under the various names, characters, relations, and offices, which He bears in the Scripture, holds out to our faith a balm for every wound, a cordial for every discouragement, and a sufficient answer to every objection which sin or Satan can suggest against our peace. If we are guilty, He is our righteousness ; if we are sick, He is our infallible Physician ; if we are weak, helpless, and defenceless, He is the compassionate and faithful Shepherd who has taken charge of us, and will not suffer any thing to disappoint our hopes, or to separate us from His love. He knows our frame, He remembers that we are but dust, and has engaged to guide us by His counsel, support us by His power, and at length to receive us to His glory, that we may be with Him for ever.

I am, with the greatest deference, &c.

LETTER IV

My Lord,   *February — 1772.*

I HAVE been sitting perhaps a quarter of an hour with my pen in my hand, and my finger upon my upper lip, contriving how I should begin my letter.—A detail of

the confused, incoherent thoughts which have succes-
sively passed through my mind, would have more than
filled the sheet ; but your Lordship's patience, and even
your charity for the writer, would have been tried to the
uttermost if I could have penned them all down. At length
my suspense reminded me of the apostle's words, Gal. v.
17 : " Ye cannot do the things that ye would." This is an
humbling but a just account of a Christian's attainments in
the present life, and is equally applicable to the strongest
and to the weakest. The weakest need not say *less*, the
strongest will hardly venture to say *more*. The Lord has
given His people a desire and will, aiming at great things ;
without this they would be unworthy the name of Chris-
tians ; but they cannot do as they would : their best desires
are weak and ineffectual, not absolutely so, (for He who
works in them to will, enables them in a measure to do
likewise,) but in comparison with the mark at which they
aim. So that while they have great cause to be thankful
for the desire He has given them, and for the degree in which
it is answered, they have equal reason to be ashamed and
abased under a sense of their continual defects, and the evil
mixtures which taint and debase their best endeavours.
It would be easy to make out a long list of particulars
which a believer would do if he could, but in which, from
first to last, he finds a mortifying inability. Permit me to
mention a few, which I need not to transcribe from books,
for they are always present to my mind.

He would willingly enjoy God in prayer :—he knows
that prayer is his duty ; but in his judgment he considers
it likewise as his greatest honour and privilege. In this
light he can recommend it to others, and can tell them of
the wonderful condescension of the great God, who humbles
Himself to behold the things that are in heaven, that He
should stoop so much lower, to afford His gracious ear to the
supplications of sinful worms upon earth. He can bid them
expect a pleasure in waiting upon the Lord, different
in kind, and greater in degree than all that the world can
afford. By prayer, he can say, You have liberty to cast all
your cares upon Him that careth for you. By one hour's
intimate access to the Throne of Grace, where the Lord
causes His glory to pass before the soul that seeks Him, you

may acquire more true spiritual knowledge and comfort
than by a day or a week's converse with the best of men,
or the most studious perusal of many folios : and in this
light he would consider it and improve it for himself. But
alas ! how seldom can he do as he would ? how often
does he find this privilege a mere task, which he would be
glad of a just excuse to omit ; and the chief pleasure he
derives from the performance is to think that his task is
finished :—he has been drawing near to God with his lips,
while his heart was far from Him. Surely this is not doing
as he would, when (to borrow the expression of an old
woman here) he is dragged before God like a slave, and
comes away like a thief.

The like may be said of reading the Scripture. He be-
lieves it to be the word of God : he admires the wisdom and
grace of the doctrines, the beauty of the precepts, the rich-
ness and suitableness of the promises ; and therefore, with
David, he accounts it preferable to thousands of gold and
silver, and sweeter than honey or the honey comb. Yet
while he thus thinks of it, and desires that it may dwell in
him richly, and be his meditation night and day, he cannot
do as he would. It will require some resolution to persist
in reading a portion of it every day ; and even then his
heart is often less engaged than when reading a pamphlet.
Here again his privilege frequently dwindles into a task.
His appetite is vitiated, so that he has but little relish for
the food of his soul.

He would willingly have abiding, admiring thoughts
of the person and love of the Lord Jesus Christ. Glad he
is, indeed, of those occasions which recall the Saviour to
his mind ; and with this view, notwithstanding all dis-
couragements, he perseveres in attempting to pray and
read, and waits upon the ordinances. Yet he cannot
do as he would. Whatever claims he may have to the
exercise of gratitude and sensibility towards his fellow-
creatures, he must confess himself mournfully ungrateful
and insensible towards his best friend and benefactor. Ah !
what trifles are capable of shutting *Him* out of our thoughts,
of whom we say, He is the beloved of our souls, who loved
us, and gave Himself for us, and whom we have deliberately
chosen as our chief good and portion. What can make us

amends for the loss we suffer here? Yet, surely if we *could* we *would* set Him always before us ; His love should be the delightful theme of our hearts,

> From morn to noon, from noon to dewy eve.

But though we aim at this good, evil is present with us ; we find we are renewed but in part, and have still cause to plead the Lord's promise, To take away the heart of stone, and give us a heart of flesh.

He would willingly acquiesce in all the dispensations of divine Providence. He believes that all events are under the direction of infinite wisdom and goodness, and shall surely issue in the glory of God, and the good of those who fear Him. He doubts not but the hairs of his head are all numbered, that the blessings of every kind which he possesses were bestowed upon him, and are preserved to him, by the bounty and special favour of the Lord whom he serves ; that afflictions spring not out of the ground, but are fruits and tokens of Divine love, no less than His comforts ;—that there is a need-be, whenever for a season he is in heaviness. Of these principles he can no more doubt than of what he sees with his eyes, and there are seasons when he thinks they will prove sufficient to reconcile him to the sharpest trials. But often when he aims to apply them in an hour of *present* distress, he cannot do what he would. He feels a law in his members warring against the law in his mind ; so that, in defiance of the clearest conviction, seeing as though he per-ceived not, he is ready to complain, murmur, and despond. Alas ! how vain is man in his best estate ! How much weakness and inconsistency, even in those whose hearts are right with the Lord ! and what reason have we to confess that we are unworthy, unprofitable servants !

It were easy to enlarge in this way, would paper and time permit. But, blessed be God, we are not under the law, but under grace. And even these distressing effects of the rem-nants of indwelling sin are over-ruled for good. By these experiences, the believer is weaned more from self, and taught more highly to prize and more absolutely to rely on Him who is appointed unto us of God, wisdom, righteous-ness, sanctification, and redemption. The more vile we are in our own eyes, the more precious He will be to us ; and a deep-rooted sense of the evil of our hearts is necessary to preclude all boasting, and to make us willing to give the whole glory of our salvation where it is due.　Again, a sense of these evils will (when hardly any thing else can do it) reconcile us to the thoughts of death ; yea, make us desirous to depart that we may sin no more, since we find depravity so deep rooted in our nature, that (like the leprous house) the whole fabric must be taken down before we can be freed from its defilement.　Then, and not till then, we shall be able to do the thing that we would : when we see Jesus, we shall be transformed into His image, and have done with sin and sorrow for ever.

I am, with great deference, &c.

LETTER V

My Lord,　　　　　　　　　　　　　　　*March —* 1772.

　　I THINK my last letter turned upon the Apostle's thought, Gal. v. 17 :　" Ye cannot do the things that ye would."　In the parallel place, Rom. vii. 19, there is another clause subjoined, " The evil which I would not, that I do." This, added to the former, would complete the dark side of my experience.　Permit me to tell your Lordship a little part, (for some things must not, cannot be told,) not of what I have read, but of what I have felt, in illustration of this passage.

　　I *would not* be the sport and prey of wild, vain, foolish, and worse imaginations ; but this evil is present with me ; my heart is like a highway, like a city without walls or gates.　Nothing so false, so frivolous, so absurd, so impossible, or so horrid, but it can obtain access, and that at any time, or in any place : neither the study, the pulpit, nor even the Lord's table, exempt me from their intrusion.　I sometimes compare my *words* to the treble of an instrument, which my *thoughts* accompany with a kind of bass, or rather antibass, in which every rule of harmony is broken, every possible combination of discord and confusion is introduced, utterly inconsistent with, and contradictory to, the intended melody.　Ah ! what music would my praying and preaching often make in the ears of the Lord of Hosts, if He listened to them as they are *mine* only! By men, the upper part only (if I may so speak) is heard; and small cause there is for self-gratulation, if *they* should happen to commend, when conscience tells me they would be struck with astonishment and abhorrence could they hear the whole.

But if this awful effect of heart-depravity cannot be wholly avoided in the present state of human nature, yet at least I would not allow and indulge it; yet this I find I do. In defiance of my best judgment and best wishes, I find something within me which cherishes and cleaves to those evils, from which I ought to start and flee, as I should if a toad or a serpent was put in my food or in my bed. Ah! how vile must the heart (at least my heart) be, that can hold a parley with such abominations, when I so well know their nature and their tendency! Surely he who finds himself capable of this, may, without the least affectation of humility, (however fair his outward conduct appears,) subscribe himself less than the least of all saints, and of sinners the very chief.

I would not be influenced by a principle of self on any occasion; yet this evil I often do. I see the baseness and absurdity of such a conduct as clearly as I see the light of the day. I do not affect to be thought ten feet high, and I know that a desire of being thought wise or good, is equally contrary to reason and truth. I should be grieved or angry if my fellow-creatures supposed I had such a desire; and therefore I fear the very principle of self, of which I complain, has a considerable share in prompting my desires to conceal it. The pride of others often offends me, and makes me studious to hide my own; because their good opinion of me depends much upon their not perceiving it. But the Lord knows how this dead fly taints and spoils my best services, and makes them no better than specious sins.

I would not indulge vain reasonings concerning the counsels, ways, and providences of God; yet I am prone to do it. That the Judge of all the earth will do right is to me as evident and necessary as that two and two make four. I believe that He has a sovereign right to do what He will with His own, and that this sovereignty is but another name for the unlimited exercise of wisdom and goodness. But my reasonings are often such, as if I had never heard of these principles, or had formally renounced them. I feel the workings of a presumptuous spirit, that would account for every thing, and venture to dispute whatever it cannot comprehend. What an evil is this, for a potsherd of the earth to contend with its Maker! I do not act thus towards my fellow-creatures ; I do not find fault with the decisions of a judge, or the dispositions of a general, because, though I know they are fallible, yet I suppose they are wiser in their respective departments than myself. But I am often ready to take this liberty when it is most unreasonable and inexcusable.

I would not cleave to a covenant of works : it should seem from the foregoing particulars, and many others which I could mention, that I have reasons enough to deter me from this. Yet even this I do. Not but that I say, and I hope from my heart, Enter not into judgment with Thy servant, O Lord. I embrace it as a faithful saying and worthy of all acceptation, that Jesus Christ came into the world to save sinners ; and it is the main pleasure and business of my life, to set forth the necessity and all-sufficiency of the Mediator between God and man, and to make mention of His right-eousness, even of His only. But here, as in every thing else, I find a vast difference between my judgment and my experience. I am invited to take the water of life *freely*, yet often discouraged, because I have nothing wherewith to pay for it. If I am at times favoured with some liberty from the above-mentioned evils, it rather gives me a more favour-able opinion of myself than increases my admiration of the Lord's goodness to so unworthy a creature ; and when the returning tide of my corruptions convinces me that *I am still the same*, an unbelieving legal spirit would urge me to conclude that the Lord is changed : at least, I feel a weari-ness of being beholden to Him for such continued multiplied forgiveness ; and I fear that some part of my striving against sin, and my desires after an increase of sanctification, arise from a secret wish that I might not be so absolutely and entirely indebted to Him.

This, my Lord, is only a faint sketch of my heart ; but it is taken from the life : it would require a volume rather than a letter to fill up the outlines. But I believe you will

not regret that I choose to say no more upon such a sub-
ject.   But though my disease is grievous, it is not desperate ;
I have a gracious and infallible Physician.   I shall not
die, but live, and declare the works of the Lord.

I remain, my Lord, &c.

LETTER VI

My Lord,   *April —* 1772.

MY two last letters turned upon a mournful subject,
the depravity of the heart, which impedes us when we
would do good, and pollutes our best intended services with
evil.   We have cause, upon this account, to go softly all our
days ; yet we need not sorrow as they who have no hope.
The Lord has provided His people relief under those com-
plaints, and teaches us to draw improvment from them.
If the evils we feel were not capable of being overruled for
good, He would not permit them to remain in us.   This
we may infer from His hatred to sin, and the love which
He bears to His people.

As to the remedy, neither our state nor His honour are
affected by the workings of indwelling sin, in the hearts of
those whom He has taught to wrestle, strive, and mourn,
on account of what they feel.   Though sin wars, it shall not
reign ;   and though it breaks our peace, it cannot separate
from His love.   Nor is it inconsistent with His holiness and
perfection to manifest His favour to such poor defiled crea-
tures, or to admit them to communion with Himself ; for
they are not considered as in themselves, but as one with
Jesus, to whom they have fled for refuge, and by whom
they live a life of faith.   They are accepted in the Beloved,
they have an Advocate with the *F*ather, who once made
an atonement for their sins, and ever lives to make inter-
cession for their persons.   Though they cannot fulfil the law,
He has fulfilled it for them ;   though the obedience of the
members is defiled and imperfect, the obedience of the head
is spotless and complete ;   and though there is much evil in
them, there is something good, the fruit of His own gracious

Spirit. They act from a principle of love, they aim at no less than His glory, and their habitual desires are supremely fixed upon Himself. There is a difference in kind between the feeblest efforts of faith in a real believer, while he is covered with shame at the thoughts of his miscarriages, and the highest and most specious attainments of those who are wise in their own eyes, and prudent in their own sight. Nor shall this conflict remain long, or the enemy finally prevail over them. They are supported by Almighty Power, and led on to certain victory. They shall not always be as they are now ; yet a little while, and they shall be freed from this vile body, which, like the leprous house, is incurably contaminated, and must be entirely taken down. They shall see Jesus as He is, and be like Him, and with Him for ever.

The gracious purposes to which the Lord makes the sense and feeling of our depravity subservient are manifold. Hereby His own power, wisdom, faithfulness, and love, are more signally displayed ; His power, in maintaining His own work in the midst of much opposition, like a spark burning in the water, or a bush unconsumed in the flames ; His wisdom, in defeating and controlling all the devices which Satan, from his knowledge of evil of our nature, is encouraged to practise against us. He has overthrown many a fair professor, and, like Goliath, he challenges the whole army of Israel ; yet he finds there are some against whom, though he thrusts sorely, he cannot prevail ; notwithstanding any seeming advantage he gains at some seasons, they are still delivered, for the Lord is on their side. The unchangeableness of the Lord's love and the riches of His mercy are likewise more illustrated by the multiplied pardons He bestows upon His people than if they needed no forgiveness at all.

Hereby the Lord Jesus Christ is more endeared to the soul ; all boasting is effectually excluded, and the glory of a full and free salvation is ascribed to Him alone. If a mariner is surprised by a storm, and after one night spent in jeopardy is presently brought safe into port ; though he may rejoice in his deliverance, it will not affect him so sensibly as if, after being tempest-tossed for a long season, and experiencing a great number and variety of hair-breadth escapes, he at last gains the desired haven. The righteous are said to be scarcely saved, not with respect to the certainty of the event, for the purpose of God in their favour cannot be disappointed, but in respect of their own apprehensions, and the great difficulties they are brought through. But when, after a long experience of their own deceitful hearts, after repeated proofs of their weakness, wilfulness, ingratitude, and insensibility, they find that none of these things can separate them from the love of God in Christ, Jesus becomes more and more precious to their souls. They love much, because much has been forgiven them. They dare not, they will not ascribe any thing to themselves, but are glad to acknowledge, that they must have perished (if possible) a thousand times over, if Jesus had not been their Saviour, their Shepherd, and their Shield. When they were wandering He brought them back, when fallen He raised them, when wounded He healed them, when fainting He revived them. By Him, out of weakness they have been made strong ; He has taught their hands to war, and covered their heads in the day of battle. In a word, some of the clearest proofs they have had of His excellence have been occasioned by the mortifying proofs they have had of their own vileness. They would not have known so much of Him, if they had not known so much of themselves.

Farther, a spirit of humiliation, which is both the *decus et tutamen*, the strength and beauty of our profession, is greatly promoted by our feeling, as well as reading, that when we would do good, evil is present with us. A broken and contrite spirit is pleasing to the Lord—He has promised to dwell with those who have it ; and experience shows, that the exercise of all our graces is in proportion to the humbling sense we have of the depravity of our nature. But that we are so totally depraved is a truth which no one ever truly learned by being only told it. Indeed, if we could receive, and habitually maintain a right judgment of ourselves, by what is plainly declared in Scripture, it would probably save us many a mournful hour ; but experience is the Lord's school, and they who are taught by Him usually learn that they have no wisdom by the mistakes they make, and that they have no strength by the slips and falls they meet with. Every day draws forth some new corruption which before was little observed, or at least discovers it in a stronger light than before. Thus by degrees they are weaned from leaning to any supposed wisdom, power, or goodness in themselves; they feel the truth of our Lord's words: "Without Me ye can do nothing;" and the necessity of crying with David: "O lead me and guide me for Thy name's sake." It is chiefly by this frame of mind that one Christian is differenced from another; for though it is an inward feeling, it has very observable outward effects, which are expressively intimated, Ezek. xvi. 63 : "Thou shalt be dumb and not open thy mouth, in the day when I am pacified towards thee, saith the Lord God." The knowledge of My full and free forgiveness, of thy innumerable backslidings and transgressions, shall make thee ashamed, and silence the unruly workings of thine heart. Thou shalt open thy mouth in praise; but thou shalt no more boast in thyself, or censure others, or repine at My dispensations. In these respects we are exceedingly prone to speak unadvisedly with our lips. But a sense of great unworthiness and much forgiveness checks these evils. Whoever is truly humbled will not be easily angry, will not be positive and rash, will be compassionate and tender to the infirmities of his fellow-sinners, knowing, that if there be a difference, it is grace that has made it, and that he has the seeds of every evil in his own heart; and under all trials and afflictions, he will look to the hand of the Lord, and lay his mouth in the dust, acknowledging that he suffers much less than his iniquities have deserved. These are some of the advantages and good fruits which the Lord enables us to obtain from that bitter root, indwelling sin.

　　　　　　　　I am, with great deference, &c. '

LETTER VII

My Lord,　　　　　　　　　　*September —* 1772.

　　Weak, unskilful, and unfaithful as I am in practice, the Lord has been pleased to give me some idea of what a Christian ought to be, and of what is actually attainable in the present life, by those whom He enables earnestly to aspire towards the prize of their high calling. They who are versed in mechanics can, from a knowledge of the combined powers of a complicated machine, make an exact calculation of what it is able to perform, and what resistance it can counteract, but who can compute the possible effects of that combination of principles and motives revealed in the Gospel upon a heart duly impressed with a sense of their importance and glory ? When I was lately at Mr. Coxe's museum, while I was fixing my attention upon some curious movements, imagining that I saw the whole of the artist's design, the person who showed it touched a little spring, and suddenly a thousand new and unexpected motions took place, and the whole piece seemed animated from the top to the bottom. I should have formed but a very imperfect judgment of it, had I seen no more than what I saw at first. I thought I might in some measure illustrate the vast difference that is observable amongst professors, even amongst those who are, it is to be hoped, sincere. There are persons who appear to have a true knowledge (in part) of the nature of the Gospel religion, but seem not to be apprised of its properties, in their comprehension and extent. If they have attained to some hope of their acceptance, if they find at seasons some communion with God in the means of grace, if they are in a measure delivered from the prevailing and corrupt customs of the world, they seem to be satisfied, as if they were possessed of all. These are indeed great things ; *sed meliora latent.* The profession of too many, whose sincerity charity would be unwilling to impeach, is greatly blemished, notwithstanding their hopes and their occasional comforts, by the breakings forth of unsanctified tempers, and the indulgence of vain hopes, anxious cares, and selfish pursuits. Far, very far, am I from that unscriptural sentiment of sinless perfection in fallen man. To those who have a due sense of the spirituality and ground of the divine precepts, and of what passes in their own hearts, there will never be wanting causes of humiliation and self-abasement on the account of sin ; yet still there is a liberty and privilege attainable by the Gospel beyond what is ordinarily thought of. Permit me to mention two or three particulars in which those who have a holy ambition of aspiring to them shall not be altogether disappointed.

A delight in the Lord's all-sufficiency, to be satisfied in Him as our present and eternal portion. This, in the sense in which I understand it, is not the effect of a present warm frame, but of a deeply-rooted and abiding principle ; the habitual exercise of which is to be estimated by the comparative indifference with which other things are regarded. The soul thus principled is not at leisure to take or to seek satisfaction in any thing but what has a known subserviency to this leading taste. Either the Lord is present, and then He is to be rejoiced in ; or else He is absent, and then He is to be sought and waited for. They are to be pitied, who, if they are at some times happy in the Lord, can at other times be happy without Him, and rejoice in broken cisterns, when their spirits are at a distance from the fountain of living waters. I do not plead for an absolute indifference to temporal blessings ; He gives us all things richly to *enjoy* ; and a capacity of relishing them is His gift likewise ; but then the consideration of His love in bestowing should exceedingly enhance their value, and a regard to His will should regulate their use. Nor can they all supply the want of *that* which we can only receive immediately from Himself. This principle likewise moderates that inordinate fear and sorrow to which we are liable upon the prospect or the occurrence of great trials, for which there is a sure support and resource provided in the all-sufficiency of infinite goodness and grace. What a privilege is this, to possess God *in all things* while we have them, and all things in God when they are taken from us !

An acquiescence in the Lord's will, founded in a persuasion of His wisdom, holiness, sovereignty, and goodness : this is one of the greatest privileges and brightest ornaments of our profession. So far as we attain to this, we are secure from disappointment. Our own limited views and short-sighted purposes and desires may be, and will be often overruled ; but then our main and leading desire, that the will of the Lord may be done, must be accomplished. How highly does it become us, both as creatures and as sinners, to submit to the appointments of our Maker ! and how necessary is it to our peace ! This great attainment is too often unthought of, and overlooked ; we are prone to fix our attention upon the second causes and immediate instruments of events ; forgetting that whatever befals us is according to His purpose, and therefore must be right and seasonable in itself, and shall in the issue be productive of good. From hence arise impatience, resentment, and secret repinings, which are not only sinful, but tormenting : whereas, if all things are in His hand, if the very hairs of our head are numbered ; if every event, great and small, is under the direction of His providence and purpose ; and if He has a wise, holy, and gracious end in view, to which every thing that happens is subordinate and subservient ;— then we have nothing to do but with patience and humility to follow as He leads and cheerfully to expect a happy issue. The path of present duty is marked out ; and the concerns of the next and every succeeding hour are in His hands. How happy are they who can resign all to Him, see His hand in every dispensation, and believe that He chooses better for them than they possibly could for themselves !

A single eye to His glory, as the ultimate scope of all our undertakings. The Lord can design nothing short of His own glory ; nor should we. The constraining love of Christ has a direct and marvellous tendency, in proportion to the measure of faith, to mortify the corrupt principle— *self*, which for a season is the grand spring of our conduct, and by which we are too much biassed after we know the Lord. But as grace prevails, self is renounced. We feel that we are not our own, that we are bought with a price ; and that it is our duty, our honour, and our happiness, to be the servants of God and of the Lord Jesus Christ. To devote soul and body, every talent, power, and faculty, to the service of His cause and will ; to let our light shine (in our several situations) to the praise of His grace ; to place our highest joy in the contemplation of His adorable perfections ; to rejoice even in tribulations and distresses, in reproaches and infirmities, if thereby the power of Christ may rest upon us, and be magnified in us ; to be content, yea, glad to be nothing, that He may be all in all ;—to obey *Him* in opposition to the threats or solicitations of men ; to trust *Him*, though all outward appearances seem against us ; to rejoice in *Him*, though we should (as will sooner or

c   c later be the case) have nothing else to rejoice in,—to live above the world, and to have our conversation in Heaven, to be like the angels, finding our own pleasure in performing His :—this, my Lord, is the prize, the mark of our high calling, to which we are encouraged with a holy ambition continually to aspire. It is true, we shall still fall short ; we shall find, that when we would do good, evil will be present with us ; but the attempt is glorious, and shall not be wholly in vain. He that gives us thus to *will*, will enable us to perform with growing success, and teach us to profit even by our mistakes and imperfections.

O blessed man ! that thus fears the Lord, that delights in His word, and derives his principles, motives, maxims, and consolations, from that unfailing source of light and strength. He shall be like a tree planted by the rivers of water, whose leaf is always green, and fruit abundant. The wisdom that is above shall direct his plans, inspire his counsels ; and the power of God shall guard him on every side, and prepare his way through every difficulty ; he shall see mountains sink into plains, and streams spring up in the dry wilderness. The Lord's enemies will be his ; and they may be permitted to fight against him, but they shall not prevail, for the Lord is with him to deliver him. The conduct of such a one, though in a narrow and retired sphere of life, is of more real excellence and importance than the most splendid actions of kings and conquerors which fill the annals of history, Prov. xvi. 32. And if the God whom he serves is pleased to place him in a more public light, his labours and cares will be amply compensated by the superior opportunities afforded him of manifesting the power and reality of true religion, and promoting the good of mankind.

I hope I *may* say, that I *desire* to be thus entirely given up to the Lord ; I am sure I *must* say, that what I have written is far from being my actual experience. Alas ! I might be condemned out of my own mouth, were the Lord strict to mark what is amiss. But, O the comfort ! we are not under the law, but under grace. The Gospel is a dispensation of sinners, and we have an Advocate with the Father. *There* is the unshaken ground of hope : a reconciled Father, a prevailing Advocate, a powerful Shepherd, a compassionate Friend, a Saviour who is able and willing to save to the uttermost. He knows our frame; He remembers that we are but dust; and has opened for us a new and blood-besprinkled way of access to the Throne of Grace, that we may obtain mercy, and find grace to help in every time of need.   I am, &c.

LETTER VIII

My Lord,   *April —* 1773.

For five or six weeks past, I have been a good deal indisposed. The ground of my complaint was a cold, attended with a slight fever, and for some time with a cough, which made me feel some inconvenience in preaching; to this succeeded a deafness, so great as to cut me off from conversation : for I could not hear the sound of a voice, unless it was spoken loud in my ear. But the Lord has mercifully removed the fever and cough, opened my ears, and I am now nearly as well as usual. I had cause to be thankful, especially for two things, under this dispensation : First, that I was enabled, though sometimes with a little difficulty, to go on with my public work. It is a singular favour I have to acknowledge, that for the space of almost nine years since I have been in the ministry, our Sabbath and weekly opportunities have not been once suspended : whereas I have seen many of the Lord's servants laid by for a considerable space within that time. My other great mercy was, that the Lord was pleased to preserve me in a peaceful resigned frame ; so that when I was deaf, and could not be certain that I should recover my hearing any more, I was in general as cheerful and easy as at other times. This was the effect of His goodness ; for though I know enough of His sovereignty, wisdom, and faithfulness, of His right to do what He pleases, and the certainty that He does all things well, to furnish me with arguments enough to prove that submission to His will is our absolute duty ; yet I am sensible, that when the trial actually comes, notwithstanding all the advice I may have offered to others, I should myself toss like a wild bull in a net ; rebel and repine ; forget that

I am a sinner, and that He is a sovereign : this I say would always and invariably be the case, unless He was graciously pleased to fulfil His words, that strength shall be according to the day. I hope my deafness has been instructive to me. The exercise of our senses is so easily and constantly performed, that it seems a thing of course ; but I was then reminded how precarious the tenure is by which we hold those blessings which seem most our own, and which are most immediately necessary to the comfortable enjoyment of life. Outward senses, mental faculties, health of body, and peace of mind, are extremely valuable ; but the continuance of them for a single moment depends upon Him, who, if He opens, none can shut, and when He shuts, none can open. A minute is more than sufficient to deprive us of what we hold most dear, or to prevent us from deriving the least comfort from it, if it is not taken away. I am not presuming to give your Lordship information ; but only mentioning the thoughts that were much upon my mind while I was incapable of conversation. These are indeed plain and obvious truths, which I have long acknowledged as indisputable ; but I have reason to be thankful when the Lord impresses them with fresh power upon my heart, even though He sees fit to do it by the medium of afflictions. I have seen of late something of the weight and importance of that admonition, Jer. ix. 23, 24. A passage which, though addressed to the wise, the mighty, and the rich, is of universal application ;—for self, unless corrected and mortified by grace, will find something whereof to glory, in the meanest characters and the lowest situation. And, indeed, when things come to be weighed in the balance of the sanctuary, the lunatics in bedlam, some of whom glory in their straw or their chains, as marks of splendour, or ensigns of royalty, have as much reason on their side, as any persons upon earth who glory in themselves. This alone is the proper ground of glory and joy, if we know the Lord. Then all is safe at present, and all will be happy for ever. Then whatever changes may affect our temporal concernments, our best interests and hopes are secured beyond the reach of change : and whatever we may lose or suffer during this little span of time will be abundantly compensated in that glorious state of eternity which is just at hand. I am, &c.

LETTER IX

My Lord,   *December* — 1772.

I LATELY employed some of my leisure hours (which, when I am not indolent, are but few) in reading the Memoirs of the Duke of Sully, which occasionally came in my way. It afforded me matter for variety of reflections. I pity the Duke of Sully, whose attachment to the name of a Protestant seems to have been little more than a point of honour, who drew all his resources from himself, and whose chief aim seems to have been to approve himself faithful to an earthly master. He acted as well as could be expected from natural principles ; and the Lord, who employed him as an instrument of His providence, rewarded his fidelity with success, honour, and riches : a reward which, though in itself a poor one, is suited to the desires of men who place their happiness in worldly things, and is so far a compensation of their services. It is given to your Lordship to act from nobler principles, and with more enlarged views. You serve a Master, of whose favour, protection, and assistance you cannot be deprived, who will not overlook or misconstrue the smallest service you attempt for Him, who will listen to no insinuations against you, who is always near to comfort, direct, and strengthen you, and who is preparing for you such honours and blessings as He only can give, an inheritance (the reverse of all earthly good) αφθαρτον, και αμιαντον και αμαραντον.* Thus animated and thus supported, assisted likewise by the prayers of thousands, may we not warrantably hope that your Lordship will be an instrument of great good, and that both church and state will be benefited by your example, counsel, and care ?

In another view, the Duke of Sully's History exhibits a comment upon the Psalmist's words, " Surely man in his best estate is altogether vanity." View him in one light, he seems to have possessed all that the most aspiring mind could aim at—the favour and confidence of his prince, accumulated wealth, great honours, and such power by his

---

* Incorruptible, undefiled, unfading.

offices and influence with the king, that he could almost do
what he pleased.   Yet he had so much to suffer from the
fatigues and difficulties of his station, and the cabals and
malice of his enemies, that in the midst of all his grandeur,
a dispassionate mind would rather pity than envy him.
And how suddenly were his schemes broken by the death
of the king ! Then he lost his friend, his protector, his
influence.   The remainder of his days were embittered by
many inquietudes ; he lived indeed (if that could afford any
consolation) in much state and pageantry afterwards ;
but after having toiled through more than fourscore years,
died at last almost of a broken heart from domestic uneasi-
ness.   And is this all that the world can do for those who are
accounted most successful ?   Alas !

Too low they build, who build below the skies.

And what a picture of the instability of human things
have we in his master, Henry !   Admired, beloved, dreaded,
full of vast designs, fondly supposing himself born to be the
arbiter of Europe, in an awful moment, and in the midst of
his friends, suddenly struck from the height of his grandeur,
and snatched into the invisible, unchangeable world.   In
that moment all his thoughts perished.

How unspeakably awful such a transition ! How re-
markable were his own forebodings of the approaching hour !
O Lord, how dost Thou pour contempt upon princes and
teach us that the great and the mean are equally in Thy
hands, and at Thy disposal, as clay in the hands of the
potter ! Poor king ! while he expected obedience to his
own commands, he lived in habitual defiance of the
commands of God.   Men may respect his memory, for his
sincerity, benevolence, and other amiable qualities ; but
besides that he was engrossed by a round of sensual
pleasures, (when business of State did not interfere,) his life
was stained with adultery.   Happy if, in the hours he spent
in retirement, when the pre-intimation of his death hung
heavy upon his mind, the Lord humbled and softened his
heart, and gave him repentance unto life ! I wish the
history afforded a proof of this.   However, in his death,
we see an affecting proof, that no human dignity or power
can ward off the stroke of the Almighty, who, by such

sudden and unexpected dispensations, often shows Himself terrible to the princes and great men of the earth. O! that they could see His hand, and wisely consider His doing in them!

But happy is the man who fears the Lord, and delights in His commandments; who sets God always before him, and acts under the constraining influence of redeeming love. *He* is the real friend and the best champion of his country, who makes not the vague notions of human wisdom and honour, but the precepts and examples of the blessed Jesus, the model and the motive of his conduct. He inculcates (as occasion offers) the great truths of religion in his conversation, and demonstrates them by his practice; yet the best part of his life is known only to God and himself. His time is divided between serving his country in public, and wrestling for it in private. Nor shall his labours or his prayers be lost. Either he shall have the desire of his heart, and shall see the religion and the liberty he so highly values transmitted to posterity; or, if he should live when wrath is decreed, and there is no remedy, the promise and the providence of God shall seal him as the peculiar charge of angels, in the midst of public calamity. And when all things are involved in confusion, when the hearts of the wicked shall shake like the leaves of the forest, he shall be kept in perfect peace, trusting in the Lord.

I am, with the greatest deference, &c.

LETTER X

My Lord,   *March — 1773.*

USUALLY for some days before I purpose writing to your Lordship, my thoughts are upon the stretch for a subject; I do not mean all day long, but it is so more or less; but I might as well spare my inquiries, I can come to no determination, and for the most part begin to write at an absolute uncertainty how I am to proceed. Since I cannot premeditate, my heart prays that it may be given me in the same hour what I shall offer. A simple dependence upon the teaching and influence of the good Spirit of God, so as not to supersede the use of appointed means, would, if it could be uniformly maintained, make every part of duty easy and successful. It would free us from much solicitude, and prevent many mistakes.—Methinks I have a subject in view already, a subject of great importance to myself, and which perhaps will not be displeasing to your Lordship : How to walk with God in the daily occurrences of life, so as to do every thing for His sake and by His strength.

When we are justified by faith, and accepted in the Beloved, we become heirs of everlasting life : but we cannot know the full value of our privileges till we enter upon the state of glory. For this, most who are converted have to wait some time after they are partakers of grace. Though the Lord loves them, hates sin, and teaches them to hate it, He appoints them to remain a while in a sinful world, and to groan under the burden of a depraved nature. He could put them in immediate possession of the Heaven for which He hath given them a meetness, but He does not. He has a service for them here, an honour which is worthy all they can suffer, and for which eternity will not afford an opportunity, namely, to be instruments of promoting His designs, and manifesting His grace in the world. Strictly speaking, this is the whole of our business here, the only reason why life is prolonged, or for which it is truly desirable, that we may fill up our connexions and situations, improve our comforts and our crosses, in such a manner as that God may be glorified in us and by us. As He is a bountiful Master and a kind Father, He is pleased to afford a variety of temporal blessings, which sweeten our service, and, as coming from His hand, are very valuable, but are by no means worth living for, considered in themselves, as they can neither satisfy our desires, nor preserve us from trouble, or support us under it. That light of God's countenance, which can pervade the walls and dissipate the gloom of a dungeon, is unspeakably preferable to all that can be enjoyed in a palace without it. The true end of life is, to live not to ourselves, but to Him who died for us ; and while we devote ourselves to His service upon earth, to rejoice in the prospect of being happy with Him for ever in Heaven. These things are generally known and acknowledged by professors ; but they are a *favoured few* who act consistently with their avowed principles; who honestly, diligently, and without reserve, endeavour to make the most of their talents and strength in promoting the Lord's service, and allow themselves in no views or designs but what are plainly subordinate and subservient to it. Yea, I believe the best of the Lord's servants see cause enough to confess, that they are not only unprofitable in comparison of what they wish to be, but in many instances unfaithful likewise. They find so many snares, hindrances, and temptations arising from without, and so much embarrassment from sin which dwells within, that they have more cause for humiliation than self-complacence, when they seem most earnest and most useful. However, we have no Scriptural evidence that we serve the Lord at all, any farther than we find an habitual desire and aim to serve Him wholly. He is gracious to our imperfections and weakness ; yet He requires all the heart, and will not be served by halves, nor accept what is performed by a divided spirit. I lately met with some profane scoffs of Voltaire upon the sentiment of doing all to the glory of God, (such as might be expected from such a man ;) however, this is the true alchymy which turns every thing to gold, and ennobles the common actions of life into acts of religion, 1 Cor. x. 31. Nor is there a grain of real goodness in the most specious actions which are performed without a reference to God's glory. This the world cannot understand ; but it will appear highly reasonable to those who take their ideas of God from the Scripture, and who have felt the necessity, and found the benefits of redemption.—We are debtors many ways. The Lord has a right to us by creation, by redemption, by conquest, when He freed us from Satan's power, and took possession of our hearts by His grace, and, lastly, by our own voluntary surrender in the day when He enabled us to fix our choice on Himself as our Lord and our portion. Then we felt the force of our obligations, we saw the beauty and honour of His service, and that nothing was worthy to stand in the least degree of competition with it. This is always equally true, though our perceptions of it are not always equally strong. But where it has been once really known, it cannot be wholly forgotten, or cease to be the governing principle of life : and the Lord has promised to revive the impression in those who wait upon Him, and thereby to renew their strength. For in proportion as we feel by what ties we are His, we shall embrace His service as perfect freedom.

Again, when the eye is thus single, the whole body will be full of light. The principle of acting simply for God will, in general, make the path of duty plain, solve a thousand otherwise dubious questions, lead to the most proper and obvious means, and preclude that painful anxiety about events, which upon no other plan can be avoided. The love of God is the best casuist ; especially as it leads us to a careful attendance to His precepts, a reliance on His promises, and submission to His will. Most of our perplexities arise from an undue, though perhaps an unperceived, attachment to self. Either we have some scheme of our own too closely connected with our general view of serving the Lord, or lay some stress upon our own management, which, though we suspect it may possibly fail us, we cannot entirely help trusting to. In these respects the Lord permits His servants occasionally to feel their own weakness ; but if they are sincerely devoted to Him, He will teach them to profit by it, and bring them by degrees to a simplicity of dependence, as well as of intention. Then all things are easy. Acting from love, and walking by faith, they can neither be disappointed nor discouraged. Duty is their part, care is His, and they are enabled to cast it upon Him. They know that, when their expedients seem to fail, He is still allsufficient. They know that, being engaged in His cause, they cannot miscarry ; and that, though in some things they may seem to fall short of success, they are sure of meeting acceptance, and that He will estimate their services, not by their actual effects, but according to the gracious principle and desire He has put into their hearts, 2 Chron. vi. 7, 8.

I am, with the greatest respect, &c.

LETTER XI

My Lord,   *June* — 1773.

My old cast-off acquaintance, Horace, occasionally
came in my way this morning—I opened it upon lib. 3.
od. 29. Did I not know the proposal to be utterly im-
practicable, how gladly should I imitate it, and send your
Lordship, in honest prose, if not in elegant verse, an invita-
tion! But I must content myself with the idea of the
pleasure it would give me to sit with you half a day under
my favourite great tree, and converse with you, not con-
cerning the comparatively petty affairs of human govern-
ments, but of the things pertaining to the kingdom of God.
How many delightful subjects would suggest themselves in
a free and retired conversation! The excellency of our
King, the permanency and glory of His kingdom, the beauty
of His administration, the privileges of His subjects, the
review of what He has done for us, and the prospect of what
He has prepared for us in future ;—and if, while we were
conversing, He should be pleased to join us, (as He did
the disciples when walking to Emmaus,) how would our
hearts burn within us! Indeed, whether we are alone, or
in company, the most interesting topics strike us but faintly,
unless He is pleased to afford His gracious influence ; but
when He is present, light, love, liberty, and joy, spring up
in the hearts that know Him. This reminds me (as I have
mentioned Horace) to restore some beautiful lines to their
proper application. They are impious and idolatrous as he
uses them, but have an expressive propriety in the mouth
of a believer ·—

> Lucem redde tuæ, dux bone, patriæ
> Instar veris enim vultus ubi tuus
> Affulsit populo, gratior it dies
> Et soles melius nitent.

But we cannot meet. All that is left for me is to use
the liberty you allow me of offering a few hints upon these
subjects by letter, not because you know them not, but
because you love them. The hour is coming, when all
impediments shall be removed. All distinctions shall

cease that are founded upon sublunary things, and the earth and all its works shall be burnt up. Glorious day! May our souls be filled with the thought, and learn to estimate all things around us now, by the view in which they will appear to us then. Then it will be of small moment who was the prince, and who was the beggar in this life ;—but who in their several situations sought, and loved, and feared, and honoured the Lord. Alas! how many of the kings of the earth, and the rich men, and the chief captains, and the mighty men, will then say (in vain) to the mountains and the rocks, Fall on us, and hide us! In this world they are, for the most part, too busy to regard the commands of God, or too happy to seek His favour ; they have their good things here ; they please themselves for a while, and in a moment they go down to the grave : in that moment their thoughts perish, their schemes are left unfinished, they are torn from their possessions, and enter upon a new, an untried, an unchangeable, a never-ending state of existence. Alas, is this all the world can afford! I congratulate you, my Lord, not because God has appointed you to appear in an elevated rank, (this, abstracted from the opportunity it affords you of greater usefulness, would perhaps be a more proper subject for condolence ;) but that He has admitted you to those honours and privileges which come *from Him only*, and which so few in the superior ranks of life think worthy of their attention. I doubt not but you are often affected with a sense of this distinguishing mercy. But though we know that we are debtors, great debtors to the grace of God, which alone has made us to differ, we know it but imperfectly at present. It doth not yet appear what we shall be, nor can we form a just conception of the misery from which we are redeemed, much less of the price paid for our redemption. How little do we know of the Redeemer's dignity and of the unutterable distress He endured when His Soul was made an offering for sin, and it pleased the Father to bruise Him, that by His stripes we might be healed. These things will strike us quite in another manner when we view them in the light of eternity. Then, to return to the thought from which I have rambled, then and there I trust we shall meet to the highest advantage, and spend an everlasting day together in happiness and praise. With this thought I endeavour to comfort myself under the regret I sometimes feel that I can have so little intercourse with you in this life.

May the cheering contemplation of the hope set before us, support and animate us to improve the interval, and fill us with a holy ambition of shining as lights in the world, to the praise and glory of His grace, who has called us out of darkness ! Encompassed as we are with snares, temptations, and infirmities, it is possible (by His promised assistance) to live in some good measure above the world while we are in it ; above the influence of its cares, its smiles, or its frowns. Our conversation, πολιτευμα, our citizenship, is in Heaven. We are not at home, but only resident here for a season, to fulfil an appointed service ; and the Lord, whom we serve, has encouraged us to hope, that He will guide us by His wisdom, strengthen us by His power, and comfort us with the light of His countenance, which is better than life. Every blessing we receive from Him is a token of His favour, and a pledge of that far more exceeding and eternal weight of glory which He has reserved for us. O l to hear Him say at last, " Well done, good and faithful servant, enter thou into the joy of thy Lord ! " will be a rich amends for all that we can lose, suffer, or forbear, for His sake.

I subscribe myself, with great sincerity, &c.

LETTER XII

My Lord,   *February — 1774.*

THE first line of Horace's epistle to Augustus, when rightly applied, suggests a grand and cheering idea. As addressed by the poet, nothing can be more blasphemous, idolatrous, and absurd ; but with what comfort and pro-priety may a Christian look up to Him to whom all power is committed in Heaven and earth, and say, *Cum tot sustineas et tanta negotia solus !* . . . Surely a more weighty and comprehensive sentence never dropped from an uninspired pen. And how beautifully and expressively

is it closed by the word *solus !* The government is upon
His shoulders : and though He is concealed by a veil of
second causes from common eyes, so that they can perceive
only the means, instruments, and contingencies, by which
He works, and therefore think He does nothing ; yet, in
reality, He does *all*, according to His own counsel and
pleasure, in the armies of Heaven, and among the
inhabitants of the earth.

Who can enumerate the *tot et tanta negotia*, which are in-
cessantly before His eye, adjusted by His wisdom, dependent
on His will, and regulated by His power in His kingdoms
of providence and grace ?   If we consider the heavens,
the works of His fingers, the moon and the stars which He
has ordained ; if we call in the assistance of astronomers
and glasses to help us in forming a conception of the number,
distances, magnitude, and motions of the heavenly bodies ;
the more we search, the more we shall be confirmed, that
these are but a portion of His ways.—But He calls them all
by their names, upholds them by His power, and without
His continual energy they would rush into confusion, or
sink into nothing.   If we speak of intelligences, He is the
life, the joy, the sun of all that are capable of happiness.
Whatever may be signified by the thrones, principalities,
and powers in the world of light, they are all dependent
upon His power, and obedient to His command ; it is
equally true of angels as of men, that without Him they can
do nothing.   The powers of darkness are likewise under
His subjection and control.   Though but little is said of
them in Scripture, we read enough to assure us that their
number must be immensely great, and that their strength,
subtilty, and malice, are such as we may tremble to think
of them as our enemies, and probably should, but for our
strange insensibility to whatever does not fall under the
cognizance of our outward senses.   But He holds them all in
a chain, so that they can do or attempt nothing but by His
permission ; and whatever He permits them to do (though
they mean nothing less) has its appointed subserviency in
accomplishing His designs.

But to come nearer home, and to speak of what seems more
suited to our scanty apprehensions,—still we may be lost
in wonder.   Before this blessed and only Potentate, all the

nations of the earth are but as the dust upon the balance, and the small drop of a bucket, and might be thought (if compared with the immensity of His works) scarcely worthy of His notice : yet here He resides, pervades, provides, protects, and rules.   In Him His creatures live, move, and have their being : from Him is their food and preservation.   The eyes of all are upon Him ; what He gives they gather, and can gather no more ; and at His word they sink into the dust.—*T*here is not a worm that crawls upon the ground, nor a flower that grows in the pathless wilderness, or a shell upon the sea shore, but bears the impress of His wisdom, power, and goodness.   With respect to men, He reigns with uncontrolled dominion over every kingdom, family, and individual.   Here we may be astonished at His wisdom, in employing free agents, the greater part of whom are His enemies, to accomplish His purposes.   But however reluctant, they all serve Him.   His patience likewise is wonderful.   Multitudes, yea, nearly our whole species, spend the life and strength which He affords them, and abuse all the bounties He heaps upon them, in the ways of sin.   His commands are disregarded, His name blasphemed, His mercy disdained, His power defied ; yet still He spares. It is an eminent part of His government to restrain the depravity of human nature, and in various ways to check its effects, which, if left to itself, without His providential control, would presently make earth the very image of hell. For the vilest of men are not suffered to perpetrate a thousandth part of the evil which their hearts would prompt them to.   The earth, though lying in the wicked one, is filled with the goodness of the Lord.   He preserveth man and beast, sustains the young lion in the forest, feeds the birds of the air, which have neither store-house nor barn, and adorns the insects and the flowers of the field with a beauty and elegance beyond all that can be found in the courts of kings.

Still more wonderful is His administration in His kingdom of grace.   He is present with all His creatures, but in a peculiar manner with His own people.   Each of these are monuments of a more illustrious display of power, than that which spread abroad the heavens like a curtain, and laid the foundations of the earth : for He finds them all in a state

of rebellion and enmity, and makes them a willing people ;
and from the moment He reveals His love to them, He
espouses their cause, and takes all their concerns into His
own hands.   He is near and attentive to every one of them,
as if there was only that one.   This high and lofty One,
who inhabits eternity, before whom the angels veil their
faces, condescends to hold communion with those whom
men despise.   He sees not as man seeth—rides on a cloud
disdainful by a Sultan or a Czar, to manifest Himself to a
humble soul in a mud-walled cottage.   He comforts them
when in trouble, strengthens them when weak, makes their
beds in sickness, revives them when fainting, upholds them
when falling, and so seasonably and effectually manages for
them, that though they are persecuted and tempted, though
their enemies are many and mighty, nothing that they feel
or fear is able to separate them from His love.

And all thus He does *solus*.   All the abilities, powers, and
instincts, that are found amongst creatures, are emanations
from His fulness.   All changes, successes, disappointments,
—all that is memorable in the annals of history, all the
risings and falls of empires, all the turns in human life, take
place according to His plan.   In vain men contrive and
combine to accomplish their own counsels, unless they are
parts of His counsel likewise ;   the efforts of their utmost
strength and wisdom are crossed and reversed by the feeblest
and most unthought-of circumstances.   But when He
has a work to accomplish, and His time is come, however
inadequate and weak the means He employs may seem to a
carnal eye, the success is infallibly secured : for all things
serve Him, and are in His hands as clay in the hands of the
potter.   Great and marvellous are Thy works, Lord God
Almighty ! just and true are Thy ways, Thou King of
Saints !

This is the God whom we adore.   This is He who invites
us to lean upon His almighty arm, and promises to guide us
with His unerring eye.   He says to you, my Lord, and even
to me, Fear not, I am with thee ; be not dismayed, I am Thy
God ;   I will strengthen thee, yea, I will help thee ;   yea,
I will uphold thee with the right hand of My righteousness.
Therefore, while in the path of duty, and following His call,
we may cheerfully pass on, regardless of apparent difficulties ;

for the Lord, whose we are, and who has taught us to make His glory our highest end, will go before us ; and at His word, crooked things become straight, light shines out of darkness, and mountains sink into plains. Faith may and must be exercised, experience must and will confirm what His word declares, that the heart is deceitful, and that man in his best estate is vanity. But His promises to them that fear Him shall be confirmed likewise, and they shall find Him, in all situations, a sun, a shield, and an exceeding great reward.

I have lost another of my people, a mother in our Israel ; a person of much experience, eminent grace, wisdom, and usefulness. She walked with God forty years : she was one of the Lord's poor ; but her poverty was decent, sanctified, and honourable : she lived respected, and her death is considered as a public loss. It is a great loss to me ; I shall miss her advice and example, by which I have been often edified and animated. But Jesus still lives. Almost her last words were, The Lord is my portion, saith my soul.

I am, &c.

LETTER XIII

My Lord, *March* 10, 1774.

For about six weeks past I have had occasion to spend several hours of almost every day with the sick and the dying. These scenes are to a minister like walking the hospitals to a young surgeon. The various cases which occur, exemplify, illustrate, and explain, with a commanding energy, many truths which may be learned indeed at home but cannot be so well understood, or their force so sensibly felt, without the advantage of experience and observation. As physicians, besides that competent general knowledge of their profession, which should be common to them all, have usually their several favourite branches of study, some applying themselves more to botany, others to chemistry, others to anatomy ; so ministers, as their inclinations and gifts differ, are led more closely to consider some particular branch of the system of divine truth. Some are directed

ç   D to state and defend the doctrines of the Gospel ; some have a talent for elucidating difficult texts of Scripture ; some have a turn for explaining the prophetical parts, and so of the rest. For myself if it be lawful to speak of myself, and so far as I can judge, anatomy is my favourite branch ; I mean the study of the human heart, with its workings and counter-workings, as it is differently affected in a state of nature or of grace, in the different seasons of prosperity, adversity, conviction, temptation, sickness, and the approach of death. The Lord, by sending me hither, provided me a good school for these purposes. I know not where I could have had a better, or affording a greater variety of characters, in proportion to the number of people ; and as they are mostly a poor people, and strangers to that address which is the result of education and converse with the world, there is a simplicity in what they say or do, which gives me a peculiar advantage in judging of their cases.

But I was about to speak of death. Though the grand evidence of those truths upon which our hopes are built, arises from the authority of God speaking them in His word, and revealing them by His Spirit, to the awakened heart, (for till the heart is awakened, it is incapable of receiving this evidence ;) yet some of these truths are so mysterious, so utterly repugnant to the judgment of depraved nature, that through the remaining influence of unbelief and vain reasoning, the temptations of Satan, and the subtile arguments with which some men, reputed wise, attack the foundations of our faith, the minds even of believers are sometimes capable of being shaken. I know no better corroborating evidence for the relief of the mind under such assaults than the testimony of dying persons, especially of such as have lived out of the noise of controversy, and who, perhaps, never heard a syllable of what has been started in these evil days against the Deity of Christ, His atonement, and other important articles. Permit me, my Lord, to relate, upon this occasion some things which exceedingly struck me in the conversation I had with a young woman whom I visited in her last illness, about two years ago. She was a sober, prudent person, of plain sense, could read her Bible, but had read little beside : her knowledge of the world was nearly confined to the parish ;

for I suppose she was seldom, if ever, twelve miles from home in her life. She had known the Gospel about seven years before the Lord visited her with a lingering consumption, which at length removed her to a better world. A few days before her death, I had been praying by her bedside, and in my prayer I thanked the Lord, that He gave her now to see that she had not followed cunningly-devised fables. When I had finished, she repeated that word, " No (she said), not cunningly-devised fables ; these are realities indeed ; I feel their truth, I feel their comfort. O tell my friends, tell my acquaintance, tell inquiring souls, tell poor sinners, tell all the daughters of Jerusalem, (alluding to Solomon's Song, v. 16, from which she had just before desired me to preach at her funeral), what Jesus has done for my soul. Tell them, that now, in the time of need, I find Him my Beloved and my Friend, and as such I commend Him to them." She then fixed her eyes steadfastly upon me, and proceeded, as well as I can recollect, as follows : " Sir, you are highly favoured in being called to preach the Gospel. I have often heard you with pleasure ; but give me leave to tell you, that I now see all you have said, or can say, is comparatively but little. Nor till you come into my situation, and have death and eternity full in your view, will it be possible for you to conceive the vast weight and importance of the truths you declare. Oh ! Sir, it is a serious thing to die ; no words can express what is needful to support the soul in the solemnity of a dying hour."

I believe it was the next day when I visited her again. After some discourse as usual, she said, with a remarkable vehemence of speech, " Are you sure I cannot be mistaken ? " I answered without hesitation, " Yes, I am sure ; I am not afraid to say, My soul for yours, that you are right." She paused a little, and then replied, " You say true ; I know I am right. I feel that my hope is fixed upon the Rock of Ages ; I know in whom I have believed. Yet, if you could see with my eyes, you would not wonder at my question. But the approach of death presents a prospect, which is till then hidden from us, and which cannot be described." She said much more to the same purpose ; and in all she spoke there was a dignity, weight, and evidence, which I suppose few professors of divinity, when lecturing from the chair, have at any time equalled. We may well say with Elihu, who teacheth like Him ? Many instances of the like kind I have met with here. I have a poor girl near me who looks like an idiot, and her natural capacity is indeed very small ; but the Lord has been pleased to make her acquainted alternately with great temptations, and proportionably great discoveries of His love and truth. Sometimes, when her heart is enlarged, I listen to her with astonishment. I think no books or ministers I ever met with have given me such an impression and understanding of what the apostle styles τα βαθη του Θεου, as I have upon some occasions received from her conversation.

But I am rambling again. My attendance upon the sick is not always equally comfortable ; but could I learn aright, it might be equally instructive. Some confirm the preciousness of a Saviour to me, by the cheerfulness with which, through faith in His name, they meet the king of terrors. Others no less confirm it, by the terror and reluctance they discover when they find they must die ; for though there are too many who sadly slight the blessed Gospel while they are in health, yet in this place most are too far enlightened to be quite thoughtless about their souls, if they retain their senses, in their last illness. Then, like the foolish virgins, they say, Give us of your oil : then they are willing that ministers and professors should pray with them and speak to them. Through the Lord's goodness, several whom I have visited in these circumstances have afforded me good hope ; they have been savingly changed by His blessing upon what has passed at the eleventh hour. I have seen a marvellous and blessed change take place in their language, views, and tempers, in a few days. I now visit a young person, who is cut short in her nineteenth year by a consumption, and I think cannot live many days. I found her very ignorant and insensible, and she remained so a good while ; but of late I hope her heart is touched. She feels her lost state, she seems to have some right desires, she begins to pray, and in such a manner as I cannot but hope the Lord is teaching her, and will reveal Himself to her before she departs. But it is sometimes otherwise. I saw a young woman die last week ; I had been often with her ; but the night she was removed she could only say, O, I cannot live, I cannot live !

She repeated this mournful complaint as long as she could speak ; for as the vital powers were more oppressed, her voice was changed into groans ; her groans grew fainter and fainter, and in about a quarter of an hour after she had done speaking she expired. Poor thing ! I thought, as I stood by her bedside, if you were a duchess, in this situation, what could the world do for you now ! I thought likewise how many things are there that now give us pleasure or pain, and assume a mighty importance in our view, which, in a dying hour, will be no more to us than the clouds which fly unnoticed over our heads. Then the truth of our Lord's aphorism will be seen, felt, and acknowledged, " One thing is needful "; and we shall be ready to apply Grotius' dying confession to (alas !) a great part of our lives, *Ah ! vitam perdidi, nihil agendo laboriose.*

Your Lordship allows me to send unpremeditated letters. I need not assure you this is one.

I am, &c.

LETTER XIV

My Lord, *March* 24, 1774.

WHAT a mercy is it to be separated in spirit, conversation, and interest, from the world that knows not God, where all are alike by nature ! Grace makes a happy and unspeakable difference. Believers were once under the same influence of that spirit who still worketh in the children of disobedience, pursuing different paths, but all equally remote from truth and peace ; some hatching cockatrice' eggs, others weaving spiders' webs. These two general heads of mischief and vanity include all the schemes, aims, and achievements of which man is capable, till God is pleased to visit the heart with His grace. The busy part of mankind are employed in multiplying evils and miseries ; the more retired, speculative, and curious, are amusing themselves with what will hereafter appear as unsubstantial, unstable, and useless as a cobweb. Death will soon sweep away all that the philosophers, the virtuosi, the mathematicians, the antiquarians, and other learned triflers, are now weaving with so much self-applauded address.   Nor will the fine-spun dresses, in which the moralist and the self-righteous clothe themselves, be of more advantage to them, either for ornament or defence than the produce of a spider.   But it is given to a few to know their present state and future destination.—These build upon the immovable Rock of Ages for eternity : these are trees springing from a living root, and bear the fruits of righteousness, which are by Jesus Christ, to the glory and praise of God : these only are awake, while the rest of the world are in a sleep, indulging in vain dreams from which likewise they will shortly awake ; but, O with what consternation, when they shall find themselves irrecoverably divorced from all their delusive attachments, and compelled to appear before that God to whom they have lived strangers, and to whom they must give an account !   O for a thousand tongues to proclaim in the ears of thoughtless mortals that important aphorism of our Lord, " One thing is needful ! " Yet a thousand tongues would be, and are employed in vain, unless so far as the Lord is pleased to send the watchman's warning, by the power and agency of His own Spirit. I think the poet tells us, that Cassandra had the gift of truly foretelling future events ; but she was afterwards laid under a painful embarrassment, that nobody should believe her words.   Such, with respect to the bulk of their auditories, is the lot of Gospel-ministers : they are enlightened to see, and sent forth to declare, the awful consequences of sin ; but, alas ! how few believe their report !   To illustrate our grief and disappointment, I sometimes suppose there is dangerous water in the way of travellers, over which there is a bridge which those who can be prevailed upon may pass with safety. By the side of this bridge watchmen are placed, to warn passengers of the danger of the waters ; to assure them, that all who attempt to go through them inevitably perish ; to invite, entreat, and beseech them, if they value their lives, to cross the bridge.   Methinks this should be an easy task : yet if we should see in fact the greater part stopping their ears to the friendly importunity ; many so much offended by it as to account the watchman's care impertinent, and only deserving of scorn and ill-treatment ; hardly one in fifty betaking themselves to the friendly bridge, the rest

eagerly plunging into the waters, from which none return, as
if they were determined to try who should be drowned first :
this spectacle would be no unfit emblem of the reception
the Gospel meets with from a blinded world.   The ministers
are rejected, opposed, vilified ; they are accounted troublers
of the world, because they dare not, cannot stand silent,
while sinners are perishing before their eyes ; and if, in the
course of many sermons, they can prevail but on one soul to
take timely warning, and to seek to Jesus, who is the way,
the truth, and the life, they may account it a mercy and an
honour, sufficient to overbalance all the labour and
reproaches they are called to endure.   From the most they
must expect no better reception than the Jews gave to
Jeremiah, who told the prophet to his face, As to the word
thou hast spoken to us in the name of the Lord, we will not
hearken to thee at all, but we will certainly do whatsoever
thing goeth forth out of our own mouth.   Surely, if the Lord
has given us any sense of the worth of our souls, any com-
passion towards them, this must be a painful exercise ;
and experience must teach us something of the meaning
of Jeremiah's pathetic exclamation, " O that my head were
waters, and mine eyes fountains of tears, that I might weep
day and night for the slain of the daughters of my people ! "
It is our *duty* to be thus affected.   Our relief lies in the
wisdom and sovereignty of God.   He reveals His salvation to
whom He pleases,—for the most part to babes ; from the
bulk of the wise and the prudent it is hidden.   Thus it has
pleased Him, and therefore it must be right.   Yea, He will
one day condescend to justify the propriety and equity of
His proceedings to His creatures :   then every mouth will
be stopped, and none will be able to reply against their
Judge.   Light is come into the world, but men prefer dark-
ness.   They hate the light, resist it, and rebel against it.
It is true all do so ; and therefore, if all were to perish under
the condemnation, their ruin would be their own act.   It is
of grace that any are saved, and in the distribution of that
grace, He does what He will with His own : a right which
most are ready enough to claim in their own concerns,
though they are so unwilling to allow it to the Lord of all.
Many perplexing and acrimonious disputes have been
started upon this subject ; but the redeemed of the Lord

are called, not to dispute, but to admire and rejoice ; to love, adore, and obey. To know that He loved us, and gave Himself for us, is the constraining argument and motive to love Him, and surrender ourselves to Him ; to consider ourselves as no longer our own, but to devote ourselves with every faculty, power, and talent to His service and glory. He deserves our all, for He parted with all for us. He made Himself poor,—He endured shame, torture, death, and the curse for us, that we through Him might inherit everlasting life. Ah ! the hardness of my heart, that I am no more affected, astonished, overpowered with this thought.

I am, &c.

LETTER XV

My Lord,   *April* 20, 1774.

I HAVE been pondering a good while for a subject, and at last begin without one, hoping that (as it has often happened) while I am writing one line, something will occur to fill up another. Indeed I have an inexhaustible fund at hand; but it is to me often like a prize in the hand of a fool, I want skill to improve it. O for a warm, a suitable, a seasonable train of thought that might enliven my own heart, and not be unworthy your Lordship's perusal I Methinks the poets can have but cold comfort, when they invocate a fabled Muse ; but we have a warrant, a right, to look up for the influence of the Holy Spirit, who ordains strength for us, and has promised to work in us. What a comfort, what an honour is this, that worms have liberty to look up to God I and that He, the high and holy One who inhabiteth eternity, is pleased to look down upon us, to maintain our peace, to supply our wants, to guide us with His eye, and to inspire us with wisdom and grace suitable to our occasions ! They who profess to know something of this intercourse, and to depend upon it, are by the world accounted enthusiasts, who know not what they mean, or perhaps hypocrites, who pretend to what they have not, in order to cover some base designs.—But we have reason to bear their reproaches with patience. Could the miser say,

——— Populus me sibilat, at mihi plaudo
Ipse domi, simul ac nummos contemplor in arca :

Well then may the believer say, Let them laugh, let them rage, let them, if they please, point at me for a fool as I walk the streets ; if I do but take up the Bible, or run over in my mind the inventory of the blessings with which the Lord has enriched me, I have sufficient amends. Jesus is mine ; in Him I have wisdom, righteousness, sanctification and redemption, an interest in all the promises and in all the perfections of God ; He will guide me by His counsel, support me by His power, comfort me with His presence while I am here, and afterwards, when flesh and heart fail, He will receive me to His glory.

Let them say what they will, they shall not dispute or laugh us out of our spiritual senses. If all the blind men in the kingdom should endeavour to bear me down, that the sun is not bright, or that the rainbow has no colours, I would still believe my own eyes. I have seen them both ; they have not. I cannot prove to their satisfaction what I assert, because they are destitute of sight, the necessary medium ; yet their exceptions produce no uncertainty in my mind : they would not, they could not hesitate a moment if they were not blind. Just so, they who have been taught of God, who have tasted that the Lord is gracious, have an experimental perception of the truth, which renders them proof against all the sophistry of infidels. I am persuaded we have many plain people here, who, if a wise man of the world was to suggest that the Bible is a human invention, would be quite at a loss how to answer him by arguments drawn from external evidences ; yet they have found such effects from this blessed book, that they would be no more moved by the insinuation, than if they were told, that a cunning man, or set of men, invented the sun, and placed it in the firmament. So, if a wise Socinian was to tell them, that the Saviour was only a man, like themselves, they would conceive just such an opinion of his skill in divinity, as a philosopher would do of a clown's skill in astronomy, who should affirm that the sun was no bigger than a cart-wheel.

It remains therefore a truth, in defiance of all the cavils of the ignorant, that the Holy Spirit does influence the hearts of all the children of God, or, in other words, they are inspired, not with new revelations, but with grace and wisdom to understand, apply, and feed upon the great things already revealed in the Scriptures, without which the Scriptures are as useless as spectacles to the blind. Were it not so, when we become acquainted with the poverty, ignorance, and wickedness of our hearts, we must sit down in utter despair of being ever able to think a good thought, to offer a single petition aright in prayer, or to take one safe step in the path of life. But now we may be content with our proper weakness, since the power and Spirit of Christ are engaged to rest upon us ; and while we are preserved in a simple dependence upon this help, though unable of ourselves to do any thing, we shall find an ability to do every thing that our circumstances and duty call for. What is weaker than a worm ? Yet the Lord's worms shall in His strength thresh the mountains, and make the hills as chaff. But this life of faith, this living and acting by a power above our own, is an inexplicable mystery, till experience makes it plain. I have often wondered that St. Paul has obtained so much quarter at the hands of some people, as to pass with them for a man of sense ; for surely the greatest part of his writings must be to the last degree absurd and unintelligible upon their principles. How many contradictions must they find, for instance, if they give any attention to what they read in that one passage, Gal. ii. 20 : " I am crucified with Christ : Nevertheless I live ; yet not I, but Christ liveth in me : and the life which I now live in the flesh, I live by faith in the Son of God, who loved me and gave Himself for me."

And as believers are thus inspired by the Holy Spirit, who furnishes them with desires, motives, and abilities, to perform what is agreeable to His will ; so I apprehend, that they who live without God in the world, whom the apostle styles *sensual, not having the Spirit,* are in a greater or less degree *ad captum recipientis,* under what I may call a *black inspiration.* After making the best allowances I can, both' for the extent of human genius and the deplorable evil of the human heart, I cannot suppose that one-half of the wicked wit, of which some persons are so proud, is properly their own. Perhaps such a one as Voltaire would neither have written, nor have been read or admired so much, if he had not been the amanuensis of an abler hand in his own way. Satan is always near when the heart is disposed to receive him ; and the Lord withdraws His restraints to heighten the sinner's ability of sinning with an *éclat*, and assisting him with such strokes of blasphemy, malice, and falsehood, as perhaps he could not otherwise have attained. Therefore I do not wonder that they are clever and smart, that they raise a laugh, and are received with applause among those who are like-minded with themselves. But unless the Lord is pleased to grant them repentance, (though it is rather to be feared some of them are given up to judicial hardness of heart) how much better would it have been for them had they been born idiots or lunatics, than to be distinguished as the willing, industrious, and successful instruments of the powers of darkness, in beguiling, perverting, and ruining the souls of men ! Alas ! what are parts and talents, or any distinctions which give pre-eminence in life, unless they are sanctified by the grace of God, and directed to the accomplishment of His will and glory ! From the expression, *Bind them in bundles and burn them*, I have been led to think, that the deceivers and the deceived, they who have prostituted their gifts or influence to encourage others in sin, and they who have perished by their means, may in another world have some peculiar and inseparable connexion, and spend an eternity in fruitless lamentations, that ever they were connected here.

Your Lordship, I doubt not, feels the force of that line,

O to grace how great a debtor !

Had not the Lord separated you for Himself, your rank, your abilities, your influence, which now you chiefly value as enlarging your opportunities of usefulness, might, nay, certainly would, have been diverted into the opposite channel.   I am, &c.

LETTER XVI

MY LORD,   *Nov.* 5, 1774.

ıI HAVE not till very lately had recourse to the expe-
dient of descanting upon a text ; but I believe it the best
method I can take to avoid ringing changes upon a few
obvious topics, which I suppose uniformly present them-
selves to my mind when I am about to write to your
Lordship.   Just now, that sweet expression of David
occurred to my thoughts, *The Lord is my Shepherd !* . . .
Permit me, without plan or premeditation, to make a few
observations upon it ; and may your Lordship feel the peace,
the confidence, the blessedness, which a believing applica-
tion of the words is suited to inspire.
The Socinians and others, in their unhappy laboured
attempts to darken the principal glory and foundation-
comfort of the Gospel, employ their critical sophistry against
those texts which expressly and doctrinally declare the
Redeemer's character ; and affect to triumph, if in any
manuscript or ancient version they can find a variation from
the received copies which seems to favour their cause.
But we may venture to wave the authority of every disputed
or disputable text, and maintain the truth against their
cavils, from the current language and tenor of the whole
Scripture.   David's words in Psa. xxiii. are alone a decisive
proof that Jesus is Jehovah, if they will but allow two things,
which I think they cannot deny :—1. That our Saviour
assumes to Himself the character of the Shepherd of His
people ;—and, 2. That He did not come into the world to
abridge those advantages which the servants of God en-
joyed before His incarnation.   Upon these premises, which
cannot be gainsayed without setting aside the whole New
Testament, the conclusion is undeniable ; for if Jehovah
was David's Shepherd, unless Jesus be Jehovah, we who live
under the Gospel have an unspeakable disadvantage in being
intrusted to the care of one who, according to the Socinians,
is a mere man ; and upon the Arian scheme, is at the most
a creature, and infinitely short of possessing those
perfections which David contemplated in his Shepherd.   He
had a Shepherd whose wisdom and power were infinite, and

might therefore warrantably conclude he should not want,
and need not fear. And we also may conclude the same,
if our Shepherd be the Lord or Jehovah, but not otherwise.
Besides, the very nature of the Shepherd's office respecting
the state of such frail creatures as we are, requires those
attributes for the due discharge of it which are incommunic-
ably divine. He must intimately know every individual
of the flock. His eye must be upon them every one, and His
ear open to their prayers, and His arm stretched out for their
relief, in all places, and in all ages. Every thought of
every heart must be open to His view, and His wisdom
must penetrate, and His arm control and overrule all the
hidden and complicated machinations of the powers of dark-
ness. He must have the administration of universal Provi-
dence over all the nations, families, and persons upon earth,
or He could not effectually manage for those who put their
trust in Him, in that immense variety of cases and circum-
stances in which they are found. Reason, as well as Scrip-
ture, may convince us, that He who gathereth the outcasts
of Israel, who healeth the broken in heart, who upholdeth
all that fall, raiseth up all that are bowed down, and upon
whom the eyes of all wait for their support, can be no other
than He who telleth the number of the stars, and calleth
them all by their names, who is great in power, and whose
understanding is infinite. To this purpose likewise the
prophet Isaiah describes this mighty Shepherd, chap. xl.
9-17, both as to His person and office.

But is not this indeed the great mystery of godliness ?
How just is the apostle's observation, that no man can say
Jesus Christ is Lord, but by the Holy Ghost ! How astonish-
ing the thought,—that the Maker of Heaven and earth,
the Holy One of Israel, before whose presence the earth
shook, the Heavens dropped, when He displayed a fa.nt
emblem of His majesty upon Sinai, should afterwards appear
in the form of a servant, and hang upon a cross, the sport
and scorn of wicked men ! I cannot wonder that to the wise
men of the world this appears absurd, unreasonable, and
impossible ; yet to right reason, to reason enlightened and
sanctified, however amazing the proposition be, yet it
appears true and necessary, upon a supposition, that a
holy God is pleased to pardon sinners in a way suited to

display the awful glories of His justice. The same arguments which prove the blood of bulls and goats insufficient to take away sin, will conclude against the utmost doings or sufferings of men or angels. The Redeemer of sinners must be mighty ; He must have a personal dignity to stamp such a value upon His undertakings, as that thereby God may appear just, as well as merciful, in justifying the ungodly for His sake ; and He must be all-sufficient to bless and almighty to protect those who come unto Him for safety and life.

Such a one is our Shepherd. This is He of whom we, through grace, are enabled to say, we are His people, and the sheep of His pasture. We are His by every tie and right ; He made us, He redeemed us, He reclaimed us from the hand of our enemies, and we are His by our own voluntary surrender of ourselves ; for though we once slighted, despised, and opposed Him, He made us willing in the day of His power : He knocked at the door of our hearts ; but we (at least I) barred and fastened it against Him as much and as long as possible. But when He revealed His love, we could stand out no longer. Like sheep, we are weak, destitute, defenceless, prone to wander, unable to return, and always surrounded with wolves. But all is made up in the fulness, ability, wisdom, compassion, care, and faithfulness of our great Shepherd. He guides, protects, feeds, heals, and restores, and will be our Guide and our God even until death. Then He will meet us, receive us, and present us unto Himself, and we shall be near Him, and like Him, and with Him for ever.

Ah, my Lord, what a subject is this ! I trust it is the joy of your heart. Placed as you are by His hand in a superior rank, you see and feel that the highest honours, and the most important concernments that terminate with the present life, are trivial as the sports of children, in comparison with the views and the privileges you derive from the glorious Gospel ; and your situation in life renders the grace bestowed upon you the more conspicuous and distinguishing. I have somewhere met with a similar reflection of Henry the Fourth of France, to this purpose, that though many came into the world the same day with him, he was probably the only one among them that was born to be a king. Your Lordship is acquainted with many, who, if not born on the same day with you, were born to titles, estates, and honours ; but how few of them were born to the honour of making a public and consistent profession of the glorious Gospel ! The hour is coming, when all honours and possessions, but this which cometh of God only, will be eclipsed and vanish ; and, like the baseless fabric of a vision, leave not a wreck behind. How miserable will they then be who must leave their all ! What a mortifying thought does Horace put in the way of those who disdain to read the Scripture—

> Linquenda tellus, et domus, et placens
> Uxor : neque harum, quas colis, arborum
> Te, præter invisas cupressos,
> Ulla brevem dominum sequetur.

But grace and faith can make the lowest state of life supportable, and make a dismission from the highest desirable. Of the former, I have many living proofs and witnesses around me. Your Lordship, I trust, will have sweet experience of the latter, when, after having fulfilled the will of God in your generation, you shall be called (I hope in some yet distant day) to enter into your Master's joy. In the meantime, how valuable are life, talents, influence, and opportunities of every kind, if we are enabled to improve and lay out all for Him who has thus loved us, thus provided for us ! As to myself, I would hope there are few who have so clear a sense of their obligations to Him, who make such unsuitable and languid returns as I do. I think I have a desire to serve Him better : but, alas ! evil is present with me. Surely I shall feel something like shame and regret for my coldness, even in Heaven ;—for I find I am never happier than when I am most ashamed of myself upon this account here.   I am, &c.

LETTER XVII

My Lord,   *December 8, 1774.*

How wonderful is the patience of God towards sinful men ! In Him they live, and move, and have their being ;

and if He were to withdraw His support for a single moment they must perish. He maintains their lives, guards their persons, supplies their wants, while they employ the powers and faculties they receive from Him in a settled course of opposition to His will. They trample upon His laws, affront His government, and despise His grace; yet still He spares. To silence all His adversaries in a moment, would require no extraordinary exertion of His power; but His forbearance towards them manifests His glory, and gives us cause to say, who is a God like unto thee ?

Sometimes, however, there are striking instances of His displeasure against sin. When such events take place, immediately upon a public and premeditated contempt offered to Him that sitteth in the Heavens, I own they remind me of the danger of standing, if I may so speak, in the Lord's way : for though His long-suffering is astonishing, and many dare Him to His face daily with seeming impunity, yet He sometimes strikes an awful and unexpected blow, and gives an illustration of that solemn word, " Whoever hardened himself against the Lord and prospered ? " But who am I to make this observation ? I ought to do it with the deepest humiliation, remembering that I once stood (according to my years and ability) in the foremost rank of His avowed opposers; and with a determined and unwearied enmity, renounced, defied, and blasphemed Him. " But He will have mercy on whom He will have mercy ; " and therefore I was spared, and reserved to speak of His goodness.

Josephus, when speaking of the death of Herod Agrippa, ascribes it to a natural cause, and says, he was seized with excruciating pains in his bowels. But Luke informs us of the *true* cause: an angel of the Lord smote him. Had we a modern history, written by an inspired pen, we should probably often be reminded of such an interposition where we are not ordinarily aware of it. For though the springs of actions and events are concealed from us for the most part, and vain men carry on their schemes with confidence, as though the Lord had forsaken the earth ; yet they are under His eye and control ; and faith, in some measure, instructed by the specimens of His government recorded in the Scriptures, can trace and admire His hand, and can see how He takes the wise in their own craftiness, stains the pride of human glory ; and that, when sinners speak proudly, He is above them, and makes everything bend or break before Him.

While we lament the growth and pernicious effects of infidelity, and see how wicked men and seducers wax worse and worse, deceiving, and being deceived ; what gratitude should fill our hearts to Him who has been pleased to call us out of the horrid darkness in which multitudes are bewildered and lost, into the glorious light of His Gospel ! Faint are our warmest conceptions of this mercy. In order to understand it fully, we should have a full and adequate sense of the evil from which we are delivered ; the glory to which we are called ; and especially of the astonishing means to which we owe our life and hope,—the humiliation, sufferings, and death of the Son of God. But our views of these points, while in our present state, are, and must be, exceedingly weak and disproportionate. We know them but in part, we see them δι' εσοπτρον, by *reflection*, rather the images than the things themselves ; and though they are faithfully represented in the mirror of God's word, to us they appear indistinct, because we see them through a gross medium of ignorance and unbelief. Hereafter every veil shall be removed ; we shall know, in another manner than we do now, the unspeakable evil of sin, and the unsupportable dreadfulness of God's displeasure against it, when we see the world in flames, and hear the final sentence denounced upon the ungodly. We shall have far other thoughts of Jesus when we see Him as He is ; and shall then be able to make a more affecting estimate of the love which moved Him to be made a substitute and a curse for us ; and we shall then know what great things God has prepared for them that love Him. Then with transport we shall adopt the Queen of Sheba's language, It was a true report we heard in yonder dark world ; but behold, the half, the thousandth part, was not told us ! In the mean time, may such conceptions as we are enabled to form of these great truths fill our hearts, and be mingled with all our thoughts, and all our concerns ; may the Lord, by faith, give us an abiding evidence of the reality and importance of the things which cannot yet be seen : so shall we be enabled to live above the world while we are in it, uninfluenced either by its blandishments or its frowns ; and, with a noble simplicity and singularity, avow and maintain the cause of God in truth, in the midst of a crooked and perverse generation. He whom we serve is able to support and protect us ; and He well deserves at our hands that we should be willing to endure, for His sake, much more than He will ever permit us to be exercised with. The believer's call, duty, and privilege, is beautifully and forcibly set forth in Milton's character of Abdiel, at the end of the fifth book :

> . . Faithful found
> Among the faithless, faithful only he
> Among innumerable false, unmov'd,
> Unshaken, unseduc'd, unterrify'd,
> His loyalty he kept, his love, his zeal ;
> Nor number, nor example, with him wrought
> To swerve from truth, or change his constant mind
> Though single .

Methinks your Lordship's situation particularly resembles that in which the poet has placed Abdiel. You are not indeed called to serve God quite alone ; but amongst those of your own rank, and with whom the station in which He has placed you necessitates you to converse, how few are there who can understand, second, or approve, the principles upon which you act, or easily bear a conduct which must impress conviction or reflect dishonour upon themselves ! But you are not alone ; the Lord's people (many of whom you will not know till you meet them in glory) are helping you here with their prayers ; His angels are commissioned to guard and guide your steps ; yea, the Lord Himself fixes His eye of mercy upon your private and your public path, and is near you at your right hand, that you may not be moved ! That He may comfort you with the light of His countenance, and uphold you with the arm of His power, is my frequent prayer.

I am, &c.

LETTER XVIII

MY LORD, *January* 20, 1775.

WE have entered upon another year! So have thousands, perhaps millions, who will not see it close! An alarming thought to the worldling! at least it should be so. I have an imperfect remembrance of an account I read, when I was a boy, of an ice-palace, built one winter at Petersburgh. The walls, the roofs, the floors, the furniture, were all of ice, but finished with taste; and every thing that might be expected in a royal palace was to be found there; the ice, while in the state of water, being previously coloured, so that to the eye all seemed formed of proper materials: but all was cold, useless, and transient. Had the frost continued till now, the palace might have been standing; but with the returning spring it melted away like the baseless fabric of a vision. Methinks there should have been one stone in the building, to have retained the inscription, *Sic transit gloria mundi*! for no contrivance could exhibit a fitter illustration of the vanity of human life. Men build and plan as if their work were to endure for ever! but the wind passes over them, and they are gone. In the midst of all their preparations, or, at farthest, when they think they have just completed their designs, their breath goeth forth, they return to their earth; in that very day their thoughts perish.

How many sleep who kept the world awake!

Yet this ice-house had something of a leisurely dissolution, though, when it began to decay, all the art of man was unable to prop it; but often death comes hastily, and, like the springing of a mine, destroys to the very foundations without previous notice. Then all we have been concerned in here (all but the consequences of our conduct, which will abide to eternity) will be no more to us than the remembrance of a dream. This truth is too plain to be denied; but the greater part of mankind act as if they were convinced it was false: they spend their days in vanity, and in a moment they go down to the grave. What cause of thankfulness have they who are delivered from this delusion, and who, by the

knowledge of the glorious Gospel, have learned their true
state and end, are saved from the love of the present world,
from the heart-distressing fear of death ; and know, that
if their earthly house were dissolved, like the ice-palace,
they have a house not made with hands, eternal in the
heavens !

Yet even these are much concerned to realize the brevity
and uncertainty of their present state, that they may be
stimulated to make the most and the best of it ; to redeem
their time, and manage their precarious opportunities, so
as may most tend to the praise and glory of Him who has
called them out of darkness into marvellous light. Why
should any that have tasted that the Lord is gracious, wish
to live another day, but that they may have the honour to
be fellow-workers with Him, instrumental in promoting
His designs, and of laying themselves out to the utmost
of their abilities and influence in His service ! To enjoy
a sense of His loving-kindness, and to have the light of His
countenance lifted up upon our souls, is indeed, respecting
ourselves, the best part of life, yea, better than life itself ;
but this we shall have to unspeakably greater advantage,
when we have finished our course, and shall be wholly freed
from the body of sin. And therefore the *great desirable*
while here seems to be—grace, that we may *serve* Him and
suffer for Him in the world. Though our first wish immedi-
ately upon our own accounts might be, to depart and be
with Jesus, which is πολλω μαλλον κρεισσον, yet a lively
thought of our immense obligations to His redeeming love,
may reconcile us to a much longer continuance here, if we
may by any means be subservient to diffuse the glory of His
name, and the blessings of His salvation, which is God's
great and principal end in preserving the world itself.
When historians and politicians descant upon the rise and
fall of empires, with all their professed sagacity in tracing
the connexion between causes and effects, they are totally
unacquainted with the great master-wheel which manages
the whole movement—that is, the Lord's design in favour
of His Church and kingdom. To this every event is sub-
ordinate ; to this every interfering interest must stoop.
How easily might this position be proved, by reviewing the
history of the period about the Reformation. Whether

Dr. Robertson considers things in this light, in his history of Charles V., I know not, as I have not seen his books ; but if not, however elaborate his performance may be in other respects, I must venture to say, it is essentially defective, and cannot give that light and pleasure to a spiritual reader of which the subject is capable. And I doubt not but some who are yet unborn, will hereafter clearly see and remark that the present unhappy disputes between Great Britain and America, with their consequences, whatever they may be, are part of a series of events, of which the extension and interests of the Church of Christ were the principal final causes. In a word, that Jesus may be known, trusted, and adored, and sinners, by the power of His Gospel, be rescued from sin and Satan, is comparatively the Το εν— the one great business for the sake of which the succession of day and night, summer and winter, is still maintained ; and when the plan of redemption is consummated, sin, which now almost fills the earth, will then set it on fire ; and the united interest of all the rest of mankind, when detached from that of the people of God, will not plead for its preservation a single day. In this view I congratulate your Lordship, that however your best endeavours to serve the temporal interests of the nation may fall short of your wishes ; yet so far as your situation gives you opportunity of supporting the Gospel cause, and facilitating its progress, you have a prospect both of a more certain and more important success. For instance, it was, under God, your Lordship's favour and influence that brought me into the ministry. And though I be nothing, yet He who put it in your heart to patronise me, has been pleased not to suffer what you then did for His sake to be wholly in vain. He has been pleased in a course of years, by so unworthy an instrument as I am, to awaken a number of persons who were at that time dead in trespasses and sins ; but now some of them are pressing on to the prize of their high calling of God in Christ Jesus ; and some of them are already before the throne. Should I suggest in some companies that the conversion of a hundred sinners (more or less) to God, is an event of more real importance than the *temporal* prosperity of the greatest nation upon earth, I should be charged with ignorance and arrogance ; but your Lordship is skilled in

Scriptural arithmetic, which alone can teach us to estimate the value of souls, and will agree with me, that one soul is worth more than the whole world, on account of its redemption-price, its vast capacities, and its duration. Should we suppose a nation to consist of forty millions, the whole and each individual to enjoy as much good as this life can afford, without abatement, for a term of fifty years each ;— all this good, or an equal quantity, might be exhausted by a single person in two thousand million of years, which would be but a moment in comparison with the eternity which would still follow. And if this good were merely temporal good, the whole aggregate of it would be evil and misery, if compared with that happiness in God, of which only they who are made partakers of a divine life are capable. On the other hand, were a whole nation to be destroyed by such accumulated miseries as attended the siege of Jerusalem, the sum total of these calamities would be but trifling, if set in competition with what every single person that dies in sin has to expect, when the sentence of everlasting destruction from the presence of the Lord, and the glory of His power, shall be executed.

What an unexpected round have my thoughts taken since I set out from the ice-palace ! It is time to relieve your Lordship, and to subscribe myself, &c.

LETTER XIX

My Lord,   *February 23, 1775.*

I ASSENT to our Lord's declaration, " Without Me ye can do nothing," not only upon the authority of the Speaker, but from the same irresistible and experimental evidence, as if He had told me, that I cannot make the sun to shine, or change the course of the seasons. Though my pen and my tongue sometimes move freely, yet the total incapacity and stagnation of thought I labour under at other times, convinces me, that in myself I have not sufficiency to think a good thought ; and I believe the case would be the same, if that little measure of knowledge and abilities, which I am too prone to look upon as my own, were a thousand times greater than it is. For every new service I stand in need of a new supply, and can bring forth nothing of my supposed store into actual exercise, but by His immediate assistance. His gracious influence is that, to those who are best furnished with gifts, which the water is to the mill, or the wind to the ship, without which the whole apparatus is motionless and useless. I apprehend that we lose much of the comfort which might arise from a sense of our continual dependence upon Him, and of course fall short of acknowledging as we ought what we receive from Him, by mistaking the manner of His operation. Perhaps we take it too much for granted, that communications from Himself must bear some kind of sensible impression that they are *His*, and, therefore, are ready to give our own industry or ingenuity credit for those performances in which we can perceive no such impression ; yet it is very possible that we may be under His influence when we are least aware : and though what we say, or write, or do, may seem no way extraordinary ; yet that we should be led to such a particular turn of thought at one time rather than at another, has, in my own concerns, often appeared to me remarkable, from the circumstances which have attended, or the consequences which have followed. How often, in the choice of a text, or in the course of a sermon, or in a letter to a friend, have I been led to speak a word in season ! and what I have expressed at large, and in general, has been so exactly suited to some case which I was utterly unacquainted with, that I could hardly have hit it so well, had I been previously informed of it. Some instances of this kind have been so striking, as hardly to admit a doubt of superior agency. And, indeed, if believers in Jesus, however unworthy in themselves, are the temples of the Holy Ghost ; if the Lord lives, dwells, and walks in them ; if He is their life and their light ; if He has promised to guide them with His eye, and to work in them to will and to do of His own good pleasure,—methinks what I have mentioned, and more, may be reasonably expected. That line in the hymn,

Help I every moment need,

is not a hyperbolical expression, but strictly and literally true, not only in great emergencies, but in our smoother hours, and most familiar paths. This gracious assistance is afforded in a way imperceptible to ourselves, to hide pride from us, and to prevent us from being indolent and careless with respect to the use of appointed means : and it would be likewise more abundantly, and perhaps more sensibly afforded, were our spirits more simple in waiting upon the Lord. But, alas ! a divided heart, an undue attachment to some temporal object, sadly deadens *our* spirits, (I speak for myself,) and grieves the Lord's Spirit ; so that we walk in darkness, and at a distance, and, though called to great privileges, live far below them. But methinks the thought of Him who is always near, and upon whom we do, and most incessantly, depend, should suggest a powerful motive for the closest attention to His revealed will, and the most punctual compliance with it ; for so far as the Lord withdraws we become as blind men, and with the clearest light, and upon the plainest ground, we are liable, or rather, sure to stumble at every step.

Though there is a principle of consciousness, and a determination of the will, sufficient to denominate our thoughts and performances our own, yet I believe mankind in general are more under an invisible agency than they apprehend. The Lord, immediately from Himself, and perhaps by the ministry of His holy angels, guides, prompts, restrains, or warns His people. So there undoubtedly is what I may call a *black inspiration*, the influence of the evil spirits who work in the hearts of the disobedient, and not only excite their wills, but assist their faculties and qualify as well as incline them to be more assiduously wicked, and more extensively mischievous, than they could be of themselves. I consider Voltaire, for instance, and many writers of the same stamp, to be little more than secretaries and amanuenses of one who has unspeakably more wit and adroitness in promoting infidelity and immorality than they of themselves can justly pretend to. They have for a while the credit (if I may so call it) of the fund from whence they draw ; but the world little imagines who is the real and original author of that philosophy and poetry, of those fine turns and sprightly inventions, which are so generally admired. Perhaps many, now applauded for their genius, would have been comparatively dolts, had they not been engaged in a cause which Satan has so much interest in supporting.

But to return to the more pleasing subject.—How great and honourable is the privilege of a true believer ! That he has neither wisdom nor strength in himself is no disadvantage, for he is connected with infinite wisdom and almighty power. Though weak as a worm, his arms are strengthened by the mighty God of Jacob, and all things become possible, yea, easy to him, that occur within the compass of his proper duty and calling. The Lord, whom he serves, engages to proportion his strength to his day, whether it be a day of service or of suffering ; and, though he be fallible and short-sighted, exceedingly liable to mistake and imposition, yet, while he retains a sense that he is so, and with the simplicity of a child asks counsel and direction of the Lord, he seldom takes a wrong step, at least not in matters of consequence ; and even his inadvertencies are overruled for good. If he forgets his true state, and thinks himself to be something, he presently finds he is indeed nothing ; but if he is content to be nothing, and to have nothing, he is sure to find a seasonable and abundant communication of all that he wants. Thus he lives, like Israel in the wilderness, upon mere bounty ; but then it is a bounty unchangeable, unwearied, inexhaustible, and all-sufficient. Moses, when speaking of the methods the Lord took to humble Israel, mentions His feeding them with manna as one method. I could not understand this for a time. I thought they were rather in danger of being proud, when they saw themselves provided for in such an extraordinary way. But the manna would not keep ; they could not hoard it up, and were therefore in a state of absolute dependence from day to day : this appointment was well suited to humble them. Thus it is with us in spirituals. We should be better pleased, perhaps, to be set up with a stock or sufficiency at once,—such an inherent portion of wisdom and power as we might depend upon, at least for common occasions, without being constrained, by a sense of indigence, to have continual recourse to the Lord for every thing we want. But His way is best. His own glory is most displayed, and our safety most secured, by keeping us quite poor and empty in ourselves, and supplying us from one minute to another, according to our need. *T*his, if anything, will prevent boasting, and keep a sense of gratitude awake in our hearts. *T*his is well adapted to quicken us to prayer, and furnishes us with a thousand occasions for praise, which would other-wise escape our notice.

But who or what are we that the Most High should thus notice us ? should visit us every morning, and water us every moment ? It is an astonishing thought, that God should thus dwell with men ! That He, before whom the mightiest earthly potentates are less than nothing, and vanity, should thus stoop and accommodate Himself to the situation, wants, and capacities of the weakest, meanest, and poorest of His children. But so it hath pleased Him. He seeth not as a man seeth.

I am, &c.

LETTER XX

M*y* L*ord*,   *August* — 1775.

I HAVE no apt preface or introduction at hand, and, as I have made it almost a rule not to study for what I should offer your Lordship, I therefore beg leave to begin abruptly. It is the future promised privilege of believers in Jesus, that they shall be as the angels ; and there is a sense in which we should endeavour to be as the angels now. *T*his is in-timated to us where we are taught to pray, Thy will be done on earth, as it is in Heaven. I have sometimes amused myself with supposing an angel should be appointed to reside a while upon earth in a human body ; not in sinful flesh like ours, but in a body free from infirmity, and still pre-serving an unabated sense of His own happiness in the favour of God, and of His unspeakable obligation to His goodness ;—and then I have tried to judge, as well as I could, how such an angel would comport himself in such a situation. I know not that I ever enlarged upon the thought, either in preaching or writing ; permit me to follow it a little in this paper.

Were I acquainted with this heavenly visitant, I am

willing to hope I should greatly reverence him, and, if permitted, be glad in some cases to consult him : in some, but not in all ; for I think my fear would be equal to my love. Methinks I could never venture to open my heart freely to him, and unfold to him my numberless complaints and infirmities ; for, as he could have no experience of the like things himself, I should suppose he would not know how fully to pity me, indeed hardly how to bear with me, if I told him all. Alas ! what a preposterous, strange, vile creature should I appear to an angel, if he knew me as I am ! It is well for me that Jesus was made lower than the angels, and that the human nature He assumed was not distinct from the common nature of mankind, though secured from the common depravity ; and because He submitted to be under the law in our name and stead, though He was free from sin Himself, yet, sin and its consequences being (for our sakes) charged upon Him, He acquired, in the days of His humiliation, an experimental sympathy with His poor people. He knows the effects of sin and temptation upon us, by that knowledge whereby He knows all things ; but He knows them likewise in a way more suitable for our comfort and relief, by the sufferings and exercises He passed through for us. Hence arises encouragement. We have not an high-priest who cannot be touched with a feeling of our infirmities, but was in all points tempted even as we are. When I add to this the consideration of His power, promises, and grace, and that He is exalted on purpose to pity, relieve, and save, I gather courage. With Him I dare be free, and am not sorry, but glad, that He knows me perfectly, that not a thought of my heart is hidden from Him. For without this infinite and exact knowledge of my disease, how could He effectually administer to my cure ? But whither am I rambling ? I seem to have lost sight of the angel already. I am now coming back, that, if he cannot effectually pity me, he may at least animate and teach me.

In the first place, I take it for granted this angel would think himself a stranger and pilgrim upon earth. He would not forget that his πολιτευμα was in heaven. Surely he would look upon all the bustle of human life (farther than the design of his mission might connect him with it) with more indifference than we look upon the sports of children, or the amusements of idiots and lunatics, which give us an uneasiness, rather than excite a desire of joining in them. He would judge of everything around him, by the reference and tendency it had to promote the will of Him that sent him˙; and the most specious or splendid appearances, considered in any other view, would make no impression upon him.

Consequently, as to his own concernment, all his aim and desire would be to fulfil the will of God. All situations would be alike to him ; whether he was commanded, as in the case of Sennacherib, to destroy a mighty army with a stroke ; or, as in the case of Hagar, to attend upon a woman, a servant, a slave ; both services would be to him equally honourable and important, because he was in both equally pleasing his Lord, which would be his element and his joy, whether he was appointed to guide the reins of empire, or to sweep the streets.

Again, the angel would doubtless exhibit a striking example of benevolence ; for, being free from selfish bias, filled with a sense of the love of God, and a knowledge of His adorable perfections, his whole heart, and soul, and strength, would be engaged and exerted, both from duty and inclination, to relieve the miseries, and advance the happiness of all around him ; and in this he would follow the pattern of Him who doth good to all, commanding His sun to rise, and His rain to fall, upon the just and the unjust ;— though, from the same pattern, He would show an especial regard to the household of faith. An angel would take but little part in the controversies, contentions, and broils, which might happen in the time of his sojourning here, but would be a friend to all, so far as consistent with the general good.

The will and glory of God being the angel's great view and having a more lively sense of the realities of an unseen world than we can at present conceive, he would certainly, in the first and chief place, have the success and spread of the glorious Gospel at heart. Angels, though not redeemed with blood, yet feel themselves nearly concerned in the work of redemption. They admire its mysteries. We may suppose them well informed in the works of creation and providence. But (unlike too many men who are satisfied with the know-

ledge of astronomy, mathematics, or history) they search
and pry into the counsels of redeeming love, rejoice at the
conversion of a sinner, and think themselves well employed
to be ministering spirits, to minister to the heirs of salvation.
It would therefore be his chief delight to espouse and pro-
mote their cause, and to employ all his talents and influence
in spreading the savour and knowledge of the name of Jesus,
which is the only and effectual means of bringing sinners out
of bondage and darkness into the glorious liberty of the sons
of God.

Lastly, though his zeal for the glory of his Lord would
make him willing to continue here till he had finished the
work given him to do, he would, I am persuaded, look for-
ward with desire to the appointed moment of his recall, that
he might be freed from beholding and mixing with the sin
and vanity of those who know not God, render his account
with joy, and be welcomed to Heaven with a " Well done,
good and faithful servant." Surely he would long for this,
as a labourer for the setting sun ; and would not form
any connexion with the things of time, which should prompt
him to wish his removal protracted for a single hour beyond
the period of his prescribed service.

Alas, why am I not more like an angel ! My views in
my better judgment are the same : my motives and obliga-
tions are even stronger ; an angel is not so deeply indebted
to the grace of God as a believing sinner, who was once upon
the brink of destruction, has been redeemed with blood,
and might justly have been, before now, shut up with the
powers of darkness, without hope ! Yet the merest trifles
are sufficient to debase my views, damp my activity, and
impede my endeavours in the Lord's service, though I profess
to have no other end or desire which can make a continuance
in life worthy my wish. I am, &c.

LETTER XXI

My Lord, *Nov. —* 1775.

Dum loquimur tempus fugit. In the midst of the hurries
and changes of this unsettled state, we glide along swiftly

towards an unchangeable world, and shall soon have as little connexion with the scenes we are now passing through, as we have with what happened before the flood. All that appears great and interesting in the present life, abstracted from its influence upon our internal character, and our everlasting allotment, will soon be as unreal as the visions of the night. This we know and confess ; but, though our judgments are convinced, it is seldom our hearts are duly affected by the thought. And, while I find it easy to write in this moralizing strain, I feel myself disposed to be seriously engaged about trifles, and trifling in the most serious concerns, as if I believed the very contrary. It is with good reason the Lord challenges, as His own prerogative, the full knowledge of the deceitfulness, desperate wickedness, and latent depths of the human heart, which is capable of making even His own people so shamefully inconsistent with themselves, and with their acknowledged principles.

I find that, when I have something agreeable in expectation, (suppose, for instance, it were a few hours' conversation with your Lordship,) my imagination paints and prepares the scene beforehand ; hurries me over the intervening space of time, as though it were a useless blank, and anticipates the pleasure I propose. Many of my thoughts of this kind are mere waking dreams ; for, perhaps, the opportunity I am eagerly waiting for never happens, but is swallowed up by some unforeseen disappointment ; or, if not, something from within or without prevents its answering the idea I had formed of it. Nor does my fancy confine itself within the narrow limits of probabilities ; it can busy itself as eagerly in ranging after chimeras and impossibilities, and engage my attention to the ideal pursuit of things which are never likely to happen. In these respects my imagination travels with wings ; so that if the wilderness, the multiplicity, the variety of the phantoms which pass through my mind in the space of a winter's day were known to my fellow-creatures, they would probably deem me, as I am so often ready to deem myself, but a more sober and harmless kind of lunatic. But if I endeavour to put this active roving power in a right track, and to represent to myself those scenes which, though not yet present, I know will soon be realized, and have a greatness which the most enlarged exercise of my powers cannot comprehend ; if I would fix my thoughts upon the hour of death, the end of the world, the coming of the Judge, or similar subjects ; then my imagination is presently tame, cold, and jaded, travels very slowly, and is soon wearied in the road of truth ; though in the fairy fields of uncertainty and folly it can skip from mountain to mountain. Mr. Addison supposes that the imagination alone, as it can be differently affected, is capable of making us either inconceivably happy or miserable. I am sure it is capable of making us miserable, though I believe it seldom gives us much pleasure, but such as is to be found in a fool's paradise. But, I am sure, were my outward life and conduct perfectly free from blame, the disorders and defilement of my imagination are sufficient to constitute me a chief sinner, in the sight of Him to whom the thoughts and intents of the heart are continually open, and who is of purer eyes than to behold iniquity.

Upon this head I cannot but lament how universally, almost, education is suited, and as it were designed, to add to the stimulus of depraved nature. A cultivated imagination is commended and sought after as a very desirable talent, though it seldom means more than the possession of a large stock of other people's dreams and fables, with a certain quickness in compounding them, enlarging upon them, and exceeding them by inventions of our own. Poets, painters, and even historians, are employed to assist us, from our early years, in forming an habitual relish for shadows and colourings, which both indispose for the search of truth, and even unfit us for its reception, unless proposed just in our own way. The best effect of the Belles Lettres upon the imaginations, seems generally expressed by the word *taste*. And what is this taste, but a certain disposition which loves to be humoured, smoothed, and flattered, and which can hardly receive or bear the most important truths, if they be not decorated and set off with such a delicacy and address as taste requires ? I say *the most important truths*, because truths of a secular importance strike so closely upon the senses, that the decision of taste perhaps is not waited for. Thus, if a man be informed of the birth of his child, or that his house is on fire, the message takes up his thoughts, and he is seldom much disgusted with the manner in which it is delivered. But what an insuperable bar is the refined taste of many to their profiting by the preaching of the Gospel, or even to their hearing it ! Though the subject of a discourse be weighty, and some just represeutation given of the evil of sin, the worth of the soul, and the love of Christ ; yet, if there be something amiss in the elocution, language, or manner of the preacher, people of taste must be possessed, in a good measure, of grace likewise, if they can hear him with tolerable patience. And, perhaps, three-fourths of those who are accounted the most sensible and judicious in the auditory, will remember little about the sermon, but the tone of the voice, the awkwardness of the attitude, the obsolete expressions, and the like ; while the poor and simple not being encumbered with this hurtful accomplishment, receive the messenger as the Lord's servant, and the truth as the Lord's word, and are comforted and edified. But I stop. Some people would say, that I must suppose your Lordship to have but little taste, or else much grace, or I should not venture to trouble you with such letters as mine.

I am, &c.

LETTER XXII

My Lord,

THE apostle speaks of a *blessedness*, which it is the design of the Gospel to impart to those who receive it. The Galatians once had it, and spoke of it. The apostle reminds them of their loss, which is left upon record as a warning to us. His expression has led me sometimes to consider wherein a Christian's present blessedness consists.—I mean that which is attainable in this state of trial, and the sense and exercise of which may be, and too often is, suspended and taken from us. It is a blessedness which, if we speak of man in a natural state, his eye hath not seen, nor his ear heard, so as to understand it, nor can the idea of it arise in his heart. It is no way dependent upon outward circumstances. Prosperity cannot impart it, preserve, or supply the want of it ; nor can adversity put it out of our reach. The wise cannot acquire it by dint of superior abilities ; nor shall the simple miss it for want of capacity.

The state of true believers, compared with that of others, is always *blessed*. If they are born from above, and united to Jesus, they are delivered from condemnation, and are heirs of eternal life, and may therefore well be accounted happy. But I consider now, not their harvest, but their first fruits ; not their portion in reversion, but the *earnest* attainable in this life ; not what they *shall* be in Heaven, but what, in an humble attendance upon the Lord, they *may be* while upon earth. There is even at present a prize of our high calling set before us. It is much to be desired, that we had such a sense of its value as might prompt us to run that we might obtain. I have thought this blessedness may be comprised in five particulars, though, in order to take a succinct view of the subject, some of these might be branched out into several others ; but I would not, by too many subdivisions, give my letter the air of a sermon.

In the first place, a clear, well-grounded, habitual per-suasion of our acceptance in the Beloved is attainable ; and, though we may be safe, we cannot be said to enjoy blessedness without it. To be in a state of suspense and uncertainty in a point of so great importance is painful, and the Lord has accordingly provided that His people may have strong consolation on this head. They are blessed, therefore, who have such views of the power, grace, and suitableness of Jesus, and the certainty and security of redemption in Him, together with such a consciousness that they have anchored their hopes, and ventured their all upon His person, work, and promise, as furnishes them with a ready answer to all the cavils of unbelief and Satan, in the apostle's manner, Rom. viii. 31-37. That Paul could thus challenge and triumph over all charges and enemies was not an appendage of his office as an apostle, but a part of his experience as a believer ; and it lies equally open to us ; for we have the same Gospel and the same promises as he had ; nor is the efficacy of the Holy Spirit's teaching a whit weakened by length of time. But many stop short of this. They have a hope, but it rather springs from their frames and feelings than from a spiritual apprehension of the Redeemer's engagements and fullness, and therefore fluctuates and changes like the weather. Could they be persuaded to pray with earnestness and importunity, as the apostle prays for them, Eph. i. 17, 18, and iii. 16, 19, they would find a blessedness which they have not yet known ; for it is said, " Ask, and ye shall receive."—And it is said likewise, " Ye receive not because ye ask not."

Could this privilege be enjoyed singly, the natural man would have no objection to it. He would (as he thinks) be pleased to know he should be saved at last, provided that while here he might live in his sins. But the believer will not, cannot think himself blessed, unless he has likewise a conscience void of offence. This was the apostle's daily exercise, though no one was farther from a legal spirit, or more dependent upon Jesus for acceptance. But if we live in any known sin, or allow ourselves in the customary omission of any known duty, supposing it possible, in such a case, to preserve a sense of our acceptance, (which can hardly be supposed ; for if the Spirit be grieved, our evidences decline of course,) yet we could not be easy. If a traveller was absolutely sure of reaching his journey's end in safety, yet, if he walked with a thorn in his foot, he must take every step in pain. Such a thorn will be felt in the conscience, till we are favoured with a simplicity of heart, and made willing in all things, great or small, to yield obedience to the authority of the Lord's precepts, and make them the standing rule of our conduct, without wilfully admitting a single exception. At the best, we shall be conscious of innumerable short-comings, and shameful defilement ; but these things will not break our peace, if our hearts are upright. But if we trifle with light, and connive at what we know to be wrong, we shall be weak, restless, and uncomfortable. How many, who we would hope are the children of the King, are lean from day to day, because some right-hand or right-eye evil, which they cannot persuade themselves to part with, keeps them halting between two opinions ; and they are as distant from happiness, as they are from the possibility of reconciling the incompatible services of God and the world ! But happy indeed is he who condemneth not himself in that thing which he alloweth.

Real communion with the Lord, in His appointed means

of grace, is likewise an important branch of this blessedness. They were instituted for this end, and are sufficient, by virtue of His power and Spirit, to answer it. I do not believe this enjoyment will be always equal. But I believe a comfortable sense of it, in some measure, is generally attainable. To read the Scriptures, not as an attorney may read a will, merely to know the sense, but as the heir reads it, as a description and proof of his interest : to hear the Gospel, as the voice of our Beloved, so as to have little leisure either for admiring the abilities, or censuring the defects of the preacher ; and, in prayer, to feel a liberty of pouring out our hearts before the Lord, to behold some glances of His goodness passing before us, and to breathe forth before Him the tempers of a child, the spirit of adoption : and thus, by beholding His glory, to be conformed more and more to His image, and to renew our strength, by drawing water out of the wells of salvation : herein is blessedness. They who have tasted it can say, It is good for me to draw nigh to God. The soul, thus refreshed by the water of life, is preserved from thirsting after the vanities of the world,—thus instructed in the sanctuary, comes down from the mount filled with heavenly wisdom, anointed with a holy unction, and thereby qualified to judge, speak, and act in character, in all the relations and occasions of secular life. In this way, besides the pleasure, a spiritual taste is acquired, something analogous to the meaning of the word *taste* when applied to music or good breeding, by which discords and improprieties are observed and avoided, as it were by instinct, and what is right is felt and followed, not so much by the force of rules, as by a habit insensibly acquired, and in which the substance of all necessary rules are, if I may so say, digested. O that I knew more of this blessedness, and more of its effects !

Another branch of blessedness is a power of reposing ourselves and our concerns upon the Lord's faithfulness and care ; and may be considered in two respects. A reliance upon Him that He will surely provide for us, guide us, protect us, be our help in trouble, our shield in danger ; so that, however poor, weak, and defenceless in ourselves, we may rejoice in His all-sufficiency as our own ;—and farther, in consequence of this, a peaceful, humble submission to His will, under all events, which, upon their first impression, are

contrary to our own views and desires. Surely, in a world
like this, where everything is uncertain, where we are exposed
to trials on every hand, and know not but a single hour
may bring forth something painful, yea, dreadful to our
natural sensations, there can be no blessedness, but so far as
we are thus enabled to entrust and resign all to the direction
and faithfulness of the Lord our Shepherd. For want of more
of this spirit, multitudes of professing Christians perplex
and wound themselves, and dishonour their high calling, by
continual anxieties, alarms, and complaints. They think
nothing safe under the Lord's keeping, unless their own eye
is likewise upon it ; and are seldom satisfied with any of His
dispensations ; for, though He gratify their desires in nine
instances, a refusal in the tenth spoils the relish of all, and
they show the truths of the Gospel can afford them little
comfort if self is crossed. But blessed is the man who
trusteth in the Lord, and whose hope the Lord is. He shall
not be afraid of evil tidings : he shall be kept in perfect peace,
though the earth be moved, and the mountains cast into the
midst of the sea.

The paper admonishes me it is time to relieve your Lord-
ship. And I have not room to detain you long upon the
fifth particular. It belongs to a believer's blessedness to
feel his spirit cheerful and active for the Lord's service in
the world. For to what other end should he wish to live ?
If he thought of himself only, it would be better to depart
and be with Jesus immediately. But he is a debtor to His
grace and love ; and, though strictly he can make no returns,
yet he longs to show his thankfulness : and if the Lord gives
him a heart to redeem his time, to devote his strength and
influence, and lay himself out for His service,—that he may
be instrumental in promoting His cause, in comforting His
people,—or enable him to let his light shine before men,
that his God and Father may be honoured,—He will account
it blessedness. This is indeed the great end of life, and he
knows it will evidently appear so at the approach of death ;
and, therefore, while others are encumbered about many
things, he esteems this the one thing needful.

I remain, my Lord, &c.

LETTER XXIII

My Lord, *July* — 1776.

THAT I may not weary you by a preamble, I oblige myself to take the turn of my letter from some passage of Scripture : and I fix upon that which just now occurred to my thoughts, a clause in that pattern of prayer which He who best knows our state has been pleased to leave for the instruction of His people, in their great concerns of waiting at His throne of grace, Matt. vi. 13,—"And lead us not into temptation." This petition is seasonable at all times, and to all persons who have any right knowledge of themselves or their spiritual calling.

The word *temptation*, taken at large, includes every kind of trial. To tempt, is to try or prove. In this sense, it is said, the Lord tempted Abraham, that is, He tried him ; for God cannot tempt to evil. He proposed such an act of obedience to him, as was a test of his faith, love, dependence, and integrity. Thus, all our afflictions, under His gracious management, are appointed to prove, manifest, exercise, and purify the graces of His children. And not afflictions only ; prosperity likewise is a state of temptation : and many who have endured sharp sufferings, and come off honourably, have been afterwards greatly hurt and ensnared by prosperity. To this purpose the histories of David and Hezekiah are in point. But by temptation we more frequently understand the wiles and force which Satan employs in assaulting our peace, or spreading snares for our feet. He is always practising against us, either directly and from himself, by the access he has to our hearts, or mediately, by the influence he has over the men and the things of this world. The words which follow confirm this sense,—"Lead us not into temptation ; but deliver us from evil," απο του πονηρου, from the *evil one*, as it might be properly rendered here, and in 1 John v. 19. The subtility and power of this adversary are very great ; he is an over-match for us ; and we have no hope of safety but in the Lord's protection. Satan's action upon the heart may be illustrated by the action of the wind upon the sea. The sea sometimes appears smooth ; but it is always disposed to swell and rage, and to obey the impulse of every storm. Thus, the heart may be sometimes quiet ; but the wind of temptation will awaken and rouse it in a moment : for it is essential to our depraved nature to be unstable and yielding as the water ; and, when it is under the impression of the enemy, its violence can only be controlled by Him who says to the raging sea, " Be still, and here shall thy proud waves be stayed." The branches of temptation are almost innumerable ; but the principal may be reduced to the several faculties of the soul, (as we commonly speak,) to which they are more directly suited.

He has temptations for the understanding. He can blind the mind with prejudices and false reasonings, and ply it with arguments for infidelity, till the most obvious truths become questionable. Even where the Gospel has been received, he can insinuate error, which for the suddenness and malignity of its effects may be properly compared to poison. A healthy man may be poisoned in a moment ; and, if he be, the baneful drug is usually mixed with his food. Many who for a while seemed to be sound in the faith have had their judgments strongly and strangely perverted, and prevailed upon to renounce and oppose the truths they once prized and defended. Such instances are striking proofs of human weakness, and loud calls to watchfulness and dependence, and to beware of leaning to our own understandings. For these purposes he employs both preachers and authors, who, by fine words and fair speeches, beguile the hearts of the unwary. And, by his immediate influence upon the mind, he is able (if the Lord permits him) to entangle those who are providentially placed out of the reach of corrupt and designing men.

He tempts the conscience. By working upon the unbelief of our hearts, and darkening the glory of the Gospel, he can hold down the soul to the number, weight, and aggravation of its sins, so that it shall not be able to look up to Jesus, nor draw any comfort from His blood, promises, and grace. How many go burdened in this manner, seeking relief from duties, and perhaps spending their strength in things not commanded, though they hear, and perhaps acknowledge the Gospel ! Nor are the wisest and most established able to withstand his assaults, if the Lord withdraw, and give him leave to employ his power and subtility unrestrained. The Gospel affords sufficient ground for an abiding assurance of hope ; nor should we rest satisfied without it. However, the possession and preservation of this privilege depend upon the Lord's presence with the soul, and His shielding us from Satan's attacks ; for I am persuaded he is able to sift and shake the strongest believer upon earth.

He has likewise temptations suited to the will. Jesus makes His people willing in the day of His power ; yet there is a contrary principle remaining within them, of which Satan knows how to avail himself. There are occasions in which he almost prevails to set self again upon the throne, as Dagon was raised after he had fallen before the ark. How else should any, who have tasted that the Lord is gracious, give way to a repining spirit, account His dispensations hard, or His precepts too strict, so as to shrink from their observance through the fear of men, or a regard to their worldly interest ?

Farther, he has snares for the affections. In managing these, he gains a great advantage from our situation in a world that knows not God. The Scripture gives Satan the title of God of this world ; and believers learn, by painful experience, how great his power is in and over the persons and things of it. So that to be steadfast in wisdom's ways requires unremitted efforts, like pressing through a crowd, or swimming against a stream. How hard is it to live in the midst of pitch and not be defiled ! The air of the world is infectious. Our business and unavoidable connexions are so interwoven with occasions of sin, and there is so much in our hearts suited to them, that, unless we are incessantly upheld by almighty strength, we cannot stand a day or an hour. Past victories afford us no greater security than they did Samson, who was shamefully surprised by enemies whom he had formerly conquered. Nor are we only tempted by compliances that are evil in themselves. With respect to these, perhaps, conscience may be awake, and we stand upon our guard ; but we are still upon Satan's ground ; and, while he may seem to allow himself defeated, he can dexterously change his method, and come upon us where we do not suspect him. For, *Perimus in licitis*. Perhaps our greatest danger arises from things in themselves lawful. He can tempt us by our nearest and dearest friends, and pervert every blessing of a kind Providence into an occasion of drawing our hearts from the Giver ; yea, spiritual blessings, gifts, comforts, and even graces, are sometimes the engines by which he practises against us, to fill us with vain confidence and self-sufficiency, or to lull us into formality and indolence.

That wonderful power which we call the imagination is, I suppose, rather the medium of the soul's perceptions, during its present state of union with the body, than a spiritual faculty, strictly speaking ; but it partakes largely of that depravity which sin has brought upon our whole frame, and affords Satan an avenue for assaulting us with the most terrifying, if not the most dangerous, of his temptations. At the best, we have but an indifferent command over it. We cannot, by an act of our own will, exclude a thousand painful, wild, inconsistent, and hurtful ideas, which are ever ready to obtrude themselves upon our minds ; and a slight alteration in the animal system, in the motion of the blood, or nervous spirits, is sufficient to withdraw it wholly from our dominion, and to leave us, like a city without walls or gates, exposed to the incursion of our enemy. We are fearfully and wonderfully made ; and, with all our boasted knowledge of other things, can form no conception of what is so vastly interesting to us, the mysterious connexion between soul and body, and the manner in which they are mutually affected by each other. The effects we too sensibly feel. The wisest of men would be accounted fools or mad were they to express in words a small part of what passes within them ; and it would appear that much of the soberest life is little better than a waking dream : but how direful are the consequences when the Lord permits some hidden pin in the human machine to be altered ! Immediately a door flies open which no hand but His can shut, and the enemy pours in like a flood, falsehood and horror, and the blackness of darkness ; the judgment is borne down and disabled, and the most distressing illusions seize us with all the apparent force of evidence and demonstration. When this is the case in a certain degree, we call it distraction ; but there are various degrees of it, which leave a person in the possession of his senses as to the things of common life, and yet are sufficient, with respect to his spiritual concerns, to shake the very foundations of his hope, and deprive him of all peace and comfort, and make him a terror to himself. All the Lord's people are not called to navigate in these deep waters of soul-distress ; but all are liable. Ah ! if we knew what some suffer, the *horribilia de Deo, et terribilia de fide*, which excruciate the minds of those over whom Satan is permitted to tyrannize in this way, surely we should be more earnest and frequent in praying, " Lead us not into temptation." From some little sense I have of the malice and subtility of our spiritual enemies, and the weakness of those barriers which we have to prevent their assaults, I am fully persuaded that nothing less than the continual exertion of that almighty power which preserves the stars in their orbits, can maintain our peace of mind for an hour or a minute. In this view, all comparative difference in external situations seems to be annihilated ; for as the Lord's presence can make His people happy in a dungeon, so there are temptations which, if we felt them, would instantly render us incapable of receiving a moment's satisfaction from an assemblage of all earthly blessings, and make the company of our dearest friends tasteless, if not insupportable.

Ah ! how little do the gay and the busy think of these things ! How little, indeed, do they think of them who profess to believe them ! How faint is the sense of our obligations to *Him*, Who freely submitted to the fiercest onsets of the powers of darkness, to free us from the punishment due to our sins ; otherwise we must have been for ever shut up with those miserable and merciless spirits, who delight in our torment, and who, even in the present state, if they get access to our minds, can make our existence a burden !

But our Lord, who knows and considers our weakness, of which we are so little aware, allows and directs us to pray, " Lead us not into temptation." We are not to expect an absolute freedom from temptation ; we are called to be soldiers, and must sometimes meet with enemies, and perhaps with wounds ; yet, considering this prayer as provided by Him who knows what we are, and where we are, it may afford us both instruction and consolation.

It calls at a constant reflection upon our own weakness. Believers, especially young ones, are prone to rest too much in grace received. They feel their hearts warm ; and, like Peter, are ready to please themselves with thinking how they would act in such or such a state of trial. It is as if the Lord had said, Poor worms, be not high-minded, but fear and pray, that, if it may be, you may be kept from learning, by bitter experience, how weak your supposed strength is. It sweetly intimates, that all our ways, and all our enemies, are in the hands of our great Shepherd. He knows our path. We are short-sighted, and cannot tell what an hour may bring forth : but we are under His protection ; and, if we depend upon Him, we need not be anxiously afraid. He will be faithful to the trust we repose in Him, and will suffer no temptation to overtake us, but what He will support us under and bring us through. But it becomes us to beware of security and presumption, to keep our eyes upon Him, and not to think ourselves safe a moment longer than our spirits feel and breathe the meaning of this petition.

It implies, likewise, the duty of watchfulness on our part, as our Lord enjoins them elsewhere, " Watch and pray." If we desire not to be led into temptation, surely we are not to *run* into it. If we wish to be preserved from error, we are to guard against a curious and reasoning spirit. If we would preserve peace of conscience, we must beware of trifling with the light and motions of the Holy Spirit ; for without His assistance we cannot maintain faith in exercise. If we would not be ensnared by the men of the world, we are to keep at a proper distance from them. The less we have to do with them the better, excepting so far as the providence of God makes it our duty, in the discharge of our callings and relations, and taking opportunities of doing them good. And, though we cannot wholly shut Satan out of our imaginations, we should be cautious that we do not wilfully provide fuel for his flame ; but entreat the Lord to set a watch upon our eyes and our ears, and to teach us to reject the first motions and the smallest appearances of evil.

I have been so intent upon my subject, that I have once and again forgot I was writing to your Lordship, otherwise I should not have let my lucubration run to so great a length, which I certainly did not intend when I began. I shall not add to this fault by making an apology. I have touched upon a topic of great importance to myself. I am one among many who have suffered greatly for want of paying more attention to my need of this prayer. O that I could be wiser hereafter, and always act and speak as knowing that I am always upon a field of battle, and beset by legions !

I am, with great respect, &c.

LETTER XXIV

My Lord,   *September* — 1776.

WITHOUT any preamble, I purpose now to wait on your Lordship, with a few thoughts on the meaning of that name which first obtained at Antioch ; in other words, what it is to be a Christian ? What are the effects which (making allowance for the unavoidable infirmities attending upon the present state of mortality) may be expected from a real experimental knowledge of the Gospel ? I would not insinuate that none are Christians who do not come up to the character I would describe ; for then I fear I should un-Christian myself : but only to consider what the Scripture encourages us to aim at as the prize of our high calling in this life. It is generally allowed and lamented, that we are too apt to live below our privileges, and to stop short of what the spirit and the promises of the Gospel point out to us as attainable.

Mr. Pope's admired line, " An honest man's the noblest work of God." may be admitted as a truth when rightly explained. A Christian is the noblest work of God in this visible world, and bears a much brighter impression of His glory and goodness than the sun in the firmament : and none but a Christian can be strictly and properly honest : all others are too much under the power of self, to do universally to others as they would others should do unto them : and nothing but a uniform conduct upon this principle deserves the name of honesty.

The Christian is a new creature, born and taught from above. He has been convinced of his guilt and misery as

a sinner, has fled for refuge to the hope set before him, has
seen the Son and believed on Him : his natural prejudices
against the glory and grace of God's salvation have been
subdued and silenced by almighty power ;   he has accepted
the Beloved, and is made acceptable in Him :   he now
knows the Lord ; has renounced the confused, distant, un-
comfortable notions he once formed of God ; and beholds
Him in Christ, who is the way, the truth, and the
life, the only door by which we can enter to any true
satisfying knowledge of God, or communion with Him.
But he sees God in Christ reconciled, a Father, a Saviour,
and a Friend, who has freely forgiven him all his sins,
and given him the spirit of adoption : he is now no longer
a servant, much less a stranger, but a son ; and, because a
son, an heir already interested in all the promises, ad-
mitted to the throne of grace, and an assured expectant of
eternal glory.   The Gospel is designed to give us not only a
peradventure or a probability, but a certainty both of our
acceptance and our perseverance, till death shall be swal-
lowed up in life.   And though many are sadly fluctuating
and perplexed upon this head, and perhaps all are so for a
season, yet there are those who can say, We know that we are
of God ;   and therefore they are steadfast and unmoveable
in His way ;   because they are confident that their labour
shall not be in vain, but that, when they shall be absent from
the body, they shall be present with the Lord.   This is
the state of the advanced, experienced Christian, who, being
enabled to make his profession the chief business of his life,
is strong in the Lord, and in the power of His might.   Every
one who has this hope in Christ, purifieth himself even as He
is pure.   I would now attempt a sketch of the Christian's
temper, formed upon these principles and hopes, under
the leading branches of its exercise, respecting God Himself,
and His fellow-creatures.
    The Christian's temper God-ward is evidenced by humility.
He has received from Gethsemane and Golgotha such a sense
of the evil of sin, and of the holiness of God, combined with
His matchless love to sinners, as has deeply penetrated
his heart ; he has an affecting remembrance of the state of
rebellion and enmity in which he once lived against this
holy and good God ; and he has a quick perception of the

defilements and defects which still debase his best services. His mouth is therefore stopped as to boasting ; he is vile in his own eyes, and is filled with wonder that the Lord should visit such a sinner with such a salvation. He sees so vast a disproportion between the obligations he is under to grace, and the returns he makes, that he is disposed, yea, constrained, to adopt the apostle's words without affectation, and to account himself less than the least of all saints ; and knowing his own heart, while he sees only the outside of others, he is not easily persuaded there can be a believer upon earth so faint, so unfruitful, so unworthy as himself. Yet, though abased, he is not discouraged, for he enjoys peace. The dignity, offices, blood, righteousness, faithfulness, and compassion of the Redeemer, in whom he rests, trusts, and lives, for wisdom, righteousness, sanctification, and redemption, are adequate to all his wants and wishes, provide him with an answer to every objection, and give him no less confidence in God, than if he were sinless as an angel. For he sees, that though sin has abounded in him, grace has much more abounded in Jesus. With respect to the past, all things are become new ; with respect to the present and future, he leans upon an almighty arm, and relies upon the word and power which made and uphold the Heavens and the earth. Though he feels himself unworthy of the smallest mercies, he claims and expects the greatest blessings that God can bestow ; and being rooted and grounded in the knowledge and love of Christ, his peace abides, and is not greatly affected, either by the variation of his own frame, or the changes of God's dispensations towards him while here. With such a sense of himself, such a heartfelt peace and heavenly hope, how can his spirit but breathe *love* to his God and Saviour ? It is indeed the perfection of his character and happiness, that his soul is united by love to the chief good. The love of Christ is the joy of his heart, and the spring of his obedience. With his Saviour's presence, he finds a Heaven begun upon earth ; and without it all the other glories of the heavenly state would not content him. The excellence of Christ, His love to sinners, especially His dying love ; His love to himself, in seeking and saving him when lost, saving him to the uttermost—but I must stop.—Your Lordship can better conceive than I can describe, how and why Jesus is dear to the heart that knows Him. That part of the Christian's life which is not employed in the active service of his Lord, is chiefly spent in seeking and maintaining communion with Him. For this he plies the throne, and studies the word of grace, and frequents the ordinances, where the Lord has promised to meet with His people. These are his golden hours; and when thus employed, how poor and trivial does all that the world calls great and important appear in his eyes! Yea, he is solicitous to keep up an intercourse of heart with his Beloved, in his busiest scenes; and so far as he can succeed, it alleviates all his labours, and sweetens all his troubles. And when he is neither communing with his Lord, nor acting for Him, he accounts his time lost, and is ashamed and grieved. The truth of his love is manifested by submission. This is twofold, and absolute and without reserve in each. He submits to His revealed will, as made known to him by precept, and by His own example. He aims to tread in his Saviour's footsteps, and makes conscience of all His commandments, without exception and without hesitation. Again, he submits to His providential will; he yields to His sovereignty, acquiesces in His wisdom; he knows he has no right to complain of any thing, because he is a sinner; and he has no reason, because he is sure the Lord does all things well. Therefore, his submission is not forced, but is an act of trust. He knows he is not more unworthy than he is unable to choose for himself, and therefore rejoices that the Lord has undertaken to manage for him; and were he compelled to make his own choice, he could only choose, that all his concerns should remain in that hand to which he has already committed them. And thus he judges of public, as well as of his personal affairs. He cannot be an unaffected spectator of national sins, nor without apprehension of their deserved consequences; he feels, and almost trembles for others; but he himself dwells under the shadow of the Almighty, in a sanctuary that cannot be forced; and, therefore, should he see the earth shaken, and the mountains cast into the midst of the sea, his heart would not be greatly moved, for God is his refuge. The Lord reigns. He sees his Saviour's hands directing every dark appearance, and overruling all to the accomplishment of His own great purposes : this satisfies him ; and though the winds and waves should be high, he can venture his own little bark in the storm, for he has an infallible and almighty Pilot on board with him. And, indeed, why should he fear when he has nothing to lose ? His best concerns are safe ; and other things he holds as gifts from his Lord, to whose call he is ready to resign them in whatever way He pleases, well knowing that creatures and instruments cannot of themselves touch a hair of his head, without the Lord's permission, and that He does permit them, it must be for the best.

I might enlarge farther.—But I shall proceed to consider the Christian's temper respecting himself. He lives godly and *soberly*. By sobriety we mean more than that he is not a drunkard ; his tempers toward God, of course, form him to a moderation in all temporal things. He is not scrupulous or superstitious : he understands the liberty of the Gospel, that every creature of God is good if it be received with thanksgiving : he does not aim at being needlessly singular, nor practice self-devised austerities. The Christian is neither a stoic nor a cynic ; yet he finds daily cause for watchfulness and restraint. Satan will not often tempt a believer to gross crimes ; our greatest snares and sorest conflicts are usually found in things lawful in themselves, but hurtful to us by their abuse, engrossing too much of our time, or of our hearts, or somehow indisposing us for communion with the Lord. The Christian will be jealous of any thing that might entangle his affections, damp his zeal, or straiten him in his opportunities of serving his Saviour. He is likewise content with his situation, because the Lord chooses it for him ; his spirit is not eager for additions and alterations in his circumstances. If divine Providence points out and leads to a change, he is ready to follow, though it should be what the world would call from a better to a worse ; for he is a pilgrim and a stranger here, and a citizen of Heaven. As people of fortune sometimes, in travelling, submit cheerfully to inconvenient accommodations, very different from their homes, and comfort themselves with thinking they are not always to live so ; so the Christian is not greatly solicitous about externals. If he has them, he will use them moderately. If he has but little of them, he can make a good shift without them ; he is but upon a journey, and will soon be at home. If he be rich, experience confirms our Lord's words, Luke xii. 15 ; and satisfies him, that a large room, a crowd of servants, and twenty dishes upon his table, add nothing to the real happiness of life. Therefore he will not have his heart set upon such things. If he be in an humbler state, he is more disposed to pity, than to envy those above him ; for he judges they must have many incumbrances from which he is freed. However, the will of God, and the light of His countenance, are the chief things the Christian, whether rich or poor, regards ; and, therefore, his moderation is made known unto all men.

A third branch of the Christian's temper respects his fellow-creatures. And here, methinks, if I had not filled a sheet already, I could enlarge with pleasure. We have, in this degenerate day, among those who claim and are allowed the name of Christian, too many of a narrow, selfish, mercenary spirit ; but in the beginning it was not so. The Gospel is designed to cure such a spirit, but gives no indulgence to it. A Christian has the mind of Christ, who went about doing good, who makes His sun to shine upon the good and the evil, and sendeth rain on the just and the unjust. His Lord's example forms him to the habit of diffusive benevolence ; he breathes a spirit of goodwill to mankind, and rejoices in every opportunity of being useful to the souls and bodies of others, without respect to parties or interests. He commiserates, and would, if possible, alleviate the miseries of all around him ; and if his actual services are restrained by want of ability, yet all share in his sympathy and prayers. Acting in the spirit of his Master he frequently meets with a measure of the like treatment ; but, if his good is requited with evil, he labours to overcome evil with good. He feels himself a sinner, and needs much forgiveness : this makes him ready to forgive. He is not haughty, captious, easily offended, or hard to be reconciled ; for at the feet of Jesus he has learned meekness ; and when he meets with unkindness or injustice, he considers, that, though he has not deserved such things from men, they are instruments employed by his heavenly Father (from whom he has deserved to suffer much more) for his humiliation and chastisement ; and is, therefore, more concerned for their sins than for his own sufferings, and prays, after the pattern of his Saviour, " Father, forgive them, for they know not what they do." He knows he is fallible, therefore cannot be positive. He knows he is frail, and therefore dares not be censorious. As a member of society, he is just, punctual in the discharge of every relative duty, faithful to his engagements and promises, rendering to all their dues, obedient to lawful authority, and acting to all men according to the golden rule, of doing as he would be done by. His conduct is simple, devoid of artifice, and consistent, attending to every branch of duty ; and in the closet, the family, the church, and in the transactions of common life, he is the same man ; for in every circumstance he serves the Lord, and aims to maintain a conscience void of offence in His sight. No small part of the beauty of his profession in the sight of men, consists in the due government of his tongue. The law of truth, and kindness, and purity, is upon his lips. He abhors lying ; and is so far from inventing a slander, that he will not repeat a report to the disadvantage of his neighbour, however true, without a proper call. His converse is cheerful, but inoffensive ; and he will no more wound another with his wit (if he has a talent that way) than with a knife. His speech is with grace, seasoned with salt, and suited to promote the peace and edification of all around him.

Such is the Christian in civil life ; but though he loves all mankind, he stands in a nearer relation, and bears an especial brotherly love to all who are partakers of the faith and hope of the Gospel. This regard is not confined within the pale of a denomination, but extended to all who love the Lord Jesus Christ in sincerity. He calls no man master himself ; nor does he wish to impose a Shibboleth of his own upon others. He rejoices in the image of God wherever he sees it, and in the work of God wherever it is carried on. Though tenacious of the truths which the Lord has taught him, his heart is open to those who differ from him in less essential points, and allows to others that right of private judgment which he claims for himself, and is disposed to hold communion in love with all who hold the Head. He cannot, indeed, countenance those who set aside the one foundation which God has laid in Zion, and maintain errors derogatory to the honour of his Saviour, or subversive of the faith and experience of His people ; yet he wishes well to their persons, pities, and prays for them, and is ready in meekness to instruct them that oppose ; but there is no bitterness in his zeal, being sensible that raillery and invective are dishonourable to the cause of truth, and quite unsuitable in the mouth of a sinner, who owes all that distinguishes him from the vilest of men to the free grace of God. In a word, he is influenced by the wisdom from above, which, as it is pure, is likewise peaceable, gentle, and easy to be entreated, full of mercy and good works, without partiality, and without hypocrisy.

I must just recur to my first head, and observe, that with this spirit and deportment, the Christian, while he is enabled to maintain a conscience void of offence towards God and man, is still sensible and mindful of indwelling sin : he has his eye more upon his rule than upon his attainments ; and therefore finds and confesses, that in every thing he comes exceedingly short, and that his best services are not only defective, but defiled ; he accounts himself an unprofitable servant, is abased in his own eyes, and derives all his hope and comfort, as well as his strength, from Jesus, whom he has known, received, and trusted, to whom he has committed his soul, in whom he rejoices, and worships God in the spirit, renouncing all confidence in the flesh, and esteeming all things as loss, for the excellency of the knowledge of Christ Jesus his Lord.

If I have lately been rather tardy in making my payments to your Lordship, I have proportionably increased the quantity.   It is high time I should now relieve your patience. I hope—I long to be a Christian indeed ; and I hope this hasty exemplification of my wishes will answer to your Lordship's experience, better than I fear it does to my own. May I beg a remembrance in your prayers, that He Who has given me to will and desire, may work in me to be and to do according to His own good pleasure.

I am, &c.

LETTER XXV

MY LORD, *Nov. — 1776.*

My London journey, which prevented my writing in October, made me amends by an opportunity of waiting upon your Lordship in person. Some seasons are not only pleasant at the time, but afford me pleasure in the review.— I could have wished the half-hour we were together by ourselves prolonged to half a day. The subject your Lordship was pleased to suggest has been often upon my mind ; and glad should I be, were I able to offer you any thing satisfactory upon it. There is no doubt but first religious impressions are usually mingled with much of a legal spirit ; and that conscience, at such a time, is not only tender, but misinformed and scrupulous : and I believe, as your Lordship intimated, that when the mind is more enlightened, and we feel a liberty from many fetters we had imposed upon ourselves, we are in danger of verging too far towards the other extreme. It seems to me that no one person can adjust the medium, and draw the line exactly for another. There are so many particulars in every situation, of which a stranger cannot be a competent judge, and the best human advices and models are mixed with such defects, that it is not right to expect others to be absolutely guided by our rules, nor is it safe for us implicitly to adopt the decisions or practices of others. But the Scripture undoubtedly furnishes sufficient and infallible rules for every person, however circumstanced ; and the throne of grace is appointed for us to wait upon the Lord for the best exposition of His precepts. Thus, David often prays to be led in the right way, in the path of judgment. By frequent prayer, and close acquaintance with the Scripture, and an habitual attention to the frame of our hearts, there is a certain delicacy of spiritual taste and discernment to be acquired, which renders a nice disquisition concerning the nature and limits of the Adiaphora, as they are called, or how near we may go to the utmost bounds of what is right, without being wrong, quite unnecessary. Love is the clearest and most persuasive casuist ; and when our love to the Lord is in lively exercise, and the rule of His word is in our eye, we seldom make

G 2

great mistakes. And, I believe, the overdoings of a young convert, proceeding from an honest simplicity of heart, and a desire of pleasing the Lord, are more acceptable in His sight, than a certain coolness of conduct which frequently takes place afterward, when we are apt to look back with pity upon our former weakness, and secretly to applaud ourselves for our present greater attainments in knowledge, though, perhaps (alas, that it should ever be so !) we may have lost as much in warmth as we have gained in light.

From the time we know the Lord, and are bound to Him by the cords of love and gratitude, the two chief points we should have in our view, I apprehend, are, to maintain communion with Him in our own souls, and to glorify Him in the sight of men. Agreeably to these views, though the Scripture does not enumerate or decide, *totidem verbis*, for or against many things which some plead for, and others condemn ; yet it furnishes us with some general canons, which, if rightly applied, will, perhaps, go a good way towards settling the debate, at least to the satisfaction of those who would rather please God than man. Some of these canons I will just remark to your Lordship :—Rom. xii. 1, 2 ; 1 Cor. viii. 13, and x. 31 ; 2 Cor. vi. 17 ; Ephes. iv. 30, and v. 11, 15, 16 ; 1 Thess. v. 22 ; Ephes. vi. 18 ; to which I may add, as suitable to the present times, Isa. xxii. 12 ; Luke xxi. 34. I apprehend the spirit of these and similar passages of Scripture (for it would be easy to adduce a larger number) will bring a Christian under such restrictions as follow :—

To avoid and forbear, for his own sake, whatever has a tendency to damp and indispose his spirit in attendance upon the means of grace ; for such things, if they be not condemned as sinful *per se*, if they be not absolutely unlawful, yea, though they be, when duly regulated, lawful and right, (for often our chief snares are entwined with our blessings,) yet, if they have a repeated and evident tendency to deaden our hearts to divine things, of which each person's experience must determine, there must be something in them, either in season, measure, or circumstance, wrong to us ; and let them promise what they will, they do but rob us of our gold to pay us with counters. For the light of God's countenance, and an open cheerfulness of spirit in walking with Him in private, is our chief joy ; and we must be already greatly hurt, if any thing can be pursued, allowed, or rested in, as a tolerable substitute for it.

For the sake of the church, and the influence example may have upon his fellow-Christians, the law of charity and prudence will often require a believer to abstain from some things, not because they are unlawful, but inexpedient. Thus the apostle, though strenuous for the *right* of his Christian liberty, would have abridged himself of the *use*, so as to eat no meat, rather than offend a weak brother, rather than mislead him to act against the present light of his conscience. Upon this principle, if I could, without hurt to myself, attend some public amusements, as a concert or oratorio, and return from thence with a warm heart to my closet, (the possibility of which, in my own case, I greatly question,) yet I should think it my duty to forbear, lest some weaker than myself should be encouraged by me to make the like experiment, though, in their own minds, they might fear it was wrong, and have no other reason to think it lawful but because I did it : in which case I should sus-peet, that though I received no harm, they would. And I have known and conversed with some who, I fear, have made shipwreck of their profession, who have dated their first decline from imitating others, whom they thought wiser and better than themselves, in such kind of compliances. And it seems that an obligation to this sort of self-denial, rises, and is strengthened, in proportion to the weight and influence of our characters. Were I in private life, I do not know that I should think it sinful to kill a partridge or a hare ; but, as a minister, I no more dare do it than I dare join in a drunken frolic, because I know it would give offence to some, and be pleaded for as a licence by others.

There is a duty, and a charity likewise, which we owe to the world at large, as well as a faithfulness to God and His grace, in our necessary converse among them. This seems to require, that though we should not be needlessly singular, yet, for their instruction, and for the honour of our Lord and Master, we should keep up a certain kind of singularity, and show ourselves called to be a separated people : that though the providence of God has given us callings and relations to fill up (in which we cannot be too exact), yet we are not of the world, but belong to another community, and act from other principles, by other rules, and to other ends, than the generality of those about us. I have observed, that the world will often leave professors in quiet possession of their notions and sentiments, and places of worship, provided they will not be too stiff in the matter of conformity with their more general customs and amusements.—But I fear many of them have had their prejudices strengthened against our holy religion by such compliances, and have thought, that if there were such joy and comfort to be found in the ways of God, as they hear from our pulpits, professors would not, in such numbers, and so often, run amongst them, to beg a relief from the burden of time hanging upon their hands. As our Lord Jesus is the great representative of His people in Heaven, He does them the honour to continue a succession of them as His representatives upon earth. Happy are they who are favoured with most of the holy unction, and best enabled to manifest to all around them, by their spirit, tempers, and conversation, what are the proper design and genuine effect of His Gospel upon the hearts of sinners.

In our way of little life in the country, serious people often complain of the snares they meet with from worldly people, and yet they must mix with them to get a livelihood. I advise them, if they can, to do their business with the world as they do it in the rain. If their business calls them abroad, they will not leave it undone for fear of being a little wet ; but then, when it is done, they presently seek shelter, and will not stand in the rain for pleasure. So providential and necessary calls of duty that lead us into the world, will not hurt us, if we find the spirit of the world unpleasant, and are glad to retire from it, and keep out of it as much as our relative duties will permit. That which is our cross is not so likely to be our snare ; but if that spirit which we should always watch and pray against, infects and assimilates our minds to itself, then we are sure to suffer loss, and act below the dignity of our profession.

The value of time is likewise to be taken into the account. —It is a precious talent, and our Christian profession opens a wide field for the due improvement of it. Much of it has been already lost, and therefore we are exhorted to redeem it. I think many things which custom pleads for will be excluded from a suitableness to a Christian, for this one reason, that they are not consistent with the simple notion of the redemption of time. It is generally said we need relaxation; I allow it in a sense; the Lord Himself has provided it; and, because our spirits are too weak to be always upon the wing in meditation and prayer, He has appointed to all men, from the king downwards, something to do in a secular way. The poor are to labour; the rich are not exempted from something equivalent. And when every thing of this sort in each person's situation is properly attended to, I apprehend, if the heart be alive, and in a right state, spiritual concernments will present themselves, as affording the noblest, sweetest, and most interesting relaxation from the cares and business of life; as, on the other hand, that business will be the best relaxation, and unbending of the mind from religious exercises, and, between the two, perhaps, there ought to be but little mere leisure time. A life in this sense, divided between God and the world, is desirable;—when one part of it is spent in retirement, seeking after, and conversing with Him whom our souls love; and the other part of it employed in active services, for the good of our family, friends, the church, and society, for His sake. Every hour which does not fall in with one or other of these views, I apprehend, is lost time.

The day in which we live seems likewise to call for something of a peculiar spirit in the Lord's people. It is a day of abounding sin, and I fear a day of impending judgment. The world, as it was in the days of Noah and Lot, is secure. We are soon to have a day of apparent humiliation; but the just causes for it are not confined to one day, but will subsist, and too probably increase, every day. If I am not mistaken in the signs of the times, there never was, within the annals of English history, a period in which the spirit and employment described, Ezek. ix. 4, could be more suitable than the present. The Lord calls for mourning and weeping, but the words of many are stout against Him; new species of dissipatiou are invented almost daily, and the language of those who bear the greatest sway in what is called the polite circle, I mean the interpretative language of their hearts, is like that of the rebellious Jews, Jer. xliv. 16, &c.: " As for the word

that thou hast spoken unto us in the name of the Lord,
we will not hearken unto thee." In short, things are coming
to a point, and it seems to be almost putting to the vote,
whether the Lord or Baal be God. In this state of affairs,
methinks, we cannot be too explicit in avowing our attach-
ment to the Lord, nor too careful in avoiding an improper
correspondence with those who are in confederacy against
Him. We know not how soon we may greatly need that
mark of providential protection which is restrained to those
who sigh and cry for our abominations. Upon the whole,
it appears to me, that it is more honourable, comfortable,
and safe, (if we cannot exactly hit the golden mean,) to be
thought by some too scrupulous and precise, than actually
to be found too compliant with those things which, if not
absolutely contrary to a divine commandment, are hardly
compatible with the genius of the Gospel, or conformable to
the mind that was in Christ Jesus, which ought also to be
in His people. The places and amusements which the world
frequent and admire, where occasions and temptations to
sin are cultivated, where the law of what is called good-breed-
ing is the only law which may not be violated with impunity,
where sinful passions are provoked and indulged, where the
fear of God is so little known or regarded, that those who do
fear Him must hold their tongues, though they should hear
His name blasphemed, can hardly be a Christian's voluntarily
chosen ground. Yet, I fear, these characters will apply to
every kind of polite amusement or assembly in the kingdom.

As to family connexions, I cannot think we are bound to
break or slight them. But as believers and their friends
often live, as it were, in two elements, there is a mutual
awkwardness, which makes their interviews rather dry and
tedious. But upon that account they are less frequent than
they would otherwise be, which seems an advantage. Both
sides keep up returns of civility and affection ; but as they
cannot unite in sentiment and leading inclination, they will
not contrive to be very often together, except there is some-
thing considerable given up by one or the other ; and I
think Christians ought to be very cautious what concessions
they make upon this account. But, as I said at the begin-
ning, no general positive rules can be laid down.

I have simply given your Lordship such thoughts as

have occurred to me while writing, without study, and
without coherence. I dare not be dogmatical; but I
think what I have written is agreeable both to particular
texts, and to the general tenour of Scripture. I submit it
to your judgment.

I am, &c.

LETTER XXVI

My Lord,   *July* — 1777.

I owe your Lordship a quire of letters for the favour
and pleasure of your late visit: and, therefore, I must
begin and write away.

I have lately read Robertson's History of Charles V.,
which, like most other histories, I consider as a comment upon
those passages of Scripture which teach us the depravity
of man, the deceitfulness of the heart, the ruinous effects
of sin, and the powerful, though secret, rule of divine provi-
dence, moving, directing, controlling the designs and
actions of men, with an unerring hand, to the accomplish-
ment of His own purposes, both of mercy and judgment.
Without the clew and the light which the word of God
affords, the history of mankind, of any, of every age, only
presents to view a labyrinth and a chaos ; a detail of wicked-
ness and misery to make us tremble, and a confused jumble
of interfering incidents, as destitute of stability, connexion,
or order, as the clouds which fly over our heads. In this
view, *Delirant reges, plectuntur Achivi*, may serve as a motto
to all the histories I have seen. But, with the Scripture
key, all is plain, all is instructive. Then I see, verily there
is a God who governs the earth, who pours contempt upon
princes, takes the wise in their own craftiness, overrules
the wrath and pride of man, to bring His own designs to pass,
and restrains all that is not necessary to that end ; blasting
the best-concerted enterprises at one time, by means appar-
ently slight, and altogether unexpected, and, at other times,
producing the most important events, from instruments
and circumstances which are at first thought too feeble and

trivial to deserve notice. I should like to see a writer of
Dr. Robertson's abilities give us a history upon this plan ;
but I think his reflections of this sort are too general, too
cold, and too few. What an empty phantom do the great
men of the world pursue, while they wage war with the peace
of mankind, and butcher (in the course of their lives) perhaps
hundreds of thousands, to maintain the shadow of authority
over distant nations, whom they can reach with no other
influence than that of oppression and devastation ! But
when we consider those who are sacrificed to their ambition,
as justly suffering for their sins, then heroes and conquerors
appear in their proper light, and worthy to be classed with
earthquakes and pestilences, as instruments of divine
vengeance. So many cares, so much pains, so many mis-
chiefs,—merely to support the idea a worm has formed of
his own grandeur, is a proof that man, by nature, is not
only depraved, but infatuated. Permit me to present my
thoughts to more advantage in the words of M. Nicole :

" Un Grand dans son idée n'est pas un seul homme ;
c'est un homme environné de tous ceux qui sont à lui, et
qui s'imagine avoir autant de bras qu'ils en ont tous ensemble,
parce qu'il en dispose et qu'il les remue. Un Général
d'armée se représente toujours à lui-même au milieu de tous
ses soldats. Ainsi chacun tâche d'occuper le plus de place
qu'il peut dans son imagination, et l'on ne se pousse, et ne
s'agrandit dans le monde, que pour augmenter l'idée que
chacun se forme de soi-même. Voilà le but de tous les
desseins ambitieux des hommes ! Alexandre et Cæsar
n'ont point eu d'autre vue dans toutes leurs batailles que
celle-là. Et si l'on demande pourquoi le Grand Seigneur a
fait depuis peu périr cent mille hommes devant Candie, on
peut repondre sûrement, que ce n'est que pour attacher
encore à cette image intérieure qu'il a de lui-même, le titre
de Conquérant."*

How awful is the case of those who live and die in such
a spirit, and who have multiplied miseries upon their fellow-
creatures, in order to support and feed it ! Perhaps they
may, upon their entrance on another state, be accosted by
multitudes, to the purport of that sarcastical language in the

---

* Essais de Morale, vol. i.

prophet's sublime ode of triumph over the king of Babylon, Isa. xiv. 5-17.

> Hic est, quem fuga, quem pavor
> Præcessit ? hic, quem terricolis gravem
> Strages secuta est, vastitasque ? hic
> Attoniti spoliator orbis ?

But though the effects of this principle of self are more extensive and calamitous, in proportion as those who are governed by it are more elevated, the principle itself is deep-rooted in every heart, and is the spring of every action, till grace infuses a new principle, and self, like Dagon, falls before the Lord of Hosts. Great and small are but relative terms ; and the passions of discontent, pride, and envy, which, in the breast of a potentate, are severely felt by one-half of Europe, exert themselves with equal strength in the heart of a peasant, though, for want of materials and opportunities, their operations are confined within narrow bounds. We are fallen into a state of gross idolatry, and self is the idol we worship. I am, &c.

EIGHT LETTERS

REV. MR. S——

LETTER I

DEAR SIR,   *June* 23, 1775.

I HAVE met with interruptions till now, or you would
have heard from me sooner. My thoughts have run much
upon the subject of your last, because I perceive it has a near
connexion with your peace. Your integrity greatly pleases
me ; far be it from me to shake the principle of your conduct ;
yet, in the application, I think there is a possibility of carry-
ing your exceptions too far.

From the account you give me of your sentiments, I
cannot but wonder you find it so difficult to accede to the
Athanasian Creed, when it seems to me you believe and
avow what the Creed chiefly sets forth. *The doctrine of
the Trinity*, some explication of the terms being subjoined,
is the Catholic faith, without the belief of which a man cannot
be saved. This damnatory clause seems to me proved by
Mark xvi. 16 : "He that believeth shall be saved," &c.
The object of faith must be *truth*. The doctrine of the Deity
of Christ, and of the Holy Spirit, in union with the Father,
so that they are not three Gods, but one God, is not merely a
proposition expressed in words, to which our assent is re-
quired, but is absolutely necessary to be known ; since,
without it, no one truth respecting salvation can be rightly
understood, no one promise duly believed, no one duty
spiritually performed. I take it for granted, that this
doctrine must appear irrational and absurd in the eye of
reason, if by reason we mean the reason of man in his fallen
state, before it is corrected and enlightened by a heavenly

Teacher. *No* man can say Jesus is Lord, but by the Holy
Ghost. I believe with you, that a man may be saved
who never heard of the Creed, who never read any book but
the *New* Testament, or, perhaps, a single Evangelist ; but
he must be taught of God the things that accompany
salvation, or I do not think he can be saved. *The mercies
of God in Christ* will not save any, (as I apprehend,) but
according to the method revealed in His word, that is, those
who are truly partakers of faith and holiness. For, as the
religion of the New Testament ascribes all power to God,
and considers all goodness in us as the effect of His com-
munication, we being by nature destitute of spiritual life or
light ; so those whom God Himself is pleased to teach will
infallibly attain the knowledge of all that they are concerned
to know. This teaching you are waiting for, and it shall
be given you ; yea, the Lord, I trust, has begun to teach you
already ; but if you consider yourself as a learner, and that
it is possible, under the Spirit's increasing illumination, you
may hereafter adopt some things which, at present, you
cannot approve, I should think it too early, as yet, to prescribe
to yourself rules and determinations for the government of
your future life. Should the will of God appoint you a
new path for service, He may, sooner than you are aware,
quiet your mind, and enable you to subscribe with as full a
persuasion of mind, as you now object to subscription. If it
depended upon me, I could be content that the Creed should
rest at the bottom of the sea, rather than embarrass a single
person of *your* disposition. *Nor* am I a warm stickler for
subscription in itself ; but something of this kind seems
necessary, upon the supposition of an Establishment.

When I think of an inclosure, some hedge, wall, bank,
ditch, &c., is, of course, included in my idea ; for who can
conceive of an inclosure without a boundary ? So, in a
National Church, there must be, I apprehend, something
marked out, the approbation or refusal of which will deter-
mine who do or do not belong to it : and for this purpose
Articles of some kind seem not improper. You think it
would be better to have these articles in Scriptural expres-
sions. But if it be lawful to endeavour to exclude from
our pulpits men who hold sentiments the most repugnant to
the truth, I wish you to consider, whether this can be in any

measure secured by Articles in which the Scripture doctrines
are not explained and stated, as well as expressed. This
proposal is strenuously pleaded for by many in our day,
upon views very different from yours. The Socinians, for
instance, would readily subscribe a Scriptural declaration
of the high priesthood, atonement, and intercession of Christ
(while they are allowed to put their own sense upon the
terms), though the sense they maintain be utterly incon-
sistent with what those who are enlightened by the Holy
Spirit learn from the same expressions.

I acknowledge, indeed, that the end is not answered by
the present method ; since there are too many like the person
you mention, who would easily subscribe 900 Articles rather
than baulk his preferment : yet the profligacy of some
seems to be no just reason why the Church, why any Church,
should not be at liberty to define the terms upon which they
will accept members or teachers, or why conscientious persons
should object to these terms, (if they think them agreeable to
the truth,) merely because they are not expressed in the
precise words of Scripture. If allowance may be made for
human infirmity in the *Liturgy*, I see not why the *Articles*
may not be entitled to the same privilege. For it seems
requisite that we should be as well satisfied with the expres-
sions we use with our lips, in frequent solemn prayer to God,
as in what we subscribe with our hands. I am persuaded
that the leaders of the Association at the Feathers Tavern,
some of them at least, though they begin with the affair
of subscription, would not (if they might have their wish)
stop there, but would go on with their projected reform till
they had overturned the Liturgy also, or, at least, weeded
it from every expression that bears testimony to the Deity
of the Saviour, and the efficacious influence of the Holy
Spirit. I bless God that you are far otherwise minded.

I hope, however, though you should not think yourself
at liberty to repeat your subscription, the Lord will make you
comfortable and useful in your present rank as a curate.
Preferment is not necessary, either to our peace or usefulness.
We may live and die contentedly, without the honours and
emoluments which aspiring men thirst after, if He be pleased
to honour us with a dispensation to preach *His* Gospel,
and to crown our endeavours with a blessing. He that

winneth souls is wise ; wise in the choice of the highest
end he can propose to himself in this life ; wise in the
improvement of the only means by which this desirable end
can be attained. Wherever we cast our eyes, the bulk
of the people are ignorant, immoral, careless. They live
without God in the world ; they are neither awed by His
authority, nor affected by His goodness, nor enabled to trust
to His promises, nor disposed to aim at His glory. If,
perhaps, they have a serious interval, or some comparative
sobriety of character, they ground their hopes upon their
own doings, endeavours, or purposes ; and treat the in-
expressible love of God revealed in Christ, and the Gospel-
method of salvation by faith in His name, with neglect,
often with contempt. They have preachers whom, perhaps,
they hear with some pleasure, because they neither alarm
their consciences by insisting on the spirituality and sanction
of the divine law, nor offend their pride by publishing the
humiliating doctrines of that Gospel which is the power of
God through faith unto salvation. Therefore, what they do
speak, they speak in vain ; the world grows worse and worse
under their instructions ; infidelity and profligacy abound
more and more ; for God will own no other doctrine but what
the apostle calls the " truth as it is in Jesus " ; that doctrine
which drives the sinner from all his vain pleas, and points
out the Lord Jesus Christ as the only ground of hope, the
supreme object of desire, as appointed of God to be wisdom,
righteousness, sanctification, and redemption to all who
believe in His name. When ministers themselves are con-
vinced of sin, and feel the necessity of an almighty Saviour,
they presently account their former gain but loss, and de-
termine, with the apostle, to know nothing but Jesus Christ,
and Him crucified. In proportion as they do this, they are
sure to be wondered at, laughed at, and railed at, if the
providence of God, and the constitution of their country,
secure them from severer treatment. But they have this
invaluable compensation, that they no longer speak without
effect. In a greater or less degree a change takes place in
their auditories :—the blind receive their sight, the deaf hear,
the lepers are cleansed ; sinners are turned from darkness
to light, and from the power of Satan to God ; sinful prac-
tices are forsaken ; and a new course of life in the converts

evidences that they have not followed cunningly-devised fables, or taken up with uncertain notions ; but that God has indeed quickened them by His Spirit, and given them an understanding to know Him that is true. The preachers, likewise, while they attempt to teach others, are taught themselves ; a blessing descends upon their studies and labours, upon their perusal of the Scripture, upon their attention to what passes within them and around them. The events of every day contribute to throw light upon the word of God ; their views of divine truth grow more enlarged, connected, and comprehensive ; many difficulties which perplexed them at their first setting out, trouble them no more ; the God whom they serve, and on whom they wait, reveals to them those great things, which, though plainly expressed in the letter of the Scripture, cannot be understood and realised without divine teaching (1 Cor. ii. 9-15). Thus they go on from strength to strength, hard things become easy, and a divine light shines upon their paths. Opposition from men, perhaps, may increase ; they may expect to be represented as those who turn the world upside down : the cry, μεγαλη ἡ Αρτεμις*, will be raised against them, the gates of the temple of preferment will be seldom open to them ; but they will have the unspeakable consolation of applying to themselves those lively words of the apostle, ὡς γυπυμενοι, αει δε χαιροντες· ὡς πτωχοι, πολλυς δε πλυτιζοντες· ὡς μηδεν εχοντες, και παντα κατεχοντες.†

It is the strain of evident sincerity which runs through your letters, that gives me a pleasing confidence the Lord is with you. A disinterested desire of knowing the truth, with a willingness to follow it through all disadvantages, is a preparation of the heart which only God can give. He has directed you to the right method—searching the Scripture, with prayer. Go on, and may His blessing attend you. You may see, from what I have written above, what is the desire of my heart for you. But I am not impatient. Follow your heavenly Leader, and, in His own time and manner, He will make your way plain. I have travelled the path before you ; I see what you yet want ; I cannot impart it to you, but He can, and I trust He will. It will rejoice my soul to

---

* Great is Diana.   † 2 Cor. vi. 10.

be in any way assistant to you ; but I am afraid I should not afford you much, either profit or satisfaction, by entering upon a dry defence of Creeds and Articles.

The truths of Scripture are not like mathematical theorems which present exactly the same ideas to every person who understands the terms. The word of God is compared to a mirror (2 Cor. iii. 18) ; but it is a mirror in which the longer we look, the more we see ; the view will be still growing upon us, and still we shall see but in part while on this side eternity. When our Lord pronounced Peter blessed, declaring he had learnt that which flesh and blood could not have taught him, yet Peter was at that time much in the dark. The sufferings and death of Jesus, though the only and necessary means of his salvation, were an offence to him. But he lived to glory in what he once could not bear to hear of. Peter had received grace to love the Lord Jesus, to follow Him, to venture all, and to forsake all, for Him : these first good dispositions were of God, and they led to further advances. So it is still. By nature, self rules in the heart ; when this idol is brought low, and we are truly willing to be the Lord's, and to apply to Him for strength and direction that we may serve Him, the good work is begun ; for it is a truth that holds universally, and without exception, a man can receive nothing, except it be given him from heaven. The Lord first *finds* us when we are thinking of something else (Isaiah lxv. 1) ; and then we begin to seek Him in good earnest, and He has promised to be *found* of us. People may, by industry and natural abilities, make themselves masters of the external evidences of Christianity, and have much to say for and against different schemes and systems of sentiment ; but all this while the heart remains untouched. True religion is not a science of the head, so much as an inward and heartfelt perception, which casts down imaginations, and every νψωμα that exalteth itself in the mind, and brings every thought into a sweet and willing subjection to Christ by faith. Here the learned have no real advantage above the ignorant ; both see when the eyes of the understanding are enlightened ; till then, both are equally blind. And the first lesson in the school of Christ is to become a little child, sitting simply at His feet, that we may be made wise unto salvation.

C.   H

I was not only prevented beginning my letter so soon as I wished, but have been unusually interrupted since I began it. *O*ften, as soon as I could well take the pen in hand, I have been called away to attend company and intervening business. Though I persuade myself, after what I have formerly said, you will put a favourable construction upon my delay, yet it has given me some pain. I set a great value upon your offer of friendship, which I trust will not be interrupted on either side, by the freedom with which we mutually express our difference of sentiments, when we are constrained to differ. You please me with intrusting me with the first rough draught of your thoughts ; and you may easily perceive, by my manner of writing, that I place equal confidence in your candour. I shall be glad to exchange letters as often as it suits us, without constraint, ceremony, or apology ; and may He, who is always present with our hearts, make our correspondence useful. I pray God to be your sun and shield, your light and strength, to guide you with His eye, to comfort you with His gracious presence in your own soul, and to make you a happy instrument of comforting many.   I am, &c.

LETTER II

My Dear Friend,   *July* 14, 1775.

I GLADLY adopt your address, and can assure you that the interchange of every letter unites my heart more closely to you. I am glad to find that your views of Articles and Creeds are not likely to hinder you from going forward in your present situation ; and if, without contracting your usefulness, they only prove a bar to your preferment, I am sure it will be no grief of mind to you at the hour of death, or at the day of judgment, that you were enabled to follow the dictates of conscience, in opposition to all the pleas of custom or interest. Since, therefore, I have no desire of shaking your resolves, may we not drop this subject entirely ? For, indeed, I act but an awkward part in it, being by no means myself an admirer of Articles and Creeds, or disposed to be a warm advocate for Church-power. The propriety of our National Establishment, or of any other, is what I have not much to do with ; I found it as it is, nor have I influence to alter it, were I willing. The question in which I was concerned was simply, Whether I, *rebus sic stantibus*, could submit to it, so as conscientiously to take a designation to the ministry under it ? I thought I could ; I accordingly did, and I am thankful that I never have seen cause to repent it.

You seem gently to charge me with a want of candour in what I observed, or apprehended, concerning the gentlemen of the Feathers Tavern. If I mistake not (for I retain no copies of my letters), I expressed myself with a double restriction, by first saying, the *leaders* of that society, and then adding, or *some of them at least*. I apprehend your candour will hardly lead you to suppose, that there are *none* amongst them who would pull down the whole fabric (that is, I mean so far as it crosses the Socinian scheme), if it was left to their choice. I apprehend I may, without the least breach of candour, suppose that the exceptions which Mr. Lindsay has made to the Liturgy, are not peculiar to himself. It seems plain in his case, and from his own writings, that the mere removal of subscriptions, which is the immediate and ostensible object of the clerical petition, could not have satisfied *him ;* and it is past a doubt with me, that there are others of the clergy like-minded with him. Indeed, I could wish to be thought candid by you ; though, I confess, I am not a friend to that lukewarmness and indifference for truth, which bears the name of candour among many in the present day. I desire to maintain a spirit of candour and benevolence to all men, to wish them well, to do them every good office in my power, and to commend what appears to me commendable in a Socinian, as readily as in a Calvinist. But, with some people, I can only go *usque ad aras*. I must judge of principles by the word of God, and of the tree by its fruit. I meddle with no man's final state, because I know that He who is exalted to give repentance and remission of sins, can do it whenever, and to whomsoever, He is pleased : yet I firmly believe, and I make no scruple of proclaiming it, that swearers, drunkards, adulterers, *continuing such*, cannot inherit the kingdom of God : and I look with no less compassion upon some persons, whose characters in common life may be respectable, when I see them unhappily blinded by their own wisdom ; and while they account themselves, and are accounted by many others, master-builders in Zion, rejecting the only foundation upon which a sinner's hope can be safely built.

I am far from thinking the Socinians all hypocrites, but I think they are all in a most dangerous error ; nor do their principles exhibit to my view a whit more of the genuine fruits of Christianity than Deism itself. You say, " If they be sincere, and fail not for want of diligence in searching, I cannot help thinking that God will not condemn them for an inevitable defect in their understandings." Indeed, my friend, I have such a low opinion of man in his depraved state, that I believe no one has real sincerity in religious matters, till God bestows it : and when *He* makes a person sincere in his desires after truth, He will assuredly guide him to the possession of it in due time, as our Lord speaks, John vi. 44, 45. To suppose that any persons can sincerely seek the way of salvation, and yet miss it through an inevitable defect of their understandings, would contradict the plain promises of the Gospel, such as Matt. vii. 7, 8 ; John vii. 16, 17 ; but to suppose that things are not necessary to be known, because some persons, who profess sincerity, cannot receive them, would be, in effect, to make the Scripture a nose of wax, and open a wide door for scepticism. I am not a judge of the heart : but I may be sure, that whoever makes the foundation-stone a rock of offence, cannot be sincere in his inquiries. He may study the Scripture accurately, but he brings his own preconceived sentiments with him, and, instead of submitting them to the touchstone of truth, he makes them a rule by which he interprets. That they who lean to their own understandings should stumble and miscarry, I cannot wonder ; for the same God who has promised to fill the hungry with good things, has threatened to send the rich empty away. So Matt. xi. 25. It is not through defect of understanding, but a want of simplicity and humility, that so many stumble, like the blind at noon-day, and can see nothing of those great truths which are written in the Gospel as with a sunbeam.

You wish me to explain myself concerning the doctrine of the Trinity. I will try ; yet I know I cannot, any farther than as He who taught me shall be pleased to bear witness in your heart to what I say. My first principle in religion is what the Scripture teaches me of the utter depravity of human nature, in connexion with the spirituality and sanction of the law of God. I believe we are by nature sinners, by practice universally transgressors ; that we are dead in trespasses and sins ; and that the bent of our natural spirit is enmity against the holiness, government, and grace of God. Upon this ground, I see, feel, and acknowledge the necessity of such a salvation as the Gospel proposes, which, at the same time that it precludes boasting, and stains the pride of all human glory, affords encouragement to those who may be thought, or who may think themselves, the weakest or the vilest of mankind. I believe, that whatever notions a person may take up from education or system, no one ever did, or ever will, feel himself, and own himself, to be such a lost, miserable, hateful sinner, unless he be powerfully and supernaturally convinced by the Spirit of God. There is, when God pleases, a certain light thrown into the soul, which differs not merely in degree, but in kind, *toto genere*, from any thing that can be effected or produced by moral suasion or argument. But (to take in another of your queries) the Holy Spirit teaches or reveals no new truths, either of doctrine or precept, but only enables us to understand what is already revealed in the Scripture. Here a change takes place, the person who was spiritually blind begins to see. The sinner's character, as described in the word of God, he finds to be a description of himself ; that he is afar off ; a stranger, a rebel ; that he has hitherto lived in vain. Now he begins to see the necessity of an atonement, an advocate, a shepherd, a comforter : he can no more trust to his own wisdom, strength, and goodness ; but accounting all his former gain but loss, for the excellency of the knowledge of Christ, he renounces every other refuge, and ventures his all upon the person, work, and promise of the Redeemer. In this way, I say, he will find the doctrine of the Trinity not only a proposition, but a principle ; that is, from his own wants and situation, he will have an abiding conviction that the Son and Holy Spirit are God, and must be possessed of the attributes and powers of Deity, to support the offices the Scriptures assign them, and to deserve the confidence and worship the Scriptures require to be placed in them, and paid to them. Without this awakened state of mind, a divine, reputed orthodox, will blunder wretchedly, even in defending his own opinions   I have seen laboured defences of the Trinity, which have given me not much more satisfaction than I should probably receive from a dissertation upon the rainbow, composed by a man blind from his birth.   In effect, the knowledge of God cannot be attained by studious discussion on our parts ; it must be by revelation on His part, Matt. xi. 27, and xvi. 17 ; a revelation, not objectively of new truth, but subjectively of new light in us.   Then he that runs may read.   Perhaps you may not quite understand my meaning, or not accede to my sentiments at present ; I have little doubt, however, but the time is coming when you will.   I believe the Lord God has given you that sincerity which He never disappoints.

Far be it from me to arrogate infallibility to myself, or to any writer or preacher ; yet, blessed be God, I am not left to float up and down the uncertain tide of opinion, in those points wherein the peace of my soul is nearly concerned.   I know, yea, I infallibly know, whom I have believed.   I am under no more doubt about the way of salvation than of the way to London.   I cannot be deceived, because the word of God cannot deceive me.   It is impossible, however, for me to give you or any person full satisfaction concerning my evidence, because it is of an experimental nature (Rev. ii. 17).   In general, it arises from the views I have received of the power, compassion, and grace of Jesus, and a consciousness that I, from a conviction of my sin and misery, have fled to Him for refuge, intrusted and devoted myself and my all to Him.   Since my mind has been enlightened, every thing within me, and every thing around me, confirm and explain to me what I read in Scripture ; and though I have reason enough to distrust my own judgment every hour, yet I have no reason to question the great essentials which the Lord Himself hath taught me.

Besides a long letter, I send you a great book.   A part of it (for I do not ask you to read the whole) may, perhaps, explain my meaning better than I have leisure to do myself. I set a high value upon this book of Mr. Halyburton's ;

so that, unless I could replace it with another, I know not if I would part with it for its weight in gold. The first and longest treatise is, in my judgment, a masterpiece ; but I would chiefly wish you to peruse the Essay concerning *F*aith, towards the close of the book. I need not beg you to read it carefully, and to read it all. The importance of the subject, its immediate connexion with your inquiries, and the accuracy of the reasoning, will render the motive of *my request* unnecessary. I cannot style him a very elegant writer ; and being a Scotsman, he abounds with the Scottish idiom. But you will prefer truth to ornament. I long to hear your opinion of it. It seems to me as much adapted to some things that have passed between us as if written on purpose.

The Inquiry concerning Regeneration and Justification, which stands last in the book, I do not desire or even wish you to read ; but if you should, and then think that you have read a speculation more curious than useful, I shall not contradict you. I think it must appear to you in that light ; but it was bound up with the rest, and therefore could not stay behind ; but I hope the Essay on Faith will please you.

I take great pleasure in your correspondence, and still more in the thought of your friendship, which I hope to cultivate to the utmost, and to approve myself sincerely and affectionately yours.

LETTER III

My Dear Friend,   *August* 11, 1775.

NEXT week I go to London, where I purpose (if nothing unforeseen prevents) to say a month. Many things, which must necessarily be attended to before my departure, abridge me of that leisure which I could wish to employ in answering your last. However, I will spare you what I can. I thank you for yours. Your objections neither displease nor weary me. While truth is the object of your inquiry, the more freedom you use with me the better. Nor do they surprise me ; for I have formerly made the like objections myself. I have stood upon your ground, and I continue to hope you will one day stand upon mine. As I have told you more than once, I do not mean to dictate to you, or to wish you to receive any thing upon my *ipse dixit ;* but, in the simplicity of friendship, I will give you my thoughts from time to time upon the points you propose, and leave the event to the divine blessing.

I am glad you do not account the Socinians master-builders. However, they esteem themselves so, and are so esteemed, not only by a few, (as you think,) but by many. I fear Socinianism spreads rapidly amongst us, and bids fair to be the prevailing scheme in this land, especially with those who profess to be the thinking part. The term *Arminian*, as at present applied, is very indiscriminate, and takes in a great variety of persons and sentiments, amongst whom, I believe, there are many who hold the funda-mental truths of the Gospel, and live a life of faith in the Son of God. I am far from supposing that God will guide every *sincere* person exactly to adopt *all* my sentiments. But there are *some* sentiments which I believe essential to the very state and character of a true Christian. And these make him a Christian, not merely by being his acknowledged sentiments, but by a certain peculiar manner in which he possesses them. There is a certain important change takes place in the heart, by the operation of the Spirit of God, before the soundest and most orthodox sentiments can have their proper influence upon us. This work or change the Scripture describes by various names, each of which is designed to teach us the marvellous effects it produces, and the almighty power by which it is produced. It is sometimes called a new birth, John iii. 3 ; sometimes a new creature or new creation, as 2 Cor. v. 17 ; sometimes the causing light to shine out of darkness, 2 Cor. iv. 6 ; sometimes the opening the eyes of the blind, Acts xxvi. 18 ; sometimes the raising the dead to life, Eph. ii. 5. Till a person has experienced this change, he will be at a loss to form a right conception of it : but it means, not being proselyted to an opinion, but receiving a principle of divine life and light in the soul. And till this is received, the things of God, the truths of the Gospel, cannot be rightly discerned or understood by the utmost powers of fallen man, who, with all his wisdom, reason, and talents, is still but what the apostle calls the natural man, till the power of God visits his heart, 1 Cor. ii. 14. This work is sometimes wrought suddenly, as in the case of Lydia, Acts xvi. 14 ; at other times very gradually. A person who before was a stranger even to the form of godliness, or at best content with a mere form—finds new thoughts arising in his mind, feels some concern about his sins, some desire to please God, some suspicions that all is not right.—He examines his views of religion, hopes the best of them, and yet cannot rest satisfied in them. To-day, perhaps, he thinks himself fixed ; to-morrow he will be all uncertainty. He inquires of others, weighs, measures, considers, meets with sentiments which he had not attended to, thinks them plausible ; but is presently shocked with objections or supposed consequences, which he finds himself unable to remove. As he goes on in his inquiry, his difficulties increase. New doubts arise in his mind ; even the Scriptures perplex him, and appear to assert contrary things. He would sound the depths of truth by the plummet of his reason ; but he finds his line is too short. Yet even now the man is under a guidance, which will at length lead him right. The importance of the subject takes up his thoughts, and takes off the relish he once had for the things of the world. He reads, he prays, he strives, he resolves ; sometimes inward embarrassments and outward temptations bring him to his wits' end. He almost wishes to stand where he is, and inquire no more ; but he cannot stop.—At length he begins to feel the inward depravity, which he had before owned as an opinion ; a sense of sin and guilt cuts him out new work. Here reasoning will stand him in no stead. This is a painful change of mind ; but it prepares the way for a blessing. It silences some objections better than a thousand arguments, it cuts the comb of his own wisdom and attainments, it makes him weary of working for life, and teaches him, in God's due time, the meaning of that text, " To him that worketh not, but believeth in Him who justifieth the ungodly, his faith is counted for righteousness." Then he learns, that Scriptural faith is a very different thing from a rational assent to the Gospel,—that it is the immediate gift of God, Ephes. ii. 8 ; the operation of God, Col. ii. 12 ; that Christ is not only the object, but the author and finisher of faith, Heb. xii. 2 ; and that faith is not so properly a part

of that obedience we owe to God, as an inestimable benefit
we receive from Him for Christ's sake ; Phil. i. 29, which is
the medium of our justification, Rom. v. 1, and the principles
by which we are united to Christ (as the branch to the vine)
John xvii. 21.   I am well aware of the pains taken to put a
different sense upon these and other seemingly mysterious
passages of Scripture ; but thus far we speak that which we
know, and testify that which we have seen.   I have des-
cribed a path in which I have known many led, and in which
I have walked myself.

The Gospel, my dear Sir, is a salvation appointed for those
who are ready to perish, and is not designed to put them in a
way to save themselves by their own works.   It speaks to us
as condemned already, and calls upon us to believe in a
crucified Saviour, that we may receive redemption through
His blood, even the forgiveness of our sins.   And the Spirit
of God, by the Gospel, first convinces us of unbelief, sin, and
misery ; and then, by revealing the things of Jesus to our
minds, enables us, as helpless sinners, to come to Christ,
to receive Him, and to behold Him, or, in other words, to
believe in Him, and expect pardon, life, and grace from Him ;
renouncing every hope and aim in which we once rested,
" and accounting all things loss and dung for the excellency
of the knowledge of Christ," John vi. 35 ; Is. xlv. 22, with
John vi. 40 ; Col. ii. 6.   In some of Omicron's letters, you
will find my thoughts more at large upon these subjects than
I have now time to write them.   For a farther illustration,
I refer you to the MSS. sent herewith.   The first part,
written in shorthand, does not so immediately concern our
present point as the second, which you may read without a
key.   It relates to a matter of indisputable fact, concerning a
person with whom (as you will perceive) I was well ac-
quainted.   You may depend upon the truth of every tittle.
I intrust it to you in the confidence of friendship, and beg
that it may not go out of your hands, and that when you
have perused it, you will return it, sealed up, by a safe con-
veyance to my house.   You will see in it the sentiments of a
man of great learning, sound reasoning, an amiable and
irreproachable character, and how little he accounted of all
these advantages, when the Lord was pleased to enlighten his
mind.

Though we have not exactly the same view of human depravity, yet as we both agree to take our measure of it from the Word of God, I trust we shall not always differ about it. Adam was created in the image of God, in righteousness and true holiness (Ephes. iv. 24). This moral image, I believe, was totally lost by sin. In that sense he died the day, the moment, he ate the forbidden fruit. God was no longer his joy and delight ; he was averse from the thoughts of His presence, and would (if possible) have hid himself from Him. His natural powers, though doubtless impaired, were not destroyed. Man, by nature, is still capable of great things. His understanding, reason, memory, imagination, &c., sufficiently proclaim that the hand that made him is divine. He is, as Milton says of Beelzebub, " majestic, though in ruins." He can reason, invent, and, by application, attain a considerable knowledge in natural things. The exertions of human genius, as specified in the characters of some philosophers, poets, orators, &c., are wonderful. But man cannot know, love, trust, or serve his Maker, unless he be renewed in the spirit of his mind. God has preserved in him, likewise, some feelings of benevolence, pity, some sense of natural justice and truth, &c., without which there could be no society : but these, I apprehend, are little more than instincts, by which the world is kept in some small degree of order ; but, being under the direction of pride and self, they do not deserve the name of virtue and goodness ; because the exercise of them does not spring from a principle of love to God, nor is directed to His glory, or regulated by the rule of His Word, till a principle of grace is super-added. You think, I will not say, " that God judicially, in punishment of one man's sin, added these corruptions to all his posterity." Let us suppose that the punishment annexed to eating the forbidden fruit had been the loss of Adam's rational powers, and that he should be degraded to the state and capacity of a brute. In this condition, had he begotten children after the Fall in his own likeness, his nature being previously changed, they must have been of course brutes like himself ; for he could not convey to them those original powers which he had lost. Will this illustrate my meaning ? Sin did not deprive him of rationality, but of spirituality. His nature became earthly, sensual, yea, devilish; and this fallen nature, this carnal mind, which is enmity against God, which is not subject to His law, neither, indeed, can be (Rom. viii. 7), we universally derive from him. Look upon children; they presently show themselves averse from good, but exceedingly propense to evil. This they can learn even without a master; but ten thousand instructors and instructions cannot instil good into them, so as to teach them to love their Creator, unless a divine power co-operates. Just as it is with the earth, which produces weeds spontaneously; but if you only see a cabbage or an apple-tree, you are sure it was planted or sown there, and did not spring from the soil. I know many hard questions may be started upon this subject, but the Lord, in due time, will clear His own cause, and vindicate His own ways. I leave all difficulties with Him. It is sufficient for me that Scripture asserts, and experience proves that it is thus in fact, Rom. iii. 9-21, Job xiv. 4. Thus, we have not only forfeited our happiness by transgression, but are, by our depravity, incapable of it, and have no more desire or taste for such a state as the Scripture describes Heaven to be, than a man, born deaf, can have for a concert of music. And, therefore, our Lord declares, that except a man be born again, he not only *shall not*, but *cannot*, see the kingdom of God. Hence a twofold necessity of a Saviour—His blood for the pardon of our sins—His life, spirit, and grace to quicken our souls, and form us anew for Himself, that we may feel His love, and show forth His praise.

St. Paul, before his conversion, was not sincere in the sense I hope you to be: he thought himself in the right, without doubt, as many have done when they killed God's servants, John xvi. 2. He was blindly and obstinately zealous: I think he did not enter into the merits of the cause, or inquire into facts with that attention which sincerity would have put upon him. You think that his sincerity and zeal were the very things that made him a chosen instrument; he himself speaks of them as the very things that made him peculiarly unworthy of that honour, 1 Cor. xv. 9: and he tells us, that he was set forth as a pattern of the Lord's long-suffering and mercy, that the very chief of sinners might be encouraged, 1 Tim. i. 15, 16.

Had he been sincerely desirous to know whether Jesus was the Messiah, there was enough in his character, doctrines, miracles, and the prophecies concerning Him, to have cleared up the point; but he took it for granted he was right in his opinion, and hurried blindly on, and was (as he said himself) exceedingly mad against them. Such a kind of sincerity is common enough. People believe themselves right, and, therefore, treat others with scorn or rage; appeal to the Scriptures, but first lay down their own pre-conceived sentiments for truths, and then examine what Scriptures they can find to countenance them. Surely a person's thinking himself right will not give a sanction to all that he does under that persuasion.

Ignorance and obstinacy are, in themselves, sinful, and no plea of sincerity will exempt from the danger of being under their influence, Is. xxvii. 11, Luke vi. 39. It appears to me, that though you will not follow any man implicitly, you are desirous of discovering your mistakes, supposing you are mistaken in any point of importance. You read and examine the word of God, not to find arms wherewith to defend your sentiments, at all events, but to know whether they are defensible or not. You pray for God's light and teaching, and, in this search, you are willing to risk what men are commonly much afraid of hazarding—character, interest, preferment, favour, &c. A sincerity of this kind I too seldom meet with; when I do, I account it a token for good, and am ready to say, " No man can do this, except God be with him." However, sincerity is not conversion; but, I believe, it is always a fore-runner of it.

I would not be uncharitable and censorious, hasty and peremptory, in judging my fellow-creatures. But if I acknowledge the word of God, I cannot avoid forming my judgment upon it. It is true, I cannot look into people's hearts; but hearts and principles are delineated to my hand in the Scripture. I read, that no murderer has eternal life in him; I read likewise, " If any man love not the Lord Jesus Christ, let him be anathema "; and, therefore, I conclude, that there are *speculative errors*, as heinous in their guilt, as destructive in their effects, as murder; and that the most moral regular man as to social life, if he loves not the Lord Jesus Christ, is, in the sight of God, the Judge of all,

as displeasing as a murderer. It has pleased God, for the
peace and support of society, to put a black mark upon those
sins which affect the peace and welfare of our neighbour,
such as adultery and murder. But, undoubtedly, the sins
committed immediately against Himself, must be more
heinous than any which offend our fellow-creatures. The
second commandment, Matt. xxii. 39, is like the first;
but it depends upon it, and is, therefore, inferior to it.
Men ordinarily judge otherwise. To live regardless of God
and the Gospel is looked upon as a peccadillo, in com-
parison with offences against society. But sooner or later
it will appear otherwise to all. A parcel of robbers may
pique themselves upon the justice, honour, and truth they
observe towards one another; but because they set up a
petty interest, which is inconsistent with the public good, they
are deservedly accounted villains, and treated as such,
notwithstanding their petty morality among themselves.
Now, such a company of robbers bears a much greater pro-
portion to a whole nation, than a nation, or all the nations
of the earth, bears to the great God. Our dependence
upon Him is absolute, our obligations to Him infinite. In
vain shall men plead their moral discharge of relative
duties to each other, if they fail in the unspeakably greater
relation under which they stand to God: and, therefore,
when I see people living without God, in the world, as all
do till they are converted, I cannot but judge them in a
dangerous state ;—not because I take pleasure in censuring,
or think myself authorized to pass sentence upon my fellow-
creature, but because the Scripture decides expressly on the
case, and I am bound to take my sentiments from thence.

The jailer was certainly a Christian when baptized, as
you observe. He trembled; he cried out, "What must I
do to be saved?" Paul did not bid him amend his life,
but believe in the Lord Jesus. He believed and rejoiced.
But the Lord blessed the apostle's words, to produce in
him that saving faith, which filled him with joy and peace.
It was, as I observed before, something more than assent to
the proposition, that Jesus is the Christ; a resting in Him for
forgiveness and acceptance, and a cleaving to Him in love.
No other faith will purify the heart, work by love, and
overcome the world.

I need not have pleaded want of leisure as an excuse for a short letter, for I have written a long one. I feel myself much interested in your concerns ;—and your unexpected frank application to me (though you well know the light in which I appear to some people), I consider as a providential call, which binds me to your service. I hope our correspondence will be productive of happy effects, and that we shall both one day rejoice in it.

I am, &c.

LETTER IV

My Dear Friend, *September* 6, 1775.

I BEGIN to fear I shall fall under a suspicion of unkindness and forgetfulness towards you,—and, therefore, I am willing to write a line by way of prevention, though I have not leisure to attempt any thing like an answer to the letter you put into my hand the evening before I left O—— ; I must, therefore, content myself with a tender of affection and respect, and an inquiry after your welfare.

Your letter will give me an opportunity of saying something farther, when time shall admit : but an endeavour to answer all the objections that may be started between us, in a way of reasoning, would require a volume, and would, likewise, interfere with the leading principle upon which my hope of giving you satisfaction, in due time, is grounded. You seem to expect that I should remove your difficulties ; but it is my part only to throw in a word occasionally, as a witness of what the Lord has been pleased to teach me from the Scriptures, and to wait for the rest, till He (who alone is able) shall be pleased to communicate the same views to you. For till we see and judge by the same medium, and are agreed in the fundamental point, that faith is not the effect of reasoning, but a special gift of God, which He bestows when, and to whom, He pleases, it will not be possible for me to convince you by dint of argument. I believe, as I have observed before, that He has already given you a desire to know His will ; and, therefore, I trust He will not disappoint your search. At present, I think you want one thing, which it is not in my power to impart. I mean, such a sense of the depravity of human nature, and the state of all mankind considered as sinners, as may make you feel the utter impossibility of attaining to the peace and hope of the Gospel in any other way, than by renouncing all hope of succeeding by any endeavours of your own, further than by humbly waiting at the throne of grace for power to cast yourself, without terms and conditions, upon Him who is able to save to the uttermost. We must feel ourselves sick before we can duly prize the great Physician, and feel a sentence of death in ourselves, before we can effectually trust in God, who raiseth the dead.

I have not brought your sermons with me, for I thought I should not have time to read them attentively, while in this hurrying place. I purpose to consider them with care, and to give you my thoughts with frankness, when I return. However, if they are upon the plan intimated in your letter, I will venture to say one thing beforehand—that they will not answer your desired end. I am persuaded you wish to be useful—to reclaim sinners from their evil ways, to inspire them with a love to God, and a sincere aim to walk in obedience to His will. May I not venture to appeal to yourself, that you meet with little success ; that the people to whom you preach, though they, perhaps, give you a patient hearing, yet remain as they were, unchanged, and unholy ? It must be so ;—there is but one sort of preaching which God blesses to these purposes—that which makes all the world guilty before God, and sets forth Jesus Christ (as the brazen serpent was proposed by Moses), that guilty and condemned sinners, by looking to Him, and believing on His name, may be healed and saved. The most pressing exhortations to repentance and amendment of life, unless they are enforced in a certain way, which only God can teach, will leave our hearers much as they find them. When we meet, or when I have leisure to write from home, I will trouble you with my thoughts more at large. Till then, permit me to assure you of my sincere regard, and best wishes, and that I am, &c.

LETTER V

My Dear Friend,   *October* 21, 1775.

THE calls and engagements which I told you engrossed and anticipated my time when I wrote last, have continued without any intermission hitherto, and I am still far behind-hand with my business. I am willing to hope, that the case has been much the same with you, and that want of leisure has been the only cause of my not having been pleasured with so much as a note from you since my return from London.

I am loath, for my own sake, to charge your silence to an unwillingness of continuing that intercourse which I have been, and still find myself, desirous to improve on my part. For though we are not agreed in our views, yet while our preliminary agreement, to allow mutual freedom, and to exercise mutual candour, in expressing our sentiments, subsists, we may, and I hope shall, be glad to hear from each other. It may seem to intimate I have a better opinion of myself than of you, that while I seem confident your freedom will not offend me, I feel now and then a fear, lest mine should prove displeasing to you. But friendship is a little suspicious when exercised with long silence, and a plain declaration of my sentiments has more than once put amiable and respectable persons to the full trial of their patience.

I now return your sermons : I thank you for the perusal ; I see much in them that I approve, and nothing in them but what I formerly espoused. But in a course of years, a considerable alteration has taken place in my judgment and experience. I hope, yea, I may boldly say I am sure, not for the worse. Then I was seeking, and now through mercy, I have found the pearl of great price. It is both the prayer and the hope of my heart, that a day is coming when you shall make the same acknowledgment. From your letters and sermons, I am encouraged to address you in our Lord's words, " Thou art not far from the kingdom of God." I am persuaded the views you have received will not suffer you to remain where you are. But fidelity obliges me to add, " Yet one thing thou lackest." " That one thing," I trust the Lord will both show you, and bestow upon you, in His due

c.   I time.   You speak somewhere of " atoning for disobedience by repentance."   Ah ! my dear sir, when we are brought to estimate our disobedience, by comparing it with such a sense of the majesty, holiness, and authority of God, and the spirituality, extent, and sanction of His holy law, as He, and He only, can impress upon the heart of a sinner, we shall be convinced, that nothing but the blood of the Son of God can atone for the smallest instance of disobedience.

I intimated, in my letter from London, one defect of your scheme, which will probably be the first to engage your notice.   I am sure you have a desire to be useful to the souls of men, to be an instrument of reclaiming them from that course of open wickedness, or lifeless formality, in which you see them enslaved ; and, in a word, to prevail with them to live soberly, righteously, and godly, according to the just and comprehensive sense you have given of those words, in your sermon on Tit. ii. 11, 12.   Now, inward experience, and a pretty extensive observation of what passes abroad, have so perfectly convinced me there is but one mode of preaching which the Holy Spirit owns to the producing these effects, that I am not afraid to pronounce confidently, you will not have the desires of your heart gratified upon your present plan : the people will give you a hearing, and remain just as they are, till the Lord leads you to speak to them as criminals condemned already, and whose first essential step it is, to seek forgiveness by the blood of Jesus, and a change of heart and state by His grace, before they can bring forth any fruit acceptable to God.

As I have little time for writing, and little hope of succeeding in a way of argumentation, I have substituted, instead of a longer letter, the heads of some sermons I preached nine or ten years ago, on our Lord's discourse with Nicodemus.   However, when I have heard that you are well, and that you are still disposed to correspond with me, I shall be ready to give a more particular answer to the subjects you pointed out to me in the letter you favoured me with the day before I left London.   I pray God to bless you in all your ways, and beg you to believe, that I am with sincerity, &c.

LETTER VI

IT never entered my pericranium, that you expected I should fully and directly answer your letter while I was in London ; and yet you reasonably might, as you knew nothing of my engagements : but, indeed, it was impracticable ; I could only send you a hasty line, as a token that I remembered you. I informed you, when I returned, that I was just going out again. Since I came home the second time, I have been engrossed by things that would admit of no delay ; and, at length, not having so much as a note from you, I thought I would wait till I heard farther. But from first to last it was my intention, and I think my promise, to answer in the manner you proposed, as soon as I could. And even now I must beg a little longer time. Believe me, that as the wise and good providence of God brought us together, without any expectation of mine, I will do all in my power to preserve the connexion, and particularly by giving my thoughts on such questions as you propose. And though, to consider your questions in the manner you wish, and to point out the agreement of detached texts (as they occur) with my views, seems in prospect to require a volume rather than a sheet, yet I am not discouraged ; only I beg you to make allowances for other things, and to be assured, that before I had the pleasure of corresponding with you, I had very little spare time. Expect, then, the best satisfaction I am able to give you, as soon as possible. To prepare the way, I will try hard for a little leisure, to give you a few thoughts upon yours, which came last night.

You complain that I have hitherto disappointed your expectations. If you have preserved my first papers, I believe you will find, that I apprised you this might probably be the event, and certainly must, unless it should please God to make what I should write a means of giving you the same views with myself. I only proposed, as a witness, to bear a simple testimony to what I have seen and known. So far as you believed me sincere, and unwilling to impose upon you, I thought you might admit, there was perhaps some weight in what I had advanced, though for the present you

could not see things in the same light.   And if you allowed a
possibility, that my changing the sentiments which I once
held in common with yourself, might be upon sufficient
grounds, you would, as I trust you do, wait upon the Great
Teacher for His instruction ; otherwise I did not expect to
convince you, nor do I yet ; only I am glad to put myself
in His hands as an instrument.

You quite misunderstood what I spoke of the light and
influence of the Spirit of God.   He reveals to me no new
truths, but has only shown me the meaning of His own
written Word ; nor is this light a particular revelation,
it is common to all who are born again.   And thus, though
you and I cannot fully agree about it, yet I almost daily meet
with persons from the east, west, north, and south, who,
though I never saw them before, I find understand me at
once.   This (as you bid me be explicit) is the one thing which
I think you at present lack.   And I limited my expression
to *one thing*, because it is our Lord's expression, and because
that *one thing* includes many.   As I said before, I cannot
give it you ; but the Lord can ; and from the desire He has
raised in your heart, I have a warm hope that He will.
You place the whole stress of your inquiries upon reason ;
I am far from discarding reason, when it is enlightened and
sanctified ; but spiritual things must be spiritually dis-
cerned, and can be received and discerned no other way ;
for to our natural reason they are foolishness, 1 Cor. ii. 14,
15 ; Matt. xi. 25.   This certain something I can no more
describe to those who have not experienced it, than I could
describe the taste of a pine-apple to a person who had never
seen one.   But Scriptural proofs might be adduced in
abundance, yet not so as to give a solid conviction of it,
till we actually experience it.   Thus it was with my friend—
whose case I sent you.   When God gave him the key,
(as he expressed it,) then the Scriptures were unlocked.
His wishing himself a Deist, some time before, was not from
any libertine exceptions he made to the precepts of the
Gospel, but from the perplexing embarrassments he had
found, by endeavouring to understand the doctrines by dint
of reason, though reason in him was as strong and penetrating
as in most men I ever met with.   Upon your present plan,
how can I hope to satisfy you, though even St. Paul asserts

it, that the carnal mind is enmity against God ? you will readily agree with me to the proposition as it stands in St. Paul's words, but I think will not so readily assent to what I have no more doubt than of my own existence, is the sense of it : that the heart of man, of any man, every man, however apparently amiable in his outward conduct, however benevolent to his fellow-creatures, however abundant and zealous in his devotions, is by nature enmity against God : not, indeed, against the idea he himself forms of God, but against the character which God has revealed of Himself in the Scripture.   Man is an enemy to the justice, sovereignty, and law of God, and to the one method of salvation He has appointed in the Gospel by faith only, by such a faith, as it is no more in his power to contribute to the production of in himself, than he can contribute to raising the dead, or making a world.   Whatever is of the flesh is flesh, and can rise no higher than its principle ; but the Lord could convince you of this by a glance of thought.

But I must break off, for want both of room and time. Let me remind you of our agreement, to use and to allow the greatest freedom, and not to be offended with what is meant well on either side.   Something in your last letter made me apprehensive you were a little displeased with me. He that knows my heart, knows that I wish you well as my own soul.

The expression, of *atoning for disobedience by repentance*, was in one of your sermons.   I considered it as *unguarded*; but, on my view of things, it were in a manner impossible I could use *that expression*, though perhaps too often unguarded myself.   I am, &c.

LETTER VII

MY DEAR FRIEND,   *November* 17, 1775.

AT length I take up your favour of August 14, with design to give a more explicit answer.   My delaying hitherto has been unavoidable.   I am sorry to have your patience put to so long a trial, and should be more sorry, but that I consider, that in my former papers, sermons, Omicron's letters, &c., you already possess the whole (in substance) of what I have to offer. My present part is but *actum agere*, to repeat what I have elsewhere expressed, only with some variety and enlargement.—You yourself well state the situation of our debate, when you say, " Nor in truth do you offer any arguments to convince me, *nor does it seem very consistent on your grounds so to do.* And if this important change is to be brought about by the intervention of some extraordinary impulse of the Holy Spirit, and cannot be brought about without it, I do not see any thing farther that I have to do, than to keep my mind as much unbiassed as I can, and to wait and pray for it." I think my letter from London was to the purport of these your own words, though you seem dissatisfied with it. While we see through a different medium, it will be easy for you to answer every text I might adduce in support of my sentiments, as you have those I have already brought, " That you understand them otherwise." In order to support my sense of one text, I should perhaps quote and argue from twenty more, and still " You would understand them otherwise." The life of man, yea, of Methuselah, would hardly suffice to prove, object, and defend all that might be alleged on both sides in this way ; and at last we should leave off as we began, more fully confirmed in our own opinions, unless the Lord by His Holy Spirit should be pleased to show the person who maintained the wrong side of the argument where his mistake lay. However, I mean to take some notice of your queries as they offer themselves.

The first which occurs is complicated.—The substance, I think, is, whether such belief and aims as you possess will stand you in no stead, unless you, likewise, believe grace irresistible, predestination absolute, faith in supernatural impulses, &c. ? You may have observed, I have several times waived speaking about predestination or election,— not that I am ashamed of the doctrine ; because, if it be indeed absurd, shocking, and unjust, the blame will not deservedly fall upon me, for I did not invent it, but upon the Scriptures, where I am sure, it is laid down in as plain terms as that God created the heavens and the earth. I own I cannot but wonder, that persons professing any reverence

for the Bible, should so openly and strongly declare their
abhorrence of what the Bible so expressly teaches, namely,
that there is a discrimination of persons by the grace and
good pleasure of God, where by nature there is no difference ;
and that all things respecting the salvation of these persons,
is infallibly secured by a Divine predestination.

I do not offer this as a rational doctrine, (though it be
highly so to me,) but it is Scriptural, or else the Scripture is
a mere nose of wax, and without a determinate meaning.
What ingenuity is needful to interpret many passages in a
sense more favourable to our natural prejudices against
God's sovereignty ! Matt. xi. 25, 26, and xiii. 10-17 ;
Mark xiii. 20, 22 ; John xvii. *passim* ; John x. 26 ; Rom.
viii. 28-30, and ix. 13-24, and xi. 7 ; Eph. i. 4, 5 ; 1 Pet.
i. 2. Were I fond of disputing, as I am not, I think I could
put a close reasoner hard to it, to maintain the truth of
Scripture-prophecies, or the belief of a particular Providence,
unless he would admit a Divine predestination of causes
and events as the ground of his arguments. However, as I
said, I have chosen to waive the point ; because, however
true and necessary in itself, the knowledge and compre-
hension of it is not necessary to the being of a true Christian,
though I can hardly conceive he can be an established con-
sistent believer without it. This doctrine is not the turning
point between you and me ; the nature of justification, and
the method of a sinner's acceptance with God, are of
much more immediate importance ; and, therefore, if I
am to speak plainly, I must say, that I look upon your pre-
sent sentiments, attainments, and advances, as you describe
them, to constitute that kind of gain the apostle speaks of,
and concerning which I hope you will one day be of his
mind, and be glad to account it all loss, that you may *win
Christ*, and *be found in Him*, " not having your own righteous-
ness, which is of the law, but the righteousness which is of
God by faith," Phil. iii. 4, 7-10. For, as you tell me, you
never remember a time when you were not conscious, before
God, of great unworthiness, and intervals of earnest en-
deavours to serve Him, though not with the same success,
yet something in the same way as at present : this is but
saying, in other words, you never remember a time when
old things passed away, and all things became new ; and yet

the apostle insists much upon this, 2 Cor. iv. 6, and v. 17.
The convictions of natural conscience, and those which are
wrought in the heart by the Holy Spirit, are different, not
only in degree, but in kind ; the light of a glowworm and of
the sun do not more essentially differ. The former are
partial and superficial, leave us in possession of a supposed
power of our own, are pacified by some appearances of an
outward change, and make us no farther sensible of the
necessity of a Saviour, than to make our doings and duties
(if I may so express myself) full weight, which, perhaps,
might otherwise be a little deficient, when brought to the
balances of the sanctuary. But *truly spiritual* convictions
give us far other views of sin ; they lead us to a deep and
awful consideration of the *root*, our total absolute depravity,
and our utter apostacy from God, by which we are incapable
of doing good, as a dead man is of performing the functions
of life. They lead us to the *rule* and *standard*, the strict,
holy, inflexible law of God, which reaches to the thoughts
and intents of the heart ; requires perfect, universal, per-
severing, obedience ; denounces a curse upon every failure,
Gal. iii. 10 ; and affords neither place nor strength for re-
pentance. Thus they sweep away every hope and refuge
we had before, and fix upon us a sense of guilt and con-
demnation, from which there is no relief, till we can look to
Jesus, as the wounded Israelite did to the brazen serpent ;
which was not to give efficacy to medicines and plasters of
their own application, but to heal them completely of itself,
by looking at it, John iii. 14, 15, and vi. 40 ; Isaiah xliii. 22.

You wish me to explain my distinction between faith and
rational assent; and though I know no two things in the
world more clearly distinct in themselves, or more expressly
distinguished in Scripture, yet, I fear, I may not easily
make it appear to you. You allow faith, in your sense, to
be the gift of God ; but, in my sense, it is, likewise, wrought
by the operation of God, Col. ii. 12, το υπερβαλλον μεγεθος της
δυναμεως αυτου—κατα την ενεργειαν του κρατους της ισχυος αυτου;*
that same energy of the power of His strength, by which the
dead body of Jesus was raised from the dead. Can these
strong expressions intend no more than a rational assent,

---

* Ephes. i. 19.

such as we give to a proposition in Euclid ? I believe fallen reason is, of itself, utterly incapable even of assenting to the great truths of revelation ; it may assent to the terms in which they are proposed, but it must put its own interpretation upon them, or it would despise them. The natural man can neither receive nor discern the things of God : and if any one would be wise, the apostle's first advice to him is, Let him become a fool, that he may be wise ; for the wisdom of the world is foolishness with God.

Indeed, when the heart is changed, and the mind enlightened, then reason is sanctified, and, if I may so say, baptized, renounces its curious disquisitions, and is content humbly to tread in the path of revelation. This is one difference ; assent may be the act of our natural reason ; faith is the effect of immediate almighty power. Another difference is, faith is always efficacious, " it worketh by love " ; whereas assent is often given where it has little or no influence upon the conduct. Thus, for instance, every one will assent to this truth, all men are mortal. Yet the greatest part of mankind, though they readily assent to the proposition, and it would be highly irrational to do otherwise, yet live as they might do if the reverse were true. But they who have Divine faith, feel, as well as say, they are pilgrims and sojourners upon earth. Again, faith gives peace of conscience, access to God, and a sure evidence and subsistence of things not seen, Rom. v. 1, 2 ; Heb. xi. 1 ; whereas, a calm, dispassionate reasoner may be compelled to assent to the external arguments in favour of Christianity, and yet remain a total stranger to that communion with God, that spirit of adoption, that foretaste of glory, which is the privilege and portion of believers. So, likewise, faith overcomes the world, which rational assent will not do. Witness the lives and tempers of thousands, who yet would be affronted if their assent to the Gospel should be questioned. To sum up all in a word, " He that believes shall be saved." But surely many, who give a rational assent to the Gospel, live and die in those sins which exclude from the kingdom of God, Gal. v. 19—21. Faith is the effect of a principle of new life implanted in the soul that was before dead in trespasses and sins ; and it qualifies not only for obeying the Saviour's precepts, but chiefly and primarily for receiving

from, and rejoicing in, His fullness, admiring His love, His
work, His person, His glory, His advocacy. It makes
Christ precious, enthrones Him in the heart, presents Him
as the most delightful object to our meditations ; as our
wisdom, righteousness, sanctification, and strength ; our
Root, Head, Life, Shepherd, and Husband. These are all
Scriptural expressions and images, setting forth, so far as
words can declare, what Jesus is in Himself and to His be-
ieving people. But how cold is the comment which rational
assent puts upon very many passages wherein the apostle
Paul endeavours (but in vain) to express the fullness of his
heart upon this subject ! A most valued friend of mine,
a clergyman, now living, had, for many years, given a rational
assent to the Gospel. He laboured with much earnestness
upon your plan, was very exemplary in his whole conduct,
preached almost incessantly, (two or three times every day
in the week, for years,) having a parish in the remote parts
of Yorkshire, of great extent, and containing five or six
different hamlets at some distance from each other. He
succeeded, likewise, with his people, so far as to break them
off from outward irregularities ; and was mentioned in a
letter to the Society for Propagating the Gospel (which I have
seen in print) as the most perfect example of a parish-priest
which this nation, or, perhaps, this age, has produced.
Thus he went on, for many years, teaching his people what
he knew, for he could teach them no more. He lived in
such retirement and recess, that he was unacquainted with
the persons and principles of any who are now branded as
enthusiasts and Methodists. One day, reading Eph. iii.
in his Greek Testament, his thoughts were stopped by
the word ανεξιχνιαστον, in verse 8. He was struck, and
led to think with himself to this purpose ; " The apostle,
when speaking of the love and riches of Christ, uses re-
markable expressions ; he speaks of heights, depths, and
lengths, and breadths, and unsearchables, where I seem to
find every thing plain, easy, and rational. He finds myster-
ies where I can perceive none. Surely, though I use the
words Gospel, faith, and grace with him, my ideas of them
must be different from his." This led him to a close exami-
nation of all his epistles, and, by the blessing of God,
brought on a total change in his views and preaching. He

no longer set his people to keep a law of faith, to trust in their sincerity and endeavours, upon some general hope that Christ would help them out where they came short ; but he preached Christ Himself, as the end of the law for righteousness to every one that believeth. He felt himself, and laboured to convince others, that there is no hope for a sinner, but merely in the blood of Jesus, and no possibility of his doing any works acceptable to God, till he himself be first made accepted in the Beloved. Nor did he labour in vain. Now his preaching effected not only an outward reformation, but a real change of heart in very many of his hearers. The word was received, as Paul expresses it, not with a rational assent only, but with demonstration, and power in the Holy Ghost, and in much assurance ; and their endeavours to observe the Gospel-precepts were abundantly more extensive, uniform, and successful, when they were brought to say with the apostle, " I am crucified with Christ : nevertheless I live, yet not I, but Christ liveth in me ; and the life I live in the flesh, I live by faith in the Son of God."

Such a change of views and sentiments I pray God my friend may experience. These things may appear uncouth to you at present, as they have done to many, who now bless God for showing them what their reason could never have taught them. My divinity is unfashionable enough at present, but it was not so always ; you will find few books written from the era of the Reformation, till a little before Laud's time, that set forth any other. There were few pulpits, till after the Restoration, from which any other was heard. A lamentable change has, indeed, since taken place ; but God has not left himself without witnesses. You think, though I disclaim infallibility, I arrogate too much in speaking with so much certainty. I am fallible indeed ; but I am sure of the main points of doctrine I hold. I am not in the least doubt, whether salvation be of faith or of works ; whether faith be of our own power, or of God's operation ; whether Christ's obedience, or our own, be the just ground of our hope ; whether a man can truly call Jesus Lord, but by the teaching of the Holy Ghost. I have no more hesitation about these points than I should have, were I asked, Whether it was God or man who created the heavens and the earth ? Besides, as I have more than once observed, your sentiments were once my own ; so that I, who have travelled both roads, may have, perhaps, some stronger reasons to determine me which is the right, than you can have who have only travelled one:

Your two sheets may lead me to write as many quires, if I do not check myself. I now come to the two queries you propose, the solution of which, you think, will clearly mark the difference of our sentiments. The substance of them is, 1st, Whether I think any sinner ever perished in his sins, (to whom the Gospel has been preached,) because God refused to supply him with such a proportion of His assistance as was absolutely necessary to his believing and repenting, or without his having previously rejected the incitements of his Holy Spirit ? A full answer to this would require a sheet. But briefly, I believe that all mankind being corrupt and guilty before God, He might, without impeachment to His justice, have left them all to perish, as we are assured He did the fallen angels. But He was pleased to show mercy, and mercy must be free. If the sinner has any claim to it, so far it is justice, not mercy. He who is to be our Judge assures us, that *few* find the gate that leadeth to life, while many throng the road to destruction. Your question seems to imply, that you think God either did make salvation equally *open to all*, or that it would have been more becoming His goodness to have done so.

But He is the potter, we are the clay : His ways and thoughts are above ours, as the heavens are higher than the earth. The Judge of all the earth *will* do right. He has appointed a day when He will manifest, to the conviction of *all*, that *he has done right*. Till then, I hold it best to take things upon His word, and not too harshly determine what it becomes Jehovah to do. Instead of saying what I think, let it suffice to remind you of what St. Paul thought, Rom. ix. 15-21. But farther, I say, that unless mercy were afforded to those who are saved, in a way peculiar to themselves, and which is not afforded to those who perish, I believe no one soul could be saved. For I believe fallen man, universally considered as such, is as incapable of doing the least thing towards his salvation, till prevented by the grace of God, (as our Article speaks,) as a dead body is of restoring itself to life. Whatever difference takes place between men, in this respect, is of grace, that is of God, undeserved. Yea, His first approaches to our hearts are undesired too ; for, till He seeks us, we cannot, we will not, seek Him, Psalm cx. 3. It is in the day of His power, and not before, His people are made willing. But, I believe, where the Gospel is preached, they who do perish do wilfully resist the light, and choose and cleave to darkness, and stifle the convictions which the truths of God, *when His true Gospel is, indeed, preached*, will, in one degree or other, force upon their minds. The cares of this world, the deceitfulness of riches, the love of other things, the violence of sinful appetites, their prejudices, pride, and self-righteousness, either prevent the reception or choke the growth of the good seed : thus their own sin and obstinacy is the proper cause of their destruction : they *will* not come to Christ that they may have life. At the same time, it is true that they cannot, unless they are supernaturally drawn of God, John v. 40 ; vi. 44. They will not, and they cannot, come. Both are equally true, and they are consistent. For a man's *cannot* is not a natural, but a moral inability ; not an impossibility in the nature of things, as it is for me to walk upon the water, or to fly in the air ; but such an inability, as, instead of extenuating, does exceedingly enhance and aggravate his guilt. He is so blinded by Satan, so alienated from God by nature and wicked works, so given up to sin, so averse from that way of salvation, which is contrary to his pride and natural wisdom, that he will not embrace it, or seek after it ; and, therefore, he cannot, till the grace of God powerfully enlightens his mind, and overcomes his obstacles. But this brings me to your second query.

Do I think that God, in the ordinary course of His providence, grants this assistance in an irresistible manner, or effects faith and conversion without the sinner's own hearty consent and concurrence ? I rather choose to term grace *invincible* than *irresistible :* For it is too often resisted even by those who believe ; but because it is invincible, it triumphs over all resistance, when He is pleased to bestow it. For the rest, I believe no sinner is converted without his own hearty will and concurrence. But he is not willing till he is made so. Why does he at all refuse ? Because he is insensible of his state ; because he knows not the evil of

sin, the strictness of the law, the majesty of God whom he
has offended, nor the total apostacy of his heart ; because he
is blind to eternity, and ignorant of the excellency of
Christ ; because he is comparatively whole, and sees not his
need of this great Physician ; because he relies upon his own
wisdom, power, and supposed righteousness. Now, in this
state of things, when God comes with a purpose of mercy, he
begins by convincing the person of sin, judgment, and
righteousness ; causes him to feel and know that he is a
lost, condemned, helpless creature, and then discovers to
him the necessity, sufficiency, and willingness of Christ to
save them that are ready to perish, without money or price,
without doings or deservings. Then he sees faith to be very
different from a rational assent, finds that nothing but the
power of God can produce a well-grounded hope in the heart
of a convinced sinner ; therefore looks to Jesus, who is the
author and finisher of faith, to enable him to believe. For
this he waits in what we call the means of grace ; he prays,
he reads the word, he thirsts for God, as the hart pants for
the water-brooks ; and though perhaps for a while he is
distressed with many doubts and fears, he is encouraged
to wait on, because Jesus has said, " Him that cometh unto
Me, I will in no wise cast out." The obstinacy of the will
remains while the understanding is dark, and ceases when
that is enlightened. Suppose a man walking in the dark,
where there are pits and precipices of which he is not aware :
you are sensible of his danger, and call after him ; but he
thinks he knows better than you, refuses your advice, and
is perhaps angry with you for your importunity. He sees
no danger, therefore will not be persuaded there is any :
but if you go with a light, get before him, and show him
plainly, that if he takes another step he falls beyond the
power of recovery ;—then he will stop of his own accord,
blame himself for not minding you before, and be ready to
comply with your farther directions. In either case man's
will acts with equal freedom ; the difference of his conduct
arises from conviction. Something like this is the case of
our spiritual concerns. Sinners are called and warned by
the Word; but they are wise in their own eyes, and take
but little notice till the Lord gives them light, which He is
not bound to give to *any*, and therefore cannot be bound to

give to *all*. They who have it, have reason to be thankful, and subscribe to the apostle's words, " By grace are ye saved, through faith ; and that not of yourselves, it is the gift of God."

I have not yet half done with the first sheet ; shall consider the rest at leisure, but send this as a specimen of my willingness to clear my sentiments to you as far as I can. Unless it should please God to make what I offer satisfactory, I well know beforehand what objections and answers will occur to you ; for these points have been often debated ; and after. a course of twenty-seven years, in which religion has been the chief object of my thoughts and inquiries, I am not entirely a stranger to what can be offered on either side. What I write, I write simply and in love ; beseeching Him, who alone can set a seal to His own truth, to guide you and bless you. This letter has been more than a week in hand ; I have been called from it I suppose ten times, frequently in the middle of a period or a line. My leisure, which before was small, is now reduced almost to a nothing. But I am desirous to keep up my correspondence with you, because I feel an affectionate interest in you, and because it pleased God to put it into your heart to apply to me. You cannot think how your first letter struck me : it was so unexpected, and seemed so improbable that you should open your mind to me, I immediately conceived a hope that it would prove for good. Nor am I yet discouraged.

When you have leisure and inclination, write ; I shall always be glad to hear from you, and I will proceed in answering what I have already by me, as fast as I can. But I have many letters now waiting for answers, which must be attended to.

I recommend you to the blessing and care of the great Shepherd ; and remain, &c.

LETTER VIII

My Dear Friend,   *December* 8, 1775.

ARE you willing I should still call you so, or are you quite weary of me? Your silence makes me suspect the latter. However, it is my part to fulfil my promise, and then leave the event to God. As I have but an imperfect remembrance of what I have already written, I may be liable to some repetitions. I cannot stay to comment upon every line in your letter, but I proceed to notice such passages as seem most to affect the subject in debate. When you speak of the Scriptures maintaining one consistent sense, which, if the Word of God, it certainly must do, you say you read and understand it in this one consistent sense; nay, you cannot remember the time when you did not. It is otherwise with me and with multitudes; we remember when it was a sealed book, and we are sure it would have been so still, had not the Holy Spirit opened our understandings. But when you add, though I pretend not to understand the whole, yet what I do understand appears perfectly consistent, I know not how far this exception may extend; for perhaps the reason why you allow you do not understand some parts, is because you cannot make them consistent with the sense you put upon other parts. You quote my words, " That when we are conscious of our depravity, reasoning stands us in no stead." Undoubtedly reason always will stand rational creatures in some stead; but my meaning is, that when we are deeply convinced of sin, all our former reasonings upon the ways of God, while we make our conceptions the standard by which we judge what is befitting Him to do, as if He were altogether such an one as ourselves— all those cobweb reasonings are swept away, and we submit to His αυτος εφη without *reasoning*, though not without *reason*. For we have the strongest reason imaginable to acknowledge ourselves vile and lost, without righteousness and strength, when we actually feel ourselves to be so.— You speak of the Gospel term of justification. This term is *faith*, Mark xvi. 16; Acts xiii. 39. The Gospel propounds, admits no other term. But this *faith*, as I endeavoured to show in my former letter, is very different from rational assent. You speak likewise of the law of *faith*, by which, if you mean what some call the remedial law, which we are to obey as well as we can, and such obedience, together with our faith, will entitle us to acceptance with God, I am persuaded the Scripture speaks of no such thing. Grace and works of any kind, in the point of acceptance with God, are mentioned by the apostle not only as opposites or contraries, but as absolutely contradictory to each other, like fire and water, light and darkness ; so that the affirmation of one is the denial of the other, Rom. iv. 5, and xi. 6. God justifies freely, justifies the ungodly, and him that worketh not. Though justifying faith be indeed an active principle, it worketh by *love*, yet not for acceptance. Those whom the apostle exhorts to work out their own salvation with " *fear and trembling*," he considers as justified already ; for he considers them as believers, in whom he supposed God had already begun a good work ; and if so, was confident he would accomplish it (Phil. i. 6). To them, the consideration that God (who dwells in the hearts of believers) wrought in them to will and to do, was a powerful motive and encouragement to them to work, that is, to give all diligence to His appointed means ; as a right sense of the sin that dwelleth in us, and the snares and temptations around us, will teach us still to work with fear and trembling. You suppose a difference between Christians (so called)who are devoted to God in baptism, and those who in the first ages were converted from abominable superstitions and idolatrous vices.—It is true, in Christian countries we do not worship heathen divinities *eo nomine*. And this is the principal difference I can find. Neither reason nor observation will allow me to think, that human nature is a whit better now than it was in the apostle's time. I know no kinds or degrees of wickedness which prevailed among heathens, which are not prevalent among nominal Christians, who have perhaps been baptized in their infancy ; and, therefore, as the streams in the life are equally worldly, sensual, devilish, I doubt not but the fountain of the heart is equally polluted and poisonous ; and that it is as true as it was in the days of Christ and His apostles, that unless a man be born again, he cannot see the kingdom of God. You sent me a sermon upon the new birth, or regeneration, and you have several of

C.

mine on the same subject. I wish you to compare them with each other, and with the Scripture ; and I pray God to show you wherein the difference consists, and on which side the truth lies.

When you desire me to reconcile God's being the author of sin with His justice, you show that you misunderstand the whole strain of my sentiments ; for I am persuaded you would not misrepresent them. It is easy to charge harsh consequences, which I neither allow, nor, indeed, do they follow from my sentiments. God cannot be the author of sin in that sense you would fix upon me : but is it possible that, upon your plan, you find no difficulty in what the Scripture teaches us upon this subject ? I conceive that those who were concerned in the death of Christ were very great sinners ; and that, in nailing Him to the cross, they committed atrocious wickedness : yet, if the apostle may be believed, all this was according to the determinate counsel and foreknowledge of God, Acts ii. 28 ; and they did no more than what His hand and purpose had determined should be done, chap. iv. 28. And, you will observe, that this wicked act (wicked with respect to the perpetrators) was not only permitted, but foreordained in the strongest and most absolute sense of the word : the glory of God, and the salvation of men depended upon its being done, and just in that manner, and with all those circumstances, which actually took place ; and yet Judas and the rest acted freely, and their wickedness was properly their own. Now, my friend, the arguments which satisfy you, that the Scripture does not present God as the author of this sin, in this appointment, will plead for me at the same time ; and when you think you easily overcome me by asking, " Can God be the author of sin ? " your imputation falls as directly upon the Word of God Himself. God is no more the author of sin, than the sun is the cause of ice ; but it is in the nature of water to congeal into ice, when the sun's influence is suspended to a certain degree. So there is sin enough in the hearts of men to make the earth the very image of hell, and to prove that men are no better than incarnate devils were He to suspend His influence and restraint. Sometimes, and, in some instances, He is pleased to suspend it considerably ; and, so far as He does, human nature quickly appears

in its true colours. Objections of this kind have been re-
peated and refuted before either you or I were born; and
the apostle evidently supposes they would be urged against
His doctrine, when he obviates the question, Why doth He
yet find fault? who hath resisted His will? To which he
gives no other answer than by referring it to God's sover-
eignty and the power which a potter has over the clay. I
think I have, in a former letter, made some reply to the
charge of positiveness in my own opinion. I acknowledge
that I am fallible; yet I must again lay claim to a certainty
about the way of salvation. I am as sure of some things as
of my own existence; I should be so, if there was no human
creature upon earth but myself. However, my sentiments
are confirmed by the suffrages of thousands who have lived
before me, of many with whom I have personally conversed
in different places and circumstances, unknown to each
other; yet all have received the same views, because taught
by the same Spirit. And I have, likewise, been greatly
confirmed by the testimony of many with whom I have
conversed in their dying hours. I have seen them rejoicing
in the prospect of death, free from fears, breathing the air
of immortality: heartily disclaiming their duties and per-
formances; acknowledging that their best actions were
attended with evil sufficient to condemn them: renouncing
every shadow of hope, but what they derived from the blood
of Christ, as the sole cause of their acceptance; yet triumph-
ing in Him over every enemy and fear, and as sure of Heaven
as if they were already there. And such were the apostle's
hopes, wholly founded on knowing whom He had believed,
and his persuasion of His ability to keep that which he had
committed unto Him. This is faith; a renouncing of every
thing we are apt to call our own, and relying wholly upon the
blood, righteousness, and intercession of Jesus. However,
I cannot communicate this my certainty to you; I only tell
you there is such a thing, in hopes, if you do not think I
wilfully lie both to God and man, you will be earnest to seek
it from Him, who bestowed it on me, and who will bestow
it upon all who will sincerely apply to Him, and patiently
wait upon Him for it.

I cannot but wonder, that while you profess to believe
the depravity of human nature, you should speak of good

qualities inherent in it. The word of God describes it as *evil, only evil*, and that *continually*. That there are such qualities as stoics and infidels call virtue, I allow. God has not left man destitute of such dispositions as are necessary to the peace of society ; but I deny there is any moral goodness in them, unless they are founded in a supreme love to God, have His glory for their aim, and are produced by faith in Jesus Christ. A man may give all his goods to feed the poor, and his body to be burned, in zeal for the truth, and yet be a mere nothing, a tinkling cymbal, in the sight of Him who seeth, not as man seeth, but judgeth the heart. Many infidels and avowed enemies to the grace and Gospel of Christ, have made a fair show of what the world calls virtue, but Christian *virtue* is *grace*, the effect of a new nature and new life ; and works thus wrought in God, are as different from the faint partial imitations of them which fallen nature is capable of producing, as a living man is from a statue. A statue may express the features and lineaments of the person whom it represents, but there is no life.

Your comment on the seventh to the Romans, latter part, contradicts my feelings. You are either of a different make and nature from me, or else you are not rightly apprised of your own state, if you do not find the apostle's complaint very suitable to yourself. I believe it applicable to the most holy Christian upon earth. But controversies of this kind are worn thread-bare. When you speak of the spiritual part of a natural man, it sounds to me like the living part of a dead man, or the seeing part of a blind man. Paul tells me, that the natural man (whatever his spiritual part may be) can neither receive nor discern the things of God. What the apostle speaks of himself, Rom. vii. is no more, when rightly understood, than what he affirms of all who are partakers of a spiritual life, or who are true believers, Gal. v. 17. The carnal natural mind is enmity against God, not subject to the law of God, neither indeed can be. When you subjoin, " Till it be set at liberty from the law of sin," you do not comment upon the text, but make an addition of your own, which the text will by no means bear. The carnal mind is enmity. An enemy may be reconciled : but enmity itself is incurable. This carnal mind, natural man, old man, flesh, for the expressions are all equivalent, and denote, and include, the heart of man as he is by nature, may be *crucified*, *must* be *mortified*, but cannot be *sanctified*. *All* that is *good* or *gracious* is the effect of a *new creation*, a *supernatural principle*, wrought in the heart by the Gospel of Christ, and the agency of His Spirit ; and till that is effected, the το υψηλον, the highest attainment, the finest qualifications in man, however they may exalt him in his own eyes, or recommend him to the notice of his fellow-worms, are but abomination in the sight of God, Luke xvi. 15. The Gospel is calculated and designed to stain the pride of human glory. It is provided, not for the wise and the righteous, for those who think they have good dispositions and good works, to plead, but for the guilty, the helpless, the wretched, for those who are ready to perish ; it fills the hungry with good things, but it sends the rich empty away. See Rev. iii. 17, 18.

You ask, If man can do nothing without an extraordinary impulse from on high, is he to sit still and careless ? By no means : I am far from saying, Man can do nothing, though I believe he cannot open his own eyes, or give himself faith. I wish every man to abstain carefully from sinful company and sinful actions, to read the Bible, to pray to God for His heavenly teaching. For this waiting upon God he has a moral ability ; and, if he persevere thus in seeking, the promise is sure, that he shall not seek in vain. But I would not have him mistake the means for the end ; think himself good because he is preserved from gross vices and follies, or trust to his religious course of duties for acceptance, nor be satisfied till Christ be revealed in him, formed within him, dwell in his heart by faith, and till he can say, upon good grounds, " I am crucified with Christ : nevertheless I live ; yet not I, but Christ liveth in me." I need not tell you these are Scriptural expressions ; I am persuaded, if they were not, they would be exploded by many as unintelligible jargon. True faith, my dear Sir, unites the soul to Christ, and thereby gives access to God, and fills it with a peace passing understanding, a hope, a joy unspeakable, and full of glory ; teaches us that we are weak in ourselves, but enables us to be strong in the Lord, and in the power of His might. To those who thus believe, Christ is precious—their beloved ; they hear and know His voice ; the very sound of His name gladdens their hearts, and *He manifests Himself to them* as *He does not* to the *world*. Thus the Scriptures speak, thus the first Christians experienced ; and this is precisely the language which, in our days, is despised as enthusiasm and folly. For it is now as it was then ; though *these things are revealed* to *babes*, and they are as sure of them as that they see the noon-day sun, they are hidden from the wise and prudent, till the Lord makes them willing to renounce their own wisdom, and to become fools, that they may be truly wise, 1 Cor. i. 18, 19 ; iii. 8 ; viii. 2. Attention to the education of children is an undoubted duty; and it is a mercy when it so far succeeds as to preserve them from gross wickedness ; but it will not change the heart. They who receive Christ are born, not of blood, nor of the will of the flesh, nor of the will of man, but of God, John i. 13.

If a man professes to love the Lord Jesus, I am willing to believe him, if he does not give me proof to the contrary ; but I am sure, at the same time, no one can love Him in the Scriptural sense, who does not know the need and the worth of a Saviour ; in other words, who is not brought, as a ruined, helpless sinner, to live upon Him for wisdom, righteousness, sanctification, and redemption. They who love Him thus, will speak highly of Him, and acknowledge that He is their all in all. And they who thus love Him, and speak of Him, will get little thanks for their pains in such a world as this :—" All that live godly in Christ Jesus must suffer persecution : the world that hated Him will hate them." And though it is possible, by His grace, to put to silence, in some measure, the ignorance of foolish men ; and though His providence can protect His people, so that not a hair of their heads can be hurt, without His permission ; yet the world will *show their teeth*, if they are not *suffered* to bite. The apostles were accounted babblers, ως περικαθαρματα του κοσμου και παντων περιψημα. I need not point out to you the force of these expressions. We are no better than the apostles ; nor have we reason to expect much better treatment, so far as we walk in their steps. On the other hand, there is a sober decent way of speaking of God, and goodness, and benevolence, and sobriety, which the world will bear well enough ;—nay, we may say a little about Jesus Christ, as ready to make up the deficiencies of our honest and good endeavours, and this will not displease them. But if we preach Him as the only foundation, lay open the horrid evils of the human heart, tell our hearers that they are dead in trespasses and sins, and have no better ground of hope in themselves than the vilest malefactors, in order to exalt the glory of Jesus, as saving those who are saved wholly and freely for His own name's sake ; if we tell the virtuous and decent, as well as the profligate, that unless they are born again, and made partakers of living faith, and count all things loss for the excellency of the knowledge of Christ, they cannot be saved ; this the world cannot bear. We shall be called knaves or fools, uncharitable bigots, and twenty hard names. If you have met with nothing like this, I wish it may lead you to suspect whether you have yet received the right key to the doctrines of Christ ; for, depend upon it, the offence of the cross is not ceased.

I am grieved and surprised that you seem to take little notice of any thing in the account of my deceased friend, but his wishing himself to be a Deist, and his having play-books about him in his illness. As to the plays, they were *Shakespeare's*, which, as a man of taste, it is no great wonder he should sometimes look into. Your remark on the other point shows, that you are not much acquainted with the exercises of the human mind, under certain circumstances. I believe I observed formerly, that it was not a libertine wish. Had you known him, you would have known one of the most amiable and unblemished characters. *F*ew were more beloved and admired for an uniform course of integrity, moderation, and benevolence ; but he was discouraged. He studied the Bible, believed it in general to be the word of God ; but his wisdom, his strong turn for reasoning, stood so in his way, that he could get no solid comfort from it. He felt the vanity of the schemes proposed by many men admired in the world as teachers of divinity ; and he felt the vanity likewise of his own. He was also a minister, and had a sincere design of doing good. He wished to reform the profligate, and comfort the afflicted by his preaching ; but as he was not acquainted with that one kind of preaching which God owns to the edification of the hearers, he found he could do neither. A sense of disappointments of this

kind distressed him.   Finding in himself none of that peace
which the Scripture speaks of, and none of the influence he
hoped for attending his ministry, he was led sometimes to
question the truth of the Scripture.   We have a spiritual
enemy always near, to press upon a mind in this desponding
situation : nor am I surprised that he should then wish
himself a Deist ; since, if there were any hope for a sinner
but by faith in the blood of Jesus, he had as much of his
own goodness to depend upon as most I have known.   As
for the rest, if you could see nothing admirable and wonder-
ful in the clearness, the dignity, the spirituality of his expres-
sions, after the Lord revealed the Gospel to him, I can only
say I am sorry for it.   This I know, that some persons
of sense, taste, learning, and reason, and far enough from
my sentiments, have been greatly struck with them.   You
say, a death-bed repentance is what you would be sorry
to give any hope of.   My dear friend, it is well for poor
sinners that God's thoughts and ways are as much above
men's as the Heavens are higher than the earth.   We agreed
to communicate our sentiments freely, and promised not
to be offended with each other's freedom if we could help it.
I am afraid of offending you by a thought just now upon
my mind, and yet I dare not in conscience suppress it :
I must, therefore, venture to say, that I hope they who
depend upon such a repentance as your scheme points out,
will repent of their repentance itself upon their death-bed
at least, if not sooner.   You and I, perhaps, should have
encouraged the fair-spoken young man, who said he had
kept all the commandments from his youth, and rather
have left the thief upon the cross to perish like a villain as
he lived.   But Jesus thought differently.   I do not encour-
age sinners to defer their repentance to their death-beds—
I press the necessity of a repentance this moment.   But
then I take care to tell them, that repentance is the gift of
God ; that Jesus is exalted to bestow it ; and that all their
endeavours that way, unless they seek to Him for grace, will
be vain as washing a blackmoor, and transient as washing
a swine, which will soon return to the mire again.   I know
the evil heart will abuse the grace of God ; the apostle
knew this likewise, Rom. iii. 8, and vi. 3.   But this did not
tempt him to suppress the glorious grace of the Gospel,

the power of Jesus to save to the uttermost, and His merciful promise that whosoever cometh unto Him, He will in no wise cast out. The repentance of a natural heart proceeding wholly from fear, like that of some malefactors, who are sorry, not that they have committed robbery or murder, but that they must be hanged for it ; this undoubtedly is nothing worth, whether in time of health or in a dying hour. But that μετανοια, that gracious change of heart, views, and dispositions, which always takes place when Jesus is made known to the soul as having died that the sinner might live, and been wounded that he might be healed ; this, at whatever period God is pleased to afford and effect it by His Spirit, brings a sure and everlasting salvation with it.

Still I find I have not done ; you ask my exposition of the parables of the talents and pounds ; but at present I can write no more. I have only just time to tell you, that when I begged your acceptance of Omicron, nothing was farther from my expectation than a correspondence with you. The frank and kind manner in which you wrote, presently won upon my heart. In the course of our letters upon Subscription, I observed an integrity and disinterestedness in you, which endeared you to me still more. Since that our debates have taken a much more interesting turn ; I have considered it as a call, and an opportunity put in my hand, by the especial providence of Him who ruleth over all. I have embraced the occasion to lay before you simply, and rather in a way of testimony than argumentation, what (in the main) I am sure is truth. I have done enough to discharge my conscience, but shall never think I do enough to answer the affection I bear you. I have done enough likewise to make you weary of my correspondence, unless it should please God to fix the subject deeply upon your mind, and make you attentive to the possibility and vast importance of a mistake in matters of everlasting concernment. I pray that the good Spirit of God may guide you into all truth. He only is the effectual Teacher. I still retain a cheerful hope, that some things you cannot at present receive, will hereafter be the joy and comfort of your heart ; but I know it cannot be till the Lord's own time. I cannot promise to give such long answers as your letters require, to clear up every text that may be proposed, and to answer every objection that may be started ; yet I shall be glad to exchange a letter now and then. At present it remains with you whether our correspondence continues or not, as this is the third letter I have written since I heard from you, and therefore must be the last till I do. I should think what remains might be better settled *vivâ voce;* for which purpose I shall be glad to see you, or ready to wait on you when leisure will permit, and when I know it will bè agreeable ; but if (as life and all its affairs are precarious) we should never meet in this world, I pray God we may meet at the right hand of Jesus, in the great day when He shall come to gather up His jewels, and to judge the world. There is an endless diversity of opinions in matters of religion ; which of them are right and safe, and will lead to eternal glory, *Dies iste indicabit.* I am still in a manner lost amidst more engagements than I have time to comply with ; but I feel and know that I am, &c.

ELEVEN LETTERS

MR. B——, &c.

LETTER I

MY DEAREST SIR, *September* 28, 1774.

I SEE the necessity of having, if possible, my principles at my fingers' ends, that I may apply them as occasions arise every hour. Certainly, if my ability was equal to my inclination, I would remove your tumour with a word or a touch ; I would exempt you instantly and constantly from every inconvenience and pain ; but you are in the hands of One who could do all this and more, and who loves you infinitely better than I can do, and yet He is pleased to permit you to suffer. What is the plain inference ? Certainly, that at the present juncture, He to whom all the concatenations and consequences of events are present in one view, sees it better for you to have this tumour than to be without it ; for I have no more idea of a tumour arising, (or any other incidental trial befalling you,) without a cause, without a need-be, without a designed advantage to result from it, than I have of a mountain or pyramid rising up of its own accord in the middle of Salisbury Plain. The promise is express and literally true, that all things, universally and without exception, shall work together for good to them that love God. But they work *together ;*—the smallest as well as the greatest events have their place and use ; like the several stones in the arch of a bridge, where no one would singly be useful, but every one in its place is necessary to the structure and support of the arch ; or rather like the movement of a watch, where, though there is an evident subordination of parts, and some pieces have a greater comparative importance than others, yet the smallest pieces have their place and use, and are so far equally important, that the whole design of the machine would be obstructed for want of them. Some dispensations and turns of divine Providence may be compared to the main spring or capital wheels, which have a more visible, sensible, and determining influence upon the whole tenour of our lives ; but the more ordinary occurrences of every day are at least pins and pivots, adjusted, timed, and suited with equal accuracy, by the hand of the same great Artist who planned and executes the whole ; and we are sometimes surprised to see how much more depends and turns upon them than we were aware of. Then we admire His skill, and say He has done all things well. Indeed, with respect to His works of providence, as well as of creation, He well deserves the title of *Maximus in minimis.* Such thoughts as these, when I am enabled to realise them, in some measure reconcile me to what He allots for myself or my friends, and convince me of the propriety of that expostulation, which speaks the language of love as well as authority, " Be still, and know that I am God." I sympathize with you in your trial, and pray and trust that your Shepherd will be your Physician ; will superintend and bless the use of means ; will give you in His good time health and cure, and at all times reveal unto you abundance of peace. His promises and power are necessary for our preservation in the smoother scenes He has allotted for us, and they are likewise sufficient for the roughest. We are always equally in danger in ourselves, and always equally safe under the shadow of His wings. No storms, assaults, sieges, or pestilence can hurt us, till we have filled up His appointed measure of service ; and when our work is done, and He has ripened us for glory, it is no great matter by what means He is pleased to call us home to Himself.

I have only room to present our joint and sincerest respects. The Lord bless you all.

I am, &c.

LETTER II

MY DEAREST SIR, *October* 15, 1774.

I THINK the greatness of trials is to be estimated rather by the impression they make upon our spirits, than by their outward appearance. The smallest will be too heavy for us if we are left to grapple with it in our own strength, or, rather, weakness ; and if the Lord is pleased to put forth His power in us, He can make the heaviest light. A lively impression of His love, or of His sufferings for us, or of the glories within the vail, accompanied with a due sense of the misery from which we are redeemed ; these thoughts will enable us to be not only submissive but even joyful in tribulations. When faith is in exercise, though the flesh will have its feelings, the spirit will triumph over them. But it is needful we should know that we have no sufficiency in ourselves, and, in order to know it, we must feel it ; and, therefore, the Lord sometimes withdraws His sensible influence, and then the buzzing of a fly will be an overmatch for our patience : at other times, He will show us what He can do in us, and for us : then we can adopt the apostle's words, and say, I can do and suffer all things through Christ strengthening me. He has said, My grace is sufficient for thee. It is observable, that the children of God seldom disappoint our expectations under great trials ; if they show a wrongness of spirit, it is usually in such little incidents that we are ready to wonder at them. For which, two reasons may be principally assigned. When great trials are in view, we run simply and immediately to our all-sufficient Friend, feel our dependence, and cry in good earnest for help ; but, if the occasion seems small, we are too apt secretly to lean to our own wisdom and strength, as if, in such slight matters, we could make shift without Him. Therefore, in these we often fail. Again, the Lord deals with us as we sometimes see mothers with their children. —When a child begins to walk, he is often very self-important : he thinks he needs no help, and can hardly bear to be supported by the finger of another. Now, in such a case, if there is no danger or harm from a fall, as if he is on a plain carpet, the mother will let him alone to try how he can walk. He is pleased at first, but, presently, down he comes ; and a few experiments of this kind convince him he is not so strong and able as he thought, and make him willing to be led.   But was he upon the brink of a river or a precipice, from whence a fall might be fatal, the tender mother would not trust him to himself, no, not for one moment.   I have not room to make the application, nor is it needful.   It requires the same grace to bear, with a right spirit, a cross word, as a cross injury ; or the breaking of a china plate, as the death of an only son.

                                                                    I am, &c.

LETTER III

My Dear Sir,   *November* 23, 1774.

    I hope to be informed, in due time, that the Lord has given you full health and cure. He has preserved me hitherto from the hands of surgeons ; but I feel as if my flesh would prove, as you say, a very coward, were it needful to submit to a painful operation. Yet I observe, when such operations are necessary, if people are satisfied of the surgeon's skill and prudence, they will not only yield to be cut at his pleasure, without pretending to direct him where, or how long, he shall make the incision, but will thank and pay him for putting them to pain, because they believe it for their advantage. I wish I could be more like them in my concerns. My body, as I said, is through mercy free from considerable ailments, but I have a soul that requires surgeon's work continually—there is some tumour to be discussed or laid open, some dislocation to be reduced, some fracture to be healed, almost daily. It is my great mercy, that One who is infallible in skill, who exercises incessant care and boundless compassion towards all His patients, has undertaken my case : and, complicated as it is, I dare not doubt His making a perfect cure. Yet, alas ! I too often discover such impatience, distrust, and complaining when under His hand ; am so apt to find fault with the instruments He is pleased to make use of ; so ready to think

the saluatary wounds He makes unnecessary, or too large ;
in a word, I show such a promptness to control, were I able,
or to direct His operations, that, were not His patience beyond
expression, He would before now have given me up. I am
persuaded no money would induce Mr. —— to attend upon
a patient who should act towards him as I have towards
my best Physician. Sometimes I indulge a hope that I am
growing wiser, and think surely, after such innumerable
proofs as I have had, that He does all things well, I shall now
be satisfied to leave myself quietly and without reserve
to His disposal. A thousand such surrenders I have made,
and a thousand times I have interpretatively retracted
them. Yet still He is gracious. O, how shall I praise Him
at last !

I thank you for your letter ; I never receive one from
you without pleasure, and, I believe, seldom without profit,
at least for the time. I believe with you, that there is much
of the proper and designed efficacy of the Gospel mystery,
which I have not yet experienced. And I suppose they
who are advanced far beyond me in the divine life, judge the
same of their utmost present attainments. Yet I have no
idea of any *permanent* state in this life, that shall make my
experience cease to be a state of warfare and humiliation.
At my first setting out, indeed, I thought to be better, and
to feel myself better, from year to year ; I expected, by
degrees, to attain everything which I *then* comprised *in
my idea* of a saint. I thought my grain of grace, by much
diligence and careful improvement, would, in time, amount
to a pound : that pound, in a farther space of time, to a
talent, and then I hoped to increase from one talent to many ;
so that supposing the Lord should spare me a competent
number of years, I pleased myself with the thoughts of dying
rich. But, alas ! these, my golden expectations, have been
like South Sea dreams ; I have lived hitherto a poor sinner,
and I believe I shall die one. Have I then gained nothing
by waiting upon the Lord ? Yes, I have gained that which
I once would rather have been without, such accumulated
proofs of the deceitfulness and desperate wickedness of my
heart, as I hope, by the Lord's blessing, have, in some
measure, taught me to know what I mean, when I say,
Behold, I am vile ! And, in connection with this, I have

gained such experience of the wisdom, power, and compassion of my Redeemer, the need, the worth of His blood, righteousness, ascension, and intercession, the glory that He displays in pardoning iniquity and sin, and passing by the transgression of the remnant of His heritage, that my soul cannot but cry out, Who is a God like unto Thee? Thus, if I have any meaner thoughts of myself, Ezek. xvi. 63, and any higher thoughts of Him than I had twenty years ago, I have reason to be thankful; every grain of this experience is worth mountains of gold. And if, by His mercy, I shall yet sink more in my own esteem, and He will be pleased to rise still more glorious to my eyes, and more precious to my heart—I expect it will be much in the same way. I was ashamed when I began to seek Him; I am more ashamed now; and I expect to be most of all ashamed when He shall appear to destroy my last enemy. But, oh! I may rejoice in Him, to think that He will not be ashamed of me.   I am, &c.

LETTER IV

My Dear Sir,   *May* 19, 1775.

I HOPE you will find the Lord present at all times, and in all places. When it is so, we are at home every where; when it is otherwise, *home* is a prison, and *abroad* a wilderness. I know what I ought to desire, and what I do desire. I point Him out to others as the all in all; I esteem Him as such in my own judgment; but, alas! my experience abounds with complaints. He is my sun; but clouds, and sometimes walls, intercept Him from my view. He is my strength; yet I am prone to lean upon reeds; He is my friend; but, on my part, there is such coldness and ingratitude, as no other friend could bear. But still He is gracious, and shames me with His repeated multiplied goodness. O for a warmer heart, a more simple dependence, a more active zeal, a more sensible deliverance from the effects of this body of sin and death! He helps me in my endeavours to keep the vineyards of others; but, alas! My own does not seem to flourish as some do around me. However, though I cannot say I labour more abundantly than they all, I have reason to say with thankfulness, by the Grace of God, I am what I am. My poor story would soon be much worse, did not He support, restrain, and watch over me every minute. Let me entreat your praises and prayers, on the behalf of me and mine; and may the Lord bless you and yours with an increase in every good.

I am, &c.

LETTER V

MY DEAR SIR,   *September 2, 1776.*

THE young woman I spoke of is still living, and not much weaker than when I left her. The Lord was pleased to relieve her on Tuesday evening, and she was comfortable the remainder of the week. But yesterday her conflicts returned, and she was in great distress. The enemy, who always fights against the peace of the Lord's children, finds great advantage against them when their spirits are weakened and worn down by long illness, and is often permitted to assault them. The reasons are hidden from us, but they are doubtless worthy of His wisdom and love, and they terminate in victory, to the praise of His glorious grace, which is more signally manifested by His leading them safely through fire and water, than if their path was always smooth. He is sovereign in His dispensations, and appoints some of His people to trials and exercises, to which others, perhaps, are strangers all their days. Believers are soldiers: all soldiers, by their profession, are engaged to fight, if called upon; but who shall be called to sustain the hottest service, and be most frequently exposed upon the field of battle, depends upon the will of the general or king. Some of our soldiers are now upon hard service in America, while others are stationed round the palace, see the King's face daily, and have no dangers or hardships to encounter. These, however, are as liable to a call as the others; but, if not called upon, they may enjoy, with thankfulness, the

C.   L more easy post assigned them. Thus, the Captain of our salvation allots to His soldiers such stations as He thinks proper. He has a right to employ whom He will, and where He will. Some are comparatively at ease ; they are not exposed to the fiercest onsets, but live near His presence ; others are, to appearance, pressed above measure, beyond strength, so that they despair even of life ; yet they are supported, and, in the end, made more than conquerors through Him who hath loved them. Long observation convinces me, that the temptations which some endure, are not chastisements brought upon them by unfaithfulness, or for anything remarkably wrong in their spirit or walk ; I often rather consider, that in *His* warfare as in worldly wars, the post of danger and difficulty is the post of honour, and, as such, assigned to those whom He has favoured with a peculiar measure of His grace. This young woman, in particular, was always, from her first awakening, remarkably humble and spiritual, and possessed of a broken and contrite spirit. I never saw her in a wrong spirit, or heard her speak an unadvised word. Yet, I believe, it is impossible to express the agonies she had endured. The effect of them is visible. Her animal frame was unable to sustain the burden. I believe they were the immediate cause of that illness which is now bringing her down to the grave. I doubt not but these cases depend, in a great measure, upon constitution ; but then the temperament of our bodies depends upon His pleasure ; for if the very hairs of our head are numbered, it is impossible that those circumstances of our frame, which, by the near connexion between body and soul, have a powerful influence upon the state of our minds, can escape His notice. He could cure such bodily disorders as affect the peace of His people in a moment; yet He does not, though He loves them. There must be, therefore, wise reasons why He does not ; and though we know them not now, we shall know them hereafter. Possibly some suffer for the instruction of the rest, that we may learn to be more thankful to Him for the peace we enjoy, and to be more humbly dependent upon Him for the continuance of it. The Lord's way is in the deep, and His path in the great waters, untraceable by our feeble reasonings ; but faith brings in a good report. We need not doubt but He does all things well, and, in due time, we shall see it. In the mean while He checks our vain inquiries, and calls upon us to be still and know that He is God.

I brought home with me a thankful sense of the kindness and friendship I am favoured with from you and all yours. I account this connexion one of the great comforts of my life ; and I hope it has been, and will be, not only pleasant, but profitable to me. Though I am but an unapt scholar, I hope I am not unwilling to learn ; and the Lord, in His merciful providence, appoints me many teachers. There is little praise due to us, if we either communicate or receive benefit in our intercourse with our fellow-disciples. In both we are but instruments under the influence of a higher hand. Were Christians to meet together without their Lord, they would either trifle or quarrel their time away. But, as He has said, " Where two or three are met, there am I in the midst of them," we may well be glad of opportunities of coming together. And though, for my own part, I am so poor an improver of such seasons, that the recollection of them, when past, is generally accompanied with shame and regret, yet He is gracious and merciful, and seldom leaves me to complain that they were wholly in vain.

I am, &c.

LETTER VI

My Dear Sir, *July 22, 1777.*

*

* * *

THE complaints you make of what passes within, encourage me under what I feel myself. Indeed, if those whom I have reason to believe are more spiritual and humble than I am, did not give some testimony that they find their hearts made of the same materials as mine is, I should be sometimes hard put to it to believe that I have any part or lot in the matter, or any real knowledge of the life of faith. But this concurrent testimony of many witnesses, confirms me in what I think the Scripture plainly teaches, that the soil of human nature, though many spots are certainly better weeded, planted, and manured than others, is everywhere the same—universally bad ; so bad that it cannot be worse, and, of itself, is only capable of producing noxious weeds, and nourishing venomous creatures. We often see the effects of culture, skill, and expense will make a garden where all was desert before. When Jesus, the good Husbandman, encloses a soil, and separates it from the waste of the world, to make it a residence for Himself, a change presently takes place ; it is planted and watered from above, and visited with beams infinitely more cheering and fertilizing than those of the material sun.

But its natural propensity to bring forth weeds still continues ; and one half of His dispensations may be compared to a company of weeders, whom He sends forth into His garden to pluck up all which He has not planted with His own hand, and which, if left to grow, would quickly overpower and overtop the rest. But, alas ! the ground is so impregnated with evil seeds, and they shoot in such quick succession, that, if this weeding work were not constantly repeated, all former labour would be lost. *Hinc illæ lachrymæ.* Hence arises the necessity of daily crosses and disappointments, daily changes of frame, and such multiplied convictions that we are nothing, and can do nothing of ourselves ; all are needful, and barely sufficient to prevent our hearts from being overrun with pride, self-dependence, and security. Yours, &c.

LETTER VII

My Dear Sir, *November* 6, 1777.

You say you are more disposed to cry *miserere* than *hallelujah*—Why not both together ? When the treble is praise, and heart-humiliation for the bass, the melody is pleasant, and the harmony good. However, if not together, we must have them alternately ; not all singing, not all sighing, but an interchange and balance, that we may be neither lifted too high, nor cast down too low, which would be the case if we were very comfortable, or very sorrowful for a long continuance. But though we change, the Saviour changes not. All our concerns are in His hands, and, therefore, safe. His path is in the deep waters, His thoughts and methods of conduct are as high above ours, at the heavens are high above the earth ; and He often takes a course for accomplishing His purposes, directly contrary to what our narrow views would prescribe. He wounds in order to heal, kills that He may make alive, casts down when He designs to raise, brings a death upon our feelings, wishes, and prospects, when He is about to give us the desire of our hearts. These things He does to *prove* us ; but He Himself knows, and has determined beforehand, what He will do. The proof, indeed, usually turns out to our shame. Impatience and unbelief show their heads, and prompt us to suppose this and the other thing, yea, perhaps, all things are against us ; to question whether He be with us, and for us, or not. But it issues, likewise, in the praise of His goodness, when we find that, maugre all our unkind complaints and suspicions, He is still working wonderfully for us, causing light to shine out of darkness, and doing us good in defiance of ourselves.

I am, &c.

LETTER VIII

To Mr. B—— jun.

DEAR SIR, *August* 24, 1774.

THE lowness of your voice, and a blameable absence of mind on my part, prevented me from understanding what you said, when you took your leave of me ; nor did I, just at that instant, recollect that you were so soon going away. I could not otherwise have parted with you, without a particular expression of my warmest wishes for your welfare, and commending you, with an emotion which my heart always feels for you, to our God, and the word of His grace. Permit me, therefore, by writing, to assure you, so far as I can answer for myself, that the request you were pleased to make for my remembrance, will not be forgotten by me.

You are going abroad ; you will carry with you, I doubt not, the best advice, strengthened by the authority and affection of parents whom you greatly love, and greatly reverence. This may seem to make anything a stranger can offer unnecessary, if not impertinent ; yet, confiding in your candour, and in your good opinion of my intention, I shall venture to let my pen run on a little longer. Not only my wishes, but my hopes, are strong in your behalf. Perhaps there is hardly a young man in the kingdom, born to a fortune, who is setting out in life upon equal advantages with yourself. How many at your years, who have been brought up in affluence, are unprincipled, uninstructed, and have already entered upon a course of dissipation and folly, in which it is impossible they themselves can find satisfaction, and which, (unless they are reclaimed from it by an Almighty arm,) will infallibly preclude them from usefulness or esteem ! whereas, your early years have been successfully employed in the pursuit of knowledge, and your education formed under the most animating and endearing influence ; and the Lord has furnished you with every natural ability of body and mind, which may qualify you to serve Him in that situation of life which His providence has allotted you.

What may I not, then, farther hope from these beginnings, especially as it is easy to observe, that He has given you an amiable and promising disposition of spirit, and has not only preserved you from being hurried down the stream of a giddy world, but enabled you to account the tender restraint under which you have been educated, not a yoke, but a privilege.

I sympathise with you at what you will feel when you are first separated from your happy family. But the Lord God, who is the sun and shield of those who fear Him, will be always near you ! His favour is the one thing needful, which no outward advantages can compensate the want of ; and the right knowledge of Him is the one thing needful, which no human teaching can communicate.

Were I more intimate with you, I could have asked the question, and, perhaps received the satisfaction to know, that you have already begun to consider Him in this light ; that you feel a vanity in science, an emptiness in creatures, and find that you have desires, which only *He* who gave them can satisfy. I trust it either is, or will be, thus. As to learning, though it is useful when we know how to make a right use of it, yet, considered as in our own power, and to those who trust to it, without seeking a superior guidance, it is usually the source of perplexity, strife, scepticism, and infidelity. It is, indeed, like a sword in a madman's hands, which gives him the more opportunity of hurting himself and others. As to what the world calls pleasure, there is so little in it, that even the philosophers of old, or many of them, though they had little of value to substitute in its room, could despise it. You will, perhaps, meet with some who will talk another language, who will pretend to be too wise to submit to the Bible, and too happy in worldly things to expect or desire any happiness beside ; but, I trust, you have seen enough to enable you to treat such persons with the pity, and such pretensions with the contempt, they deserve.

Should we set our concerns with an *eternal world* aside for a moment, it would be easy to demonstrate that religion is necessary, in order to make the most of this life, and to enjoy temporal good with the highest relish. In such a world as this, where we are every moment liable to so many unforeseen and unavoidable contingencies, a man without religion may be compared to a ship in a storm, without either rudder, anchor, or pilot. But then, the religion which *only* deserves the name, must come from above ; it must be suited to the state and wants of a sinner, it must be capable of comforting the heart, it must take away the sting and dread of death, and fix our confidence upon One who is always able to help us. Such is the religion of Jesus, such are its effects, and such are the criteria whereby we are to judge of the various forms and schemes under which it is proposed to us. But I forbear ; I am only reminding you of what you know, and what you have known to be verified by *living* and *dying* examples. This happiness, my dear Sir, is open to you, to all who seek. He is enthroned in Heaven, but prayer will bring Him down to the heart. Indeed, He is always beforehand with us ; and if we feel one desire towards Him, we may accept it as a token that He gave it us to encourage us to ask for more.

May He be your guide and guard, be with you at all times, and in all places, and bring you back to your father's house in peace !   Should I live to see that day, you have few friends whose congratulations would be warmer, or more sincere, than mine ; and if, when you are settled, and at leisure, you will afford me a letter it will be both a pleasure and a favour, to, dear Sir,   Yours, &c.

LETTER IX

To Miss M—— B——

My DEAR MISS M——   *Nov.* 11, 1775.

OUR late visit to —— was very pleasant to myself ; if anything passed that was of service to you, we know to whom the thanks are due ; for we can neither communicate nor receive anything but so far as He is pleased to enable us. One reason why He often disappoints us is, that we may learn to depend on Him alone. We are prone, as you observe, to rest too much upon sensible comforts, yet they are very desirable ; only, as to the measure and seasons, it is well to be submissive to His will, to be thankful for them when we have them, and humbly waiting for them when we have them not. They are not, however, the proper ground of our hope ; a good hope springs from such a sense of our wants, and such a persuasion of His power and grace, as engages the heart to venture, upon the warrant of His promises, to trust in Him for salvation. In a sense, we are often hindering Him by our impatience and unbelief ; but, strictly speaking, when He really begins the good work, and gives us a desire which will be satisfied with nothing short of Himself, *He will not be hindered from carrying it on ;* for He has said, I will work, and none shall let it. Ah ! had it depended upon myself, upon my wisdom or faithfulness, I should have hindered Him to purpose, and ruined myself long ago. How often have I grieved and resisted His

Spirit! but hereby I have learned more of His patience and tenderness than I could otherwise have known. He knows our frame, and what effects our evil nature, fomented by the artifices of Satan, will have; He sees us from first to last. A thousand evils arise in our hearts, a thousand wrongnesses in our conduct, which, as they do arise, are new to ourselves, and, perhaps, at some times we were ready to think we were incapable of such things; but none of them are new to Him, to whom past, present, and future are the same. The foresight of them did not prevent His calling us by His grace. —Though He knew we were vile, and should prove ungrateful and unfaithful, yet He would be found of us; He would knock at the door of our hearts, and gain Himself an entrance. Nor shall they prevent His accomplishing His gracious purpose. It is our part to be abased before Him, and quietly to hope and wait for His salvation in the use of His appointed means. The power, success, and blessing, are wholly from Himself. To make us more sensible of this, He often withdraws from our perception: and as, in the absence of the sun, the wild beasts of the forest roam abroad; so when Jesus hides Himself, we presently perceive what is in our hearts, and what a poor shift we can make without Him; when He returns, His light chases the evils away, and we are well again. However, they are not dead, when most controlled by His presence.

It is your great and singular mercy, my dear Miss, that He has taught you to seek Him so early in life. You are entered in the way of salvation, but you must not expect all at once. The work of grace is compared to the corn, and to a building; the growth of the one, and the carrying forward of the other, are gradual. In a building, for instance, if it be large, there is much to be done in preparing and laying the foundation, before the walls appear above ground; much is doing within, when the work does not seem, perhaps, to advance without; and when it is considerably forward, yet being encumbered with scaffolds and rubbish a by-stander sees it at a great disadvantage, and can form but an imperfect judgment of it. But all this while the architect himself, even from the laying of the first stone, conceives of it according to the plan and design he has formed; he prepares and adjusts the materials, disposing each in its proper time and place, and views it, in idea, as already finished. In due season it is completed, but not in a day. The top-stone is fixed, and then the scaffolds and rubbish being removed, it appears to others as he intended it should be. Men, indeed, often plan what, for want of skill or ability, or from unforeseen disappointments, they are unable to execute. But nothing can disappoint the heavenly Builder ; nor will He ever be reproached with forsaking the work ,of His own hands, or beginning that which He could not, or would not, accomplish, Phil. i. 6. Let us, therefore, be thankful for beginnings, and patiently wait the event. His enemies strive to retard the work, as they did when the Jews, by His order, set about rebuilding the temple. Yet it was finished, in defiance of them all.

Believe me to be, &c.

LETTER X

My Dear Miss M——   *April* 29, 1776.

I THANK you for your last ; and I rejoice in the Lord's goodness to you. To be drawn by love, exempted from those distressing terrors and temptations which some are beset with ; to be favoured with the ordinances and means of grace, and connected with those, and with those only, who are disposed and qualified to assist and encourage you in seeking the Saviour—these are peculiar advantages, which all concur in your case ; He loves you, He deals gently with you, He provides well for you, and accompanies every outward privilege with His special blessing ; and I trust He will lead you on from strength to strength, and show you still greater things than you have yet seen. They whom He teaches are always increasing in knowledge, both of themselves and of Him. The heart is deep, and, like Ezekiel's vision, presents so many chambers of imagery, one within another, that it requires time to get a considerable acquaintance with it, and we shall never know it thoroughly. It is now more than twenty-eight years since the Lord began to open mine to my own view ; and, from that time to this, almost every day has discovered to me something which, till then, was unobserved ; and the farther I go, the more I seem convinced that I have entered but a little way. A person that travels in some parts of Derbyshire may easily be satisfied that the country is cavernous ; but how large, how deep, how numerous the caverns may be, which are hidden from us by the surface of the ground, and what is contained in them, are questions which our nicest inquirers cannot fully answer. Thus I judge of my heart that it is very deep and dark, and full of evil ; but as to particulars, I know not one of a thousand.

And if our own hearts are beyond our comprehension, how much more incomprehensible is the heart of Jesus ! If sin abounds in us, grace and love superabound in Him : His ways and thoughts are higher than ours, as the heavens are higher than the earth ; His love has a height, and depth, and length, and breadth, that passeth all knowledge ; and His riches of grace are unsearchable riches, Eph. iii. 8, 18, 19. All that we have received, or can receive, from Him, or know of Him in this life, compared with what He *is* in Himself, or what He *has* for us, is but as the drop of a bucket compared with the ocean, or a single ray of light in respect of the sun. The waters of the sanctuary flow to us, at first, almost upon a level, ankle deep, so graciously does the Lord condescend to our weakness ; but they rise as we advance, and constrain us to cry out with the apostle, O the depth ! We find before us, as Dr. Watts beautifully expresses it,

> A sea of love and grace unknown,
> Without a bottom or a shore.

O the excellency of the knowledge of Christ ! It will be growing upon us through time, yea, I believe, through eternity. What an astonishing and what a cheering thought, that this high and lofty One should unite Himself to our nature, that so, in a way worthy of His adorable perfections, He might, by His Spirit, unite us to Himself ! Could such a thought have arisen in our hearts, without the warrant of His word (but it is a thought which no created mind was capable of conceiving till He revealed it) it would have been presumption and blasphemy ; but now He has made it known, it is the foundation of our hope, and an inexhaustible spring of life and joy. Well may we say, Lord, what is man, that Thou shouldst thus visit him ?

I am, &c.

LETTER XI ·

MY DEAR MISS M——   *September* 3, 1776.

WE saw no danger upon the road homeward ; but my judgment tells me we are always upon the brink of danger, though we see it not ; and that, without the immediate protection and care of Him who preserveth the stars in their courses, there could be no travelling safely a few miles, nor even sitting in safety by the fire-side. But with Him we are safe in all places and circumstances, till our race is done, and His gracious purposes concerning us in the present life are completely answered ; then He will call us home, that we may see His face, and be with Him for ever, and then it will not much signify what messenger He shall be pleased to send for us.

While He took care of us abroad, He watched over our concerns at home, likewise ; so that we found all well upon our return, and met with nothing to grieve us. Many go out and return home no more, and many find distressing things have happened in their absence ; but we have to set up our Ebenezer, and to say, Hitherto He has helped us. Assist me to praise Him. The Lord is leading you in the good old way, in which you may perceive the footsteps of His flock who have gone before you. They had, in their day, the same difficulties, fears, and complaints as we have, and, through mercy, we partake of the same consolation which supported and refreshed them ; and the promises which they trusted, and found faithful, are equally sure to us. It is still true, that they who believe shall never be confounded. If left to ourselves, we should have built upon sand ; but He has provided and revealed a sure foundation, removed our natural prejudices against it ; and now, though rains, and floods, and storms assault our building, it cannot fall, for it is founded upon a Rock. The suspicions and fears which arise in an awakened mind, proceed, in a good measure, from remaining unbelief: but not wholly so; for there is a jealousy and diffidence of ourselves, a wariness, owing to a sense of the deceitfulness of our hearts, which is a grace and a gift of the Lord. Some people who have much zeal, but are destitute of this jealous fear, may be compared to a ship that spreads a great deal of sail, but is not properly ballasted, and is, therefore, in danger of being overset whenever a storm comes. A sincere person has many reasons for distrusting his own judgment; is sensible of the vast importance of the case, and afraid of too hastily concluding in his own favour, and, therefore, not easily satisfied. However, this fear, though useful, especially to young beginners, is not comfortable; and they who simply wait upon Jesus, are gradually freed from it, in proportion as their knowledge of Him, and their experience of His goodness, increases. He has a time for settling and establishing them in Himself, and His time is best. We are hasty, and would be satisfied at once, but His word is, Tarry thou the Lord's leisure. The work of grace is not like Jonah's gourd, which sprang up and flourished in a night, and as quickly withered, but rather like the oak, which, from a little acorn, and a tender plant, advances, with an almost imperceptible growth, from year to year, till it becomes a broad, spreading, and deep-rooted tree, and then it stands for ages. The Christian oak shall grow and flourish for ever. When I see any, soon after they appear to be awakened, making a speedy profession of great joy, before they have a due acquaintance with their own hearts, I am in pain for them. I am not sorry to hear them afterwards complain that their joys are gone, and they are almost at their wits' end; for without some such check, to make them feel their weakness and dependence, I seldom find them turn out well: either their fervour insensibly abates till they become quite cold, and sink into the world again (of which I have seen many instances) or, if they do not give up all, their walk is uneven, and their spirit has not that savour of brokenness and true humility, which is a chief ornament of our holy profession. If they do not feel the plagues of their hearts at first, they find it out afterwards, and too often manifest it to others. Therefore, though I know the Spirit of the Lord is free, and will not be confined to our rules, and there may be excepted cases ; yet, in general, I believe the old proverb, " Soft and fair goes far," will hold good in Christian experience. Let us be thankful for the beginnings of grace, and wait upon our Saviour patiently for the increase. And, as we have chosen Him for our physician, let us commit ourselves to His management and not prescribe to Him what He shall prescribe for us. He knows us, and He loves us better than we do ourselves, and will do all things well.

You say, " It never came with power and life to my soul, that He died for me." If you mean, you never had any extraordinary, sudden manifestation, something like a vision or a voice from Heaven, confirming it to you, I can say the same. But I know He died for sinners ; I know I am a sinner ; I know He invites them that are ready to perish ; I am such a one ; I know, upon His own invitation, I have committed myself to Him : and I know by the effects, that He has been with me hitherto, otherwise I should have been an apostate long ago ; and, therefore, I know that He died for me ; for had He been pleased to kill me (as He justly might have done) He would not have shown me such things as these.

> If I must perish, would the Lord
> Have taught my heart to love His word ?
> Would He have given me eyes to see
> My danger and my remedy ?
> Reveal'd His name, and bid me pray,
> Had He resolv'd to say me nay ?

I know that I am a child, because He teaches me to say, Abba, Father. I know that I am *His*, because He has enabled me to choose Him for *mine*. For such a choice and desire could never have taken place in my heart, if He had not placed it there Himself. By nature I was too blind to know Him, too proud to trust Him, too obstinate to serve Him, too base-minded to love Him. The enmity I was filled with against His government, righteousness, and grace, was too strong to be subdued by any power but His own. The love I bear Him is but a faint and feeble spark, but it is an emanation from Himself : He kindled it, and He keeps it alive ; and, because it is His work, I trust many waters shall not quench it.

I have only room to assure you that I am, &c.

FOUR LETTERS

TO THE

REV. MR. R——

LETTER I

MY DEAR SIR,   *April* 15, 1776.

*   *   *

I OFTEN rejoice on your behalf. Your call out of the world was a singularly comfortable instance of the power of grace. And when I consider the difficulties and snares of your situation, and that you have been kept in the middle path, preserved from undue compliances on the one hand and unnecessary singularities on the other, I cannot doubt but the Lord has hitherto helped and guided you. Indeed, you have need of His guidance. At your years, and with your expectations in life, your health firm, and your natural spirits lively, you are exposed to many snares : yet, if the Lord keeps you sensible of your danger, and dependent upon Him, you will walk safely. Your security, success, and comfort, depend upon Him ; and in the way of means, chiefly upon your being preserved in a humble sense of your own weakness. It is written, " Fear not, I am with thee." It is written again, " Blessed is the man who feareth always." There is a perfect harmony in those seemingly different texts. May the wisdom that cometh from above teach you and me to keep them both united in our view. If the Lord be with us, we have no cause of fear. His eye is upon us, His arm over us, His ear open to our prayer —His grace sufficient, His promise unchangeable. Under His protection, though the path of duty should lie through fire and water, we may cheerfully and confidently pursue it. On the other hand, our hearts are so deceitful, fallible,

175

and frail ; our spiritual enemies so subtle, watchful, and powerful ; and they derive so many advantages from the occasions of every day, in which we are unavoidably and unexpectedly concerned ; there is so much combustible within, and so many temptations arising from without, capable of setting all in a flame, that we cannot be too jealous of ourselves and our circumstances. The Duke of Devonshire's motto (if I mistake not) well suits the Christian, *Cavendo tutus.* When we can say in the Psalmist's spirit, *Hold thou me up*, we may warrantably draw his conclusion— *and I shall be safe ;* but the moment we lean to our own understanding, we are in imminent danger of falling. The enemy who wars against our souls is a consummate master in his way, fertile in stratagems, and equally skilful in carrying on his assaults by sap or by storm. He studies us, if I may so say, all around, to discover our weak sides ; and he is a very Proteus for changing his appearances, and can appear as a sly serpent, a roaring lion, or an angel of light, as best suits his purpose. It is a great mercy to be in some measure acquainted with his devices, and aware of them. They who wait humbly upon the Lord, and consult carefully at His word and throne of grace, are made wiser than their enemy, and enabled to escape and withstand his wiles. I know you will not expect me to apologize for putting you in mind of these things, though you know them. I have a double warrant : the love I bear you, and the Lord's command, Heb. iii. 13. Use the like freedom with me ; I need it, and hope to be thankful for it, and accept it as one of the best proofs of friendship.

The Lord bless and keep you. Pray for us, and believe me to be sincerely yours.

LETTER II

My Dear Sir, *July* 13, 1776.

The Lord, who mercifully called you out of a state of thoughtless dissipation, and has hitherto been with you, will, I trust, sweeten all your trials, and cause His light to shine upon your paths. It seems probable, that if you pay a just regard to your father's negative, which, I really think, He has a right to expect from you, and, at the same time, make a steady and conscientious use of that negative, which he generously allows you to put upon his proposals, to which, I think, you have an equal right—I say, while things remain in this situation, and you continue to think differently, it seems probable that the hour of your exchanging a single for the married state is yet at some distance. But let not this grieve you. The Lord is all-sufficient. A lively sense of His love, a deep impression of eternity, a heart filled with zeal for His cause, and a thirst for the good of souls, will, I hope, enable you to make a cheerful sacrifice of whatever has no necessary connection with your peace and His service. And you may rest assured, that whenever He who loves you better than you do yourself, sees it best for you, upon the whole, to change your condition, He will bring it about, He will point out the person, prepare the means, and secure the success, by His providence, and the power He has over every heart. And you shall see that all previous difficulties were either gracious preventions, which He threw in the way to prevent your taking a wrong step, or temporary bars, which, by His removing them afterwards, should give you opportunity of more clearly perceiving His care and interposition in your favour. In the meantime, remember your high calling—you are a minister and ambassador of Christ : you are entrusted with the most honourable and important employment that can engage and animate the heart of man. Ταῦτα μελετα, ἐν τ*υ*τοις ἴσθι᾿ ἐπιμενε αὐτοῖς.*

Filled and fired with a constraining sense of the love of Jesus, and the worth of souls ; impressed with an ardour to carry war into Satan's kingdom, to storm his strongholds, and rescue his captives—you will have little leisure to think of anything else. How does the love of glory stimulate the soldier, make him forget and forego a thousand personal tendernesses, and prompt him to cross oceans, to traverse deserts, to scale mountains, and plunge into the greatest hardships and the thickest dangers ! They do it for a corruptible crown, a puff of breath, an empty fame ; their

---

* 1 Tim. iv. 15, 16.

highest prospect is the applause and favour of their prince. We, likewise, are soldiers ; we have a Prince and Captain who deserves our all. They who know Him, and have hearts to conceive of His excellence, and to feel their obligations to Him, cannot indeed seek their own glory, but His glory is dearer to them than a thousand lives. They owe Him their souls, for He redeemed them with blood, His own blood : and, by His grace, He subdued and pardoned them when they were rebels, and in arms against Him. Therefore they are not their own, they would not be their own. When His standard is raised, when His enemies are in motion, when His people are to be rescued, they go forth clothed with His panoply, they fight under His eye, they are sure of His support, and He shows them the conqueror's crown. O when they think of that εν δυλε αγαθε,* with which He has promised to welcome them home when the campaign is over, hard things seem easy, and bitter things sweet ; they count nothing, not even their own lives, dear, so that they may finish their course with joy. May the Lord make us thus minded ; give us a hearty concern for *His* business, and He has engaged to take care of *ours ,* and nothing that can conduce to our real comfort and usefulness shall be withheld.

Believe me to be sincerely yours.

LETTER III

MY DEAR FRIEND,   *December 21, 1776.*

YOUR letter brought me tidings of joy, and then furnished me with materials for a bonfire upon the occasion. It was an act of passive obedience to burn it, but I did obey. I congratulate you upon the happy issue to which the Lord has brought your affairs. I see that His good Spirit and good providence have been, and are, with you. I doubt not but your union with Miss—— will be a mutual blessing, and, on your part, heightened by being connected with such

---

* Well done, good servant.

a family. I could enlarge upon this head, if my letter, likewise, was to be burnt as soon as you have read it. I look upon the friendship the Lord has given me there, as one of my prime privileges ; and I hope I shall always be thankful that it proved a means of introducing you into it.

I congratulate you, likewise, upon your accession to ——, not because it is a good living, in a genteel neighbour-hood, and a fine country ; but because I believe the Lord sends you there for fulfilling the desires He has given you, of being useful to souls. Church preferment, in any other view, is dreadful : and I would as soon congratulate a man upon seeing a millstone tied about his neck, to sink him into the depths of the sea, as upon his obtaining what is called a good living, except I thought him determined to spend and be spent in the cause of the Gospel. A parish is an awful millstone, indeed, to those who see nothing valuable in the flock but the fleece ; but the Lord has impressed your heart with a sense of the glory and importance of His truth, and the worth of souls, and animated your zeal by the most powerful motive, the knowledge of His constraining love. Your case is extraordinary. Perhaps, when you review in your mind the circle of your former gay acquaint-tance, you may say with Job's servant, " I only am escaped alive " : the rest are either removed into an eternal state, or are still hurrying down the stream of dissipation, and living without God in the world. Yet there was a time when there seemed no more probability on your side than on theirs, that you should obtain mercy, and be called to the honour of preaching the glorious Gospel. You are setting out with every possible advantage—in early life, with a cheerful flow of spirits, affluent circumstances ; and now, to crown all, the Lord gives you the very choice of your heart in a partner ; one who, besides deserving and meeting your affection, will, I am persuaded, be a real help-mate to you in your spiritual walk. How much is here to be thankful for !

I trust the Lord has given you, and will maintain in you, a right spirit, so as not to rest in His gifts, but to hold them in connection with the love and favour of the Giver. It is a low time with us when the greatest assemblage of earthly blessings can seem to satisfy us without a real communion with Him. His grace is sufficient for you; but, undoubtedly, such a scene of prosperity as seems to lie before you, is full of snares, and calls for a double effort of watchfulness and prayer. Your situation will fix many eyes upon you, and Satan will, doubtless, watch you, and examine every corner of the hedge around you, to see if he can find a gap by which to enter. We have but few rich Gospel-Ministers; but it is too evident that he has found a way to damp the zeal, and hurt the spirits, of some of those few, who, for a time, acted nobly, and seemed to walk out of the reach of the allurements of the world. I am not jealous of you; I feel a comfortable persuasion that the Lord has taken a fast hold of your heart, and given you a fast hold of His almighty arm: yet I believe you will not be displeased with me for dropping a hint of this kind, and at this time.

You have heard of the trial with which the Lord has been pleased to visit us; it still continues, though considerably alleviated. It is tempered with many mercies, and, I hope, He disposes us, in a measure, to submission. I trust it will be for good. My dear friend, you are now coming into my school, where you will learn, as occasions offer, to feel more in the person of another than in your own. But be not discouraged; the Lord only afflicts for our good. It is necessary that our sharpest trials should sometimes spring from our dearest comforts, else we should be in danger of forgetting ourselves, and setting up our rest here. In such a world, and with such hearts as we have, we shall often need something to prevent our cleaving to the dust, to quicken us to prayer, and to make us feel that our dependence for one hour's peace is upon the Lord alone. I am ready to think I have known as much of the good and happiness which this world can afford, as most people who live in it. I never saw the person with whom I wished to exchange in temporals. And, for many years past, I have thought my trials have been light and few, compared with what many, or most, of the Lord's people have endured. And yet, though in the main possessed of my own wishes, when I look back upon the twenty-seven years past, I am ready to style them, with Jacob, few and evil; and to give the sum-total of their contents in Solomon's words—All is vanity. If I take these years to pieces, I see a great part of them was filled up with sins, sorrows, and inquietudes. The pleasures too are gone, and have no more real existence than the baseless fabric of a dream. The shadows of the evening will soon begin to come over us; and, if our lives are prolonged, a thousand pains and infirmities, from which the Lord has, in a remarkable measure, exempted us hitherto, will probably overtake us; and, at last, we must feel the parting pang. *Sic transit gloria mundi.* Sin has so envenomed the soil of this earth, that the amaranth will not grow upon it. But we are hastening to a better world, and bright unclouded skies, where our sun will go down no more, and all tears shall be wiped from our eyes.

I am, &c.

LETTER IV

My Dear Friend,   *September 27, 1777.*

MR. —— called on us Thursday evening, and, from that hour, my thoughts, when awake, have seldom been absent from ——. Few people are better qualified to feel for *you*, yourself and the family excepted; perhaps, there is no person living more nearly interested in what concerns Mrs. —— than myself. I could not, therefore, at such a time as this, refrain from writing; and glad should I be, if the Lord may help me to drop a suitable word, and accompany it with a blessing to you in the reading.

I am glad to be assured (though I expected no less) that Mrs. —— happily feels herself safe in the Lord's hand, and under the care of the good Shepherd and Saviour, to whom she has often committed herself; and finds Him faithful to His promise, giving her strength in her soul according to her day, and enabling her quietly to submit to His holy, wise, and gracious will. And it is my prayer, that He may strengthen you likewise, and reveal His own all-sufficiency so clearly and powerfully to your heart, that you may not be afraid of any event, but cheerfully rely upon Him, to be

all that to you, in every circumstance and change, which
His promise warrants you to expect.

I am willing to hope that this is but a short season of
anxiety, appointed for the exercise of your faith and patience,
and to give you, in his good time, a signal proof of His power
and goodness in answering prayer. He sometimes brings
us into such a situation, that the help of creatures is utterly
unavailing, that we may afterwards be more clearly sensible
of His interposition. Then we experimentally learn the
vanity of all things here below, and are brought to a more
immediate and absolute dependence upon Himself. We
have need of having these lessons frequently inculcated upon
us ; but when His end is answered, how often, after He has
caused grief, does He show His great compassions, and
save us from our fears by an outstretched arm, and such a
seasonable and almost unexpected relief, as constrains us
to cry out, What has God wrought ; and who is a God like
unto Thee ? Such, I hope, will be the issue of your present
trial, and that He, who gave her to you at first, will restore
her to you again. I see you in the furnace ; but the Lord
is sitting by it as a refiner of silver, to moderate the fire,
and manage the process, so that you shall lose nothing but
dross, and be brought forth refined as gold, to praise His
name. Apparent difficulties, however great, are nothing
to Him. If He speaks, it is done ; for to God the Lord
belong the issues from death. Should His pleasure be other-
wise, and should He call your dear partner to a state of glory
before you, still I know He is able to support you. What
He does, however painful to the flesh, must be right, because
He does it. Having bought us with His blood, and saved
our souls from hell, He has every kind of right to dispose of
us and ours as He pleases ; and this we are sure of, He will
not lay so much upon us as He freely endured for us ; and
He can make us amends for all we suffer, and for all we lose,
by the light of His countenance. A few years will set all
to rights ; and they who love Him, and are beloved by Him,
though they may suffer as others, shall not sorrow as others ;
for the Lord will be with them here, and He will soon
have them with Him : there all tears shall be wiped from
their eyes.

Perhaps I know as well how to calculate the pain of such

a separation, as any one who has not actually experienced it. Many a time the desire of my eyes has been threatened, many a time my heart has been brought low ; but, from what I have known at such seasons, I have reason to hope, that had it been His pleasure to bring upon me the thing that I feared, His everlasting arm would have upheld me from sinking under the stroke. As ministers, we are called to comfort the Lord's afflicted people, and to tell them the knowledge of His love is a cordial able to keep the soul alive under the sharpest trials. We must not wonder that He sometimes puts us in a way of showing that we do not deal in unfelt truths, but that we find ourselves that solid consolation in the Gospel which we encourage others to expect from it. You have now such an occasion of glorifying the Lord ; I pray He may enable you to improve it, and that all around you may see that He is with you, and that His good word is the support and anchor of your soul. Then I am sure, if it, upon the whole, is best for you, He will give you the desire of your heart, and you shall yet live to praise Him together. I am, &c.

A LETTER

REV. MR. O——

LETTER I

My Dearest Sir,   *April* 3, 1759.

You see I have prevented you in your promise of writing first ; and having found a pretext for troubling Mr. ——, I was willing to venture upon you without any, unless you would let me plead a desire of showing you, how welcome your correspondence would be to me. I know not if my heart was ever more united to any person, in so short a space of time, than to you ; and what engaged me so much was, the spirit of meekness and of love (that peculiar and inimitable mark of true Christianity) which I observed in you. I mean it not to your praise. May all the praise be to Him from whom every good and perfect gift cometh, who alone maketh the best to differ from the worst : but I think I may well mention, to your encouragement, that all who conversed with you greatly regret your speedy departure ; and I am persuaded, the same temper, the same candour, will make you acceptable, honourable, and useful, wherever you go. Blessed are the poor in spirit, the meek, the merciful, and the peace-makers ; they shall obtain the mercy they want, and possess the peace they love. They shall inherit the earth. The earth, sinful and miserable as it is, shall be worthy to be called an inheritance to them, for they shall enjoy a comparative heaven in it. They shall be called the children of God, though dignified with no title among men. Alas ! how much are these things overlooked, even by many who, I would hope, are real believers. Methinks, a very different spirit from that of the church of

184

Laodicea is to be seen amongst us, though, perhaps, it is not easy to say which is the best of the two. That was neither cold nor hot ; this (*mirabile dictu*) is both cold and hot at once, and both to the extreme—hot, hasty, and arbitrary in those few things where mediocrity is a virtue ; but cool and remiss in those great points, where the application of the whole heart, and soul, and mind, and strength is so absolutely necessary, and so positively enjoined. Surely there is too much room for this observation, and I, perhaps, stand self-condemned in making it.

I hope you will take opportunity to improve your interest in Mr. ———— by letter. He expressed much satisfaction in the hour he spent with you before you sailed, and a great regard for you ; therefore would, I doubt not, give you a fair hearing ; and the phrase *litera scripta manet* is true in more senses than one. He makes such large concessions sometimes, that I am apt to think he is conscious of the weakness of his own argument ; and then he is so soon angry with himself for complying as far, and flies off to the other extreme. Yet, for the most part, when he speaks plain, and is not restrained by complaisance for particular persons, he appears not only a stranger to experimental religion, but averse to the notion, and generally inclined to treat it with levity. His obstacles are very many and very great ; his reputation as a learned man, his years, his regular life, and, perhaps, above all, his performances in print, especially his last book, are so many barriers that must be broke through before conviction can reach him. But the grace of God can do all this and more ; and, indeed, when I think of the many truly valuable parts of his character, and the indefatigable pains he has taken in his researches after truth, I am willing to hope, that the Lord will, at length, teach him the true wisdom, and enable him (however hard it may seem) to give up his own attainments, and sit down, like a little child, at the feet of Jesus.

I hope to hear soon and often from you. I number my Christian correspondents among my principal blessings, a few judicious pious friends, to whom, when I can get leisure to write, I send my heart by turns. I can trust them with my inmost sentiments, and can write with no more disguise than I think. I shall rejoice to add you to the number, if

you can agree to take me as I am (as I think you will) and
suffer me to commit my whole self to paper, without respect
to names, parties, and sentiments.   I endeavour to observe
my Lord's commands, to call no man master upon earth :
yet I desire to own and honour the image of God, wherever
I find it.   I dare not say I have no bigotry, for I know not
myself ; and remember, to my shame, that formerly, when I
ignorantly professed myself free from it, I was, indeed,
overrun with it : but this I can say, I allow it not ; I strive
and pray against it ; and thus far, by the grace of God, I have
attained, that I find my heart as much united to many who
differ from me in some points, as to any who agree with me
in all.   I set no value upon any doctrinal truth, farther than
as it has a tendency to promote practical holiness.   If others
should think those things hindrances, which I judge to be
helps, in this respect, I am content they should go on in their
own way, according to the light God has given them, pro-
vided they will agree with me ἐν τῷ Ἐπαναγκες.   If it should
be asked, Which are the necessary things ?   I answer,
Those in which the spiritual worshippers of all ages and
countries have been agreed.   Those, on the contrary, are
mere subordinate matters, in which the best men, those who
have been the most eminent for faith, prayer, humility, and
nearness to God, always have been, and still are, divided
in their judgments.   Upon this plan I should think it no
hard matter to draw up a form of sound words (whether
dignified with the name of a creed or not, I care not) to which
true believers of all sort and sizes would unanimously sub-
scribe.   Suppose it ran something in the following manner :
I believe that sin is the most hateful thing in the world ;
that I and all men are, by nature, in a state of wrath and
depravity, utterly unable to sustain the penalty or to fulfil
the commands, of God's holy law ; and that we have no
sufficiency of ourselves to think a good thought.   I believe
that Jesus Christ is the chief among ten thousands ; that He
came into the world to save the chief of sinners, by making
a propitiation for sin by His death, by paying a perfect
obedience to the law, in our behalf ; and that He is now
exalted on high, to give repentance and remission of sins
to all that believe ; and that He ever liveth to make inter-
cession for us.   I believe that the Holy Spirit (the gift of

God through Jesus Christ) is the sure and only guide into all truth, and the common privilege of all believers ; and, under His influence, I believe the Holy Scriptures are able to make us wise unto salvation, and to furnish us thoroughly for every good work. I believe that love to God, and to man for God's sake, is the essence of religion, and the fulfilling of the law ; that without holiness no man shall see the Lord ; that those who, by a patient course in well-doing, seek glory, honour, and immortality, shall receive eternal life ; and I believe that this reward is not of debt, but of grace, even to the praise and glory of that grace, whereby He has made us accepted in the Beloved. Amen.

I pretend not to accuracy in this hasty draught ; they are only outlines, which, if you please to retouch, and fill up at your leisure, I hope you will favour me with a sight of. I fear I have tired you—shall only add my prayers, that the Lord may be with you, and crown your labours of love with success, that you may hereafter shine among those who have been instrumental in turning many to righteousness.

I am, &c.

SEVEN LETTERS

TO THE

REV. MR. P——

LETTER I

Dear Sir,

THE account which I received by Mr. C———, and by the letter which he brought from you, of your welfare, and the welfare of your people, was very pleasing, though, indeed, no more than I expected. I believed, from the first of your going to S——, that you would like the people, and I believed the Lord had given you that frame of spirit which He has promised to bless. What reason have we to praise Him for the knowledge of His Gospel, and for the honour of being called to preach it to others ; and, likewise, that He has been pleased to cast your lot and mine amongst a people who value it, and to crown our poor labours with some measure of acceptance and usefulness ! How little did we think, in the unawakened part of our life, to what it was His good pleasure to reserve us !

The Lord is pleased, in a measure, to show me the suitableness and necessity of a humble, dependent frame of heart, a ceasing from self, and a reliance upon Him in the due use of appointed means ; I am far from having attained, but I hope I am pressing, at least seeking, after it. I wish to speak the word simply and experimentally, and to be so engaged with the importance of the subject, the worth of souls, and the thought that I am speaking in the name and presence of the Most High God, as that I might, if possible, forget everything else. This would be an attainment, indeed ! More good might be expected from a broken discourse, delivered in such a frame, than from the most advantageous display of knowledge and gifts without it.

Not that I would undervalue propriety and pertinence of expression : it is our duty to study to find out acceptable words, and to endeavour to appear as workmen that need not be ashamed ; but those who have most ability in this way, have need of a double guard of grace and wisdom, lest they be tempted to trust in it, or to value themselves upon it. They that trust in the Lord shall never be moved ; and they that abase themselves before Him, He will exalt. I am well persuaded that your conduct and view have been agreeable to these sentiments ; and, therefore, the Lord has supported, encouraged, and owned you ; and, I trust, He will still bless you, and make you a blessing to many. He that walketh humbly, walketh surely.

Believe me to be, &c.

LETTER II

My Dear Sir,   *August* 14, 1770.

Your letter did me good when I received it, at least, gave me much pleasure ; and I think it has given me a lift while I have been just now reading it. I know not that I ever had those awful views of sin which you speak of ; and though, I believe, I should be better for them, I dare not seriously wish for them. There is a petition which I have heard in public prayer—Lord, show us the evil of our hearts. To this petition I cannot venture to set my Amen, at least, not without a qualification. Show me enough of Thyself to balance the view, and then show me what Thou pleasest. I think I have a very clear and strong conviction, in my *judgment*, that I am vile and worthless, that my heart is full of evil, only evil, and that continually. I know something of it, too, experimentally ; and, therefore, judging of the whole by the sample, though I am not suitably affected with what I do see, I tremble at the thought of seeing more. A man may look with some pleasure upon the sea in a storm, provided he stands safe upon the land himself ; but to be *upon* the sea in a storm is quite another thing. And yet, surely, the coldness, worldliness, pride, and twenty other evils under which I groan, owe much of their strength to the want of that feeling sense of my own abominations with which you have been favoured : I say, favoured ; for I doubt not but the Lord gave it you in mercy, and that it has proved, and will prove, a mercy to you, to make you more humble, spiritual, and dependent, as well as to increase your ability for preaching the Gospel of His grace. Upon these accounts, I can assure you that, upon a first reading, and till I stopped a moment to count the cost, I was ready to envy you all that you had felt. I often seem to know what the Scripture teaches, both of sin and grace, as if I knew them not ; so faint and languid are my perceptions, I often seem to think and talk of sin without any sorrow, and of grace without any joy.

I have had some people awakened by dreams, as you had by streamers : but, for aught I know, we are no less instrumental to the good of these, than to any other person, upon whom, when we look, our hearts are ready to exult, and say, See what the Lord has done by me. I do not think that, strictly speaking, all the streamers of the north are able to awaken a dead soul. I suppose people may be terrified by them, and made thoughtful, but awakened only by the *word*. The streamers either sent them to hear the Gospel, or roused them to attend to it ; but it was the knowledge of the truth brought home to the heart that did the business. Perhaps the streamers reminded them of what they had heard from you before. Two persons here, who lived like heathens, and never came to church, were alarmed by some terrifying dreams, and came out to hearing forthwith. There the Lord was pleased to meet with them. One of them died triumphing ; the other, I hope, will do so when her time comes. Whatever means, instruments, or occasions He is pleased to employ, the work is all His own ; and, I trust, you and I are made willing to give Him all the glory, and to sink into the dust at the thought that He should ever permit us to take His holy name upon our polluted lips.

I am, &c.

LETTER III

MY DEAR SIR,   *June* 13, 1772.

YOU say that your experience agrees with mine. It must be so, because our hearts are alike. The heart is deceitful and desperately wicked, destitute of good, and prone to evil. This is the character of mankind universally, and those who are made partakers of grace are renewed but in part ; the evil nature still cleaves to them, and the root of sin, though mortified, is far from being dead.—While the cause remains, it will have effects ; and while we are burdened with the body of this death, we must groan under it. But we need not be swallowed up with overmuch sorrow, since we have in Jesus a Saviour, a Righteousness, an Advocate, a Shepherd. " He knows our frame, and remembers that we are but dust." If sin abounds in us, grace abounds much more in Him ; nor would He suffer sin to remain in His people, if He did not know how to overrule it, and make it an occasion of endearing His love and grace so much the more to their souls. The Lord forbid that we should plead His goodness as an encouragement to sloth and indifference. Humiliation, godly sorrow, and self-abasement become us ; but, at the same time, we may rejoice in the Lord. Though sin remains, it shall not have dominion over us ; though it wars in us, it shall not prevail against us. We have a mercy-seat sprinkled with blood, we have an Advocate with the Father, we are called to this warfare, and we fight under the eye of the Captain of our salvation, who is always near to renew our strength, to heal our wounds, and to cover our heads in the heat of battle. As ministers, we preach to those who have like passions and infirmities with ourselves, and by our own feelings, fears, and changes, we learn to speak a word in season to them that are weary, to warn those who stand, and to stretch out a hand of compassion towards them that are fallen ; and to commend it to others from our own experience, as a faithful saying. Besides, if the Lord is pleased to give us some liberty, acceptance, and success in preaching the Gospel, we should be in great danger of running mad with spiritual pride, if the Lord did not permit us to feel the depravity and vileness of our hearts, and thereby keep us from forgetting *what we are in ourselves.*

With regard to your young people, you must expect to meet with some disappointment. Perhaps, not every one of whom you have conceived hopes will stand, and some who do belong to the Lord are permitted to make sad mistakes for their future humiliation. It is our part to watch, warn, and admonish, and we ought, likewise, to be concerned for those slips and miscarriages which we cannot prevent. A minister, if faithful, and of a right spirit, can have no greater joy than to see his people walking honourably and steadily in the truth ; and hardly anything will give him more sensible grief, than to see any of them taken in Satan's wiles. Yet still the Gospel brings relief here. He is wiser than we are, and knows how to make those things subservient to promote his work, which we ought to guard against as evils and hindrances. We are to use the means—He is to rule the whole. If the faults of some are made warnings to others, and prove, in the end, occasions of illustrating the riches of divine grace, this should reconcile us to what we cannot help, though such considerations should not slacken our diligence in sounding an alarm, and reminding our hearers of their continual danger.　　　　　　　　　　I am, &c.

LETTER IV

Dear Sir,　　　　　　　　　　　*January 26, 1775.*

I lately read a sermon of Mr. Baxter's (in the fifth volume of the *Morning Exercises*) on Matt. v. 16. My mind is somewhat impressed with the subject, and with his manner of treating it. Some of Mr. Baxter's sentiments in divinity are rather cloudy ; and he sometimes, upon that account, met with but poor quarter from the staunch Calvinists of his day. But, by what I have read of him, where he is quiet, and not ruffled by controversy, he appears to me, notwithstanding some mistakes, to have been one of the greatest men of his age, and, perhaps, in fervour, spirituality, and success, more than equal, both as a minister and a Christian, to some twenty taken together, of those who affect to undervalue him in this present day. There is a spirit in some passages of his *Saint's Rest*, his *Dying Thoughts*, and others of his practical treatises, compared with which, many modern compositions, though well written and well meant, appear to me to a great disadvantage. But I was speaking of his sermon. He points out the way at which we should aim to let our light shine in the world, for the glory of God, and the conviction and edification of men. I have mentioned where it is to be found, that, if you have the *Morning Exercises*, or they should come in your way, you may look at it. I think you would like it. The perusal suggested to me some instruction, and much reproof. Alas! my friend, are we not too often chargeable with a sad, shameful selfishness and narrowness of spirit, far, very far different from that activity, enlargement, and generosity of soul, which such a Gospel as we have received might be expected to produce? For myself, I must plead guilty. It seems as if my heart was always awake, and keenly sensible to my *own* concernments, while those of my Lord and Master affect me much less forcibly, at least, only by intervals. Were a stranger to judge of me by what I sometimes say in the pulpit, he might think that, like the angels, I had but two things in view, to do the will of God, and to behold His face. But, alas! would he not be almost as much mistaken, as if, seeing Mr. G—— in the character of a tragedy-hero, he should suppose him to be the very person whom he only represents? I hope Satan will never be able to persuade me that I am a *mere hypocrite* and *stage-player;* but sure I am that there is so much hypocrisy in me, so many littlenesses and self-seekings insinuating into my plan of conduct, that I have humbling cause to account myself unworthy and unprofitable, and to say, "Enter not into judgment with Thy servant, O Lord." I have some tolerable idea of what a Christian ought to be, and it is, I hope, what I desire to be. A Christian should be conformable to Christ in his spirit and in his practice; that is, he should be spiritually minded, dead to the world, filled with zeal for the glory of God, the spread of the Gospel, and the good of souls. He should be humble, patient, meek, cheerful, thankful under all events and changes. He should account it the business and honour of his life to imitate Him who pleased not Himself, Who went about doing good, and has expressed to us the very feelings of His heart, in that divine aphorism, which surpasses all the fine admired sayings of the philosophers, as much as the sun outshines a candle, " It is more blessed to give than to receive."   The whole deportment of a Christian should show, that the knowledge of Jesus, which he has received from the Gospel, affords him all he could expect from it : a balm for every grief, an amend for every loss, a motive for every duty, a restraint from every evil, a pattern for everything which he is called to do or suffer, and a principle sufficient to constitute the actions of every day, even in common life, acts of religion.   He should (as the children of this world are wise to do in their genera-tion) make every occurrence through which he passes, subservient and subordinate to his main design.   Gold is the worldly man's god, and his worship and service are uniform and consistent, not by fits and starts, but from morning to night ; from the beginning to the end of the year, he is the same man.   He will not slip an opportunity of adding to his pelf to-day, because he may have another to-morrow, but he heartily and eagerly embraces both ; and, so far as he carries his point, though his perseverance may expose him to the ridicule or reproach of his neigh-bours, he thinks himself well paid, and says,

> Populus me sibilat ; at mihi plaudo
> Ipse domi, simul ac nummos contemplor arca.

I am, &c.

LETTER V

DEAR SIR,   *Jan.— 1776.*

I MAY learn (only I am a sad dunce) by small and com-mon incidents, as well as by some more striking and import-ant turns in life, that it is not in man that walketh to direct his steps. It is not for me to say, to-day or to-morrow, I will do this or that. I cannot write a letter to a friend without leave or without help ; for neither opportunity nor ability are at my own disposal. It is not needful that the Lord should raise a mountain in my way, to stop my purpose ; if He only withdraw a certain kind of imperceptible support, which in general I have and use without duly considering whose it is, then in a moment I feel myself unstrung and disabled, like a ship that has lost her masts, and cannot proceed till He is pleased to refit me and renew my strength. My pride and propensity to self-independence render frequent changes of this kind necessary to me, or I should soon forget what I am, and sacrifice to my own drag. Therefore, upon the whole, I am satisfied, and see it best, that I should be absolutely poor and penniless in myself, and forced to depend upon the Lord for the smallest things as well as the greatest. And if, by His blessing, my experience should at length tally with my judgment in this point, that without Him I can do nothing, then I know I shall find it easy, through Him, to do all things ; for the door of His mercy is always open, and it is but ask and have. But, alas ! a secret persuasion (though contrary to repeated convictions) that I have something at home, too often prevents me going to Him for it, and then no wonder I am disappointed. The life of faith seems so simple and easy in theory, that I can point it out to others in few words ; but in practice it is very difficult, and my advances are so slow, that I hardly dare say I get forward at all. It is a great thing indeed to have the spirit of a little child, so as to be habitually afraid of taking a single step without leading.

I have heard of you more than once since I heard from you, and am glad to know the Lord is still with you ; I trust He has not withdrawn wholly from us. We have much call for thankfulness, and much for humiliation. Some have been removed, some are evidently ripening for glory, and now and then we have a new inquirer. But the progress of wickedness amongst the unconverted here is awful. Convictions repeatedly stifled in many, have issued in a hardiness and boldness in sinning which, I believe, is seldom found but in those places where the light of the

Gospel has been long resisted and abused. If my eyes suitably affected my heart, I should weep day and night upon this account ; but alas ! I am too indifferent. I feel a woful defect in my zeal for God and compassion for souls ; and when Satan and conscience charge me with cowardice, treachery, and stupidity, I know not what to reply. I am generally carried through my public work with some liberty ; and because I am not put to shame before the people, I seem content and satisfied. I wish to be more thankful for what the Lord is pleased to do amongst us, but, at the same time, to be more earnest with Him for a further outpouring of His Spirit. Assist me therein with your prayers.

As to my own private experience, the enemy is not suffered to touch the foundation of my faith and hope ; thus far I have peace. But my conflicts and exercises, with the effects of indwelling sin, are very distressing. I cannot doubt of my state and acceptance ; and yet it seems no one can have more cause for doubts and fears than myself, if such doubtings were at all encouraged by the Gospel ; but I see they are not ; I see that what I want and hope for, the Lord promises to do, for His own name's sake, and with a *non obstante* to all my vileness and perverseness ; and I cannot question but He has given me (for how else could I have it ?) a thirst for that communion with Him in love, and conformity to His image, of which, as yet, I have experienced but very faint and imperfect beginnings. But if He has begun, I venture, upon His word, that He will not forsake the work of His own hands.

On public affairs I say but little. Many are censuring men and measures ; but I would lay all the blame upon sin. It appears plain to me that the Lord has a controversy with us ; and, therefore, I fear what we have yet seen is but the beginning of sorrows. I am ready to dread the event of this summer ; but I remember the Lord reigns. He has His own glory and the good of His church in view, and will not be disappointed. He knows how likewise to take care of those who fear Him. I wish there were more sighing and mourning amongst professors, for the sins of the nation and the churches. But I must conclude, and am, &c.

LETTER VI

DEAR SIR,

No very considerable alteration has taken place since I wrote, except the death of Mrs. L———, who was removed to a better world in September last. The latter part of her course was very painful; but the Lord made her more than conqueror, and she had good cause to apply the apostle's words, 2 Tim. iv. 7, 8. She repeated that passage in her last illness, and chose it for her funeral-text. She was a Christian indeed. Her faith was great, and so were her trials. Now she is above them all, now she is before the throne. The good Lord help us to be followers of those who through faith and patience have attained to the hope set before them.

The number of professors still increases with us, and a greater number of persons affords a greater variety of cases, and gives greater scope to observe the workings of the heart and Satan. For seven years I had to say that I had not seen a person of whom I had conceived a good hope go back, but I have met with a few disappointments since. However, upon the whole, I trust the Lord is still with us. The enemy tries to disturb and defile us, and if the Lord did not keep the city, the poor watchman would wake in vain. But the eye that never slumbereth nor sleepeth has been upon us for good; and though we have cause of humiliation and complaint, we have likewise much cause of thankfulness. My health is still preserved; and I hope that the Lord does not suffer my desires of personal communion with Him, and of usefulness in the ministry, to decline. He supplies me with fresh strength and matter in my public work; I hear now and then of one brought to inquire the way: and His presence is at times made known to many in the ordinances.

To combine zeal with prudence is indeed difficult. There is often too much self in our zeal, and too much of the fear of man in our prudence. However, what we cannot attain by any skill or resolution of our own, we may hope in measure to receive from Him who giveth liberally to those who seek Him, and desire to serve Him. Prudence is a word much abused; but there is a Heavenly wisdom, which

the Lord has promised to give to those who humbly wait
upon Him for it.   It does not consist in forming a bundle
of rules and maxims, but in a spiritual taste and discern-
ment, derived from an experimental knowledge of the truth,
and of the heart of man, as described in the word of God ;
and its exercise consists much in a simple dependence upon
the Lord, to guide and prompt us in every action.   We
seldom act wrong, when we truly depend upon Him, and
can cease from leaning to our own understanding.   When
the heart is thus in a right tune and frame, and His word
dwells richly in us, there is a kind of immediate perception of
what is proper for us to do in present circumstances, without
much painful inquiry ; a light shines before us upon the
path of duty ; and if He permits us in such a spirit to make
some mistakes, He will likewise teach us to profit by them ;
and our reflections upon what was wrong one day, will
make us to act more wisely the next.   At the best, we must
always expect to meet with new proofs of our own weakness
and insufficiency ; otherwise how should we be kept humble,
or know how to prize the liberty He allows us of coming to
the throne of grace, for fresh forgiveness and direction every
day ?   But if He enables us to walk before Him with a
single eye, He will graciously accept our desire of serving
Him better if we could, and His blessing will make our feeble
endeavours in some degree successful, at the same time that
we see defects and evils attending our best services, sufficient
to make us ashamed of them.   I am, &c.

LETTER VII

DEAR SIR,   *January* 11, 1777.

WE all need, and at the seasons the Lord sees best,
we all receive chastisement.   I hope you likewise have
reason to praise Him, for supporting, sanctifying, and
delivering mercy.   The coward flesh presently sinks under
the rod, but Faith need not fear it, for it is in the hand of
One who loves us better than we do ourselves, and who

knows our frame, that we are but dust, and therefore will not suffer us to be overdone and overwhelmed.

I feel as a friend should feel for Mr. B——; were I able, I would soon send him health. If the Lord, who is able to remove his illness in a minute, permits it to continue, we may be sure, upon the whole, it will be better for him. It is, however, very lawful to pray that his health may be restored, and his usefulness prolonged. I beg you to give my love to him, and tell him that my heart bears him an affectionate remembrance ; and I know the God whom he serves will make every dispensation supportable and profitable to him.

If, as you observe, the Song of Solomon describes the experience of his church, it shows the dark as well as the bright side. No one part of it is the experience of every individual at any particular time. Some are in his banqueting-house, others upon their beds. Some sit under His banner, supported by His arm ; while others have a faint perception of Him at a distance, with many a hill and mountain between. In one thing, however, they all agree, that He is the leading object of their desires, and that they have had such a discovery of His person, work, and love, as makes Him precious to their hearts. Their judgment of Him is always the same, but their sensibility varies. The love they bear Him, though rooted and grounded in their hearts, is not always equally in exercise, nor can it be so. We are like trees, which, though alive, cannot put forth their leaves and fruit without the influence of the sun. They are alive in winter as well as in summer ; but how different is their appearance in these different seasons ! Were we always alike, could we always believe, love, and rejoice, we should think the power inherent and our own ; but it is more for the Lord's glory, and more suited to form us to a temper becoming the Gospel, that we should be made deeply sensible of our own inability and dependence, than that we should be always in a lively frame. I am persuaded, a broken and a contrite spirit, a conviction of our vileness and nothingness, connected with a cordial acceptance of Jesus as revealed in the Gospel, is the highest attainment we can reach in this life. Sensible comforts are desirable, and we must be sadly declined when they do not appear to us ; but I believe there may be a real exercise of faith and growth in grace when our sensible feelings are faint and low. A soul may be in as thriving a state when thirsting, seeking, and mourning after the Lord, as when actually rejoicing in Him ; as much in earnest when fighting in the valley, as when singing upon the mount ; nay, dark seasons afford the surest and strongest manifestations of the power of faith. To hold fast the word of promise, to maintain a hatred of sin, to go on steadfastly in the path of duty, in defiance both of the frowns and the smiles of the world, when we have but little comfort, is a more certain evidence of grace, than a thousand things which we may do or forbear when our spirits are warm and lively. I have seen many who have been upon the whole but uneven walkers, though at times they have seemed to enjoy, at least have talked of, great comforts. I have seen others, for the most part, complain of much darkness and coldness, who have been remarkably humble, tender, and exemplary in their spirit and conduct. Surely were I to choose my lot, it should be with the latter.

I am, &c.

THREE LETTERS

MRS. G——

LETTER I

MADAM, *June* 20, 1776.

IT would be both unkind and ungrateful in me, to avail myself of any plea of business, for delaying the acknowledgment I owe you for your acceptable favour from——, which, though dated the 6th instant, I did not receive till the 10th.

Could I have known in time that you were at Mr. ——'s, I should have endeavoured to have called upon you while there ; and very glad should I have been to have seen you with us. But they who fear the Lord may be sure, that whatever is not practicable is not necessary. He could have overruled every difficulty in your way, had He seen it expedient ; but He is pleased to show you, that you depend not upon them, but upon Himself ; and that, notwithstanding your connections may exclude you from some advantages in point of outward means, He who has begun a good work in you, is able to carry it on, in defiance of all seeming hindrances, and make all things (even those which have the most unfavourable appearances) work together for your good.

A sure effect of His grace, is a desire and longing for Gospel ordinances ; and when they are afforded, they cannot be neglected without loss. But the Lord sees many souls who are dear to Him, and whom He is training up in a growing meetness for His kingdom, who are, by His providence, so situated, that it is not in their power to attend upon Gospel preaching ; and, perhaps, they have seldom either Christian minister or Christian friend to assist or comfort them. Such a situation is a state of trial ; but Jesus is all-sufficient, and He is always near. They cannot be debarred from His word of grace, which is everywhere at hand, nor from His throne of grace ; for they who feel their need of Him, and whose hearts are drawn towards Him, are always at the foot of it. Every room in the house, yea, every spot they stand on, fields, lanes, and hedge-rows, all is holy ground to them ; for the Lord is there. The chief difference between us and the disciples, when our Saviour was upon earth, is in this : they then walked by sight, and we are called to walk by faith. They could see Him with their bodily eyes, we cannot ; but He said, before He left them, " It is expedient for you that I go away." How could this be, unless that spiritual communion, which He promised to maintain with His people after his ascension, were preferable to that intercourse He allowed them whilst He was visibly with them ? But we are sure it is pre- ferable, and they who had tried both were well satisfied He had made good His promise ; so that though they had known Him after the flesh, they were content not to know Him so any more. Yes, Madam, though we cannot see Him, he sees us ; He is nearer to us than we are to ourselves. In a natural state, we have very dark, and indeed, dishon- ourable thoughts of God ; we conceive of Him as at a dis- tance. But when the heart is awakened, we begin to make Jacob's reflection, " Surely the Lord is in this place, and I knew it not." And when we receive faith, we begin to know that this ever-present God is in Christ ; that the government of heaven and earth, the dispensations of the kingdom of nature, providence, and grace, are in the hands of Jesus : that it is He with whom we have to do, who once suffered agony and death for our redemption, and whose com- passion and tenderness are the same, now He reigns over all blessed for ever, as when He conversed amongst men in the days of His humiliation. Thus God is made known to us by the Gospel, in the endearing views of a Saviour, a Shep- herd, a Husband, a Friend ; and a way of access is opened for us through the vail, that is, the human nature of our Redeemer, to enter, with humble confidence, into the holiest of all, and to repose all our cares and concerns upon the strength of that everlasting arm which upholds Heaven and earth, and upon that infinite love which submitted to the shame, pain, and death of the cross, to redeem sinners from wrath and misery.

Though there is a height, a breadth, a length, and a depth, in this mystery of redeeming love, exceeding the comprehension of all finite minds ; yet the great and leading principles which are necessary for the support and comfort of our souls, may be summed up in a very few words. Such a summary we are favoured with in Titus ii. 11-14, where the whole of salvation, all that is needful to be known, experienced, practised, and hoped for, is comprised within the compass of four verses. If many books, much study, and great discernment, were necessary, in order to be happy, what must the poor and simple do ? Yet for them especially is the Gospel designed ; and few but such as these attain the knowledge and comfort of it. The Bible is a sealed book till the heart be awakened ; and then he that runs may read. The propositions are few. I am a sinner, therefore, I need a Saviour, one who is able and willing to save to the uttermost ; such a one is Jesus ; He is all that I want— wisdom, righteousness, sanctification, and redemption. But will He receive me ? Can I answer a previous question ? Am I willing to receive Him ? If so, and if His word may be taken, if He meant what He said, and promised no more than He can perform, I may be sure of a welcome ; He knew, long before, the doubts, fears, and suspicions, which would arise in my mind when I should come to know what I am, what I have done, and what I have deserved ; and, therefore, He declared, before He left the earth, "Him that cometh to Me, I will in no wise cast out." I have no money or price in my hand, no worthiness to recommend me ; and I need none, for He saveth freely for His own name's sake. I have only to be thankful for what He has already shown me, and to wait upon Him for more. It is my part to commit myself to Him as the physician of sin-sick souls, not to prescribe to Him how He shall treat me. To begin, carry on, and perfect the cure, is His part.

The doubts and fears you speak of, are in a greater or lesser degree, the common experience of all the Lord's people, at least for a time ; whilst any unbelief remains in the heart, and Satan is permitted to tempt, we shall feel these things. In themselves they are groundless and evil ; yet the Lord permits and overrules them for good. They tend to make us know more of the plague of our own hearts, and feel more sensibly the need of a Saviour, and make His rest (when we attain it) doubly sweet and sure. And they likewise qualify us for pitying and comforting others. Fear not ; only believe, wait, and pray. Expect not all at once. A Christian is not of hasty growth, like a mushroom, but rather like the oak, the progress of which is hardly perceptible, but, in time, becomes a great deep-rooted tree. If my writings have been useful to you, may the Lord have the praise. To administer any comfort to His children is the greatest honour and pleasure I can receive in this life. I cannot promise to be a very punctual correspondent, having many engagements ; but I hope to do all in my power to show myself, Madam, Yours, &c.

LETTER II

MADAM, *August* 20, 1776.

THOUGH, in general, I think myself tolerably punctual when I can answer a letter in six or seven weeks after the receipt, yet I feel some pain for not having acknowledged yours sooner. A case like that which you have favoured with an account of, deserved an immediate attention, and when I read it, I proposed writing within a post or two ; and I can hardly allow any plea of business to be sufficient excuse for delaying it so long ; but our times are in the Lord's hands : may He now enable me to send you what may prove a word in season.

Your exercises have been by no means singular, though they may appear so to yourself ; because, in your retired situation, you have not (as you observe) had much opportunity of knowing the experience of other Christians ; nor has the guilt with which your mind has been so greatly burdened been properly your own. It was a temptation forced upon you by the enemy, and he shall answer for it.

Undoubtedly it is a mournful proof of the depravity of our nature, that there is that within us which renders us so easily susceptive of his suggestions ; a proof of our extreme weakness, that after the clearest and most satisfying evidences of the truth, we are not able to hold fast our confidence, if the Lord permits Satan to sift and shake us. But I can assure you these changes are not uncommon. I have known persons, who, after walking with God comfortably, in the main, for forty years, have been at their wits' end from such assaults as you mention, and been brought to doubt, not only of the reality of their own hopes, but of the very ground and foundation upon which their hopes were built. Had you remained, as it seems you once were, attached to the vanities of a gay and dissipated life, or could you have been contented with a form of godliness, destitute of the power, it is probable you would have remained a stranger to these troubles. Satan would have employed his arts in a different and less perceptible way, to have soothed you into a false peace, and prevented any thought or suspicion of danger from arising in your mind. But when he could no longer detain you in his bondage, or seduce you back again into the world, then, of course, he would change his method, and declare open war against you. A specimen of his power and malice you have experienced : and the Lord whom you loved, because He first loved you, permitted it, not to gratify Satan, but for your benefit—to humble and prove you, to show you what is in your heart, and to do you good in the issue. These things, for the present, are not joyous, but grievous ; yet, in the end, they yield the peaceable fruits of righteousness. In the mean time His eye is upon you ; He has appointed bounds both to the degree and the duration of the trial ; and He does and will afford you such support that you shall not be tried beyond what you are enabled to bear. I doubt not but your conflicts and sorrows will, in due time, terminate in praise and victory, and be sanctified to your fuller establishment in the truth.

I greatly rejoice in the Lord's goodness to your dying parent. How wisely timed, and how exactly suited, was that affecting dispensation, to break the force of those suggestions with which the enemy was aiming to overwhelm your spirit ! He could not stand against such an illustrious demonstrative attestation, that the doctrines you had embraced were not cunningly-devised fables. He could proceed no farther in that way ; but He is fruitful in re-sources. His next attempt, of course, was to fix guilt upon your conscience, as if you had yourself formed, and willingly entertained, those thoughts, which, indeed, you suffered with extreme reluctance and pain. Here, likewise, I find he succeeded for a time ; but He who broke the former snare, will deliver you from this likewise.

The dark and dishonourable thoughts of God, which I hinted at as belonging to a natural state, are very different from the thoughts of your heart concerning Him. You do not conceive of Him as a hard Master, or think you could be more happy in the breach than in the observance of His precepts. You do not prefer the world to His favour, or think you can please Him, and make amends for your sins, by an obedience of your own. These, and such as these, are the thoughts of the natural heart—the very reverse of yours. One thought, however, I confess you have indulged, which is no less dishononrable to the Lord than uncomfortable to yourself. You say, " I dare not believe that God will not impute to me as sin, the admission of thoughts which my soul ever abhorred, and to which my will never consented." Nay, you fear lest they should not only be imputed, but unpardonable. But how can this be possible ? Indeed I will not call it your *thought*, it is your *temptation.* You tell me you have children. Then you will easily feel a plain illustration, which just now occurs to me. Let me suppose a case which has sometimes happened : a child three or four years of age, we will say, while playing incautiously at a little distance from home, should be suddenly seized and carried away by a gipsy. Poor thing ! how terrified, how distressed must it be ! Methinks I hear its cries. The sight and violence of the stranger, the recollection of its dear parents, the loss of its pleasing home, the dread and uncer-tainty of what is yet to befal it. Is it not a wonder that it does not die in agonies ? But see, help is at hand ! the gipsy is pursued, and the child recovered. Now, my dear Madam, permit me to ask you, if this were your child, how would you receive it ? Perhaps, when the first transports of your joy for its safety would permit you, you might gently chide it for leaving your door. But would you disinherit it? Would you disown it? Would you deliver it up again to the gipsy with your own hands, because it had suffered a violence which it could not withstand, *which it abhorred, and to which its will never consented?* And yet what is the tenderness of a mother, of ten thousand mothers, to that which our compassionate Saviour bears to every poor soul that has been enabled to flee to Him for salvation? Let us be far from charging that to Him, of which we think we are utterly incapable ourselves. Take courage, Madam; resist the devil and he will flee from you. If he were to tempt you to anything criminal you would start at the thought, and renounce it with abhorrence. Do the same when he tempts you to question the Lord's compassion and goodness. But there he imposes upon us with a show of humility, and persuades us that we do well to oppose our unworthiness as a sufficient exception to the many express promises of the word. It is said, the blood of Jesus cleanseth from all sin; that all manner of sin shall be forgiven for its sake; that whoever cometh He will in no wise cast out; and that He is able to save to the uttermost. Believe His word, and Satan shall be found a liar. If the child had deliberately gone away with the gipsy, had preferred that wretched way of life, had refused to return, though frequently and tenderly invited home; perhaps its parent's love might, in time, be too weak for the pardon of such continued obstinacy. But, indeed, in this manner we have all dealt with the Lord; and yet, whenever we are willing to return, He is willing to receive us with open arms, and without an upbraiding word, Luke xv. 20-22. Though our sins have been deep-dyed with scarlet and crimson, enormous as mountains, and countless as the sands, the sum total is, *sin has abounded;* but where sin hath abounded, grace has much more abounded. After all, I know the Lord keeps the key of comfort in His own hands, yet He has commanded us to attempt comforting one another. I should rejoice to be His instrument of administering comfort to you. I shall hope to hear from you soon; and that you will then be able to inform me He has restored to you the joys of His salvation. But if not, yet wait for Him, and you shall not wait in vain.

I am, &c.,

LETTER III

My Dear Madam,   *June* — 1777.

TEMPTATIONS may be compared to the wind, which, when it has ceased raging from one point, after a short calm, frequently renews its violence from another quarter. The Lord silenced Satan's former assaults against you, but he is permitted to try you again in another way. Be of good courage, Madam : wait upon the Lord, and the present storm shall likewise subside in good time. You have an infallible Pilot, and are embarked in a bottom against which the winds and waves cannot prevail ; you may be tossed about, and think yourself in apparent jeopardy, but sink you shall not, except the promises and faithfulness of God can fail. Upon an attentive consideration of your complaint, it seems to me to amount only to this, that though the Lord has done great things for you, He has not yet brought you to a state of dependence on Himself, nor released you from that impossibility, which all His people feel, of doing anything without Him. And is this indeed a matter of complaint ? Is it not every way better, more for His glory, and more suited to keep us mindful of our obligations to Him, and in the event more for our safety, that we should be reduced to a happy necessity of receiving daily out of His fulness (as the Israelites received the manna) than to be set up with something of a stock of wisdom, power, and goodness of our own? Adam was thus furnished at the beginning with strength to stand ; yet, mutability being essential to a creature, he quickly fell and lost all. We, who are by nature sinners, are not left to so hazardous an experiment. He has Himself engaged to keep us, and treasured up all fulness of grace for our support, in a Head who cannot fail. Our gracious Saviour will communicate all needful supplies to His members, yet in such a manner that they shall feel their need and weakness, and have nothing to boast of from first to last, but His wisdom, compassion, and care. We are in no worse circumstances than the apostle Paul, who, though eminent and exemplary in the Christian life, found, and freely confessed, that he had no sufficiency in himself to think a good thought. Nor did he wish it otherwise ; he even gloried in his infirmities, that the power of Christ might rest upon him. Unbelief, and a thousand evils, are still in our hearts : though their reign and dominion is at an end, they are not slain or eradicated ; their effects will be felt more or less sensibly, as the Lord is pleased more or less to afford or abate His gracious influence. When they are kept down, we are no better in ourselves, for they are not kept down by us ; but we are very prone to think better of ourselves at such a time, and therefore He is pleased to permit us at seasons to feel a difference, that we may never forget how weak and how vile we are. We cannot absolutely conquer these evils, but it becomes us to be humbled for them ; and we are to fight, and strive, and pray against them. Our great duty is to be at His footstool, and to cry to Him who has promised to perform all things for us. Why are we called soldiers, but because we are called to a warfare ? And how could we fight, if there were no enemies to resist ? The Lord's soldiers are not merely for show, to make an empty parade in a uniform, and to brandish their arms when none but friends and spectators are around them. No, we must stand upon the field of battle ; we must face the fiery darts ; we must wrestle (which is the closest and most arduous kind of fighting) with our foes ; nor can we well expect wholly to escape wounds : but the leaves of the tree of life are provided for their healing. The Captain of our salvation is at hand, and leads us on with an assurance, which might make even a coward bold—that in the end we shall be more than conquerors through Him who has loved us.

I am ready to think, that some of the sentiments in your letters are not properly yours, such as you yourself have derived from the Scriptures, but rather borrowed from authors or preachers, whose judgments your humility has led you to prefer to your own. At least I am sure the Scripture does not authorize the conclusion which distresses you, that if you were a child of God you should not feel such changes and oppositions. Were I to define a Christian, or rather to describe him at large, I know no text I would choose sooner as a ground for the subject, than Gal. v. 17. A Christian has noble aims, which distinguish him from the bulk of mankind. His leading principles, motives, and desires, are all supernatural and divine. Could he do as he would, there is not a spirit before the throne should excel him in holiness, love, and obedience.   He would tread in the very footsteps of his Saviour, fill up every moment in His service, and employ every breath in His praise.   This he would do, but, alas! he cannot.   Against this desire of the spirit, there is a contrary desire and working of a corrupt nature, which meets him at every turn.   He has a beautiful copy set before him : he is enamoured with it, and though he does not expect to equal it, he writes carefully after it, and longs to attain to the nearest possible imitation.   But indwelling sin and Satan continually jog his hand, and spoil his strokes. You cannot, Madam, form a right judgment of yourself, except you make due allowance for those things which are not peculiar to yourself, but common to all who have spiritual perception, and are indeed the inseparable appendages of this mortal state.   If it were not so, why should the most spiritual and gracious people be so ready to confess themselves vile and worthless?   One eminent branch of our holiness is a sense of shame and humiliation for those evils which are only known to ourselves, and to Him who searches our hearts, joined with an acquiescence in Jesus, who is appointed of God—wisdom, righteousness, sanctification, and redemption.   I will venture to assure you, that though you will possess a more stable peace, in proportion as the Lord enables you to live more simply upon the blood, righteousness, and grace of the Mediator, you will never grow into a better opinion of yourself than you have at present. The nearer you are brought to Him, the quicker sense you will have of your continual need of Him, and thereby your admiration of His power, love, and compassion, will increase likewise from year to year.

I would observe farther, that our spiritual exercises are not a little influenced by our constitutional temperament. As you are only an ideal correspondent, I can but conjecture about you upon this head.   If your frame is delicate, and your nervous system very sensible and tender, I should probably ascribe some of your apprehensions to this cause. It is an abstruse subject, and I will not enter into it ; but according to the observations I have made, persons of this habit seem to live more upon the confines of the invisible world, if I may so speak, and to be more susceptive of impressions from it, than others. That complaint which, for want of a better name, we call lowness of spirits, may probably afford the enemy some peculiar advantages and occasions of distressing you. The mind then perceives objects as through a tinctured medium, which gives them a dark and discouraging appearance ; and I believe Satan has more influence and address than we are aware of in managing the glass. And when this is not the case at all times, it may be so occasionally, from sickness, or other circumstances. You tell me that you have lately been ill, which, together with your present situation, and the prospect of your approaching hour, may probably have such an effect as I have hinted. You may be charging yourself with guilt, for what springs from indisposition, in which you are merely passive, and which may be no more properly sinful, than the headache or any of the thousand natural shocks the flesh is heir to. The enemy can take no advantage but what the Lord permits him ; and He will permit him none but what He designs to overrule for your greater advantage in the end. He delights in your prosperity ; and you should not be in heaviness for an hour, were there not a need-be for it. Notwithstanding your fears, I have a good hope, that He who you say has helped you in six troubles, will appear for you in the seventh ; that you will not die, but live and declare the works of the Lord, and come forth to testify to His praise, that He has turned your mourning into joy.

I am, &c.

TWO LETTERS

TO

MISS F——

LETTER I

DEAR MADAM, *October* 3, 1778.

You would have me tell you what are the best means
to be used by a young person, to prevent the world, with all
its opening and ensnaring scenes, from drawing the heart
aside from God. It is an important question : but I appre-
hend your own heart will tell you, that you are already
possessed of all the information concerning it which you can
well expect from me. I could only attempt to answer it
from the Bible, which lies open to you likewise. If your
heart is like mine, it must confess, that when it turns aside
from God, it is seldom through ignorance of the proper means
or motives which should have kept us near Him, but rather
from an evil principle within, which prevails against our
better judgment, and renders us unfaithful to light already
received.

I could offer you rules, cautions, and advices in abundance ;
for I find it comparatively easy to preach to others. But
if you should further ask me, how you shall effectually
reduce them to practice, I feel that I am so deficient, and
so much at a loss in this matter *myself*, that I know not well
what to say to *you*. Yet something must be said.

In the first place, then, I would observe, that though it
be our bounden duty, and the highest privilege we can
propose to ourselves, to have our hearts kept close to the
Lord ; yet we must not expect it absolutely or perfectly,
much less all at once ; we shall keep close to Him, in pro-
portion as we are solidly convinced of the infinite disparity

212

between Him and the things which would presume to stand in competition with Him, and the folly, as well as ingratitude, of departing from Him. But these points are only to be learned by experience, and by smarting under a series of painful disappointments in our expectations from creatures. Our judgments may be quickly satisfied that His favour is better than life, while yet it is in the power of a mere trifle to turn us aside. The Lord permits us to feel our weakness, that we may be sensible of it; for though we are ready in words to confess that we are weak, we do not properly know it, till that secret, though unallowed, dependence we have upon some strength in ourselves, is brought to the trial and fails us. To be humble, and like a little child, afraid of taking a step alone, and so conscious of snares and dangers around us as to cry to Him continually to hold us up that we may be safe, is the sure, the infallible, the only secret of walking closely with Him.

But how shall we attain this humble frame of spirit? It must be, as I said, from a real and sensible conviction of our weakness and vileness, which we cannot learn (at least I have not been able to learn it) merely from books or preachers. The providence of God concurs with His Holy Spirit, in His merciful design of making us acquainted with ourselves. It is, indeed, a great mercy to be preserved from such de-clensions as might fall under the notice of our fellow-crea-tures; but when *they* can observe nothing of consequence to object to us, things may be far from right with us in the sight of Him who judges not only actions, but the thoughts and first motions of the heart. And indeed could we for a season so cleave to God as to find little or nothing in ourselves to be ashamed of, we are such poor creatures, that we should presently grow vain and self-sufficient, and expose ourselves to the greatest danger of falling.

There are, however, means to be observed on our part; and though you know them, I will repeat the principal, because you desire me. The *first* is prayer: and here, above all things, we should pray for humility. It may be called both the guard of all other graces, and the soil in which they grow. The *second*, attention to the Scripture. Your question is directly answered in Psalm cxix. 9. The precepts are our rule and delight, the promises our strength and encouragement; the good recorded of the saints is proposed for our encouragement; their miscarriages are as landmarks set up to warn us of the rocks and shoals which lie in the way of our passage. The study of the whole scheme of Gospel-salvation, respecting the person, life, doctrine, death, and glory of our Redeemer, is appointed to form our souls to a spiritual and divine taste; and so far as this prevails and grows in us, the trifles that would draw us from the Lord will lose their influence, and appear divested of the glare with which they strike the senses, mere vanity and nothing. The *third* grand means is, consideration of recollection, a careful regard to those temptations and snares to which, from our tempers, situations, or connexions, we are more immediately exposed, and by which we have been formerly hindered. It may be well in the morning, ere we leave our chambers, to forecast, as far as we are able, the probable circumstances of the day before us. Yet the observance of this, as well as of every rule that can be offered, may dwindle into a mere form. However, I trust the Lord, who has given you a desire to live to Him, will be your Guard and Teacher. There is none that teacheth like Him.

I am, &c.

LETTER II

DEAR MADAM,   *March* — 1779.

OUR experiences pretty much tally; they may be drawn out into sheets and quires, but the sum total may be comprised in a short sentence, " Our life is a warfare." For our encouragement the apostle calls it a *good* warfare. We are engaged in a good cause, fight under a good Captain, the victory is sure beforehand, and the prize is a crown, a crown of life. Such considerations might make even a coward bold. But then we must be content to fight; and considering the nature, number, situation, and subtlety of our enemies, we may expect sometimes to receive a wound; but there is a medicinal tree, the leaves of which are always at hand to heal us. We cannot be too attentive to the evil which is always working in us, or to the stratagems which are employed against us ; yet our attention should not be wholly confined to these things. We are to look upwards likewise to Him, who is our Head, our Life, our Strength. One glance of Jesus will convey more effectual assistance than poring upon our own hearts for a month. The one is to be done, but the other should upon no account be omitted. It was not by counting their wounds, but by beholding the brazen serpent, the Lord's instituted means of cure, that the Israelites were healed. That was an emblem for our instruction. One great cause of our frequent conflicts is, that we have a secret desire to be rich, and it is the Lord's design to make us poor. *We* want to gain an ability of doing something ; and He suits His dispensations, to convince us that we can do nothing. *We* want a stock in ourselves, and He would have us absolutely dependent upon Him. So far as we are content to be weak, that His power may be magnified in us, so far we shall make our enemies know that we are strong, though we ourselves shall never be directly sensible that we are so; only by comparing what we are, with the opposition we stand against, we may come to a comfortable conclusion, that the Lord worketh mightily in us (Psa. xli. 11).

If our views are simple, and our desires towards the Lord, it may be of use to consider some of your faults and mine, not as the faults of you and me in particular, but as the fault of that depraved nature, which is common with us to all the Lord's people, and which made Paul groan as feelingly and as heartily as we can do. But this consideration, though true and Scriptural, can only be safely applied when the mind is sincerely, and in good earnest, devoted to the Lord. There are too many unsound and half professors, who eagerly catch at it, as an excuse for those evils they are unwilling to part with. But I trust I may safely recommend it to you. This evil nature, this indwelling sin, is a living principle, an active, powerful cause ; and a cause that is active will necessarily produce an effect. Sin is the same thing in believers as in the unregenerate ; they have, indeed, a contrary principle of grace, which counteracts and resists it, which can prevent its outbreakings, but will not suppress its risings. As grace resists sin, so sin resists grace, Gal. v. 17. The proper tendency of each is mutually weakened on both sides ; and, between the two, the poor believer, however blameless and exemplary in the sight of men, appears, in his own view, the most inconsistent character under the sun. He can hardly think it is so with others ; and, judging of *them* by what he *sees*, and of *himself* by what he *feels*, in lowliness of heart, he esteems others better than himself. This proves him to be right ; for it is the will of God concerning him, Phil. ii. 3. This is the warfare. But it shall not always be so. Grace shall prevail. The evil nature is already enervated, and ere long it shall die the death. Jesus will make us more than conquerors.

I am, &c.

TWO LETTERS

MR. A—— B——

LETTER I

DEAR SIR,   1758.

I SUPPOSE you will receive many congratulations on
your recovery from your late dangerous illness ; most of
them, perhaps, more sprightly and better turned, but none,
I persuade myself, more sincere and affectionate than mine.
I beg you would prepare yourself by this good opinion of
me, before you read further ; and let the reality of my regard
excuse what you may dislike in my manner of expressing it.

When a person is returned from a doubtful distant voy-
age, we are naturally led to inquire into the incidents he has
met with, and the discoveries he has made.   Indulge me in
a curiosity of this kind, especially as my affection gives me
an interest and concern in the event.   You have been, my
friend, upon the brink, the very edge, of an eternal state ;
but God has restored you back to the world again.   Did you
meet with, or have you brought back, nothing *new* ?   Did
nothing occur to stop or turn your usual train of thought ?
Were your apprehensions of invisible things exactly the same
in the height of your disorder, when you were cut off from
the world and all its engagements, as when you were in perfect
health, and in the highest enjoyment of your own inclina-
tions ?   If you answer me, " Yes, all things are just the same
as formerly, the difference between sickness and health
only excepted," I am at a loss how to reply.   I can only
sigh and wonder ; *sigh*, that it should be thus with any, that
it should be thus with you, whom I dearly love ; and
wonder, since this unhappy case, strange as it seems in one
view, is yet so frequent, why it was not always thus with

myself : for long and often it was just so. Many a time, when sickness had brought me, as we say, to death's door, I was as easy and insensible as the sailor, who, in the height of a storm, should presume to sleep upon the top of the mast, quite regardless that the next tossing wave might plunge him into the raging ocean, beyond all possibility of relief. But, at length, a day came, which, though the most terrible day I ever saw, I can now look back upon with thankfulness and pleasure : I say the time came, when, in such a helpless extremity, and under the expectation of immediate death, it pleased God to command the veil from my eyes, and I saw things, in some measure, as they really were. Imagine, with yourself, a person trembling upon the point of a dreadful precipice, a powerful and inexorable enemy eager to push him down, and an assemblage of all that is horrible waiting at the bottom for his fall ; even this will give you but a faint representation of the state of my mind at that time. Believe me, it was not a whim or a dream which changed my sentiments and conduct, but a powerful conviction which will not admit the least doubt, an evidence which, like that I have of my own existence, I cannot call in question without contradicting all my senses. And though my case was, in some respects, uncommon, yet something like it is known by one and another every day ; and I have myself conversed with many, who, after a course of years spent in defending Deistical principles, or indulging libertine practices, when they have thought themselves confirmed in their schemes by the cool assent of what they then deemed impartial reason, have been, like me, brought to glory in the Cross of Christ, and to live by that faith which they had before slighted and opposed. By these instances, I know that nothing is too hard for the Almighty. The same power which humbled me, can, undoubtedly, bring down the most haughty infidel upon earth ; and as I likewise know that, to show His power, He is often pleased to make use of weak instruments, I am encouraged, notwithstanding the apparent difficulty of succeeding, to warn those over whom friendship or affection gives me any influence, of the evil and the danger of a course of life formed upon the prevailing maxims of the world. So far as I neglect this, I am unfaithful in my professions both to God and man.

I shall not, at present, trouble you in an argumentative way. If, by dint of reasoning, I could effect some change in your notions, my arguments, unless applied by a superior power, would still leave your heart unchanged and untouched. A man may give his assent to the Gospel, and be able to defend it against others, and yet not have his own spirit truly influenced by it. This thought I shall leave with you, that if your scheme be not true to a demonstration, it must necessarily be false ; for the issue is too important to make a doubt on the dangerous side tolerable. If the Christian could possibly be mistaken, he is still upon equal terms with those who pronounce him to be so ; but if the Deist be wrong (that is, if we are in the right) the consequence to him must be unavoidable and intolerable. This, you will say, is a trite argument : I own it ; but, beaten as it is, it will never be worn out or answered.

Permit me to remind you, that the points in debate between us are already settled in themselves, and that our talking cannot alter or affect the nature of things ; for they will be as they are, whatever apprehensions we may form of them : and remember, likewise, that we must all, each one for himself, experience on which side the truth lies. I used a wrong word when I spoke of your *recovery :* my dear friend, look upon it only as a *reprieve ;* for you carry the sentence of death about with you still ; and unless you should be cut off (which God of His mercy forbid !) by a sudden stroke, you will as surely lie upon a death-bed, as you have been now raised from a bed of sickness. And remember, likewise (how can I bear to write it !) that, should you neglect my admonitions, they will, notwithstanding, have an effect upon you, though not such an effect as I could wish : they will render you more inexcusable. I have delivered my own soul, by faithfully warning you : but if you will not examine the matter with that seriousness it calls for ; if you will not look up to God, the former of your body, and the preserver of your Spirit, for direction and assistance how to please Him ; if you will have your reading and conversation only on one side of the question ; if you determine to let afflictions and dangers, mercies and deliverances, all pass without reflection and improvement ; if you will spend your life as though you thought you were sent into the world only to eat, sleep, and play, and, after a course of years, be extinguished like the snuff of a candle—why, then, you must abide the consequences. But assuredly, sooner or later, God will meet you. My hearty daily prayer is, that it may be in a way of mercy, and that you may be added to the number of the trophies of His invincible grace.

I am, &c.

LETTER II

Dear Sir,　　　　　　　　　　　　　　　　　1760.

Though I truly love you, and have no reason to doubt of the reality of your friendship to me, yet I cannot but apprehend that, notwithstanding our mutual regard, and my frequent attempts to be witty (if I could) for your diversion, there is something in most of my letters (which I cannot, dare not, wholly suppress) that disgusts and wearies you, and makes you less inclined to keep up a frequent intercourse than you would otherwise be. Rather than lose you quite, I will in general spare you as much as I can ; but at present you must bear with me, and allow me full scope. You have given me a challenge, which I know not how to pass over ; and since you so far justify my preaching as to condescend to preach (in your way) yourself, permit me for this time to preach again, and to take some passages in your letter for my text.

In the present debate I will accept your compliment, and suppose myself to be, as you say, a man of sense. You allow, then, that all the sense is not on your side. This, indeed, you cannot deny ; for, whatever becomes of me, it is needless to tell you, that Hale, Boyle, and other great names I could mention, were men of as great penetration and judgment, had as good opportunities, and took as much pains to be informed of the truth, as any of the advocates for infidelity can pretend to. And you cannot, with any modesty or conscience, absolutely determine, that they had not as good grounds for thinking themselves right as you can have for concluding they are wrong.

But, declining the advantage of human authority, I am

content the point shall rest between you and me. And here I beg you to observe, that I have one evident advantage over you in judging, namely, that I have experienced the good and evil on both sides, and you only on one. If you were to send me an inventory of your pleasures, how charmingly your time runs on, and how dexterously it is divided between the coffee-houses, play-house, the card-table, and tavern, with intervals of balls, concerts, &c., I could answer, that most of these I have tried and tried again, and know the utmost they can yield, and have seen enough of the rest most heartily to despise them all. Setting religion entirely out of the question, I profess I had rather be a worm to crawl upon the ground, than to bear the name of MAN upon the poor terms of whiling away my life in an insipid round of such insignificant and unmanly trifles. I will return your own expression—I believe you to be a person of sense ; but, alas ! how do you prostitute your talents and capacity, how far do you act below yourself, if you know no higher purpose of life than these childish dissipations, together with the more serious business of rising early and sitting up late, to amass money that you may be able to enlarge your expenses ! I am sure, while I lived in these things, I found them unsatisfying and empty to the last degree ; and the only advantage they afforded (miserable are they who are forced to deem it an advantage) was, that they only relieved me from the trouble and burden of thinking. If you have any other pleasures than these, they are such as must be evil and inconvenient even upon your own plan ; and therefore my friendship will not allow me to bring them into the account. I am willing to hope you do not stoop still lower in pursuit of satisfaction. Thus far we stand upon even ground. You know all that a life of pleasure can give, and I know it likewise.

On the other hand, if I should attempt to explain to you the source and streams of *my* best pleasures, such as a comfortable assurance of the pardon of my sins, an habitual communion with the God who made Heaven and earth, a calm reliance on the Divine providence, the cheering prospect of a better life in a better world, with the pleasing foretastes of Heaven in my own soul ; should I, or could I, tell you the pleasure I often find in reading the Scripture, in the exercise of prayer, and in that sort of preaching and conversation which you despise ; I doubt not but you would think as meanly of my happiness as I do of yours. But here lies the difference, my dear friend ; you condemn that which you have never tried. You know no more of these things than a blind man does of colours ; and, notwithstanding all your flourishes, I defy you to be at all times able to satisfy yourself that things may not possibly be as I have represented them.

Besides, what do I lose upon my plan that should make me so worthy of your pity ? Have you a quicker relish in the prudent use of temporal comforts ? Do you think I do not eat my food with as much pleasure as you can do, though, perhaps, with less cost and variety ? Is your sleep sounder than mine ? Have not I as much satisfaction in social life ? It is true, to join much with the gay fluttering tribe, who spend their days in laugh and sing-song, is equally contrary to my duty and inclination. But I have friends and acquaintance as well as you. Among the many who favour me with their esteem and friendship, there are some who are persons of sense, learning, wit, and (what perhaps may weigh as much with you) of fortune and distinction. And if you should say, " Aye, but they are all enthusiasts like yourself," you would say nothing to the purpose, since, upon your maxim, that " happiness is according to opinion," it cannot be an objection, but the contrary, to have my acquaintance to my own taste. Thus much for the brighter side of your situation—or let me add one thing more. I know you have thoughts of marriage ; do you think, if you should enter into this relation, your principles are calculated to make you more happy in it than I am ? You are well acquainted with our family life. Do you propose to know more of the peace and heart-felt joy of domestic union than I have known, and continue to know to this hour ? I wish you may equal us ; and, if you do, we shall still be as before, but upon even ground. I need not turn Deist, to enjoy the best and the most that this life can afford.

But I need not tell you that the present life is not made up of pleasurable incidents only. Pain, sickness, losses, disappointments, injuries, and affronts, will, more or less, at one time or other, be our lot. And can you bear these

trials better than I ? You will not pretend to it. Let me
appeal to yourself : how often do you toss and disquiet
yourself, like a wild bull in a net, when things cross your
expectations ? As your thoughts are more engrossed by
what you see, you must be more keenly sensible of what
you feel. You cannot view these trials as appointed by a
wise and Heavenly Father, in subservience to your good ;
you cannot taste the sweetness of His promises, nor feel the
secret supports of His strength in an hour of affliction ;
you cannot so cast your burden and care upon Him, as to
find a sensible relief to your spirit thereby, nor can you see
His hand engaged and employed in effecting your deliver-
ance. Of these things you know no more than of the art
of flying ; but I seriously assure you, and I believe my testi-
mony will go farther with you than my judgment, that they
are realities, and that I have found them to be so. When
my worldly concerns have been most thorny and discourag-
ing, I have once and again felt the most of that peace which
the world can neither give nor take away. However, I may
state the case still lower. You do pretty well among your
friends ; but how do you like being alone ? Would you not
give something for that happy secret, which could enable
you to pass a rainy day pleasantly, without the assistance
of business, company, or amusement ? Would it not mortify
you greatly to travel for a week on an unfrequented road,
where you shall meet with no lively incidents to recruit and
raise your spirits ? Alas ! what a poor scheme of pleasure
is yours, that will not support an interval of reflection !

What you have heard is true ; I have a few friends
who meet at my house once a fortnight, and we spend
an hour or two in worshipping the God who made us. And
can this move your indignation, or your compassion ? Does
it show a much nobler spirit, a more refined way of thinking,
to live altogether without God in the world ? If I kept
a card-assembly at those times, it would not displease you.
How can you, as a person of sense, avoid being shocked
at your own unhappy prejudice ? But I remember how it
was once with myself, and forbear to wonder. May He
who has opened my eyes, open yours ! He only can do it !
I do not expect to convince you by anything I can say as of
myself ; but, if He be pleased to make use of me as His

instrument, then you will be convinced. How should I then rejoice! I should rejoice to be useful to any one; but especially to you, whom I dearly love. May God show you your true self, and your true state; then you will attentively listen to what you now disdain to hear of, His goodness in providing redemption and pardon for the chief of sinners, through Him who died upon the Cross for sins not His own! Keep this letter by you at my request; and, when you write, tell me that you receive it in good part, and that you still believe me to be

Your sincere and affectionate friend.

FOUR LETTERS

LETTER I

DEAR SIR,   *April* 17, 1776.

BY this time I hope you are both returned in peace, and happy together in your stated, favoured tract : rejoicing in the name of Jesus yourselves, and rejoicing to see the savour of it spreading like a precious perfume among the people. Every day I hope you find prejudices wearing off, and more disposed to hear the words of Life. The Lord has given you a fine first fruits, which I trust will prove the earnest of a plentiful harvest. In the meantime, He will enable you to sow the seed in patience, leaving the event in His hands. Though it does not spring up visibly at once, it will not be lost. I think He would not have sent you, if He had not a people there to call ; but they can only come forth to view as He is pleased to bring them. Satan will try to hinder and disturb you, but he is in a chain which he cannot break, nor go a step further than he is permitted. And, if you have been instrumental to the conversion of but a few, in those few you have an ample reward already for all the difficulties you have or can meet with. It is more honourable and important to be an instrument of saving one soul, than to rescue a whole kingdom from temporal ruin. Let us, therefore, while we earnestly desire to be more useful, not forget to be thankful for what the Lord has been pleased already to do for us ; and let us expect, knowing whose servants we are, and what a Gospel we preach, to see some new miracles wrought from day to day ; for, indeed, every real conversion may be accounted miraculous, being no less than an immediate exertion of that power which made the heavens, and commanded the light to shine out of darkness. Your little telescope is safe. - I wish I had more of that clear air and sunshine you speak of, that with you I might have more distinct views of the land of promise. I cannot say my prospect is greatly clouded by doubts of my reaching it at last ; but then there is such a languor and deadness hangs upon my mind, that it is almost amazing to me how I can entertain any hopes at all. It seems, if doubting could ever be reasonable, there is no one who has greater reason for doubting than myself. But I know not how to doubt, when I consider the faithfulness, grace, and compassion of Him who has promised. If it could be proved that Christ had not died, or that He did not speak the words which are ascribed to Him in the Gospel, or that He is not able to make them good, or that His word cannot safely be taken ; in any of these cases I should not doubt to purpose, and lie down in despair.   I am, etc.

LETTER II

My Dear Sir,   *July* 15, 1777.

I begin with congratulations first to you and Mrs.——, on your safe journey and good passage over the formidable Humber. Mrs. —— has another river to cross (may it be many years before she approaches the bank) over which there is no bridge. Perhaps, at seasons, she may think of it with that reluctance which she felt before she saw the Humber ; but, as her fears were then agreeably disappointed, and she found the experiment, when called to make it, neither terrifying nor dangerous, so I trust she will find it in the other case. Did not she think, The Lord knows where I shall be, and He will meet me there with a storm, because I am such a sinner ? Then how the billows will foam and rage at me, and what a long passage I shall have, and perhaps I shall sink in the middle, and never set my foot in Hull ! It is true, I am not so much afraid of the

journey I go by land, though I know that every step of
the way, the horses or the chaise may fall, and I be killed ;
but how do I know but He may preserve me on the road,
on purpose to drown me in the river ! But, behold, when
she came to it, all was calm ; or, what was better, a gentle,
fair breeze, to waft her pleasantly over before she was
aware. Thus we are apt perversely to reason : He guides
and guards me through life ; He gives me new mercies,
and new proofs of His power and care every day ; and,
therefore, when I come to die, He will forsake me, and
let me be the sport of winds and waves. Indeed, the
Lord does not deserve such hard thoughts at our hands
as we are prone to form of Him. But, notwithstanding
we make such returns, He is and will be gracious, and
shame us out of our unkind, ungrateful, unbelieving fears
at last. If, after my repeated kind reception at your
house, I should always be teasing Mrs. —— with suspicions
of her good will, and should tell everybody I saw, that
I verily believed the next time I went to see her she would
shut the door in my face, and refuse me admittance, would
she not be grieved, offended, and affronted ? Would
she not think, What reason can he assign for this treatment ?
He knows I did everything in my power to assure him
of a welcome, and told him so over and over again. Does
he count me a deceiver ? Yes, he does : I see his friendship
is not worth preserving; so farewell. I will seek friends
among such as believe my words and actions. Well, my
dear Madam, I am clear I always believed you ; I make
no doubt but you will treat me kindly next time, as you
did the last. But pray, is not the Lord as worthy of being
trusted as yourself ; and are not His invitations and pro-
mises as hearty and as honest as yours ? Let us, therefore,
beware of giving way to such thoughts of Him, as we could
hardly forgive in our dearest friends if they should harbour
the like of us.

I have heard nothing of Mr. P —— yet, but that he is in
town, very busy about that precious piece of furniture called
a wife. May the Lord direct and bless His choice ! In
Captain Cook's voyage to the South Sea, some fish were
caught which looked as well as others, but those who ate of
them were poisoned : alas ! for the poor man who catches a

poisonous wife! There are such to be met with in the
matrimonial seas, that look passing well to the eye, but a
connexion with them proves baneful to domestic peace, and
hurtful to the life of grace. I know two or three people,
perhaps a few more, who have great reason to be thankful to
Him who sent the fish with the money in its mouth to
Peter's hook. He secretly instructed and guided us where
to angle ; and if we have caught prizes, we owe it not to our
own skill, much less to our deserts, but to His goodness.

I am, &c.

LETTER III

MY DEAR SIR, *September* 4, 1777.

———— ·Poor little boy ! it is mercy indeed that he re-
covered from such a formidable hurt. The Lord wounded,
and the Lord healed. I ascribe, with you, what the world
calls accident, to Him, and believe, that without His per-
mission, for wise and good ends, a child can no more pull a
bowl of boiling water on itself, than it could pull the moon
out of its orbit. And why does He permit such things ?
One reason or two is sufficient for us : it is to remind us of
the uncertainty of life and all creature-comforts ; to make
us afraid of cleaving too closely to pretty toys, which are so
precarious, that often while we look at them they vanish ;
and to lead us to a more entire dependence upon Himself ;
that we might never judge ourselves or our concerns safe
from outward appearances only, but that the Lord is our
keeper, and were not His eye upon us, a thousand dangers
and painful changes, which we can neither foresee nor
prevent, are lurking about us at every step, ready to break
in upon us every hour. Men are but children of a larger
growth. How many are labouring and planning in the
pursuit of things, the event of which, if they obtain them, will
be but like pulling scalding water upon their own heads !
They *must* have the bowl by all means, but they are not
aware what is in it till they feel it.

I am, &c.

LETTER IV

SIR, *July 7, 1777.*

I HAVE had a letter from your minister since his arrival at ——. I hope he will be restored to you again before long, and that he and many of your place will rejoice long in each other. Those are favoured places which are blessed with a sound and faithful Gospel ministry, if the people know and consider the value of their privileges, and are really desirous of profiting by them : but the kingdom of God is not in word, but in power. I hope those who profess the Gospel with you will wrestle in prayer for grace to walk worthy of it. A minister's hands are strengthened, when he can point to his people as so many living proofs that the doctrines he preaches are doctrines according to godliness ; when they walk in mutual love ; when each one, in their several places, manifests a humble, spiritual, upright conduct ; when they are Christians, not only at church, but in the family, the shop, and the field ; when they fill up their relations in life, as husbands or wives, masters or servants, parents or children, according to the rule of the word ; when they are evidently a people separated from the world while conversant in it, and are careful to let their light shine before men, not only by talking, but by acting as the disciples of Christ : when they go on steadily, not by fits and starts, prizing the means of grace without resting in them : when it is thus, we can say, Now we live, if you stand fast in the Lord. Then we come forth with pleasure, and our service is our delight, and we are encouraged to hope for an increasing blessing. But if the people in whom we have rejoiced sink into formality or a worldly spirit ; if they have dissensions and jealousies among themselves ; if they act improperly, and give the enemies occasion to say, There, there, so would we have it ; then our hearts are wounded and our zeal damped, and we know not how to speak with liberty. It is my heart's desire and prayer for you, that whether I see you, or else be absent from you, I may know that you stand fast in one spirit and one mind striving together for the faith of the Gospel.

I am, &c,

SEVEN LETTERS

TO

MRS. ——

LETTER I

MY DEAR MADAM,   *Nov.* 1775.

Too much of that impatience which you speak of, to-
wards those who differ from us in some religious sentiments,
is observable on all sides. I do not consider it as the fault
of a few individuals, or of this or that party, so much as
the effect of that inherent imperfection which is common
to our whole race. Anger and scorn are equally unbecom-
ing in those who profess to be followers of the meek and
lowly Jesus, and who acknowledge themselves to be both
sinful and fallible ; but too often something of this leaven
will be found cleaving to the best characters, and mixed
with honest endeavours to serve the best cause. But
thus it was from the beginning ; and we have reason to
confess that we are no better than the apostles were, who,
though they meant well, manifested once and again a
wrong spirit in the zeal, Luke ix. 54. *O*bservation and
experience contribute, by the grace of God, gradually to
soften and sweeten our spirits ; but then there will always
be ground for mutual forbearance and mutual forgiveness on
this head. However, so far as I may judge of myself, I
think this hastiness is not my most easy besetting sin.
I am not, indeed, an advocate for that indifference and luke-
warmness to the truths of God, which seem to constitute
the candour many plead for in the present day. But
while I desire to hold fast the sound doctrines of the Gospel
towards the persons of my fellow-creatures, I wish to

exercise all moderation and benevolence : Protestants or Papists, Socinians or Deists, Jews, Samaritans, or Mahometans, all are my neighbours, they have all a claim upon me for the common offices of humanity. As to religion, they cannot all be right ; nor may I compliment them, by allowing that differences between us are but trivial when I believe, and know they are important ; but I am not to expect them to see with my eyes. I am deeply convinced of the truth of John Baptist's aphorism, John iii. 27, " A man can receive nothing, except it be given him from Heaven." I well know, that the little measure of knowledge I have obtained in the things of God, has not been owing to my own wisdom and docility, but to His goodness. Nor did I get it all at once : He has been pleased to exercise much patience and long-suffering towards me for about twenty-seven years past, since He first gave me a desire of learning from Himself. He has graciously accommodated Himself to my weakness, borne with my mistakes, and helped me through innumerable prejudices, which, but for His mercy, would have been insuperable hindrances : I have therefore no right to be angry, impatient, or censorious, especially as I have still much to learn, and am so poorly influenced by what I seem to know. I am weary of controversies and disputes, and desire to choose for myself, and to point out to others Mary's part—to sit at Jesus' feet, and to hear His words. And, blessed be His name ! so far as I have learned from Him, I am favoured with a comfortable certainty ; I know whom I have believed, and am no longer tossed about by the various winds and tides of opinions, by which I see many are dashed one against the other. But I cannot, I must not, I dare not contend ; only as a witness for God, I am ready to bear my simple testimony to what I have known of His truth, whenever I am properly called to it.

I agree with you, that some, accounted evangelical teachers, have too much confined themselves to a few leading and favourite topics ; I think this a fault : and believe, when it is constantly so, the auditories are deprived of much edification and pleasure, which they might receive from a more judicious and comprehensive plan. The whole Scripture, as it consists of histories, prophecies, doctrines,

precepts, promises, exhortations, admonitions, encourage-
ments, and reproofs, is the proper subject of the Gospel-
ministry : and every part should in its place and course be
attended to ; yet so as that, in every compartment we
exhibit, Jesus should be the capital figure, in whom the
prophecies are fulfilled, the promises established : to
whom, in a way of type and emblem, the most important
parts of Scripture-history have an express reference ; and
from, whom alone ˙we can receive that life, strength, and
encouragement, which are necessary to make obedience
either pleasing or practicable. And where there is *true
spiritual faith* in the heart, and in exercise, I believe a person
will not so much need a detail of what he is to practise,
as to be often greatly at a loss without it. Our Saviour's
commandments are plain and clear in themselves ; and
that love which springs from faith is the best casuist and
commentator to apply and enforce them.

You are pleased to say, " Forgive me if I transgress :
I know the place whereon I stand is holy ground." Permit
me to assure you, my dear Madam, that were I ˌa person
of some importance, which I am not, you would run no
hazard of offending me by the controverting any of my
sentiments : I hold none (knowingly) which I am not
willing to submit to examination ; nor am I afraid of offend-
ing you by speaking freely, when you point out my way.
I should wrong you, if I thought to please you by palliating
or disguising the sentiments of my heart ; and if I attempted
to do so, you would see through the design, and despise it.
There may perhaps be an improper manner of chiming upon
the name of Jesus, and I am not for vindicating any impro-
priety ; yet could I feel what I ought to mean when I pro-
nounce that name, I should not fear mentioning it too often.
I am afraid of no excess in thinking highly of it, because I
read it is the will of God that all men should honour the Son
as they honour the Father. Laboured explications of the
Trinity I always avoid. I am afraid of darkening counsel
by words without knowledge. Scripture, and even reason,
assures me, there is but one God, whose name *alone* is
Jehovah. Scripture likewise assures me, that Christ is God,
that Jesus is Jehovah. I cannot say that reason assents
with equal readiness to this proposition as to the former.

But, admitting what the Scripture teaches concerning the evil of sin, the depravity of human nature, the method of salvation, and the offices of the Saviour ; admitting that God has purposed to glorify, not His mercy only but His justice, in the work of redemption ; that the blood upon the cross is a proper, adequate satisfaction for sin ; and that the Redeemer is at present the Shepherd of those who believe in Him, and will hereafter be the Judge of the world ; that, in order to give the effectual help which we need, it is necessary that He be always *intimately with those* who depend upon Him, in every age, in every place ; must know the thoughts and intents of every heart ; must have His eye always upon them, His ear always open to them ; His arm ever stretched out for their relief ; that they can receive nothing but what He bestows ; can do nothing but as He enables them, nor stand a moment but as He upholds them ; admitting these and the like promises with which the word of God abounds, reason must allow, whatever difficulties may attend the thought, that only He who is God over all, blessed for ever, is able or worthy to execute this complicated plan, every part of which requires the exertion of infinite wisdom and almighty power ; nor am I able to form any clear, satisfactory, comfortable thoughts of God, suited to awaken my love, or engage my trust, but as He has been pleased to reveal Himself in the person of Jesus Christ. I believe with the apostle, that God was once manifested in the flesh upon earth ; and that He is now manifested in the flesh in Heaven ; and that the worship, not only of redeemed sinners, but of the holy angels, is addressed to the Lamb that was slain, and who, in that nature in which He suffered, now exercises universal dominion, and has the government of Heaven, earth, and hell upon His shoulders. This truth is the foundation upon which my hope is built, the fountain from whence I derive all my strength and consolation, and my only encouragement for venturing to the throne of grace, for grace to help in time of need.

> Till God in human flesh I see,
> My thoughts no comfort find ;
> The holy, just, and sacred Three
> Are terrors to my mind.

But if Immanuel's face appear,
My hope, my joy begins ;
His name forbids my slavish fear,
His grace removes my sins.

I am, however, free to confess to you, that, through the pride and unbelief remaining in my heart, and the power of Satan's temptations, there are seasons when I find no small perplexity and evil reasonings upon this high point ; but ,it is so absolutely essential to my peace, that I cannot part with it ; for I cannot give it up, without giving up all hope of salvation on the one hand, and giving up the Bible, as an unmeaning, contradictory fable, on the other ; and through mercy, for the most part, when I am in my right mind, I am as fully persuaded of this truth as I am of my own existence ; but from the exercises I have had about it, I have learned to subscribe to the apostle's declaration, that " no man can say that Jesus Christ is Lord, but by the Holy Ghost." I am well satisfied, it will not be a burden to me at the hour of death, nor be laid to my charge at the day of judgment, that I have thought too highly of Jesus, expected too much from Him myself, or laboured too much in commending and setting Him forth to others, as the Alpha and Omega, the true God and eternal life. On the contrary, alas ! alas ! my guilt and grief are, that my thoughts of Him are so faint, so infrequent, and my commendations of Him so lamentably cold and disproportionate to what they ought to be.

I know not whose letters are rapturous, but I wish mine were more so ; not that I am a friend to ungrounded sallies of imagination, flights of animal passions, or heat without light. But it would be amazing to me, were I not aware of human depravity, (of which I consider this as one of the most striking proofs,) that they who have any good hope of an interest in the Gospel-salvation, do not find their hearts (as Dr. Watts expresses it) all on fire ; and that their very looks do not express a transport of admiration, gratitude, and love, when they consider from what misery they are redeemed, to what happiness they are called, and what a price was paid for their souls. I wish to be more like the apostle Paul in this respect, who, though he often forms and compounds new words, seems at a loss for any that could suitably describe the emotions of his heart. But I am persuaded you would not object to the just fervour of Scriptural devotion. But this holy flame can seldom be found unsullied in the present life. The temper, constitution, and infirmities of individuals, will mix more or less with what they say or do. Allowances must be made for such things in the present state of infirmity; for who can hope to be perfectly free from them? If the heart is right with God, and sincerely affected with the wonders of redeeming love, our gracious High Priest, who knows our weakness, pities and pardons what is amiss, accepts our poor efforts, and gradually teaches us to discern and avoid what is blameable. The work of grace, in its first stages, I sometimes compare to the lighting of a fire, where for a while, there is abundance of smoke, but it burns clearer and clearer. There is often, both in letters and books, what might be very well omitted; but if a love to God and souls be the leading principle, I pass as gentle censure upon the rest as I can, and apply to some eccentric expressions, what Mr. Prior somewhere says of our civil dissensions in this land of liberty,

A bad effect, but from a noble cause.

I am, &c.

LETTER II

My Dear Madam, *February* 16, 1776.

It gave me great comfort to find, that what I wrote concerning the divine character of Jesus as God manifest in the flesh, met with your approbation. This doctrine is, in my view, the great foundation-stone upon which all true religion is built; but alas! in the present day, it is the stumbling-stone and rock of offence, upon which too many, fondly presuming upon their own wisdom, fall and are broken. I am so far from wondering that any should doubt of it, that I am firmly persuaded none can truly believe it, however plainly set forth in Scripture, unless it be revealed to them from Heaven; or, in the apostle's words, that "no one can call Jesus Christ Lord, but by the Holy Ghost." I believe there are many who think they believe it, because they have taken it for granted, and never attentively consider the difficulties with which it is attended in the eye of fallen reason. Judging by natural light, it seems impossible to believe that the title of the true God and eternal life should properly belong to that despised Man who hung dead upon the cross, exposed to the insults of His cruel enemies. I know nothing that can obviate the objections the reasoning mind is ready to form against it, but a real conviction of the sinfulness of sin, and the state of a sinner as exposed to the curse of the holy law, and destitute of every plea and hope in himself. Then the necessity of a Redeemer, and the necessity of this Redeemer's being almighty, is seen and felt, with an evidence which bears down all opposition ; for neither the efficacy of His atonement and intercession, nor His sufficiency to guide, save, protect, and feed those who trust in Him, can be conceived of without it. When the eyes of the understanding are opened, and the soul made acquainted with and attentive to its own state and wants, he that runs may read this truth, not in a few detached texts of a dubious import, and liable to be twisted and tortured by the arts of criticism, but as interwoven in the very frame and texture of the Bible, and written, as with a sun-beam, throughout the principal parts both of the Old and New Testament. If Christ be the Shepherd and the Husband of His people under the Gospel, and if His coming into the world did not abridge those who feared God of the privileges they were entitled to before His appearance, it follows by undeniable consequence, " that He is God over all, blessed for ever." For David tells us, that his Shepherd was Jehovah; and the Husband of the Old Testament Church was the Maker and God over the whole earth, the Holy One of Israel, whose name is the Lord of Hosts, Psa.'xxiii. 1., Is. liv. 8, with xlvii. 4. I agree with you, Madam, that among the many attempts which have been made to prove and illustrate the Scripture doctrine, that the Father, the Word, and the Holy Spirit, are one God, there have been many injudicious, unwarrantable things advanced, which have perplexed instead of instructing, and of which the enemies of the truth have known how to make their advantage. However, there have been tracts upon these sublime subjects which have been written with judgment and an unction, and I believe attended with a blessing. I seem to prefer Mr. Jones's book on the Trinity to any I have seen, because he does little more than state some of the Scripture evidence for it, and draws his inferences briefly and plainly ; though even he has admitted a few texts, which may perhaps be thought not quite full to the point ; and he has certainly omitted several of the most express and strongest testimonies. The best and happiest proof of all, that this doctrine is true in itself, and true to us, is the experience of its effects. They who know His name will put their trust in Him : they who are right impressed with His astonishing condescension and love, in emptying Himself, and submitting to the death of the cross for our sakes, will find themselves under a sweet constraint to love Him again, and will feel a little of that emotion of heart which the Apostle expresses in that lively passage, Gal. vi. 14. The knowledge of Christ crucified (like Ithuriel's spear) removes the false appearances by which we have been too long cheated, and shows us the men and the things, the spirit, customs, and maxims of the world, in their just light. Were I perfectly master of myself and my subject, I would never adduce any text in proof of a doctrine or assertion from the pulpit, which was not direct and conclusive ; because, if a text is pressed into an argument, to which it has no proper relation, it rather encumbers than supports it, and raises a suspicion that the cause is weak, and better testimonies in its favour cannot be obtained. Some misapplications of this kind have been so long in use, that they pass pretty current, though, if brought to the assay, they would be found not quite sterling : but I endeavour to avoid them to the best of my judgment. Thus, for instance, I have often heard Rom. xiv. 23, " Whatever is not of faith is sin," quoted to prove, that without a principle of saving faith, we can perform nothing acceptable to God ; whereas it seems clear from the context, that faith is there used in another sense, and signifies a firm persuasion of mind respecting the lawfulness of the action. However, I doubt not but the proposition in itself is strictly true in the other sense, if considered detached from the connexion in which it stands ; but I should rather choose to prove it from other passages, where it is directly affirmed, as Heb. xi. 6 ; Matt. xii. 33. In such cases, I think hearers should be careful not to be prejudiced against a doctrine merely because it is not well supported : for, perhaps, it is capable of solid proof, though the preacher was not so happy as to hit upon that which was most suitable ; and extempore preachers may sometimes hope for a little allowance upon his head, from the more candid part of their auditory, and not be made offenders for an inadvertence, which they cannot perhaps always avoid in the hurry of speaking. With respect to the application of some passages in the Old Testament to our Lord and Saviour, I hold it safest to keep close to the specimens the Apostles have given us, and I would venture with caution, if I go beyond their line ; yet it is probable they have only given us a specimen, and that there are a great number of passages which have a direct reference to Gospel-truths, though we may run some hazard in making out the allusion. If St. Paul had not gone before me, I should have hesitated to assert, that the prohibition, " Thou shalt not muzzle the ox that treadeth out the corn," was given, not upon the account of oxen, but altogether, for our sakes ; nor should I, without his assistance, have found out, that the history of Sarah and Hagar was a designed allegory, to set forth the difference between the law and Gospel covenants. Therefore, when I hear ministers tracing some other allusions I cannot be always sure that they push them too far, though perhaps they are not quite satisfactory to my judgment ; for it may be, they have a farther insight into the meaning of the places than myself. And I think Scriptures may be sometimes used to advantage, by way of accommodation in popular discourses, and in something of a different sense from what they bear in the place where they stand, pro-vided they are not alleged as proofs, but only to illustrate a truth already proved or acknowledged. Though Job's friends and Job himself were mistaken, there are many great truths in their speeches, which, as such, may, I think, stand as the foundation of a discourse. Nay, I either have, or have often intended, to borrow a truth from the mouth even of Satan, " Hast Thou not set a hedge about him ? "

such a confession extorted from our grand adversary placing the safety of the Lord's people under His providential care in a very striking light.

I perfectly agree with you, Madam, that our religious sensations and exercises are much influenced and tinctured by natural constitution ; and that, therefore, tears and warm emotions on the one hand, or a comparative dryness of spirit on the other, are no sure indications of the real state of the heart. Appearances may agree in different persons or vary in the same person, from causes merely natural : even a change of weather may have some influence in raising or depressing the spirits, where the nerves are very delicate, and I think such persons are more susceptive of impressions from the agency of invisible powers, both good and evil ; an agency which, though we cannot explain, experience will not permit us to deny. However, though circumstantials rise and fall, the real difference between nature and grace remains unalterable. That work of God upon the heart, which is sometimes called a new birth, at others a new creation, is as distant from the highest effects of principles, or the most specious imitations which education or resolutions can produce, as light is from darkness, or life from death. Only He who made the world can either make a Christian, or support and carry on His own work. A thirst after God as our portion ; a delight in Jesus as the only way and door ; a renunciation of self and of the world, so far as it is opposite to the spirit of the Gospel ; these and the like fruits of that grace which bringeth salvation, are not only beyond the power of our fallen nature, but contrary to its tendency ; so that we can have no desires of this kind till they are given us from above, and can for a season hardly bear to hear them spoken of, either as excellent or necessary.

I am, &c.

LETTER III

My Dear Madam, *September* 17, 1776.

We are much indebted to you for your kind thoughts of us. Hitherto I feel no uneasiness about what is before me ; but I am afraid my tranquillity does not wholly spring from trust in the Lord and submission to His will, but that a part of it at least is derived from the assurances Mr. W. gave me, that the operation would be neither difficult nor dangerous. I have not much of the hero in my constitution ; if in great pains or sharp trials I should ever show a becoming fortitude, it must be given me from above. I desire to leave all with Him in whose hands my ways are, and who has promised me strength according to my day.

I rejoice that the Lord has not only made you desirous of being useful to others in their spiritual concerns, but has given you, in some instances, to see that your desires and attempts have not been in vain. I shall thankfully accept of the commission you are pleased to offer me, and take a pleasure in perusing any papers you may think proper to put into my hands, and offer you my sentiments with that simplicity which I am persuaded will be much more agreeable to you than compliments. Though I know there is in general a delicacy and difficulty in services of this kind, yet with respect to yourself I seem to have nothing to fear.

I have often wished we had more female pens employed in the service of the sanctuary. Though few ladies encumber themselves with the apparatus of Latin or Greek, or engage in voluminous performances ; yet, in the article of essay writing, I think many are qualified to succeed better than most men, having a peculiar easiness of style, which few of us can imitate. I remember you once showed me a paper, together with the corrections and alterations proposed by a gentleman whose opinion you had asked. I thought his corrections had injured it, and given it an air of stiffness, which is often observable when learned men write in English. Grammatical rules, as they are called, are wholly derived from the mode of speaking or writing which obtains amongst those who best understand the language ; for the language must be supposed established before any grammar can be made for it ; and therefore women who, from the course of their education and life, have had an opportunity of reading the best written books, and conversing with those who speak well, though they do not burden themselves with the formality of grammar, have often more skill in the English language than the men who can call every figure of speech by a Latin or a Greek name. You may be sure, Madam, I shall not wish your papers suppressed, merely because they were not written by a learned man. Language and style, however, are but the dress. Trifles, however adorned, are trifles still. A person of spiritual discernment would rather be the author of one page, written in the humble garb of Bunyan, upon a serious subject, than be able to rival the sprightliness and elegance of Lady M. W. Montague, unless it could be with a view to edification. The subjects you propose are important ; and with respect to sacramental meditations, and all devotional exercises so called, I perfectly agree with you, that to be affecting and useful, they must be dictated rather by the heart than by the head ; and are most likely to influence others when they are the fruits and transcripts of our own experience. So far as I know, we are but scantily provided with specimens of this sort in print, and therefore I shall be glad to see an accession to the public stock. Your other thought, of helps to recollection on Saturday evenings, is, I think, an attempt in which none have been beforehand with you. So that, according to the general appearance, I feel myself disposed to encourage you to do as you have purposed. On the other hand, if I meet with anything on the perusal of the papers which, in my view, may seem to need alteration, I will freely and faithfully point it out.

I can almost smile *now* to think you once classed me among the *Stoics*. If I dare speak with confidence of myself in anything, I think I may lay claim to a little of that pleasing, painful thing, sensibility. I need not boast of it, for it has too often been my snare, my sin, and my punishment. Yet I would be thankful for a spice of it, as the Lord's gift, and, when rightly exercised, it is valuable ; and I think I should make but an awkward minister without it, especially here. Where there is this sensibility in the natural temper, it will give a tincture or cast to our religious expression. Indeed I often find this sensibility weakest where it should

c. Q

be strongest, and have reason to reproach myself that I am not more affected by the character, love, and sufferings of my Lord and Saviour, and my own peculiar personal obligations to Him.   However, my views of religion have been, for many years, such as I supposed more likely to make me deemed to be an enthusiast than a Stoic.   A moon-light head-knowledge, derived from a system of sentiments, however true in themselves, is in my judgment a poor thing : nor, on the other hand, am I an admirer of those rapturous sallies, which are more owing to a warm imagination than to a just perception of the power and importance of Gospel truth.   The Gospel addresses both head and heart ; and where it has its proper effect, where it is received as the word of God, and is clothed with the authority and energy of the Holy Spirit, the understanding is enlightened, the affections awakened and engaged, the will brought into subjection, and the whole soul delivered to its impression, as wax to the seal—when this is the case, when the affections do not take the lead, and push forward with a blind impulse, but arise from the principles of Scripture, and are governed by them, the more warmth the better.   Yet in this state of infirmity nothing is perfect ; and our natural temperament and disposition will have more influence upon our religious sensations than we are ordinarily aware.   It is well to know how to make proper allowances and abatements upon this head, in the judgment we form both of ourselves and of others.   Many good people are distressed, and alternately elated by frames and feelings which perhaps are more constitutional than properly religious experiences.   I dare not tell you, Madam, what I am, but I can tell you what I wish to be.   The love of God, as manifested in Jesus Christ, is what I would wish to be the abiding object of my contemplation ; not merely to speculate upon it as a doctrine, but so to feel it, and my own interest in it, as to have my heart filled with its effects, and transformed into its resemblance ; that with this glorious exemplar in my view, I may be animated to a spirit of benevolence, love, and compassion, to all around me ; that my love may be primarily fixed upon Him who has so loved me, and then for His sake, diffused to all His children, and to all His creatures.   Then, knowing that much is forgiven to me, I should be prompted to the ready exercise of forgiveness, if I have aught against any. Then I should be humble, patient, and submissive under all His dispensations ; meek, gentle, forbearing, and kind to my fellow-worms. Then I should be active and diligent in improving all my talents and powers in His service, and for His glory ; and live not to myself, but to Him who loved me and gave Himself for me.

I am, &c.

LETTER IV

MY DEAR MADAM, *Nov.* 29, 1776.

I AM persuaded you need not be told, that though there are perhaps supposable extremities, in which self would prevail over all considerations, yet in general it is more easy to suffer in our own persons, than in the persons of those whom we dearly love ; for through such a medium our apprehensions possibly receive the idea of the trouble enlarged beyond its just dimensions ; and it would sit lighter upon us, if it were properly our own case, for then we should feel it all, and there would be no room for imagination to exaggerate.

But though I feel grief, I trust the Lord has mercifully preserved me from impatience and murmuring, and that, in the midst of all the pleadings of flesh and blood, there is exception, " *Not* my will, but Thine be done."

It is a comfortable consideration, that He with whom we have to do, our great High Priest who once put away our sins by the sacrifice of Himself, and now for ever appears in the presence of God for us, is not only possessed of sovereign authority and infinite power, but wears our very nature, and feels and exercises in the highest degree those tendernesses and commiserations, which I conceive are essential to humanity in its perfect state. The whole history of His wonderful life is full of inimitable instances of this kind. His bowels were moved before His arm was exerted ; He condescended to mingle tears with mourners, and wept over distresses which He intended to relieve. He is still the same in His exalted state ; compassions dwell within His heart. In a way inconceivable to us, but consistent with His supreme dignity and perfection of happiness and glory, He still feels for His people.   When Saul persecuted the members upon earth, the Head complained from Heaven ; and sooner shall the most tender mother sit insensible and inattentive to the cries and wants of her infant, than the Lord Jesus be an unconcerned spectator of His suffering children.   No ; with the eye, and the ear, and the heart of a friend, He attends to their sorrows ; He counts their sighs, puts their tears in His bottle ; and when our spirits are overwhelmed within us, He knows our path, and adjusts the time, the measure of our trials, and everything that is necessary for our present support and seasonable deliverance, with the same unerring wisdom and accuracy as He weighed the mountains in scales, and the hills in a balance, and meted out the heavens with a span.   Still more, besides His benevolent, He has an experimental, sympathy.   He knows our sorrows, not merely as He knows all things, but as one who has been in our situation, and who, though without sin Himself, endured, when upon earth, inexpressibly more for us than He will ever lay upon us.   He has sanctified poverty, pain, disgrace, temptation, and death, by passing through these states ; and in whatever states His people are, they may by faith have fellowship with Him in their sufferings, and He will, by sympathy and love, have fellowship and interest with them in theirs.   What then, shall we fear, or of what shall we complain, when all our concerns are written upon His heart, and their management, to the very hairs of our head, are under His care and Providence ; when He pities us more than we can do ourselves, and has engaged His almighty power to sustain and relieve us ?   However, as He is tender, He is wise also ; He loves us, but especially with regard to our best interests.   If there were not something in our hearts and our situation that required discipline and medicine, He so delights in our prosperity, that we should never be in heaviness.   The innumerable comforts and mercies with which He enriches even those we call our darker days, are sufficient proofs that He does not willingly grieve us ; but when He sees a need-be for chastisement, He will not withhold it, because He loves us ; on the contrary, that is the very reason why He afflicts. He will put His silver into the fire to purify it ; but He sits by the furnace as a refiner, to direct the process, and to secure the end He has in view, that we may neither suffer too much, nor suffer in vain.

I am, &c.

LETTER V

My Dear Madam,   *Dec.* — 1776.

I HAVE often preached to others of the benefit of affliction ; but my own path for many years has been so smooth, and my trials, though I have not been without trials, comparatively so light and few, that I have seemed to myself to speak by rote upon a subject of which I had not a proper feeling. Yet the many exercises of my poor afflicted people, and the sympathy the Lord has given me with them in their troubles, has made this a frequent and favourite topic of my ministry among them. The advantages of afflictions, when the Lord is pleased to employ them for the good of His people, are many and great. Permit me to mention a few of them ; and the Lord grant, that we may all find those blessed ends answered to ourselves, by the trials He is pleased to appoint us.

Afflictions quicken us to prayer. It is a pity it should be so ; but experience testifies, that a long course of ease and prosperity without painful changes, has an unhappy tendency to make us cold and formal in our secret worship ; but troubles rouse our spirits, and constrain us to call upon the Lord in good earnest, when we feel a need of that help which we only can have from Him.

They are useful, and in a degree necessary, to keep alive in us a conviction of the vanity and unsatisfying nature of the present world, and all its enjoyments ; to remind us that this is not our rest, and to call our thoughts upwards, where our true treasure is, and where our conversation ought to be. When things go on much to our wish, our hearts are too prone to say, " It is good to be here." It is probable, that had Moses, when he came to invite Israel to Canaan, found them in prosperity, as in the days of Joseph, they would have been very unwilling to remove ; but the afflictions they were previously brought into made his message welcome. Thus the Lord, by pain, sickness, and disappointments, by breaking our cisterns, and withering our gourds, weakens our attachment to this world, and makes the thought of quitting it more familiar and more desirable.

A child of God cannot but greatly desire a more enlarged and experimental acquaintance with His Holy Word; and this attainment is greatly promoted by our trials. The far greater part of the promises in Scripture are made and suited to a state of affliction; and though we may believe they are true, we cannot so well know their sweetness, power, and suitableness, unless we ourselves are in a state to which they refer.   The Lord says, " Call upon Me in the day of trouble, and I will deliver."   Now, till the day of trouble comes, such a promise is like a city of refuge to an Israelite, who, not having slain a man, was in no danger of the avenger of blood.   He had a privilege near him, of which he knew not the use and value, because he was not in the case for which it was pro-vided.   But some can say, I not only believe this promise upon the authority of the speaker, but I can set my seal to it ; I have been in trouble, I took this course for relief, and I was not disappointed.   The Lord verily heard and de-livered me.   Thus afflictions likewise give occasion of our knowing and noticing more of the Lord's wisdom, power, and goodness, in supporting and relieving, than we should otherwise have known.

I have not time to take another sheet ; must, therefore, contract my homily.   Afflictions evidence to ourselves, and manifest to others, the reality of grace.   And when we suffer as Christians, exercise some measure of that patience and submission, and receive some measure of these supports and supplies, which the Gospel requires and promises to believers, we are more confirmed that we have not taken up with mere notions ; and others may be con-vinced, that we do not follow cunningly-devised fables. They likewise strengthen, by exercise, our graces : as our limbs and natural powers would be feeble if not called to daily exertion ; so the graces of the Spirit would languish,

unless something were provided to draw them out to use.
And, to say no more, they are honourable, as they advance
our conformity to Jesus our Lord, who was a man of sorrows
for our sake. Methinks, if we might go to Heaven without
suffering, we should be unwilling to desire it. Why should
we ever wish to go by any other path than that which He has
consecrated and endeared by His own example ? especially
as His people's sufferings are not penal ; there is no wrath
in them ; the cup He puts in their hands is very different
from that which He drank for their sakes, and is only
medicinal to promote their chief good. Here I must stop ;
but the subject is fruitful, and might be pursued through a
quire of paper.

I am,˙&c.

LETTER VI

My Dear Madam, *August,* — 1768.

YOUR obliging favour of the 22nd from B ——, which
I received last night, demands an immediate acknowledg-
ment. Many things which would have offered by way of
answer, must, for the present, be postponed ; for the same
post brought information which turns my thoughts to *one*
subject. What shall I say ? Topics of consolation are at
hand in abundance ; they are familiar to your mind ; and
were I to fill the sheet with them, I could suggest nothing
but what you already know. Then are they consolatory
indeed, when the Lord Himself is pleased to apply them to
the heart. This He has promised, and therefore we are en-
couraged to expect it. This is my prayer for you ; I sin-
cerely sympathise with you : I cannot comfort you ; but
He can, and I trust He will. How impertinent would it
be to advise you to forget or suspend the feelings which
such a stroke must excite ! who can help feeling ? nor is
sensibility in itself sinful. Christian resignation is very
different from that stoical stubbornness, which is most
easily practised by those unamiable characters, whose regards
centre wholly in self : nor could we, in a proper manner,

exercise submission to the will of God under our trials, if we did not feel them.   He who knows our frame, is pleased to allow that afflictions for the present are not joyous, but grievous.   But to them that fear Him, He is near at hand, to support their spirits, to moderate their grief, and in the issue to sanctify it ; so that they shall come out of the furnace refined, more humble, and more spiritual.   There is, however, a part assigned us : we are to pray for the help in need ; and we are not wilfully to give way to the impression of overwhelming sorrow.   We are to endeavour to turn our thoughts to such considerations as are suited to alleviate it : our deserts as sinners, the many mercies we are still indulged with, the still greater afflictions which many of our fellow-creatures endure, and, above all, the sufferings of Jesus, that man of sorrows, who made Himself intimately acquainted with grief for our sakes.

When the will of the Lord is manifested to us by the event, we are to look to Him for grace and strength, and be still to know that He is God, that He has a right to dispose of us and ours as He pleases, and that in the exercise of this right He is most certainly good and wise.   We often complain of losses ; but this expression is rather improper. Strictly speaking, we can lose nothing, because we have no real property in anything.   Our earthly comforts are lent us ; and when recalled, we ought to return and resign them with thankfulness to Him who has let them remain so long in our hands.   But, as I said above, I do not mean to enlarge in this strain : I hope the Lord, the only Comforter, will bring such thoughts with warmth and efficacy to your mind.   Your wound, while fresh, is painful ; but faith, prayer, and time, will, I trust, gradually render it tolerable.   There is something fascinating in grief ; painful as it is, we are prone to indulge it, and to brood over the thoughts and circumstances which are suited (like fuel to fire) to heighten and prolong it.   When the Lord afflicts, it is His design that we should grieve : but in this, as in all other things, there is a certain moderation which becomes a Christian, and which only grace can teach ; and grace teaches us, not by books or by hearsay, but by experimental lessons : all beyond this should be avoided, and guarded against as sinful and hurtful.   Grief, when indulged and excessive, preys upon the spirits, injures health, indisposes us for duty, and causes us to shed tears, which deserve more tears. This is a weeping world. Sin has filled it with thorns and briers, with crosses and calamities. It is a great hospital, resounding with groans in every quarter. It is as a field of battle, where many are falling around us continually ; and it is more wonderful that we escape so well, than that we are sometimes wounded. We *must* have some share ; it is the unavoidable lot of our nature and state ; it is likewise needful, in point of discipline. The Lord will certainly chasten those whom He loves, though others may seem to pass for a time with impunity. That is a sweet, instructive, and important passage, Heb. xii. 5, 11. It is so plain, that it needs no comment ; so full, that a comment would but weaken it. May the Lord inscribe it upon your heart, my dear Madam, and upon mine l

I am, &c.

LETTER VII

My Dear Madam,   *Nov. —* 1778.

YOUR obliging favour raised in me a variety of emotions when I first received it, and has revived them this morning while perusing it again. I have mourned and rejoiced with you, and felt pain and pleasure in succession, as you diversified the subject. However, the weight of your grief I was willing to consider as a thing that is past ; and the thought that you had been mercifully supported under it, and brought through it, that you were restored home in safety, and that at the time of writing you were tolerably well and composed, made joy upon the whole preponderate ; and I am more disposed to congratulate you, and join you in praising the Lord for the mercies you enumerate, than to prolong my condolence upon the mournful parts of your letter. Repeated trying occasions have made me well acquainted with the anxious inquiries with which the busy poring mind is apt to pursue departed friends : it can hardly be otherwise under some circumstances. I have found prayer the best relief. I have thought it very allowable to avail myself to the utmost of every favourable consideration; but I have had the most comfort, when I have been enabled to resign the whole concern into His .hands, whose thoughts and ways, whose power and goodness, are infinitely superior to our conceptions. I consider in such cases, that the great Redeemer can save to the uttermost, and the great Teacher can communicate light, and impress truth, when and how He pleases. I trust the power of His grace and compassion will hereafter triumphantly appear in many instances of persons, who, on their dying beds, and in the last moments, have been by His mercy constrained to feel the importance and reality of truths which they did not properly understand and attend to in the hour of health and prosperity. Such a salutary change I have frequently, or at least more than once, twice, or thrice, been an eye-witness to, accompanied with such evidence as I think has been quite satisfactory. And who can say such a change may not often take place, when the person who is the subject of it is too much enfeebled to give an account to bystanders of what is transacting in his mind? Thus I have encouraged my hope. But the best satisfaction of all is, to be duly impressed with the voice that says, " Be still, and know that I am God." These words direct us not only to His sovereignty, His undoubted right to do what He will, with His own, but to all His adorable and amiable perfections, by which He has manifested Himself to us in the Son of His love.

As I am not a Sadducee, the account you give of the music which entertained you on the road does not put my dependence upon your veracity or your judgment to any trial. We live upon the confines of the invisible world, or rather, perhaps, in the midst of it. That unseen agents have a power of operating upon our minds, at least, upon that mysterious faculty we call the imagination, is with me not merely a point of opinion, or even of faith, but of experience. That evil spirits can, when permitted, disturb, distress, and defile us, I know, as well as I know that the fire can burn me ; and though their interposition is perhaps more easily and certainly distinguishable, yet, from analogy, I conclude that good spirits are equally willing, and equally able, to employ their kind offices for our relief and comfort. I have formed in my mind a kind of system upon this subject, which, for the most part, I keep pretty much to myself; but I can entrust my thoughts to you as they occasionally offer. I apprehend that some persons (those particularly who rank under the class of nervous) are more open and accessible to these impressions than others, and probably the same persons more so at some times than at others. And though we frequently distinguish between imaginary and real (which is one reason why nervous people are so seldom pitied) yet an impression upon the imagination may, as to the agent that produces it, and to the person that receives it, be as much a reality as any of the sensible objects around him ; though a by-stander, not being able to share in the perception, may account it a mere whim, and suppose it might be avoided or removed by an act of the will. Nor have any a right to withhold their assent to what the Scriptures teach, and many sober persons declare, of this invisible agency, merely because we cannot answer the questions, How? or Why? The thing may be certain though *we* cannot easily explain it ; and there may be just and important reasons for it, though *we* should not be able to assign them. If what you heard, or (which in my view is much the same) what you thought you heard, had a tendency to compose your spirit, and to encourage your application to the Lord for help, at the time when you were about to stand in need of especial assistance, then there is a sufficient and suitable reason assigned for it at once, without looking further. It would be dangerous to make impressions a *rule* of duty ; but if they strengthen us, and assist us in the performance of what *we know* to be our duty, me way be thankful for them.

You have taken leave of your favourite trees, and the scenes of your younger life, but a few years sooner than you must have done, if the late dispensation had not taken place. All must be left soon ; for all below is polluted, and in its best state is too scanty to afford us happiness. If we are believers in Jesus, all we *can* quit is a mere nothing, compared with what we shall obtain. To exchange a dungeon for a palace, earth for Heaven, will call for no self-denial when we stand upon the threshold of eternity, and shall have a clearer view than we have now of the vanity of what is passing from us, and the glory of what is before us. The partial changes we meet with in our way through life are designed to remind us of, and prepare us for, the great change which awaits us at the end of it. The Lord grant that we may find mercy of the Lord in that solemn hour !

I am, &c.

FOUR LETTERS

MRS. T——

LETTER I

MY DEAR MADAM,   *March* 12, 1774.

MY heart is full, yet I must restrain it. Many thoughts which crowd my mind, and would have vent were I writing to another person, would to you be unseasonable. I write not to remind you of what you have lost, but of what you have which you cannot lose. May the Lord put a word into my heart that may be acceptable ; and may His good Spirit accompany the perusal, and enable you to say with the apostle, that as sufferings abound, consolations also abound by Jesus Christ ! Indeed I can sympathise with you. I remember, too, the delicacy of your frame, and the tenderness of your natural spirits ; so that, were you not interested in the exceeding great and precious promises of the Gospel, I should be ready to fear you must sink under your trial. But I have some faint conceptions of the all-sufficiency and faithfulness of the Lord, and may address you in the king's words to Daniel, " Thy God, whom thou servest continually, He will deliver thee." Motives for resignation to His will abound in His word ; but it is an additional and crowning mercy, that He has promised to apply and enforce them in time of need. He has said, " My grace shall be sufficient for thee : and as thy day is, so shall thy strength be." This I trust you have already experienced. The Lord is so rich and so good, that He can by a glance of thought compensate His children for whatever His wisdom sees fit to deprive them of. If He gives them a lively sense of what He has delivered them from, and prepared for them, or of what He Himself submitted to endure for their sakes, they find at once light springing up out of darkness ; hard things become easy, and bitter sweet. I remember to have read of a good man in the last century (probably you may have met with the story) who, when his beloved and only son lay ill, was for some time greatly anxious about the event. One morning he stayed longer than usual in his closet ; while he was there his son died. When he came out, his family were afraid to tell him, but, like David, he perceived it by their looks ; and when upon inquiry they said it was so, he received the news with a composure that surprised them. But he soon explained the reason, by telling them, that for such discoveries of the Lord's goodness as he had been favoured with that morning, he could be content to lose a son every day. Yes, Madam, though every stream must fail, the fountain is still full and still flowing. All the comfort you ever received in your dear friend was from the Lord, who is abundantly able to comfort you still ; and He is gone but a little before you. May your faith anticipate the joyful and glorious meeting you will shortly have in a better world ! Then your worship and converse together will be to unspeakable advantage, without imperfecting, interruption, abatement or end. Then all tears shall be wiped away, and every cloud removed ; and then you will see that all your concernments here below (the late afflicting dispensation not excepted) were appointed and adjusted by infinite wisdom and infinite love.

The Lord, who knows our frame, does not expect or require that we should aim at a stoical indifference under His visitations. He allows, that afflictions are at present not joyous, but grievous ; yea, He was pleased when upon earth to weep with His mourning friends when Lazarus died. But He has graciously provided for the prevention of that anguish and bitterness of sorrow, which is' upon such occasions, the portion of such as live without God in the world, and has engaged that all shall work together for good, and yield the peaceable fruits of righteousness. May He bless you with a sweet serenity of spirit, and a cheerful hope of the glory that shall be shortly revealed !

I intimated that I would not trouble you with my own sense

and share of this loss. If you remember the great kindness
I always received from Mr. T.—— and yourself, as often
as opportunity afforded, and if you will believe me possessed
of any sensibility or gratitude, you will conclude that
my concern is not small. I feel likewise for the public.
Will it be a consolation to you, Madam, to know that you
do not mourn alone ? A character so exemplary, as a friend,
a counsellor, a Christian, and a minister, will be long and
deeply regretted ; and many will join with me in praying,
that you who are most nearly interested may be signally
supported, and feel the propriety of Mrs. Rowe's acknow-
ledgment,

> Thou dost but take the dying lamp away
> To bless me with Thine own unclouded day.

We join in most affectionate respects and condolence.
May the Lord bless you and keep you, lift up the light of
His countenance upon you, and give you peace !

I am, &c.

LETTER II

My Dear Madam, *April* 8, 1775.

I HAVE long and often purposed waiting upon you with
a second letter, though one thing or other still caused delay ;
for though I could not but wish to hear from you, I was
far from making that a condition of my writing. If you have
leisure and spirits to favour me with a line now and then,
it will give us much pleasure ; but if not, it will be a suffi-
cient inducement with me to write, to know that you give
me liberty, and that you will receive my letters in good
part. At the same time I must add, that my various
engagements will not permit me to break in upon you so often
as my sincere affection would otherwise prompt me to do.

I heartily thank you for yours, and hope my soul desires
to praise the Lord on your behalf. I am persuaded that
His goodness to you, in supporting you under a trial so
sharp in itself, and in the circumstances that attended it,

has been an encouragement and comfort to many. It is in such apparently severe times that the all-sufficiency and faithfulness of the Lord, and the power and proper effects of His precious Gospel, are most eminently displayed. I would hope, and I do believe, that the knowledge of your case has animated some of the Lord's people against those anxious fears which they sometimes feel when they look upon their earthly comforts with too careful an eye, and their hearts are ready to sink at the thought. What should I do, ånd how should I behave, were the Lord pleased to take away my desire with a stroke? But we see He can supply their absence, and afford us superior comforts without them. The Gospel reveals one thing needful, the pearl of great price; and supposes that they who possess this are provided for against all events, and have ground of unshaken hope, and a source of never-failing consolation under every change they can meet with during their pilgrimage state. When His people are enabled to set their seal to this, not only in theory when all things go smooth, but practically when called upon to pass through the fire and water, then His grace is glorified in them and by them; then it appears both to themselves and to others, that they have neither followed cunningly devised fables, nor amused themselves with empty notions; then they know in themselves, and it is evidenced to others, that God is with them of a truth. In this view a believer, when in some good measure divested from that narrow selfish disposition which cleaves so closely to us by nature, will not only submit to trials, but rejoice in them, notwithstanding the feelings and reluctance of the flesh. For if I am redeemed from misery by the blood of Jesus, and if He is now preparing me a mansion near Himself, that I may drink of the rivers of pleasure at His right hand for evermore, the question is not (at least ought not to be)—How may I pass through life with the least inconvenience—How may my little span of life be made most subservient to the praise and glory of Him Who loved me, and gave Himself for me? Where the Lord gives this desire, He will gratify it: and as afflictions for the most part afford the fairest opportunities of this kind, therefore it is, that those whom He is pleased eminently to honour are usually called, at one time or another, to the heaviest trials ; not because He loves to grieve them, but because He hears their prayers, and accepts their desires of doing Him service in the world. The post of honour in war is so called, because attended with difficulties and dangers which but few are supposed equal to ; yet generals usually allot these hard services to their favourites and friends, who, on their parts, eagerly accept them as tokens of favour, and marks of confidence. Should we, therefore, not account it an honour and a privilege, when the Captain of our salvation assigns us a difficult post since He can and does (which no earthly commander can) inspire His soldiers with wisdom, courage and strength, suitable to their situation (2 Cor. xii. 9, 10) ? I am acquainted with a few who have been led thus into the fore-front of the battle : they suffered much ; but I have never heard them say they suffered too much ; for the Lord stood by them and strengthened them. Go on, my dear Madam : yet a little while and Jesus will wipe away all tears from your eyes ; you will see your beloved friend again, and he and you will rejoice together for ever.

I am, &c.

LETTER III

MY DEAR MADAM, *October* 24, 1775.

THE manner in which you mention "*Omicron's* Letters," I hope, will rather humble me than puff me up. Your favourable acceptance of them, if alone, might have the latter effect ; but, alas ! I feel myself so very defective in those things, the importance of which I endeavour to point out to others, that I almost appear to myself to be one of those who say, but do not. I find it much easier to speak to the hearts of others than to my own. Yet I have cause, beyond many, to bless God, that He has given me some idea of what a Christian ought to be, and I hope a real desire of being one myself ; but verily I have attained but a very little way. A friend hinted to me, that the character I have given of C. or grace in the full ear, must be from my own experience, or I could not have written it. To myself, however, it appears otherwise ; but I am well convinced, that the state of C. is attainable, and more to be 'desired than mountains of gold and silver. But I find you complain likewise ; though it appears to me, and I believe to all who know you, that the Lord has been peculiarly gracious to you, in giving you much of the spirit in which He delights, and by which His name and the power of His Gospel are glorified. It seems, therefore, that we are not competent judges either of ourselves or of others. I take it for granted, that they are the most excellent Christians who are most abased in their own eyes ; but lest you should think upon this ground that I am something, because I can say so many humiliating things of myself, I must prevent your over-rating me, by assuring you, that my confessions rather express what I know I ought to think of myself, than what I actually do. Naturalists suppose, that if the matter of which the earth is formed were condensed as much as it is capable of, it would occupy but a very small space ; in proof of which they observe, that a cubical pane of glass, which appears smooth and impervious to us, must be exceedingly porous in itself ; since in every assignable point it receives and transmits the rays of light ; and yet gold, which is the most solid substance we are acquainted with, is about eight times heavier than glass, which is made up (if I may say so) of nothing but pores. In like manner, I conceive that inherent grace, when it is dilated, and appears to the greatest advantage in a sinner, would be found to be very small and inconsiderable, if it was condensed, and absolutely separated from every mixture. The highest attainments in this life are very inconsiderable, compared with what should properly result from our relation and obligations to a God of infinite holiness. The nearer we approach to Him, the more we are sensible of this. While we only hear of God as it were by the ear, we seem to be something ; but when, as in the case of Job, He discovers Himself more sensibly to us, Job's language becomes ours, and the height of our attainment is, to abhor ourselves in dust and ashes.

I hope I do not write too late to meet you at Bath. I pray that your health may be benefited by the waters, .

and your soul comforted by the Lord's blessing upon His ordinances, and the converse of His children. If any of the friends you expected to see are still there, to whom we are known, and my name should be mentioned, I beg you to say, we desire to be respectfully remembered to them. Had I wings I would fly to Bath while you are there. As it is, I endeavour to be with you in spirit. There certainly is a real, though secret, a sweet, though mysterious, communion of saints, by virtue of their common union with Jesus. Feeding upon the same bread, drinking of the same fountain, waiting at the same mercy-seat, and aiming at the same ends, they have fellowship one with another, though at a distance. Who can tell how often the Holy Spirit, who is equally present with them all, touches the hearts of two or more of His children at the same instant, so as to excite a sympathy of pleasure, prayer, or praise, on each other's account? It revives me sometimes in a dull and dark hour to reflect, that the Lord has in mercy given me a place in the hearts of many of His people; and perhaps some of them may be speaking to Him on my behalf, when I have hardly power to utter a word for myself. For kind services of this sort, I persuade myself, I am often indebted to you. O that I were enabled more fervently to repay you in the same way! I can say that I attempt it: I love and honour you greatly, and your concernments are often upon my mind.

We spent most of a week with Mr. B—— since we returned from London, and he has been once here. We have reason to be very thankful for his connexion; I find but few like-minded with him, and his family is filled with the grace and peace of the Gospel. I never visit them but I meet with something to humble, quicken, and edify me. O! what will Heaven be, where there shall be all who love the Lord Jesus, and they only; where all imperfection, and whatever now abates or interrupts their joy in their Lord, and in each other, shall cease for ever? There at last I hope to meet you, and spend an eternity with you, in admiring the riches and glory of redeeming love.

We join in a tender of the most affectionate respects.

I am, &c.

R 2

LETTER IV

My Dear Madam,   *October 28, 1777.*

WHAT can I say for myself, to let your obliging letter
remain so long unanswered, when your kind solicitude for
us induced you to write? I am ashamed of the delay.
You would have heard from me immediately, had I been
at home. But I have reason to be thankful that we were
providentially called to London a few days before the fire;
so that Mrs. —— was mercifully preserved from the alarm
and shock she must have felt, had she been upon the spot.
Your letter followed me hither, and was in my possession
more than a week before my return. I purposed writing
every day, but indeed I was much hurried and engaged.
Yet I am not excused; I ought to have saved time from
my meals or my sleep, rather than appear negligent or
ungrateful. I now seize the first post I could write by
since I came home. The fire devoured twelve houses; and
it was a mercy, and almost a miracle, that the whole
town was not destroyed; which must, humanly speaking,
have been the case, had not the night been calm, as two-thirds
of the buildings were thatched. No lives were lost, no
person considerably hurt; and I believe the contributions
of the benevolent will prevent the loss from being greatly
felt. It was at the distance of a quarter of a mile from my
house.

Your command limits my attention, at present, to a
part of your letter, and points me out a subject. Yet,
at the same time, you lay me under a difficulty. I would not
willingly offend you, and I hope the Lord has taught me
not to aim at saying handsome things. I deal not in com-
pliments, and religious compliments are the most unseemly
of any. But why might I not express my sense of the
grace of God manifested in you as well as in another? I be-
lieve our hearts are all alike destitute of every good, and
prone to every evil. Like money from the same mint, they
bear the same impression of total depravity; but grace
makes a difference, and grace deserves the praise. Perhaps
it ought not greatly to displease you, that others do, and
must, and will, think better of you than you do of yourself.

If I do, how can I help it, when I form my judgment entirely from what you say and write ?   I cannot consent that you should seriously appoint me to examine and judge of your state.   I thought you knew, beyond the shadow of a doubt, what your views and desires are ; yea, you express them in your letter, in full agreement with what the Scripture declares of the principles, desires, and feelings of a Christian. It is true that you feel contrary principles, that you are conscious of defects and defilements ; but it is equally true that you could not be right if you did not feel these things.   To be conscious of them, and humbled for them, is one of the surest marks of grace ; and to be more deeply sensible of them than formerly, is the best evidence of growth in grace.   But when the enemy would tempt us to doubt and distrust, because we are not perfect, then he fights, not only against our peace, but against the honour and faithfulness of our dear Lord.   Our righteousness is in Him, and our hope depends, not upon the exercise of grace in us, but upon the fulness of grace and love in Him, and upon His obedience unto death.

There is, my dear Madam, a difference between the holiness of a sinner and that of an angel.   The angels have never sinned, nor have they tasted of redeeming love ; they have no inward conflicts, no law of sin warring in their members ; their obedience is perfect ; their happiness is complete.   Yet if I be found among redeemed sinners, I need not wish to be an angel.   Perhaps God is not less glorified by your obedience, and, not to shock you, I will add, by mine, than by Gabriel's.   It is a mighty manifestation of His grace indeed, when it can live, and act, and conquer, in such hearts as ours ; when, in defiance of an evil nature and an evil world, and all the force and subtlety of Satan, a weak worm is still upheld, and enabled not only to climb, but to thresh the mountains ; when a small spark is preserved through storms and floods.   In these circumstances, the work of grace is to be estimated, not merely from its imperfect appearance, but from the difficulties it has to struggle with and overcome ; and, therefore, our holiness does not consist in great attainments, but in spiritual desires, in hungerings, thirstings, and mournings ; in humiliation of heart, poverty of spirit, submission, meekness; in cordial admiring thoughts of Jesus, and dependence upon Him alone for all we want. Indeed these may be said to be great attainments; but they who have most of them are most sensible that they, in and of themselves, are nothing, have nothing, can do nothing, and see daily cause for abhorring themselves, and repenting in dust and ashes.

Our view of death will not always be alike, but in proportion to the degree in which the Holy Spirit is pleased to communicate His sensible influence. We may anticipate the moment of dissolution with pleasure and desire in the morning, and be ready to shrink from the thought of it before night. But though our frames and perceptions vary, the report of faith concerning it is the same. The Lord usually reserves dying strength for a dying hour. When Israel was to pass Jordan, the ark was in the river; and though the rear of the host could not see it, yet as they successively came forward and approached the banks, they all beheld the ark, and all went safely over. As you are not weary of living, if it be the Lord's pleasure, so I hope, for the sake of your friends and the people whom you love, He will spare you amongst us a little longer; but when the time shall arrive which He has appointed for your dismission, I make no doubt but He will overpower all your fears, silence all your enemies, and give you a comfortable, triumphant entrance into His kingdom. You have nothing to fear from death; for Jesus, by dying, has disarmed it of its sting, has perfumed the grave, and opened the gates of glory for His believing people. Satan, so far as He is permitted, will assault our peace, but He is a vanquished enemy : our Lord holds him in a chain, and sets him bounds which he cannot pass. He provides for us likewise the whole armour of God, and has promised to cover our heads Himself in the days of battle, to bring us honourably through every skirmish, and to make us more than conquerors at last. If you think my short unexpected interview with Mr. C—— may justify my wishing he should know that I respect his character, love his person, and rejoice in what the Lord has done and is doing for him and by him, I beg you to tell him so; but I leave it entirely to you.

We join in most affectionate respects.   I am, &c.

FIVE LETTERS

TO

MR. ——

LETTER I

DEAR SIR,   *March 7, 1765.*

YOUR favour of the 19th February came to my hand yesterday. I have read it with attention, and very willingly sit down to offer you my thoughts. Your case reminds me of my own : my first desires towards the ministry were attended with great uncertainties and difficulties, and the perplexity of my own mind was heightened by the various and opposite judgments of my friends. The advice I have to offer is the result of painful experience and exercise, and for this reason, perhaps, may not be unacceptable to you. I pray our gracious Lord to make it useful.

I was long distressed, as you are, about what was or was not a proper call to the ministry ; it now seems to me an easy point to solve, but perhaps will not be so to you, till the Lord shall make it clear to yourself in your own case. I have not room to say as much as I could : in brief, I think it principally includes three things :

1. A warm and earnest desire to be employed in this service. I apprehend, the man who is once moved by the Spirit of God to this work, will prefer it, if attainable, to thousands of gold and silver ; so that though he is at times intimidated by a sense of its importance and difficulty, compared with his own great insufficiency, (for it is to be presumed a call of this sort, if indeed from God, will be accompanied with humility and self-abasement,) yet he cannot give it up. I hold it a good rule to inquire on this point, whether the desire to preach is most fervent in our most lively and

spiritual frames, and when we are most laid in the dust before the Lord ? If so, it is a good sign. But if, as is sometimes the case, a person is very earnest to be a preacher to others, when he finds but little hungerings and thirstings after grace in his own soul, it is then to be feared, his zeal springs rather from a selfish principle, than from the Spirit of God.

2. Besides this affectionate desire and readiness to preach, there must in due season appear some competent sufficiency, as to gifts, knowledge and utterance. Surely if the Lord sends a man to teach others, He will furnish him with the means. I believe many have intended well in setting up for preachers, who yet went beyond or before their call in so doing. The main difference between a minister and a private Christian seems to consist in these ministerial gifts, which are imparted to him, not for his own sake, but for the edification of others. But then I say, these are to appear in due season : they are not to be expected instantaneously, but gradually, in the use of proper means. They are necessary for the discharge of the ministry ; but not necessary as pre-requisites to warrant our desires after it. In your case, you are young, and have time before you ; therefore, I think you need not as yet perplex yourself with inquiring if you have these gifts already : it is sufficient if your desire is fixed, and you are willing, in the way of prayer and diligence, to wait upon the Lord for them, as yet you need them not.

3. That which finally evidences a proper call, is a correspondent opening in providence, by a gradual train of circumstances, pointing out the means, the time, the place, of actually entering upon the work. And till this coincidence arrives, you must not expect to be always clear from hesitation in your own mind. The principal caution on this head, is not to be too hasty in catching at first appearances. If it be the Lord's will to bring you into His ministry, He has already appointed your place and service ; and though you know it not at present, you shall at a proper time. If you had the talents of an angel, you could do no good with them till His hour is come, and till He leads you to the people whom He has determined to bless by your means. It is very difficult to restrain ourselves within the bounds of

prudence here ; when our zeal is warm, a sense of the love
of Christ upon our hearts, and a tender compassion for
poor sinners, are ready to prompt us to break out too soon ;
—but he that believeth shall not make haste. I was about
five years under this constraint : sometimes I thought I
must preach, though it was in the streets. I listened to
every thing that seemed plausible, and to many things which
were not so. But the Lord graciously, and as it were
insensibly, hedged up my way with thorns ; otherwise, if I
had been left to my own spirit, I should have put it quite out
of my power to have been brought into such a sphere of
usefulness, as He in His good time has been pleased to lead
me to. And I can now see clearly, that at the time I would
first have gone out, though my intention was, I hope, good
in the main, yet I overrated myself, and had not that
spiritual judgment and experience which are requisite for
so great a service. I wish you, therefore, to take time ;
and if you have a desire to enter into the Established Church,
endeavour to keep your zeal within moderate bounds,
and avoid every thing that might unnecessarily clog your
admission with difficulties. I would not have you hide your
profession, or to be backward to speak for God ; but avoid
what looks like preaching, and be content with being a
learner in the school of Christ for some years. The delay
will not be lost time ; you will be so much the more
acquainted with the Gospel, with your own heart, and with
human nature ; the last is a necessary branch of a minister's
knowledge, and can only be acquired by comparing what
passes within us, and around us, with what we read in the
word of God.

I am glad to find you have a distaste both for Arminian
and Antinomian doctrines ; but let not the mistakes of
others sit too heavy upon you. Be thankful for the grace
that has made you to differ : be ready to give a reason of
the hope that is in you, with meekness and fear ; but beware
of engaging in disputes, without evident necessity, and
some probable hope of usefulness. They tend to eat out
the life and savour of religion, and to make the soul lean and
dry. Where God has begun a real work of grace, incidental
mistakes will be lessened by time and experience ; where
He has not, it is of little signification what sentiments

people hold, or whether they call themselves Arminians or Calvinists.

I agree with you, it is time enough for you to think of Oxford yet; and that if your purpose is fixed, and all circumstances render it prudent and proper to devote yourself to the ministry, you will do well to spend a year or two in private studies. It would be further helpful, in this view, to place yourself where there is Gospel preaching, and, a lively people. If your favourable opinion of this place should induce you to come here, I shall be very ready to give you every assistance in my power. As I have trod exactly the path you seem to be setting out in, I might so far perhaps, be more serviceable than those who are in other respects much better qualified to assist you. I doubt not but in this, and every other step, you will intreat the Lord's direction; and I hope you will not forget to pray for,

Sir, your affectionate friend, &c.

LETTER II

Dear Sir,   *January* 7, 1767.

I MUST beg you (once for all) to release me from any constraint about the length or frequency of my letters. Believe that I think of you, and pray for you, when you do not hear me. Your correspondence is not quite so large as mine, therefore you may write the oftener: your letters will be always welcome; and I will write to you when I find a leisure hour, and have any thing upon my mind to offer.

You seem insensible where your most observable failing lies, and to take reproof and admonition concerning it in good part; I therefore hope and believe the Lord will give you a growing victory over it. You must not expect habits and tempers will be eradicated instantaneously; but by perseverance and prayer, and observation upon the experience of every day, much may be done in time. Now and then you will (as is usual in the course of war) lose a battle; but be not discouraged, but rally your forces, and

return to the fight. There is a comfortable word, a leaf of
the tree of life, for healing the wounds we receive, in 1 John
ii. 1. If the enemy surprises you, and your heart smites
you, do not stand astonished as if there was no help, nor give
way to sorrow as if there was no hope, nor attempt to heal
yourself; but away immediately to the throne of grace,
to the Great Physician, to the compassionate High Priest,
and tell Him all. Satan knows, that if he can keep
us from confession, our wounds will rankle; but do
you profit by David's experience, Psa. xxxii. 3-5. When
we are simple and open hearted in abasing ourselves before
the Lord, though we have acted foolishly and ungratefully,
He will seldom let us remain long, without affording us a
sense of His compassion; for He is gracious; He knows our
frame, and how to bear with us though we can hardly bear
with ourselves, or with one another.

The main thing is to have the heart right with God:
this will bring us in the end safely through many mistakes
and blunders: but a double mind, a selfish spirit, that
would halve things between God and the world, the Lord
abhors. Though I have not yet had many opportunities
of commending your prudence, I have always had a good
opinion of your sincerity and integrity; if I am not mistaken
in this, I make no doubt of your doing well. If the Lord is
pleased to bless you, He will undoubtedly make you hum-
ble; for you cannot be either happy or safe, or have any
probable hope of abiding usefulness, without it. I do not
know that I have had any thing so much at heart in my
connexions with you, as to impress you with a sense of the
necessity and advantages of an humble frame of spirit:
I hope it has not been in vain. O! to be little in our
own eyes!—this is the groundwork of every grace; this
leads to a continual dependence upon the Lord Jesus;
this is the spirit which He has promised to bless; this
conciliates us good-will and acceptance amongst men;
for he that abaseth himself is sure to be honoured. And
that this temper is so hard to attain and preserve, is a
striking proof of our depravity. For are we not sinners?
Were we not rebels and enemies before we knew the Gospel?
and have we not been unfaithful, backsliding, and unprofit-
able ever since? Are we not redeemed by the blood of

Jesus—and can we stand a single moment except He upholds us? Have we any thing which we have not received—or have we received any thing which we have not abused? Why then is dust and ashes proud?

I am glad you have found some spiritual acquaintance in your barren land. I hope you will be helpful to them, and they to you. You do well to guard against every appearance of evil. If you are heartily for Jesus, Satan owes you a grudge. One way or other he will try to cut you out work, and the Lord may suffer him to go to the length of his chain. But though you are to keep your eye upon him, and expect to hear from him at every step, you need not be slavishly afraid of him; for Jesus is stronger and wiser than he, and there is a complete suit of armour provided for all who are engaged on the Lord's side.

I am, &c.

LETTER III

DEAR SIR,   *October* 20, 1767.

A CONCERN for the perplexity you have met with, from objections which have been made against some expressions in my printed sermons, and, in general, against exhorting sinners to believe in Jesus, engages me to write immediately; otherwise I should have waited a little longer; for we are now upon the point of removing to the vicarage, and I believe this will be the last letter I shall write from the old house. I shall chiefly confine myself at present to the subject you propose.

In the first place, I beg you to be upon your guard against a reasoning spirit. Search the Scriptures; and where you can find a plain rule or warrant for any practice, go boldly on; and be not discouraged because you may not be clearly able to answer or reconcile every difficulty that may either occur to your own mind, or be put in your way by others. Our hearts are very dark and narrow, and the very root of all apostacy is a proud disposition to question the necessity or propriety of Divine appointments.

But the child-like simplicity of faith is to follow God without reasoning ; taking it for granted a thing must be right if He directs it, and charging all seeming inconsistencies to the account of our own ignorance.

I suppose the people that trouble you upon this head are of two sorts : 1st, Those that preach upon Arminian principles and suppose a free will in man, in a greater or less degree, to turn to God when the Gospel is proposed. These, if you speak to sinners at large, though they will approve of your doing so, will take occasion perhaps to charge you with acting in contradiction to our own principles. So it seems Mr. —— has said. I love and honour that man greatly, and I beg you will tell him so from me ; and tell him farther, that the reason why he is not a Calvinist, is because he misapprehends our principles. If I had a proper call, I would undertake to prove the direct contrary ; namely that to exhort and deal plainly with sinners, to stir them up to flee from the wrath to come, and to lay hold of eternal life, is an attempt not reconcileable to sober reason upon any other grounds than those doctrines which we are called Calvinists for holding ; and that all the absurdities which are charged upon us, as consequences of what we teach, are indeed truly chargeable upon those who differ from us in these points. I think this unanswerably proved by Mr. Edwards, in his discourse on the freedom of the will ; though the chain of reasoning is so close, that few will give attention and pains to pursue it. As to myself, if I were not a Calvinist, I think I should have no more hope of success in preaching to men, than to horses or cows.

But these objections are more frequently urged by Calvinists themselves ; many of them, I doubt not, good men, but betrayed into a curiosity of spirit which often makes their ministry (if ministers) dry and inefficacious, and their conversation sour and unsavoury. Such a spirit is too prevalent in many professors, that if a man discovers a warm zeal for the glory of God, and is enabled to bear a faithful testimony to the Gospel truths ; yea, though the Lord evidently blesses him, they overlook all, and will undervalue a sermon, which upon the whole they cannot but acknowledge to be Scriptural, if they meet with a single sentence contrary to the opinion they have taken up. I am sorry to see such a spirit prevailing. But this I observe, that the ministers who give in to this way, though good men and good preachers in other respects, are seldom very useful or very zealous; and those who are in private life, are more ready for dry points of disputation, at least harping upon a string of doctrines, than for experimental and heart-searching converse, whereby one may warm and edify another. Blessed be God, who has kept me and my people from this turn : if it should ever creep in or spread amongst us, I should be ready to write *Ichabod* upon our assemblies.

I advise you, therefore, to keep close to the Bible and prayer; bring your difficulties to the Lord, and entreat Him to give you, and maintain in you, a simple spirit. Search the Scriptures. How did Peter deal with Simon Magus? We have no right to think worse of any who can hear us than the apostle did of him. He seemed almost to think his case desperate, and yet he advised him to repentance and prayer. Examine the same apostle's discourse, Acts iii., and the close of St. Paul's sermon, Acts xiii. The power is all of God; the means are likewise of His appointment; and He always is pleased to work by such means as may show that the power is His. What was Moses's rod in itself; or the trumpets that threw down Jericho? What influence could the pool of Siloam have, that the eyes of the blind man by washing in it should be opened; or what could Ezekiel's feeble breath contribute to the making dry bones live? All these means were exceedingly disproportionate to the effect ; but He who ordered them to be used, accompanied them with His power. Yet if Moses had gone without his rod, if Joshua had slighted the rams' horns, if the prophet had thought it foolishness to speak to dry bones, or the blind man refused to wash his eyes, nothing could have been done. The same holds good on the present subject : I do not reason, expostulate, and persuade sinners, because I think I can prevail with them, but because the Lord hath commanded it. He directs me to address them as reasonable creatures ; to take them by every handle ; to speak to their consciences ; to tell them of the terrors of the Lord, and of His tender mercies ; to argue with them what good they find in sin ; whether they do not need a Saviour ; to put them in mind of death, judgment, and eternity, &c. When I have done all, I know it is to little purpose, except the Lord speaks to their hearts ; and this to His own, and at His own time, I am sure He will, because He has promised it. See Isaiah lv. 10, 11 ; Matt. xxviii. 20. Indeed I have heard expressions in the warmth of delivery, which I could not wholly approve, and therefore do not imitate. But, in general, I see no preaching made very useful for the gathering of souls, where poor sinners are shut out of the discourse. I think one of the closest and most moving addresses to sinners I ever met with is in Dr. Owen's Exposition of the 130th Psalm (in my edition, from p. 243 to 276). If you get it and examine it, I think you will find it all agreeable to Scripture ; and he was a steady, deep-sighted Calvinist. I wish you to study it well, and make it your pattern. He handles the same point likewise in other places, and shows the weakness of the exceptions taken somewhere at large, but I cannot just now find the passage. Many thnik themselves quite right, because they have not had their thoughts exercised at large, but have confined themselves to one track. There are extremes in everything. I pray God to show you the golden mean.

I am, &c.

LETTER IV

DEAR SIR,   *August* 30, 1770.

I WOULD steal a few minutes here to write, lest I should not have leisure at home. I have not your letter with me, and therefore can only answer so far as I retain a general remembrance of the contents.

You will doubtless find rather perplexity than advantage from the multiplicity of advice you may receive, if you endeavour to reconcile and adopt the very different sentiments of your friends. I think it will be best to make use of them in a full latitude, that is, to correct and qualify them one by another, and to borrow a little from each, without confining yourself entirely to any. You will probably be advised to different extremes, it will then be impossible to follow both ; but it may be practicable to find a middle path between them : and I believe this will generally prove the best and safest method. Only consult your own temper, and endeavour to incline rather to that side to which you are the least disposed by the ordinary strain of your own inclination ; for on that side you will be in the least danger of erring. Warm and hasty dispositions will seldom move too slowly, and those who are naturally languid and cool are as little liable to over-act their part.

With respect to the particulars you instance, I have generally thought you warm and enterprising enough, and therefore thought it best to restrain you ; but I meant only to hold you in, till you had acquired some farther knowledge and observation both of yourself and of others. I have the pleasure to hope (especially of late) that you are become more self-diffident and wary than you were some time ago. And, therefore, as your years and time are advancing, and you have been for a tolerable space under a probation of silence, I can make no objection to your attempting sometimes to speak in select societies ; but let your attempts be confined to such, I mean where you are acquainted with the people, or the leading part of them, and be upon your guard against opening yourself too much among strangers ; and again, I earnestly desire you would not attempt any thing of this sort in a very public way, which may, perhaps, bring you under inconveniences, and will be inconsistent with the part you ought to act (in my judgment) from the time you receive episcopal ordination. You may remember a simile I have sometimes used of green fruit : children are impatient to have it while it is green, but persons of more judgment will wait till it is ripe. Therefore, I would wish your exhortations to be brief, private, and not very frequent. Rather give yourself to reading, meditation, and prayer.

As to speaking without notes, in order to do it successfully, a fund of knowledge should be first possessed. Indeed, in such societies as I hope you will confine your attempts to, it would not be practicable to use notes ; but I mean, that if you design to come out as a preacher without notes from the first, you must use double diligence in study : your reading must not be confined to the Scriptures : you should be acquainted with church-history, have a general view of divinity as a system, know something of the state of controversies in past times and at present, and, indeed, of the general history of mankind. I do not mean that you should enter deeply into these things ; but you will need to have your mind enlarged, your ideas increased, your style and manner formed ; you should read, think, write, compose, and use all diligence to exercise and strengthen your faculties. If you would speak extempore as a clergyman you must be able to come off roundly, and to fill up your hour with various matter, in tolerable coherence, or else you will not be able to overcome the prejudice which usually prevails among the people. Perhaps it may be as well to use some little scheme in the note way, especially at the beginning ; but a little trial will best inform you what is the most expedient.

Let your backwardness to prayer and reading the Scripture be ever so great, you must strive against it. The backwardness, and the doubts you speak of, are partly from your own evil heart, but perhaps chiefly temptations of Satan : he knows it, if he can keep you from drawing water out of the wells of salvation, he will have much advantage. My soul goes often mourning under the same complaints, but at times the Lord gives me a little victory. I hope He will overrule all our trials to make us more humble, and dependent, and to give us tenderness of spirit towards the distressed. The exercised and experienced Christian, by the knowledge he has gained of his own heart, and the many difficulties he has had to struggle with, acquires a skill and compassion in dealing with others ; and without such exercise, all our study, diligence, and gifts in other ways, would leave us much at a loss in some of the most important parts of our calling.

You have given yourself to the Lord for the ministry ; His providence has thus far favoured your views ; therefore harbour not a thought of flinching from the battle, because the enemy appears in view, but resolve to endure hardships as a good soldier of Jesus Christ. Lift up your banner in His name ; trust in Him, and He will support you ; but, above all things, be sure not to be either enticed or terrified from the privilege of a throne of grace.

Who your enemies are, or what they say, I know not ; for I never conversed with them.   Your friends here have thought you at times harsh and hasty in your manner, and rather inclining to self-confidence.   These things I have often reminded you of ; but I considered them as blemishes usually attendant upon youth, and which experience, temptation, and prayer would correct.   I hope and believe you will do well.   You will have a share in my prayers and best advice ; and when I see occasion to offer a word of reproof, I shall not use any reserve.

Yours, &c.

LETTER V

DEAR SIR,   *July 25, 1772.*

I AM glad to hear you are accommodated at D——
where I hope your best endeavours will not be wanting to make yourself agreeable, by a humble, inoffensive, and circumspect behaviour.

I greatly approve of your speaking from one of the lessons in the afternoon : you will find it a great help to bring you gradually to that habit and readiness of expression which you desire ; and you will, perhaps, find it make more impression upon your hearers, than what you read to them from the pulpit.   However, I would not discourage or dissuade you from reading your sermons for a time. The chief inconvenience respecting yourself is that which you mention.   A written sermon is something to lean upon ; but it is best for a preacher to lean wholly upon the Lord. But set off gradually ; the Lord will not despise the day of small things : pray heartily, that your spirit may be right with Him, and then all the rest will be well.   And keep on writing : if you compose one sermon, and should find your heart enlarged to preach another, still your labour in writing will not be lost.   If your conscience bears you witness, that you desire to serve the Lord, His promise (now He has brought you into the ministry) of a sufficiency and ability for the work, belongs to you as much as to another. Your borrowing help from others may arise from a diffidence of yourself, which is not blameable ; but it may arise, in part, likewise from a diffidence of the Lord, which is hurtful. I wish you may get encouragement from that word, Exodus iv. 11, 12. It was a great encouragement to me. While I would press you to diligence in every rational means for the improvement of your stock in knowledge, and your ability of utterance, I would have you remember, that preaching is a *gift*. It cannot be learned by industry and imitation only, as a man may learn to make a chair or a table : it comes from above ; and if you patiently wait upon God, He will bestow this gift upon you, and increase it in you. It will grow by exercise. " To him that hath shall be given, and he shall have more abundantly." And be chiefly solicitous to obtain an unction upon what you do say. Perhaps those sermons in which you feel yourself most deficient, may be made most useful to others. I hope you will endeavour likewise to be plain and familiar in your language and manner, though not low or vulgar, so as to suit yourself as much as possible to the apprehensions of the most ignorant people. There are in all congregations some persons exceedingly ignorant : yet they have precious souls, and the Lord often calls such. I pray the Lord to make you wise to win souls. I hope He will. You cannot be too jealous of your own heart ; but let no such instances as Mr. —— discourage you. Cry to Him who is able to hold you up, that you may be safe, and you shall not cry in vain. It is indeed an alarming thought, that a man may pray and preach, be useful and acceptable for a time, and yet be nothing. But still the foundation of God standeth sure. I have a good hope, that I shall never have cause to repent the part I have taken in your concerns. While you keep in the path of duty, you will find it the path of safety. Be punctual in waiting upon God in secret. This is the life of everything, the only way, and the sure way, of maintaining and renewing your strength.

I am, &c.

EIGHT LETTERS

TO THE

REV. MR. ——

LETTER I

DEAR SIR, *June* 29, 1757.

I ENDEAVOUR to be mindful of you in my prayers, that you may find both satisfaction and success, and that the Lord Himself may be your Light to discover to you every part of your duty. I would earnestly press you and myself to be followers of those who have been followers of Christ ; to aim at a life of self-denial ; to renounce self-will, and to guard against self-wisdom. The less we have to do with the world the better ; and even in conversing with our brethren, we have been, and, unless we watch and pray, shall often be, ensnared. Time is precious, and opportunities once gone are gone for ever. Even by reading, and what we call studying, we may be comparatively losers. The shorter way is to be closely waiting upon God in humble, secret, fervent prayer. The treasures of wisdom and knowledge are in His hands ; and He gives bountifully, without upbraiding. On the other hand, whatever we may undertake with a sincere desire to promote His glory, we may comfortably pursue : nothing is trivial that is done for Him. In this view, I would have you, at proper intervals, pursue your studies, especially at those times when you are unfit for better work. Pray for me that I may be enabled to break through the snares of vanity that lie in my way ; that I may be crucified with Christ, and live a hidden life by faith in Him who loved me and gave Himself for me. Adieu.

276

LETTER II

DEAR SIR, *August* 31, 1757.

I WISH you much of that spirit which was in the apostle, which made him content to become all things to all men, that he might gain some. I am persuaded that love and humility are the highest attainments in the school of Christ, and the brightest evidences that He is indeed our Master. If any should seem inclined to treat you with less regard, because you are or have been a Methodist teacher, you will find forbearance, meekness, and long suffering, the most prevailing means to conquer their prejudices. Our Lord has not only taught us to expect persecution from the world (though this alone is a trial too hard to flesh and blood) but we must look for what is much more grievous to a renewed mind, to be in some respects slighted, censured, and misunderstood, even by our Christian brethren, and that, perhaps, in cases where we are really striving to promote the glory of God, and the good of souls, and cannot, without the reproach of our consciences, alter our conduct, however glad we should be to have their approbation. Therefore we are required, not only to resist the world, the flesh, and the devil, but likewise to bear one another's burdens : which plainly intimates there will be something to be borne with on all hands ; and happy indeed is he that is not offended. You may observe what unjust reports and surmises were received, even at Jerusalem, concerning the apostle Paul ; and it seems he was condemned unheard, and that by many thousands too, Acts xxi. 20, 21 ; but we do not find he was at all ruffled, or that he sought to retort anything upon them, though, doubtless, had he been so disposed, he might have found something to have charged them with in his turn ; but he calmly and willingly complied with everything in his power to soften and convince them. Let us be followers of this pattern, so far as he was a follower of Christ ; for even Christ pleased not Himself. How did He bear with the mistakes, weakness, intemperate zeal, and imprudent proposals, of His disciples while on earth; and how does He bear with the same things from you and me, and every one of His followers now ! and do we, can we, think much to bear with each other for His sake ? Have we all a full remission of ten thousand talents, which we owed him, and were utterly unable to pay, and do we wrangle amongst ourselves for a few pence ? Good forbid !

If you should be numbered among the regular Independents, I advise you not to offend any of them by unnecessary singularities. I wish you not to part with any truth, or with anything really expedient ; but if the omitting anything of an indifferent nature will obviate prejudices, and increase a mutual confidence, why should not so easy a sacrifice be made ? Above all, my dear friend, let us keep close to the Lord in a way of prayer : He giveth wisdom that is profitable to direct ; He is the Wonderful Counsellor ; there is no teacher like Him. Why do the living seek the dead ? Why do we weary our friends, and our selves, in running up and down, and turning over books for advice ? If we shut our eyes upon the world and worldly things, and raise our thoughts upwards in humility and silence, should we not often hear the secret voice of the Spirit of God whispering to our hearts, and pointing out to us the way of truth and peace ? Have we not often gone astray, and hurt either ourselves or our brethren, for want of attending to this divine instruction ? Have we not sometimes mocked God, by pretending to ask direction from Him when we had fixed our determination beforehand ? It is a great blessing to know that we are sincere ; and, next to this, to be convinced of our insincerity, and to pray against it.

I am, &c.,

LETTER III

Dear Sir,   *November* 21, 1757.

Can you forgive so negligent a correspondent ? I am indeed ashamed ; but (if that is any good excuse) I use you no worse than my other friends. Whatever I write, I am obliged to begin with an apology ; for, what with business and the incidental duties of every day, my time is always mortgaged before it comes into my hands,

especially as I have so little skill in redeeming and improving
it. I long to hear from you, and I long to see you ; and,
indeed, from the terms of yours, I expected you here before
this, which has been partly a cause of my delay. I have
mislaid your letter, and cannot remember the particulars ;
in general, I remember you were well, and going on com-
fortably in your work, which was matter of joy to me ;
and my poor prayers are for you, that the Lord may own
and prosper you more and more. The two great points we
are called to pursue in this sinful divided world, are peace
and holiness : I hope you are much in the study of them.
These are the peculiar characteristics of a disciple of Jesus ;
they are the richest part of the enjoyments of Heaven ;
and so far as they are received into the heart, they bring
down Heaven upon earth ; and they are more inseparably
connected between themselves than some of us are aware.
The longer I live, the more I see of the vanity and the
sinfulness of our unchristian disputes : they eat up the
very vitals of religion. I grieve to think how often I have
lost my time and my temper in that way, in presuming to
regulate the vineyards of others, when I have neglected my
own ; when the beam in my own eye has so contracted
my sight, that I could discern nothing but the mote in
my neighbour's. I am now desirous to choose a better
part. Could I speak the publican's words with a proper
feeling, I wish not for the tongue of men or angels to fight
about notions or sentiments. I allow that every branch of
Gospel truth is precious, that errors are abounding, and that
it is our duty to bear an honest testimony to what the Lord
has enabled us to find comfort in, and to instruct with
meekness such as are willing to be instructed ; but I cannot
see it my duty, nay, I believe it would be my sin, to attempt
to beat my notions into other people's heads. Too often
I have attempted it in time past ; but now I judge, that both
my zeal and my weapons were carnal. When our dear
Lord questioned Peter, after his fall and recovery, He said
not, Art thou wise, learned, and eloquent ? nay, he said
not, Art thou clear, and sound, and orthodox ? But this
only, " Lovest thou Me ? " An answer to this was sufficient
then ; why not now ? Any other answer, we may believe,
would have been insufficient then. If Peter had made the

most pompous confession of his faith and sentiments, still the first question would have recurred, " Lovest thou Me ? " This is a Scripture precedent. Happy the preacher, whoever he be, my heart and my prayers are with him, who can honestly and steadily appropriate Peter's answer! Such a man, I say, I am ready to hear, though he should be as much mistaken in some points as Peter afterwards appears to have been in others. What a pity it is, that Christians in succeeding ages should think the constraining force of the love of Christ too weak, and suppose the end better answered by forms, subscriptions, and questions of their own devising! I cannot acquit even those churches who judge themselves nearest the primitive rule in this respect. Alas ! will-worship and presumption may creep into the best external forms. But the misfortune both in churches and private Christians is, that we are too prone rather to compare ourselves with others, than to judge by the Scriptures ; and while each can see that they give not in to the errors and mistakes of the opposite party, both are ready to conclude that they are right : and thus it happens, that an attachment to a supposed Gospel order will recommend a man sooner and farther to some churches, than an eminency of Gospel practice. I hope you will beware of such a spirit, whenever you publicly assume the independent character ; this, like the worm at the root, has nipt the grace and hindered the usefulness, of many a valuable man ; and those who change sides and opinions are the most liable to it. For the pride of our heart insensibly prompts us to cast about, far and near, for arguments to justify our own behaviour, and makes us too ready to hold the opinions we have taken up to the very extreme, that those amongst whom we are newly come may not suspect our sincerity. In a word, let us endeavour to keep close to God, to be much in prayer, to watch carefully over our hearts, and leave the busy warm spirits to make the best of their work. The secret of the Lord is with them that fear Him, and that wait on Him continually ; to these He will show His covenant, not notionally, but experimentally. A few minutes of the Spirit's teaching will furnish us with more real useful knowledge, than toiling through whole folios of commentators and expositors ; they are useful in their places, and are not to be undervalued by those who can perhaps, in general, do better without them ; but it will be our wisdom to deal less with the streams, and be more close in applying to the fountain-head. The Scripture itself, and the Spirit of God, are the best and the only sufficient expositors of Scripture. Whatever men have valuable in their writings, they got it from hence ; and the way is as open to us as to any of them. There is nothing required but a teachable humble spirit ; and learning, as it is commonly called, is not necessary in order to this. I commend you to the grace of God, and remain,

Yours, &c.

LETTER IV

DEAR SIR, *January 10, 1760.*

    I HAVE procured Cennick's sermons ; they are in my judgment sound and sweet. O that you and I had a double portion of that spirit and unction which is in them ! Come, let us not despair ; the fountain is as full and as free as ever—precious fountain, ever flowing with blood and water, milk and wine. This is the stream that heals the wounded, refreshes the weary, satisfies the hungry, strengthens the weak, and confirms the strong ; it opens the eyes of the blind, softens the heart of stone, teaches the dumb to speak, and enables the lame and paralytic to walk, to leap, to run, to fly, to mount up with eagle's wings : a taste of this stream raises earth to Heaven, and brings down Heaven upon earth. Nor is it a fountain only ; it is a universal blessing, and assumes a variety of shapes to suit itself to our wants. It is a sun, a shield, a garment, a shade, a banner, a refuge ; it is bread, the true bread, the very staff of life ; it is life itself, immortal, eternal life !

> The cross of Jesus Christ my Lord,
> Is food and med'cine, shield and sword.

Take that for your motto ; wear it in your heart ; keep it in your eye ; have it often in your mouth, till you can find

something better. The cross of Christ is the tree of life
and the tree of knowledge combined. Blessed be God, there
is neither prohibition nor flaming sword to keep us back,
but it stands like a tree by the highway-side, which affords
its shade to every passenger without distinction. Watch
and pray. We live in sifting times : error gains ground
every day. May the name and love of our Saviour Jesus
keep us and all His people ! Either write or come very soon
to
                                              Yours, &c.

LETTER V

DEAR SIR,   *November* 15, 1760.
    IF your visit should be delayed let me have a letter.
I want either good news or good advice : to hear that
your soul prospers, or to receive something that may quicken
my own. The apostle says, " Ye know the grace of our Lord
Jesus Christ " ; alas ! we know how to say something about
it, but how faint and feeble are our real perceptions of it.
Our love to Him is the proof and measure of what we know
of His love to us. Surely, then, we are mere children in this
kind of knowledge, and every other kind is vain. What
should we think of a man who would neglect his business,
family, and all the comforts of life, that he might study
the Chinese language, though he knows beforehand he
would never be able to attain it, nor ever find occasion or
opportunity to use it ? The pursuit of every branch of
knowledge that is not closely connected with the one thing
needful, is no less ridiculous.
    You know something of our friend Mrs. B ——. She
has been more than a month confined to her bed, and I
believe her next remove will be to her coffin. The Lord has
done great things for her. Though she has been a serious,
exemplary person all her life, when the prospect of death
presented itself, she began to cry out earnestly, " What shall
I do to be saved ? " But her solicitude is at an end ; she
has seen the salvation of God, and now for the most part

rejoices in something more than hope. This you will account good news, I am sure. Let it be your encouragement and mine. The Lord's arm is not shortened, nor is His presence removed ; He is near us still, though we perceive Him not. May He guide you with His eye in all your public and private concerns, and may He in particular bless our communications to our mutual advantage !

I am, &c.

LETTER VI

DEAR SIR, *July* 29, 1761.

ARE the quarrels made up ? Tell those who know what communion with Jesus is worth, that they will never be able to maintain it if they give way to the workings of pride, jealousy, and anger. This will provoke the Lord to leave them dry, to command the clouds of His grace that they rain no rain upon them. These things are sure signs of a low frame, and a sure way to keep it so. Could they be prevailed upon, from a sense of the pardoning love of God to their own souls, to forgive each other as the Lord forgives us, freely, fully, without condition, and without reserve, they would find this like breaking down a stone wall, which has hitherto shut up their prayers from the Lord's ears, and shut out His blessing from filling their hearts. Tell them, I hope to hear that all animosities, little and big, are buried by mutual consent in the Redeemer's grave. Alas ! the people of God have enemies enough. Why, then, will they weaken their own hands ? Why will they help their enemies to pull down the Lord's work ? Why will they grieve those that wish them well, cause the weak to stumble, the wicked to rejoice, and bring a reproach upon their holy profession ? Indeed, this is no light matter : I wish it may not lead them to something worse ; I wish they may be wise in time, lest Satan gain further advantage over them, and draw them to something that shall make them (as David did) roar under the pains of broken bones. But I must break off. May God give you wisdom, faithfulness, and patience ! Take care that you do not catch an angry spirit yourself, while you aim to suppress it in others : this will spoil all, and you will exhort, advise, and weep in vain. May you rather be an example and pattern to the flock : and in this view, be not surprised if you yourself meet some hard usage ; rather rejoice, that you will thereby have an opportunity to exemplify your own rules, and to convince your people, that what you recommend to them you do not speak by *rote,* but from the experience of your heart. One end why our' Lord was tempted for the encouragement of His poor followers, that they might know Him to be a High Priest suited to them, having had a fellow-feeling in their distresses. For the like reason he appoints His ministers to be sorely exercised, both from without and within, that they may sympathize with their flock, and know in their own hearts the deceitfulness of sin, the infirmities of the flesh, and the way in which the Lord supports and bears with all that trust Him. Therefore be not discouraged ; usefulness and trials, comforts and crosses, strength and exercise, go together. But remember He has said, " I will never leave thee, nor forsake thee ; be thou faithful unto death, and I will give thee a crown of life." When you get to Heaven, you will not complain of the way by which the Lord brought you. Farewell. Pray for us.

Yours, &c.

LETTER VII

Dear Sir, *December* 14, 1761.

I pray the Lord to accompany you ; but cannot help fearing you go on too fast. If you have not (as I am sure you ought not) made an absolute promise, but only a conditional one, you need not be so solicitous ; depend upon it, when the Lord is pleased to remove you, He will send one to supply your place. I am grieved that your mind is so set upon a step which, I fear, will occasion many inconveniences to a people who have deserved your best regard. Others may speak you fairer, but none wishes you better, than myself ; therefore I hope you allow me to speak my mind plainly, and believe that it is no pleasure to me to oppose your inclinations. As to your saying they will take no denial, it has no weight with me. Had they asked what you were exceedingly averse to, you would soon have expressed yourself so as to convince them it was to no purpose to urge you ; but they saw something in your manner or language that encouraged them ; they saw the proposal was agreeable to you, that you were not at all unwilling to exchange your old friends for new ones ; and this is the reason they would take no denial. If you should live to see those who are most forward in pressing you become the first to discourage you, you will think seriously of my words.

If I thought my advice would prevail, it should be this Call the people together, and desire them (if possible) to forget you ever intended to depart from them ; and promise not to think of a removal, till the Lord shall make your way so clear, that even they shall have nothing reasonable to object against it. You may keep your word with your other friends too ; for when a proper person shall offer, as likely to please and satisfy the people as yourself, I will give my hearty consent to your removal.

Consider what it is you would have in your office, but maintenance, acceptance, and success. Have you not those where you are ? Are you sure of having them where you are going ? Are you sure the Spirit of God (without which you will do nothing) will be with you there, as He has been with you hitherto ? Perhaps, if you act in your own spirit, you may find as great a change as Samson. I am ready to weep when I think what difficulties were surmounted to accomplish your ordination ; and now, when the people thought themselves fixed, that you should so soon disappoint them.

Yours, &c.

LETTER VIII

DEAR SIR, *February* 15, 1762.

I HAVE been often thinking of you since your removal, and was glad to receive your letter to-day. I hope you will still go on to find more and more encouragement to believe, that the Lord has disposed and led you to the step you have taken. For though I wrote with the greatest plainness and earnestness, and would, if in my power, have prevented it while under deliberation, yet, now it is done and past recall, I would rather help than dishearten you. Indeed, I cannot say that my view of the affair is yet altered. The best way not to be cast down hereafter, is not to be too sanguine at first. You know there is something pleasing in novelty ; as yet you are new to them, and they to you : I pray God that you may find as cordial a regard from them as at present, when you have been with them as many years as in the place you came from. And if you have grace to be watchful and prayerful, all will be well ; for we serve a gracious Master, who knows how to over-rule even our mistakes to His glory and our own advantage. Yet I observe, that when we do wrong, sooner or later we smart for our indiscretion ; perhaps many years afterwards. After we have seen and confessed our fault, and received repeated proofs of pardoning love, as to the guilt ; yet chastisement, to remind us more sensibly of our having done amiss, will generally find us out. So it was with David in the matter of Uriah ; the Lord put away his sin, healed his broken bones, and restored unto him the light of His countenance ; yet many troubles, in consequence of this affair, followed one upon another, till at length (many years afterwards) he was driven from Jerusalem by his own son. So it was with Jacob : he dealt deceitfully with his brother Esau ; notwithstanding this, the Lord appeared to him and blessed him, gave him comfortable promises, and revealed Himself to him from time to time ; yet, after an interval of twenty years, his fault was brought afresh to his remembrance, and his heart trembled within him when he heard his brother was coming with armed men to meet him. And thus I have found it in my own experience :

things which I had forgotten a long while have been brought to my mind by providential dispensations which I little expected, but the first rise of which I have been able to trace far back, and forced to confess, that the Lord is indeed He that judgeth the heart and trieth the reins. I hint this for your caution : you know best upon what grounds you have proceeded ; but if, (though I do not affirm it, I hope otherwise,) I say, if you have acted too much in your own spirit, been too hasty and precipitate ; if you have not been sufficiently tender of your people, nor thoughtful of the consequences which your departure will probably involve them in ; if you have been impatient under the Lord's hand, and instead of waiting His time and way of removing the trials and difficulties you found, have ventured upon an attempt to free and mend yourself : I say, if any of these things have mixed with your determinations, something will fall out to show you your fault : either you will not find the success you hope for, or friends will grow cold, or enemies and difficulties you dream not of will present themselves, or your own mind will alter, so that what seems now most pleasant will afford you little pleasure. Yet though I write thus, I do not mean (as I said before) to discourage you, but that you may be fore-warned, humble, and watchful. If you should at any time have a different view of things, you may take comfort from the instances I have mentioned. The trials of David and Jacob were sharp ; but they were short, and they proved to their advantage, put them upon acts of humiliation and prayer, and ended in a double blessing. Nothing can harm us that quickens our earnestness and frequency in applying to a throne of grace : only trust the Lord and keep close to Him, and all that befalls you shall be for good. Temptations end in victory ; troubles prove an increase of consolation ; yea, our very falls and failings tend to increase our spiritual wisdom, to give us a greater knowledge of Satan's devices, and make us more habitually upon our guard against them. Happy case of the believer in Jesus ! when bitten by the fiery serpent he needs not go far for a remedy ; he has only to look to a bleeding Saviour, and be healed.

I think one great advantage that attends a removal

into a new place is, that it gives an easy opportunity of forming a new plan, and breaking off any little habits which we have found inconvenient, and yet perhaps could not so readily lay aside where our customs and acquaintance had been long formed. I earnestly recommend to you to reflect, if you cannot recollect some things which you have hitherto omitted, which may properly be now taken up ; some things formerly allowed, which may now with ease and convenience be laid aside. I only give the hint in general ; for I have nothing in particular to charge you with. I recommend to you to be very choice of your time, especially the fore part of the day ; let your morning hours be devoted to prayer, reading, and study ; and suffer not the importunity of friends to rob you of the hours before noon, without a just necessity : and if you accustom yourself to rise early in the morning, you will find a great advantage. Be careful to avoid losing your thoughts, whether in books or otherwise, upon any subjects which are not directly subservient to your great design, till towards dinner time ; the afternoon is not so favourable to study ; this is a proper time for paying and receiving visits, conversing among your friends, or unbending with a book of instructive entertainment, such as history, &c., which may increase your general knowledge, without a great confinement of your attention ; but let the morning hours be sacred. I think you would likewise find advantage in using your pen more ; write short notes upon the Scriptures you read, or transcribe the labours of others ; make extracts from your favourite authors, especially those who, besides a fund of spiritual and evangelical matter, have a happy talent of expressing their thoughts in a clear and lively, or pathetic manner ; you would find a continued exercise in this way would be greatly useful to form your own style, and help your delivery and memory ; you would become insensibly master of their thoughts, and find it more easy to express yourself justly and clearly : what we only read we easily lose, but what we commit to paper is not so soon forgotten. Especially remember, (what you well know, but we cannot too often remind each other,) that frequent secret prayer is the life of all we do.   If any man lack wisdom let him ask of God, and it shall be given ; but all our diligence will fail if we are remiss in this particular. I am glad it is not thought necessary for you to go to London on this occasion. I hope you will not think it necessary upon any other account. Rather keep close to the work you have undertaken, and endeavour to avoid anything that looks like ostentation, or a desire to be taken notice of. You see I advise you with the freedom of a friend who loves you, and longs to see your work and your soul prosper.

You will, I doubt not, endeavour to promote the practice of frequent prayer in the houses that receive you. I look upon prayer-meetings as the most profitable exercises (excepting the public preaching) in which Christians can engage ; they have a direct tendency to kill a worldly, trifling spirit, to draw down a Divine blessing upon all our concerns, compose differences, and enkindle (at least to maintain) the flame of Divine love amongst brethren. But I need not tell you the advantages ; you know them : I only would exhort you ; and the rather, as I find in my own case the principal cause of my leanness and unfruitfulness is owing to an unaccountable backwardness to pray. I can write, or read, or converse, or hear, with a ready will ; but prayer is more spiritual and inward than any of these ; and the more spiritual any duty is, the more my carnal heart is apt to start from it. May the Lord pour forth His precious spirit of prayer and supplication in both our hearts !

I am not so well pleased with the account you give of so many dry bones. It increases my wonder that you could so readily exchange so much plump flesh and blood as you had about you, for a parcel of skeletons. I wish they may not haunt you, and disturb your peace. I wish these same dry bones do not prove thorns in your sides and in your eyes. You say, now you have to pray and prophesy, and wait for the four winds to come and put life into those bones. God grant that your prayers may be answered ; but if I knew a man who possessed a field in a tolerable soil, which had afforded him some increase every year ; and if this man, after having bestowed seven years' labour in cultivating, weeding, manuring, fencing, &c., just when he has brought his ground (in his neighbour's judgment) into good order, and might reasonably hope for larger crops than he had ever yet seen, should suddenly forego all his advantages, leave his good seed for the birds to eat, pull up the young fences which cost him so much pains to plant, and all this for the sake of making a new experiment upon the top of a mountain, though I might heartily wish him great success, I could not honestly give him great encouragement. You have parted with that for a trifle, which in my eyes seems an inestimable jewel; I mean the hearts and affections of an enlightened people. This appears to me, one of the greatest honours and greatest pleasures a faithful minister can possess, and which many faithful and eminent ministers have never been able to obtain. This gave you a vast advantage ; your gift was more acceptable there than that of any other person, and more than you will probably find elsewhere. For I cannot make a comparison between the hasty approbation of a few, whose eyes are but beginning to open, and their affections and passions warm, so that they must, if possible, have the man that first catches their attention; I say I cannot think this worthy to be compared to the regard of a people who understood the Gospel, were able to judge of men and doctrines, and had trial of you for so many years. It is, indeed, much to your honour, (it proves that you were faithful, diligent, and exemplary,) that the people proved so attached to you ; but that you should force yourself from them, when they so dearly loved you, and so much needed you, this has made all your friends in these parts to wonder, and your enemies to rejoice ; and I, alas ! know not what to answer in your behalf to either. Say not, " I hate this Micaiah, for he prophesies not good of me, but evil " ; but allow me the privilege of a friend. My heart is full when I think of what has happened, and what will probably be the consequence. In a few words, I am strongly persuaded you have taken an unadvised step, and would therefore prepare you for the inconvenience and uneasiness you may probably meet with. And if I am (as I desire I may prove) mistaken, my advice will do no harm ; you will want something to balance the caresses and success you meet with.

We should be very glad to see you, and hope you will take your measures, when you do come, to lengthen your usual stay, in proportion to the difference of the distance. Pray for us. I am, &c.

FOUR LETTERS

TO

MRS. P——

LETTER 1

My Dear Madam,   *May* — 1774.

I HAVE had sudden notice, that I may send you a hasty line, to express our satisfaction in hearing that you had a safe though perilous journey : I hope I shall be always mindful to pray that the Lord may guide, bless, and comfort you, and give you such a manifestation of His person, power, and grace, as may set you at liberty from all fear, and fill you with abiding peace and joy in believing. Remember that Jesus has all power, the fulness of compassion, and embraces with open arms all that come to Him for life and salvation.

I know not whether Mrs. ——'s illness was before or since my last. Through mercy she is better again ; and I remain so, though death and illness are still walking about the town. O for grace to take warning by the sufferings of others, and sit loose to the world, and so number our days as to incline our hearts to the one thing needful ! Indeed, that one thing includes many things, sufficient to engage the best of our thoughts and the most of our time, if we were duly sensible of their importance : but I may adopt the Psalmist's expression, " My soul cleaveth to the dust." How is it that the truths of which I have the most undoubted conviction, and which are of all others the most weighty, should make so little impression upon me ? Oh ! I know the cause ; it is deeply rooted. An evil nature cleaves to me ; so that when I would do good, evil is present with me. It is, however, a mercy to be made sensible of it, and in any measure humble for it. Ere long it will be dropped in the grave ; then all compliments shall cease. That thought gives relief. I shall not always live this poor dying life ; I hope one day to be all ear, all heart, all tongue ; when I shall see the Redeemer as He is, I shall be like Him. This will be a Heaven indeed, to behold His glory without a veil, to rejoice in His love without a cloud, and to sing His praises, without one jarring or wandering note, for ever. In the mean time, may He enable us to serve Him with our best. O that every power, faculty, and talent, were devoted to Him ! He deserves all we have, and ten thousand times more if we had it ; for He has loved us, and washed us from our sins in His own blood. He gave Himself for us. In one sense, we are well suited to answer His purpose ; for if we were not vile and worthless beyond expression, the exceeding riches of His grace would not have been so gloriously displayed. His glory shines more in redeeming one sinner, than in preserving a thousand angels. Poor Mr. —— is still in the dark valley, but we trust prayer shall yet bring him out. Mighty things have been done in answer to prayer, and the Lord's arm is not shortened, neither is His ear heavy. It is our part to wait till we have an answer. One of His own hymns says,

> The promise may be long deferr'd,
> But never comes too late.

I suppose you have heard of the death of Mr. T——, of R——. This is apparently a heavy blow. He was an amiable, judicious, candid man, and an excellent preacher, in a great sphere of usefulness ; and his age and constitution gave hopes that he might have been eminently serviceable for many years. How often does the Lord write "vanity" upon all our expectations from men. He visited a person ill of a putrid fever, and carried the seeds of infection with him to London, where he died. Mrs. —— is a very excellent and accomplished woman, but exceedingly delicate in her frame and spirits. How can she bear so sudden and severe a stroke ! But yet I hope she will afford a proof of the Lord's all-sufficiency and faithfulness. Oh, Madam, the Lord our God is a great God ! If He frowns, the smiles of the whole creation can afford no comfort ; and if He is pleased to smile, He can enable the soul under the darkest dispensations to say, " All is well." Yet the flesh will feel, and it ought ; otherwise the exercise of faith, patience, and resignation, would be impracticable. I have lost in him one of my most valued and valuable friends ; but what is my loss to that of his people ?

The Lord bless you and keep you. The Lord increase you more and more, you and your children. The Lord lift up the light of His countenance upon you, and give you His peace. I thank Him for leading you to us, but especially for making your visit there in any measure agreeable and profitable to yourself. If I have been an instrument in His hand for your comfort, I have reason to remember it among the greatest favours He has conferred upon me. And now, dear Madam, once more, farewell. If the Lord spares our lives, I hope we shall see each other again upon earth. But above all, let us rejoice in the blessed Gospel, by which immortality is brought to light, and a glorious prospect opened beyond the grave.

> There sits our Saviour thron'd in light,
> Clothed with a body like our own.

There at last, after all the changes and trials of this state, we shall meet to part no more.

I am, &c.

LETTER II

My Dear Madam, 1775.

I should have been more uneasy at being prevented writing immediately, had I any reason to apprehend my advice necessary upon the point you propose, which by this time I suppose is settled as it should be without me. I smiled at Miss M——'s disappointment. However, if the Lord favours her with a taste for the library of my proposing, she will be like the merchant man seeking goodly pearls, and will count all other books but pebbles in comparison of those four volumes, which present us with something new and important whenever we look into them.   I shall be much obliged to her, if she will commit the third chapter of Proverbs to her memory, and I shall pray the Lord to write it in her heart.

You surprise me when you tell me that the incident of my birthday was noticed by those I never saw.   Be so good as to return my thanks to my unknown friends, and tell them that I pray our common Lord and Saviour to bless them abundantly.   His people, while here, are scattered abroad, separated by hills and rivers, and too often by names and prejudices ; but, by and bye, we shall all meet where we shall all know and acknowledge each other, and rejoice together for evermore.   I have lately read with much pleasure, and I hope with some profit, the history of the Greenland Mission.   Upon the whole, it is a glorious work. None who love the Lord will refuse to say, it is the finger of God indeed.   For my own part, my soul rejoices in it ; and I honour the instruments, as men who have hazarded their lives in an extraordinary manner for the sake of the Lord Jesus.   Sure I am, that none could have sustained such discouragements at first, or have obtained such success afterwards, unless the Lord had sent, supported, and owned them.

I hope we shall have an interest in your prayers.   I trust the Lord is yet with us.   We have some ripe for the sickle, and some just springing up ; some tokens of His gracious presence amongst us ; but sin and Satan cut us out abundance of work as individuals, though, through mercy, as a society we walk in peace.

The " toad and spider " is an exhibition of my daily experience.   I am often wounded, but the Lord is my health.   Still I am a living monument of mercy ; and I trust that word, " Because I live, you shall live also," will carry me to the end.   I am poor, weak, and foolish ; but Jesus is wise, strong, and abounding in grace.   He has given me a desire to trust my all in His hands, and He will not disappoint the expectation which He Himself has raised. At present I have but little to say, and but little time to say it in.   When you think of this place, I hope you will think and believe, that you have friends here most cordially interested in your welfare, and often remembering you in

prayer.   May the Lord be your guide and shield, and give
you the best desires of your heart !   I pray Him to establish
and settle you in the great truths of His word.   I trust He
will.   We learn more, and more effectually, by one minute's
communication with Him through the medium of His
written word, than we could from an assembly of divines, or
a library of books.

I am, &c.

LETTER III

My Dear Madam,   *August* 17, 1775.

It is not owing to forgetfulness that your letter has been
thus long unanswered.   It has lain within my view this
fortnight, demanding my first leisure hour ;   but affairs of
daily occurrence have been so many and so pressing, that
I have been constrained to put it off till now.   I trust the
Lord, by His Spirit and providence, will direct and prosper
the settlement of your children.   I desire my love to Miss
M——.   My idea of her enlarges.   Methinks I see her
aspiring to be as tall as her mamma.   I hope, likewise, that
she increases in grace and wisdom, as in years and stature ;
and that hearing our Lord's flock is a little flock, she feels
an earnest thirst to be one of the happy number which
constitutes His fold.

> There the Lord dwells amongst them upon His own hill,
> With the flocks all around Him, awaiting His will.

If she has such a desire, I can tell who gave it her, for I am
persuaded it was not born with her :   and where the good
Husbandman sows, there will He also reap.   Therefore,
dear Miss M——, press forward :   knock, and it shall be
opened unto you, for yet there is room.   O what a fold !
O what a pasture !   O what a Shepherd !   Let us love,
and sing, and wonder.

I hope the good people at Bristol, and everywhere else,
are praying for our sinful distracted land, in this dark day.
The Lord is angry, the sword is drawn, and I am afraid

nothing but the spirit of wrestling prayer can prevail for the returning it into the scabbard. Could things have proceeded to these extremities except the Lord had withdrawn his salutary blessing from both sides? It is a time of prayer. We see the beginning of trouble, but who can foresee the possible consequences? The fire is kindled, but how far it may spread, those who are above may, perhaps, know better than we. I meddle not with the disputes of party, nor concern myself about any political maxims, but such as are laid down in Scripture. There I read that righteousness exalteth a nation, and that sin is the reproach, and if persisted in, the ruin, of any people. Some people are startled at the enormous sum of our national debt : they who understand spiritual arithmetic, may be well startled if they sit down and compute the debt of national sin. *Imprimis*, Infidelity : *Item*, Contempt of the Gospel : *Item*, The profligacy of manners : *Item*, Perjury : *Item*, The cry of blood, the blood of thousands, perhaps millions, from the East Indies. It would take sheets, yea, quires, to draw out the particulars under each of these heads, and then much would remain untold. What can we answer, when the Lord saith, " Shall not I visit for these things? Shall not my soul be avenged on such a nation as this ? " Since we received the news of the first hostilities in America, we have had an additional prayer-meeting. Could I hear that professors in general, instead of wasting their breath in censuring men and measures, were plying the throne of grace I should still hope for a respite. Poor New England ! once the glory of the earth, now likely to be visited with fire and sword. They have left their first love, and the Lord is sorely contending with them. Yet surely their sins as a people are not to be compared with ours. I am just so much affected with these things as to know that I am not affected enough. Oh ! my spirit is sadly cold and insensible, or I should lay them to heart in a different manner : yet I endeavour to give the alarm as far as I can. There is one political maxim which comforts me, " The Lord reigns." His hand guides the storm ; and He knows them that are His, how to protect, support, and deliver them. He will take care of His own cause, yea, he will extend His kingdom, even by these formidable methods. Men have one thing in view, He has another ; and His counsel shall stand.

The chief piece of news since my last is concerning B. A. She has finished her course, and is now with the great multitude who have overcome by the blood of the Lamb, and by the word of His testimony. Tuesday, the 1st of February, she was in our assembly, was taken ill the next day, and died while we were assembled the Tuesday following. She had an easy dissolution, retained her senses and her speech till the last minute, and went without a struggle or a sigh. She was not in raptures during her illness, but was composed, and maintained a strong and lively faith. She had a numerous levee about her bed daily, who were all witnesses to the power of faith, and to the faithfulness of the Lord, enabling her to triumph over the approaches of death ; for she was well known and well respected. She will be much missed ; but I hope He will answer the many prayers she put up for us, and raise up others in her room. " Blessed are the dead who die in the Lord." Blessed are they who know whom they have believed, and when death comes, can cheerfully rest their hopes on Him who died that we might live. B—— had been long a precious and honourable woman ; but her hope in the trying hour rested not on what she had done for the Lord, but upon what He had done for her ; not upon the change His grace had wrought in her, but upon the righteousness He had wrought out for her by His obedience unto death. This supported her, for she saw nothing in herself but what she was ashamed of. She saw reason to renounce her own goodness, as well as her own sins, as to the point of acceptance with God, and died, as St. Paul lived, " determined to know nothing but Jesus Christ and Him crucified."

The time when Mr. and Mrs. C—— remove to Scotland drawing near, Mrs. —— is gone to spend a week or two with them, and take her leave. She feels something at parting with a sister, who is indeed a valuable person ; and from children with whom they have always lived in the most tender intimacy and uninterrupted friendship. But all beneath the moon (like the moon itself) is subject to incessant change. Alterations and separations are graciously appointed of the Lord, to remind us that this is not our rest, and to prepare our thoughts for that approaching change which shall fix us for ever in an unchangeable state. O, Madam! what shall we poor worms render to Him who has brought life and immortality to light by the Gospel, taken away the sting of death, revealed a glorious prospect beyond the grave, and given us eyes to see it? Now the reflection, that we must ere long take a final farewell of what is most capable of pleasing us upon earth, is not only tolerable, but pleasant. For we know we cannot fully possess our best Friend, our chief Treasure, till we have done with all below: nay, we cannot till then properly see each other. We are cased up in vehicles of clay, and converse together, as if we were in different coaches, with the blinds close drawn round. We see the carriage, and the voice tells us that we have a Friend within; but we shall know each other better, when death shall open the coach doors, and hand out the company successively, and lead them into the glorious apartments which the Lord has appointed to be the common residence of them that love Him. What an assembly will there be! What a constellation of glory, when each individual shall shine like the sun in the kingdom of their Father! No sins, sorrows, temptations; no veils, clouds, or prejudices, shall interrupt us then. All names of idle distinction (the fruits of present remaining darkness, the channels of bigotry, and the stumbling-block of the world) will be at an end.

The description you give of your present residence pleases me much, and chiefly because it describes and manifests to me something still more interesting, I mean the peaceable situation of your mind. Had He placed you in an Eden some months ago it would hardly have awakened your descriptive talent. But He whom the winds and seas obey has calmed your mind, and I trust will go on to fill you with all joy and peace in believing. It is no great matter where we are, provided we see that the Lord has placed us there, and that He is with us.

I am, &c.

LETTER IV

1766.

So, my dear Madam, I hope we have found you out, and that this letter will reach you in good time to welcome you in our names to London. We are ready to take it for granted, that you will now most certainly make us a visit. Do come as soon, and stay as long as you possibly can. Methinks you will be glad to get out of the smell and noise as soon as possible. If we did not go to London now and then, we should perhaps forget how people live there. Especially I pity professors ; they are exposed to as many dangers as people who live in mines ; chilling damps, scorching blasts, epidemical disorders, owing to the impure air. Such are the winds of false doctrines, the explosions of controversy, the blights of worldly conversation, the contagion of evil custom. In short, a person had need have a good constitution of grace, and likewise to be well supplied with antidotes, to preserve a tolerable share of spiritual health in such a situation.

And now, how shall I fill up the rest of the paper ? It is a shame for a Christian and a minister to say he has no subject at hand, when the inexhaustible theme of redeeming love is ever pressing upon our attention. I will tell you, then, though you know it, that the Lord reigns. He who once bore our sins, and carried our sorrows, is seated upon a throne of glory, and exercises all power in Heaven, and on earth. Thrones, principalities, and powers, bow before Him. Every event in the kingdoms of providence and of grace is under His rule. His providence pervades and manages the whole, and is as minutely attentive to every part, as if there were only that single object in His view. From the tallest archangel to the meanest ant or fly, all depend on Him for their being, their preservation, and their powers. He directs the sparrows where to build their nests, and to find their food. He overrules the rise and fall of nations, and bends with an invincible energy and unerring wisdom, all events ; so that, while many intend nothing less, in the issue their designs all concur and coincide in the accomplishment of His holy will. He restrains, with a mighty hand the still more formidable efforts of the powers of darkness ; and Satan, and all his hosts, cannot exert their malice a hair's breadth beyond the limits of His permission. This is He who is the Head and Husband of His believing people. How happy are they whom it is His good pleasure to bless ! How safe are they whom He has engaged to protect ! How honoured and privileged are they to whom He is pleased to manifest Himself, and whom He enables and warrants to claim Him as their friend and their portion ! Having redeemed them by His own blood, he sets a high value upon them ; He esteems them His treasure, His jewels, and keeps them as the apple of His eye. They shall not want ; they need not fear ; His eye is upon them in every situation, His ear is open to their prayers, and His ever-lasting arms are under them for their sure support. On earth, He guides their steps, controls their enemies, and directs all His dispensations for their good ; while in Heaven, He is pleading their cause, preparing them a place, and communicating down to them reviving foretastes of the glory that shall be shortly revealed. O how is this mystery hidden from an unbelieving world ! Who can believe, till it is made known by experience, what an intercourse is maintained in this land of shadows between the Lord of glory and sinful worms ? How should we praise Him that He has visited us ; for we were once blind to His beauty and insensible to His love, and should have remained so to the last, had He not prevented us with His goodness, and been found of us when we sought Him not.

Mrs. —— presents her love The bite of the leech, which I mentioned to you, has confined her to the house ever since ; but I hope she will be able to go out to-morrow. We were for a while apprehensive of worse consequences ; but the Lord is gracious ; He shows us, in a variety of instances, what dependent creatures we are ; how blind to events, and how easily the method which we take to relieve ourselves from a small inconvenience may plunge us into a greater. Thus we learn (happy, indeed, if we can effectually learn it) that there is no safety but in His protection, and that nothing can do us good but by His blessing. As for myself, I see so many reasons why He might contend with me, that I am amazed He affords me and mine so much peace, and appoints us so few trials. We live as upon a field of battle ;

many are hourly suffering and falling around us, and I can give no reason why we are preserved, but that He is God, and not man. What a mercy that we are only truly known to Him who is alone able to bear us !

May the Lord bless you and yours ; may He comfort you, guide you, and guard you ! Come quickly to

Yours, &c.

SIX LETTERS

LETTER I

REV. AND DEAR SIR,   *Sept.* 14, 1765.

WHEN I was at London in June last, your name first
reached me, and from that time I have been desirous to
wish you success in the name of the Lord.   A few weeks
ago I received a further account from Mrs. ——, with a
volume of your sermons : she likewise gave me a direction
where to write, and an encouragement that a letter would
not be unacceptable.   The latter, indeed, I did not much
need when I had read your book.   Though we have no
acquaintance, we are already united in the strictest ties of
friendship, partakers of the same hope, servants of the same
Lord, and in the same part of His vineyard : I, therefore,
hold all apologies needless.   I rejoice in the Lord's goodness
to you ; I pray for His abundant blessing upon your labours ;
I need an interest in your prayers ; I have an affectionate
desire to know more concerning you :   these are my motives
for writing.

Mrs. —— tells me that you have read my Narrative ;
I need not tell you, therefore, that I am one of the most
astonishing instances of the forbearance and mercy of God
upon the face of the earth.   In the close of it, I mention a
warm desire I had to the ministry : this the Lord was pleased
to keep alive for several years, through a succession of views
and disappointments.   At length His hour came, and my
way was made easy.   I have been here about fifteen months.
The Lord has led me by a way that I little expected, to a
pleasant lot, where the Gospel has been many years known,

and is highly valued by many. We have a large Church and congregation, and a considerable number of lively, thriving believers ; and in general, go on with great comfort and harmony. I meet with less opposition from the world than is usual where the Gospel is preached. This burden was borne by Mr. B—— for ten years, and in that course of time, some of the fiercest opposers were removed, some wearied, and some softened ; so that we are now remarkably quiet in that respect. May the Lord teach us to improve the privilege, and preserve us from indifference ! How unspeakable are our obligations to the grace of God ! What a privilege is it to be a believer ! They are comparatively few, and we by nature were no nearer than others ; it was grace, free grace, that made the difference. What an honour to be a minister of the everlasting Gospel ! These upon comparison are perhaps fewer still. How wonderful that one of these few should be sought for among the wilds of Africa, reclaimed from the lowest state of impiety and misery, and brought to assure other sinners, from His own experience that " there is, there is forgiveness with Him, that He may be feared ! " And you, Sir, though not left to give such flagrant proofs of the wickedness of the heart and the power of Satan, yet owe your present views to the same almighty grace. If the Lord had not distinguished you from your brethren, you would have been now in the character of a minister misleading the people, and opposing those precious truths you are now labouring to establish. Not unto us, O Lord ! but unto Thy name, be the glory. I shall be thankful to hear from you at your leisure. Be pleased to inform me, whether you received the knowledge of the truth before or since you were in orders ; how long you have preached the joyful sound of salvation by Jesus, and what is the state of things in your parts.

We are called to an honourable service, but it is arduous. What wisdom does it require to keep the middle path in doctrines, avoiding the equally dangerous errors on the right hand and on the left ! What steadiness, to speak the truth boldly and faithfully in the midst of a gainsaying world ! What humility, to stand against the tide of popularity ! What meekness, to endure all things for the elect's sake, that they may be saved ! " Who is sufficient for these things ? " We are not in ourselves, but there is an all-sufficiency in Jesus. Our enemy watches us close ; he challenges and desires to have us, that he may sift us as wheat ; he knows he can easily shake us if we are left to ourselves; but we have a Shepherd, a Keeper, who never slumbers nor sleeps. If He permits us to be exercised, it is for our good ; He is at hand to direct, moderate, and sanctify every dispensation ; He has prayed for us that our faith may not fail and He has promised to maintain His fear in our hearts, that we may not depart from Him. When we are prone to wander, He calls us back ; when we say, " My feet slip," His mercy holds us up ; when we are wounded, He heals ; when we are ready to faint, He revives. The people of God are sure to meet with enemies, but especially the ministers : Satan bears them a double grudge : the world watches for their halting, and the Lord will suffer them to be afflicted, that they may be kept humble, that they may acquire a sympathy with the sufferings of others, that they may be experimentally quali-fied to advise and help them, and to comfort them with the comforts with which they themselves have been comforted of God. But the Captain of our salvation is with us ; His eye is upon us, His everlasting arm beneath us ; in His name, therefore, may we go on, lift up our banners, and say, " If God be for us, who can be against us ? Nay, in all these things we are more than conquerors, through Him that has loved us." The time is short : yet a little while, and He will wipe all tears from our eyes, and put a crown of life upon our heads with His own gracious hand. In this sense, how beautiful are those lines :—

> Temporis illius
> Me consolor imagine
> Festis quum populus me reducet choris,
> Faustisque excipiet vocibus, et Dei
> Pompa cum celebri, me comitabitur
> Augusta ad penetralia.
>
> BUCH, in Ps. 32.

If any occasions should call you into these parts, my house and pulpit will be glad to receive you. Pray for us, dear Sir, and believe me to be

Yours, &c.

LETTER II

Very Dear Sir,   *Nov.* 2, 1765.

YOUR letter of the 4th ult. gave me great pleasure. I thank you for the particular account you have favoured me with. I rejoice with you, sympathize with you, and find my heart opened to correspond with unreserved freedom. May the Lord direct our pens, and help us to help each other The work you are engaged in is great, and your difficulties many ; but faithful is He that hath called you, who also will do it. The weapons which He has now put into your hands are not carnal, but mighty through God to the pulling down of strongholds. Men may fight, but they shall not prevail against us, if we are but enabled to put our cause simply into the Lord's hands, and keep steadily on in the path of duty. He will plead our cause and fight our battles ; He will pardon our mistakes, and teach us to do better. My experience as a minister is but small, having been but about eighteen months in the vineyard ; but for about twelve years I have been favoured with an increasing acquaintance among the people of God, of various ranks and denominations, which, together with the painful exercises of my own heart, gave me opportunity of making observations which were of great use to me when I entered upon the work myself : and ever since, I have found the Lord graciously supplying new lights and new strength as new occurrences arise. So I trust it will be with you. I endeavour to avail myself of the examples, advice, and sentiments of my brethren ; yet at the same time to guard against calling any man master. This is the prerogative of Christ. The best are but men ; the wisest may be mistaken ; and that which may be right in another might be wrong in me, through a difference of circumstances. The Spirit of God distributes variously, both in gifts and dispensations ; and I would no more be tied to act strictly by others' rules, than to walk in shoes of the same size. My shoes must fit my own feet.

I endeavour to guard against extremes : our nature is prone to them ; and we are liable likewise, when we have found the inconvenience of one extreme, to revert insensibly

c.   u

(sometimes to fly suddenly) to the other. I pray to be led in the midst of the path. I am what they call a Calvinist ; yet there are flights, niceties, and hard sayings, to be found among some of that system, which I do not choose to imitate. I dislike those sentiments against which you have borne your testimony in the note at the end of your preface ; but having known many precious souls in that party, I have been taught, that the kingdom of God is not in names and ,'sentiments, but in righteousness, faith, love, peace, and joy in the Holy Ghost. I should, however, upon some occasions, oppose those tenets, if they had any prevalence in my neighbourhood ; but they have not ; and in general, I believe, the surest way to refute or prevent error is to preach the truth. I am glad to find you are aware of that spirit of enthusiasm which has so often broken loose and blemished hopeful beginnings, and that the foundation you build upon is solid and Scriptural : this will, I hope, save you much trouble, and prevent many offences. Let us endeavour to make our people acquainted with the Scripture, and to impress them with a high sense of its authority, excellence, and sufficiency. Satan seldom remarkably imposes on ministers or people, except where the Word of God is too little consulted or regarded. Another point in which I aim at a medium, is in what is called *prudence.* There is certainly such a thing as Christian prudence, and a remarkable deficiency of it is highly inconvenient. But caution too often degenerates into cowardice ; and if the fear of man, under the name of prudence, gets within our guard, like a chilling frost it nips everything in the bud. Those who trust the Lord, and act openly, with an honest freedom and consistence, I observe He generally bears out, smooths their way, and makes their enemies their friends, or at least restrains their rage ; while such as halve things, temporize, and aim to please God and men together, meet with double disappointment, and are neither useful nor respected. If we trust to Him, He will stand by us ; if we regard men, He will leave us to make the best we can of them.

I have set down hastily what occurred to my pen, not to dictate to you, but to tell you how I have been led, and because some expressions in your letter seemed to imply that you would not be displeased with me for so doing. As to books, I think there is a medium here likewise. I have read too much in time past ; yet I do not wholly join with some of our brethren, who would restrain us entirely to the Word of God. Undoubtedly this is the fountain ; here we should dwell : but a moderate and judicious perusal of other authors may have its use ; and I am glad to be beholden to such helps, either to explain what I do not understand, or to confirm me in what I do. Of these, the writings of the last age afford an immense variety.

But, above all, may we, dear Sir, live and feed upon the precious promises, John xiv. 16, 17, 26 ; and xvi. 13—15. There is no teacher like Jesus, who, by His Holy Spirit, reveals Himself in His word to the understanding and affections of His children. When we thus behold His glory in the Gospel glass, we are changed into the same image. Then our hearts melt, our eyes flow, our stammering tongues are unloosed. That this may be your increasing experience is the prayer of, dear Sir,

Yours, &c.

LETTER III

Dear Sir, *Jan. 21, 1766.*

Your letters gave me the sincerest pleasure. Let us believe that we are daily thinking of and praying for each other, and write when opportunity offers, without apologies. I praise the Lord, that He has led so soon to a settled judgment in the leading truths of the Gospel. For want of this, many have been necessitated, with their own hands, to pull down what, in the first warm emotions of their zeal, they had laboured hard to build. It is a mercy likewise, to be enabled to acknowledge what is excellent in the writings or conduct of others, without adopting their singularities, or discarding the whole on account of a few blemishes. We should be glad to receive instruction from all, and avoid being led by the *ipse dixit* of any. *Nullus jurare in verbum,* is a fit motto for those who have one Master, even Christ. We may grow wise apace in opinions, by books and men ;

but vital experimental knowledge can only be received from the Holy Spirit, the great Instructor and Comforter of His people. And there are two things observable in His teaching : 1. That He honours the means of His own appointment, so that we cannot expect to make any great progress without diligence on our parts : 2. That He does not teach all at once, but by degrees. Experience is His school ; and by this I mean the observation and improvement of what, passeth between us and around us in the course of every day. The Word of God affords a history in miniature of the heart of man, the devices of Satan, the state of the world, and the method of grace. And the most instructing and affecting commentary on it, to an enlightened mind may be gathered from what we see, feel, and hear, from day to day. *Res, ætas, usus semper aliquid apportent novi;* and no knowledge in spiritual things but what we acquire in this way is properly our own, or will abide the time of trial. This is not always sufficiently considered : we are ready to expect that others should receive upon our word, in half an hour's time, those views of things which have cost us years to attain. But none can be brought forward faster than the Lord is pleased to communicate inward light. Upon this ground, controversies have been multiplied among Christians to little purpose ; for plants of different standings will be (*cæteris paribus*) in different degrees of forwardness. A young Christian is like a green fruit : it has perhaps a disagreeable austerity, which cannot be corrected out of its proper course ; it wants time and growth ; wait a while, and by the nourishment it receives from the root, together with the action of the sun, wind, and rain, in succession from without, it will insensibly acquire that flavour and maturity, for the want of which an unskilful judge would be ready to reject it as nothing worth. We are favoured with many excellent books in our tongue, but I with you agree in assigning one of the first places (as a teacher) to Dr. Owen. I have just finished his discourse on the Holy Spirit, which is an epitome, if not the masterpiece, of his writings. I should be glad to see the republication you speak of ; but I question if the booksellers will venture upon it. I shall perhaps mention it to my London friends. As to Archbishop Leighton, besides his select works, there are two octavo volumes published at Edinburgh, in the year 1748, and since reprinted at London. They contain a valuable commentary on St. Peter's First Epistle, and lectures on Isa. vi. Psal. xxxix. cxxx. iv. and a part of Rom. xii. I have likewise a small quarto in Latin of his Divinity Lectures, when Professor at Edinburgh : the short title is *Prælectiones Theologiæ.* Mine was printed in London, 1698. I believe this book is scarce ; I set the highest value upon it. He has wonderfully united the simplicity of the Gospel with all the captivating beauties of style and language. Bishop Burnet says, he was the greatest master of the Latin tongue he ever knew, of which together with his compass of learning he has given proof in his Lectures ; yet in his gayer dress, his eminent humility and spirituality appear to no less advantage than when clad in plain English. I think it may be said to be a diamond set in gold. I could wish it translated, if it was possible (which I almost question) to preserve the beauty and spirit of the original.

Edwards on Free-will I have read with pleasure, as a good answer to the proud reasoners in their own way ; but a book of that sort cannot be generally read where the subject-matter is unpleasing, and the method of treating it requires more attention than the Athenian spirit of the times will bear. I wonder not if it is uncalled for; and am afraid we shall not see him upon Original Sin, if it depends upon the sale of the other. This answer to Dr. Taylor, which you speak of, is not a MS., but has been already printed at Boston.

You send us good news, indeed, that two more of your brethren are declaring on the Gospel side. The Lord confirm and strengthen them, and yet to your numbers, and make you helps and comforts to each other ! Surely He is about to spread His work. Happy those whom He honours to be fellow-workers with Him. Let us account the disgrace we suffer for His name's sake to be our great honour. Many will be against us ; but there are more for us. All the praying souls on earth, all the glorified saints in heaven, all the angels of God, yea, the God of angels Himself, are all on our side. Satan may rage, but he is a chained enemy. Men may contradict and fight, but they cannot prevail. Two things we shall especially need, courage and patience, that we

neither faint before them, nor upon any provocation act
in their spirit. If we can pity and pray for them, return
good for evil, make them sensible that we bear them a hearty
good-will, and act as the disciples of Him who wept for His
enemies, and prayed for His murderers ; in this way we shall
find the Lord will plead our cause, soften opposers, and by
degrees give us a measure of outward peace. Warmth and
imprudence have often added to the necessary burden of
the cross. I rejoice that the Lord has led you in a different
way ; and I hope your doctrine and example will make your
path smoother every day ; you find it so in part already. As
the Lord brings you out a people, witnesses for you to the truth
of His word, you will find advantage in bringing them often
together. The interval from Sabbath to Sabbath is a good
while, and affords time for the world and Satan to creep
in. Intermediate meetings for prayer, &c., when properly
conducted, are greatly useful. I could wish for larger
sheets and longer leisure ; but I am constrained to say
adieu, in our dear Lord and Saviour,

Yours, &c.

LETTER IV

DEAR SIR,   *Dec.* 12, 1767.

THIS is not intended as an answer to your last acceptable
letter, but an occasional line in consequence of the account
Mr. T—— has given me of your late illness. I trust this
dispensation will be useful to you ; and I wish the knowledge
of it may be so to me. I am favoured with an unusual
share of health, and an equal flow of spirits If the blow
you have received should be a warning to me, I shall have
cause to be thankful. I am glad to hear you are better ;
I hope the Lord has no design to disable you from service,
but rather (as He did Jacob) to strengthen you by wounding
you ; to maintain and increase in you that conviction which,
through grace, you have received of the vanity and uncer-
tainty of everything below ; to give you a lively sense of
the value of health and opportunities, and to add to the

treasury of your experience new proofs of His power and goodness, in supporting, comforting, and healing you ; and likewise to quicken the prayers of your people for you, and to stir them up to use double diligence in the present improvement of the means of grace, while by this late instance they see how soon and suddenly you might have been removed from them.

I understand you did not feel that lively exercise of faith and joy which you would have hoped to have found at such a season : but let not this discourage you from a firm confidence, that when the hour of dismission shall come, the Lord will be faithful to His gracious promise, and give you strength sufficient to encounter and vanquish your last enemy. You had not this strength lately because you needed it not : for though you might think yourself near to death, the Lord intended to restore you ; and He permitted you to feel weakness, that you might know your strength does not consist in grace received, but in His fulness, and His promise to communicate from Himself as your occasions require. O it is a great thing to be strong in the grace that is in Christ Jesus ! but it is a hard lesson ; it is not easy to understand it in theory ; but when the Lord has taught us so far, it is still more difficult to reduce our knowledge to practice. But this is one end He has in view, permitting us to pass through such a variety of inward and outward exercises, that we may cease from trusting in ourselves, or in any creature, or frame, or experiences, and be brought to a state of submission and dependence upon Him alone. I was once visited somewhat in the same way, seized with a fit of the apoplectic kind, which held me nearly an hour and left a disorder in my head, which quite broke the scheme of life I was then in, and was consequently one of the means the Lord appointed to bring me into the ministry ; but I soon perfectly recovered. From the remembrance Mrs. —— has of what she then suffered, she knows how to sympathize with Mrs. B—— in her share of your trial. And I think dear Mr. —— some years since had a sudden stroke on a Christmas day, which disabled him from duty for a time. To him and to me these turns were only like the caution which Philip of Macedon ordered to be repeated to him every morning, " Remember thou art a man."

I hope it will be no more to you, but that you shall live to praise Him, and to give many cause to praise Him on your behalf. Blessed be God, we are in safe hands ; the Lord Himself is our keeper ; nothing befals us but what is adjusted by His wisdom and love. Health is His gift ; and sickness, when sanctified, is a token of love likewise. Here we may meet with many things which are not joyous, but grievous to the flesh ; but He will, in one way or other, sweeten every bitter cup, and ere long He will wipe away all tears from our eyes. O that joy, that crown, that glory which awaits the believer ! Let us keep the prize of our high calling in view, and press forward in the name of Jesus the Redeemer, and He will not disappoint our hopes.

I am but just come off from a journey, am weary, and it grows late ; must therefore break off. When you have leisure and strength to write, oblige me with a confirmation of your recovery, for I shall be somewhat anxious about you.

I am, &c.

LETTER V

My Dear Friend,   *March* 14, 1775.

I THOUGHT you long in writing, but am afraid I have been longer. A heavy family affliction called me from home in December, which put me out of my usual course, and threw me behind-hand in my correspondence ; yet I did not suspect the date of your last letter was so old by two months as I find it. Whether I write more frequently, or more seldom, the love of my heart to you is the same, and I shall believe the like of you ; yet, if it can be helped, I hope the interval will not be so long again on either side. I am glad that the Lord's work still flourishes in your parts, and that you have a more comfortable prospect at home than formerly ; and I was pleased with the acceptance you found at S—— ; which I hope will be an earnest of greater things. I think affairs in general, with respect to this land, have a dark appearance ; but it is comfortable to observe,

that amidst the aboundings of iniquity, the Lord is spreading
His Gospel ; and that, though many oppose, yet in most
places whither the word is sent, great numbers seem disposed
to hear. I am going (if the Lord please) into Leicestershire
on Friday. This was lately such a dark place as you describe
your country to be, and much of it is so still ; but the Lord
has visited three of the principal towns with Gospel-light.
I have a desire of visiting these brethren in the vineyard,
to bear my poor testimony to the truths they preach, and
to catch, if I may, a little fire and fervour among them. I
do not often go abroad ; but I have found a little excursion
now and then (when the way is made plain) has its advan-
tages, to quicken the spirits, and enlarge the sphere of obser-
vation. On these accounts, the recollection of my N——
journey gives me pleasure to this day ; and very glad should
I be to repeat it ; but the distance is so great, that I consider
it rather as desirable than practicable.

My experiences vary as well as yours : but possibly your
sensations, both of the sweet and of the bitter, may be
stronger than mine. The enemy assaults me more by sap
than storm ! and I am ready to think I suffer more by
languor than some of my friends do by the sharper conflicts
to which they are called. So likewise in these seasons,
which comparatively I call my best hours, my sensible
comforts are far from lively. But I am in general enabled
to hold fast my confidence, and to venture myself upon the
power, faithfulness, and compassion of that adorable Saviour
to whom my soul has been directed and encouraged to flee
for refuge. I am a poor, changeable, inconsistent creature ;
but He deals graciously with me ; He does not leave me
wholly to myself ; but I have such daily proofs of the
malignity of the sin that dwelleth in me, as ought to cover
me with shame and confusion of face, and make me thankful
if I am permitted to rank with the meanest of those who sit
at His feet. That I was ever called to the knowledge of His
salvation, was a singular instance of His sovereign grace ;
and that I am still preserved in the way in defiance of all
that has arisen from within and from without to turn me
aside, must be wholly ascribed to the same sovereignty ;
and if, as I trust, He shall be pleased to make me a conqueror
at last, I shall have peculiar reason to say, " Not unto me,

not unto me, but unto Thy name, O Lord, be the glory and the praise ! "

> How oft have sin and Satan strove
> To rend my soul from Thee, my God !
> But everlasting is Thy love,
> And Jesus seals it with His blood.

The Lord leads me in the course of my preaching to insist much on a life of communion with Himself, and of the great design of the Gospel to render us conformable to Him in love; and as by His mercy nothing appears in my outward conduct remarkably to contradict what I say, many who only can judge by what they see, suppose I live a very happy life. But, alas ! if they knew what passes in my heart, how dull my spirit is in secret, and how little I am myself affected by the glorious truths I propose to others, they would form a different judgment. Could I be myself what I recommend to them, I should be happy indeed. Pray for me, my dear friend, that now the Lord is bringing forward the pleasing spring, He may favour me with a spring season in my soul ; for indeed I mourn under a long winter.

> I am, &c.

LETTER VI

My Dear Friend, *April* 16, 1772.

I hope the Lord has contracted my desires and aims almost to the one point of study, the knowledge of His truth. All other acquisitions are transient, and comparatively vain. And yet, alas ! I am a slow scholar ; nor can I see in what respect I get forward, unless that every day I am more confirmed in the conviction of my own emptiness and inability to all spiritual good. And as notwithstanding this, I am still enabled to stand my ground, I would hope, since no effect can be without an adequate cause, that I have made some advance, though in a manner imperceptible to myself, towards a more simple dependence upon Jesus as my all in all. It is given me to thirst and to taste, if it is not given me to drink abundantly ; and I would be thankful for

the desire. I see and approve the wisdom, grace, suit-
ableness, and sufficiency of the Gospel-salvation ; and
since it is for sinners, and I am a sinner, and the promises
are open, I do not hesitate to call it mine. I am a weary,
laden soul ; Jesus has invited me to come, and has enabled
me to put my trust in Him. I seldom have an uneasy doubt,
at least not of any continuance, respecting my pardon,
acceptance, and interest in all the blessings of the New
Testament. And, amidst a thousand infirmities and evils
under which I groan, I have the testimony of my conscience
when under the trial of His word, that my desire is sincerely
towards Him, that I choose no other portion, that I allowedly
serve no other master. When I told our friend —— lately
to this purpose, he wondered, and asked, " How is it possible
that, if you can say these things, you should not be always
rejoicing ? " Undoubtedly I derive from the Gospel a peace
at bottom which is worth more than a thousand worlds :
but so it is, I can only speak for myself though I rest and
live upon the truths of the Gospel, they seldom impress me
with a warm and lively joy. In public, indeed, I sometimes
seem in earnest, and much affected ; but even then it appears
to me rather as a part of the gift intrusted to me for the
edification of others, than as a sensation which is properly
my own. For when I am in private, I am usually dull and
stupid to a strange degree, or the prey to a wild and ungov-
erned imagination ; so that I may truly say, when I would
do good, evil, horrid evil, is present with me. Ah, how
different is this from sensible comfort ! and if I were to
compare myself to others, to make their experience my
standard, and were not helped to retreat to the sure Word of
God as my refuge, how hard should I find it to maintain a
hope, that I had either part or lot in the matter ! What I
call my good times are, when I can find my attention in
some little measure fixed to what I am about, which indeed
is not always nor frequently my case in prayer, and still
seldomer in reading the Scripture. My judgment embraces
these means as blessed privileges, and Satan has not prevailed
to drive me from them ; but in the performance, I too often
find them tasks,—feel a reluctance when the seasons return,
—and am glad when they are finished. O what a mystery
is the heart of man ! What a warfare is the life of faith (at

least in the path the Lord is pleased to lead me)! What reason have I to lie in the dust as the chief of sinners! and what cause for thankfulness that salvation is wholly of grace! Notwithstanding all my complaints, it is still true that Jesus died and rose again, that He ever liveth to make intercession, and is able to save to the uttermost. But, on the other hand, to think of that joy of heart in which some of His people live, and to compare it with that apparent deadness and want of spirituality which I feel, this makes me mourn. However, I think there is a Scriptural distinction between faith and feeling, grace and comfort ; they are not insepar able, and perhaps when together, the degree of the one is not often the just measure of the other. But though I pray that I may be ever longing and panting for the light of His countenance, yet I would be so far satisfied, as to believe the Lord has wise and merciful reasons for keeping me so short of the comforts which He has taught me to desire and value more than the light of the sun.

I am, &c.

NINE LETTERS

TO THE

REV. MR. R——

LETTER I

Dear Sir, *Jan.* 16, 1772.

It is true, I was apprehensive, from your silence, that I had offended you ; but when your letter came, it made me full amends ; and now I am glad I wrote as I did, though I am persuaded I shall never write to you again in the same strain. I am pleased with the spirit you discover ; and your bearing so well to be told of the mistakes I pointed out to you, endears you more to me than if you had not made them. Henceforward I can converse freely with you, and shall be glad when I have the opportunity.

As to your view of justification, I did not oppose it ; I judge for myself, and I am willing others should have the same liberty, If we hold the head, and love the Lord, we agree in Him ; and I should think my time ill employed in disputing the point with you. I only meant to except against the positive manner in which you had expressed yourself. My end is answered, and I am satisfied. Indeed, I believe the difference between a judicious Supra-lapsarian, and a sound Sub-lapsarian, lies more in a different way of expressing their sentiments than is generally thought. At the close of Halyburton's Insufficiency of Natural Religion, he has an Inquiry into the Nature of Regeneration and Justification, wherein he proposes a scheme, in which, if I mistake not, the moderate of both parties might safely unite. I have used the epithets judicious and sound, because, as I acknowledge some of the one side are not quite *sound*, so I think some on the other side are not so

317

judicious as I could wish; that is, I think they do not sufficiently advert to the present state of human nature, and the danger which may arise from leading those who are weak in faith and judgment, into inquiries and distinctions evidently beyond the line of their experience, and which may be hurtful; because, admitting them to be true when properly explained, they are very liable to be misunderstood. To say nothing of Mr. Hussey (in whose provisions I have frequently found more bones than meat, and the whole seasoned with much of an angry and self-important spirit), I have observed passages in other writers, for whom I have a higher esteem, which, to say the least, appear to me paradoxical, and hard to be understood; though perhaps I can give my consent to them, if I had such restrictions and limitations as the authors would not refuse. But plain people are easily puzzled. And though I know several in the Supra-lapsarian scheme, at whose feet I am willing to sit and learn, and have found their preaching and conversation savoury and edifying, yet I must say I have met with many who have appeared to be rather wise than warm, rather positive than humble, rather captious than lively, and more disposed to talk of speculations than experience. However, let us give ourselves to the study of the Word and to prayer; and may the great Teacher make every Scriptural truth food to our souls. I desire to grow in knowledge, but I want nothing which bears that name, that has not a direct tendency to make sin more hateful, Jesus more precious to my soul, and at the same time to animate me to a diligent use of every appointed means, and an unreserved regard to every branch of duty. I think the Lord has shown me in a measure, there is a consistent sense running through the whole Scripture, and I desire to be governed and influenced by it all : doctrines, precepts, promises, warnings, all have their proper place and use ; and I think many of the inconveniences which obtain in the present day, spring from separating those things which God hath joined together, and insisting on some parts of the word of God, almost to the exclusion of the rest.

I have filed my paper with what I did not intend to say a word of when I began, and I must leave other things which were more upon my mind for another season. I thank you for saying you pray for me. Continue that kindness; I both need it and prize it.

I am, &c.

LETTER II

DEAR SIR, *July* 31, 1773.

I RECEIVED your sorrowing epistle yesterday, and, in order to encourage you to write, I answer it to-day.

The ship was safe when Christ was in her, though He was *really* asleep. At present I can tell you good news, though you know it; He is wide awake, and His eyes are in every place. You and I, if we could be pounded together, might perhaps make two tolerable ones. You are too anxious, and I am too easy in some respects. Indeed I cannot be too easy, when I have a right thought that all is safe in His hands; but if your anxiety makes you pray, and my composure makes me careless, you have certainly the best of it. However, the ark is fixed upon an immovable foundation; and if we think we see it totter, it is owing to a swimming in our heads. Seriously, the times look dark and stormy, and call for much circumspection and prayer; but let us not forget that we have an infallible Pilot, and that the power, and wisdom, and honour of God are embarked with us. At Venice they have a fine vessel called the *Bucentaur*, in which, on a certain day of the year, the doge and nobles embark, and go a little way to sea, to repeat the foolish ceremony of marriage between the Republic and the Adriatic (in consequence of some flying, antiquated Pope's bull, by which the banns of matrimony between Venice and the Gulf were published in the dark ages), when, they say, a gold ring is very gravely thrown overboard. Upon this occasion, I have been told, when the honour and government of Venice are shipped on board the *Bucentaur*, the pilot is obliged by his office to take an oath that he will bring the vessel safely back again *in defiance of wind and weather*. Vain mortals! If this be true, what an instance of God's long-suffering is it, that they have never yet sunk as lead in the mighty waters ! But my story will probably remind you, that Jesus has actually entered into such an engagement in behalf of His Church. And well He may, for both wind and 'weather are at His command ; and He can turn the storm into a calm in a moment. We may, therefore, safely and confidently leave the government upon His shoulders. Duty is our part, the care is His.

A revival is wanted with us as well as with you, and I trust some of us are longing for it. We are praying and singing for one ; and I send you, on the other side, a hymn that you (if you like it) may sing with us. Let us take courage ; though it may seem marvellous in our eyes, it is not so in the Lord's. He changed the desert into a fruitful field, and bade dry bones live. And if we prepare our hearts to pray, he will surely incline His ear to hear.

The miscarriages of professors are grievous ; yet such things must be ; how else could the Scriptures be fulfilled ? But there is One who is able to keep us from falling. Some who have distressed us, perhaps never were truly changed ; how then could they stand ? We see only the outside. Others who are sincere are permitted to fall for our instruction, that we may not be high-minded, but fear. However, he that walketh humbly, walketh surely.

Believe me, &c.

LETTER III

DEAR SIR, *Feb.* 22, 1774.

YOUR letter by last post surprised and grieved me. We knew nothing of the subject, though Mrs. —— remembers when W—— was here, a hint or two were dropped which she did not understand ; but no name was mentioned.

This instance shows the danger of leaning to impressions. Texts of Scripture, brought powerfully to the heart, are very desirable and pleasant, if their tendency is to humble us, to give us a more feeling sense of the preciousness of Christ, or of the doctrines of grace ; if they make sin more hateful, enliven our regard to the means, or increase our confidence in the power and faithfulness of God. But if they are understood as intimating our path of duty in particular circumstances, or confirming us in purposes we may have already formed, not otherwise clearly warranted by the general strain of the Word, or by the leadings of Providence, they are for the most part ensnaring, and always to be suspected. Nor does their coming into the mind at the time of prayer give them more authority in this respect. When the mind is intent upon any subject, the imagination is often watchful to catch at anything which may seem to countenance the favourite pursuit. It is too common to ask counsel of the Lord when we have already secretly determined for ourselves ; and in this disposition we may easily be deceived by the sound of a text of Scripture, which, detached from the passage in which it stands, may seem remarkably to tally with our wishes. Many have been deceived in this way ; and sometimes, when the event has shown them they were mistaken, it has opened a door for great distress, and Satan has found occasion to make them doubt even of their most solid experiences.

I have sometimes talked to —— upon this subject, though without the least suspicion of anything like what has happened. As to the present case, it may remind us all of our weakness. I would recommend prayer, patience, much tenderness towards her, joined with faithful expostulation. Wait a little while, and I trust the Lord who loves her will break the snare. I am persuaded, in her better judgment, she would dread the thoughts of doing wrong ; and I hope and believe the good Shepherd, to whom she has often committed her soul and her ways, will interpose to restore and set her to rights. * * * * *
* * * * * * * * * *
* * I am sorry you think any of whom you have hoped well are going back ; but be not discouraged. I say again, pray and wait, and hope the best. It is common for young professors to have a slack time ; it is almost necessary, that they may be more sensible of the weakness and deceitfulness of their hearts, and be more humbled in future when the Lord shall have healed their breaches, and restored their souls. We join love to you and yours. Pray for us,

I am, &c.

C.   X

LETTER IV

DEAR SIR,   *Feb.* 3, 1775.

It would be wrong to make you wait long for an answer to the point you propose in your last. It is an important one. I am not a casuist by profession, but I will do my best. Suppose I imitate your laconic manner of stating the question and circumstances.

I doubt not but it is very lawful at your age to think of marriage, and, in the situation you describe, to think of money likewise. I am glad you have no persons, as you say, *fixedly in view*; in that case, advice comes a post or two too late. But your expression seems to intimate, that there is one *transiently in view*. If so, since you have no settlement, if she has no money, I cannot but wish she may pass on till she is out of sight and out of mind. I see this will not do; I must get into my own grave way about this grave business. I take it for granted, that my friend is free from the love of filthy lucre; and that money will never be the turning point with you in the choice of a wife. Methinks I hear you say, if I wanted money, I would either dig or beg for it; but to preach or marry for money, that be far from me. I commend you. However, though the love of money be a great evil, money itself, obtained in a fair and honourable way, is desirable upon many accounts, though not for its own sake. Meat, clothes, fire and books, cannot easily be had without it; therefore, if these be necessary, money, which procures them, must be a necessary likewise. If things were otherwise than you represent them, if you were able to provide for a wife yourself, then I would say, Find a gracious girl (if she be not found already), whose person you like, whose temper you think will suit; and then, with your father and mother's consent (without which I think you would be unwilling to move), thank the Lord for her, marry her, and account her a valuable portion, though she should not have a shilling. But while you are without income or settlement, if you have thoughts of marriage, I hope they will be regulated by a due regard to consequences. They who set the least value upon money, have in some respects the most need of it. A generous mind will feel a thousand pangs in strait circumstances, which some unfeeling hearts would not be sensible of. You could perhaps endure hardships alone, yet it might pinch you to the very bone to see the person you love exposed to them. Besides, you might have a John, a Thomas, and a William, and a half dozen more to feed (for they must all eat) ; and how this could be done without a competency on one side or the other, or so much on both sides as will make a competency when united, I see not. Besides, you would be grieved not to find an occasional shilling in your pocket to bestow upon one or other of the Lord's poor, though you should be able to make some sort of a shift for those of your own house.

But is it not written, " The Lord will provide " ? It is : but it is written again, " Thou shalt not tempt the Lord thy God." Hastily to plunge ourselves into difficulties upon a persuasion that He will find some way to extricate us, seems to me a species of tempting Him.

Therefore, I judge it so far lawful for you to have a regard to money in looking out for a wife, that it would be wrong, that is, in other words, unlawful for you to omit it, supposing you have a purpose of marrying in your present situation.

Many serious young women have a predilection in favour of a minister of the Gospel : and I believe among such, one or more may be found as spiritual, as amiable, as suitable to make you a good wife, with a tolerable fortune to boot, as another who has not a penny. If you are not willing to trust your own judgment in the search, intreat the Lord to find her for you. He chose well for Isaac and Jacob ; and you, as a believer, have warrant to commit your way to Him, and many more express promises than they had for your encouragement. He knows your state, your wants, what you are at present, and what use He designs to make of you. Trust in Him, and wait for Him : prayer, and faith, and patience, are never disappointed. I commend you to His blessing and guidance. Remember us to all in your house.

I am, &c.

LETTER V

DEAR SIR, *May* 28, 1775.

* ¯' *   *   *   *   *   *   *

*   *   *   * You must not expect a long letter this morning; we are just going to Court, in hopes of seeing the King, for He has promised to meet us. We can say He is mindful of his promise; and yet it is not strange that though we are all in the same place, and the King in the midst of us, it is but here and there one (even of those who love Him) can see Him at once! However, in our turns, we are all favoured with a glimpse of Him, and have had cause to say, How great is His goodness! How great is His beauty! We have the advantage of the Queen of Sheba, a more glorious object to behold, and not so far to go for the sight of it. If a transient glance exceed all that the world can afford for a long continuance, what must it be to dwell with Him! If a day in His courts be better than a thousand, what will eternity be in His presence! I hope the more you see, the more you love; the more you drink, the more you thirst; the more you do for Him, the more you are ashamed you can do so little; and that the nearer you approach to your journey's end, the more your pace is quickened. Surely, the power of spiritual attraction should increase as the distance lessens. O that heavenly load-stone! May it so draw us, that we may not creep, but run. In common travelling, the strongest become weary if the journey be very long; but in the spiritual journey we are encouraged with the hope of going on from strength to strength; *instaurabit iter vires*, as Johnson expresses it. No road but the road to Heaven can thus communicate refreshment to those who walk in it, and make them more fresh and lively when they are just finishing their courses than when they first set out.

I am, &c.

LETTER VI

DEAR SIR,   *April* 18, 1776.

ARE you sick, or lame of your right hand, or are you busy in preparing a folio for the press, that I hear nothing from you ? You see, by the excuses I would contrive, I am not willing to suppose you have forgotten me, but that your silence is rather owing to a *cannot* than a *will not*.

I hope your soul prospers. I do not ask you, if you are always filled with sensible comfort ; but, do you find your spirit more bowed down to the feet and will of Jesus, so as to be willing to serve Him for the sake of serving Him, and to follow Him, as we say, through thick and thin, to be willing to be anything or nothing, so that He may be glorified. I could give you plenty of good advice upon this head ; but I am ashamed to do it, because I so poorly follow myself. I want to live with Him by the day, to do all for Him, to receive all from Him, to possess all in Him, to live all to Him, to make Him my hiding-place and my resting-place. I want to deliver up that rebel Self to him in chains ; but the rogue, like Proteus, puts on so many forms, that he slips through my fingers : but I think I know what I would do if I could fairly catch him.

My soul is like a besieged city : a legion of enemies without the gates, and a nest of restless traitors within, that hold a correspondence with them without ; so that I am deceived and counteracted continually. It is a mercy that I have not been surprised and overwhelmed long ago : without help from on high, it would soon be over with me. How often have I been forced to cry out, O God, the heathen are got into thine inheritance ; thy holy temple have they defiled, and defaced all thy work ! Indeed, it is a miracle that I still hold out. I trust, however, I shall be supported to the end, and that the Lord will at length raise the siege, and cause me to shout deliverance and victory.

Pray for me, that my walls may be strengthened, and wounds healed. We are all pretty well as to the outward man, and join in love to all friends.

                                                I am, &c.

LETTER VII

DEAR SIR, *July* 6, 1776.

I WAS abroad when your letter came, but employ the first post to thank you for your confidence. My prayers (when I can pray) you may be sure of ; as to advice, I see not that the case requires much. Only be a quiet child, and lie patiently at the Lord's feet. He is the best *Friend* and Manager in these matters, for He has a key to open every heart. * * * * * * * * * *
* * * * * * * * I should not have taken Mr. Z——'s letter for a denial, as it seems you did. Considering the years of the parties, and other circumstances, a prudent parent could hardly say more, if he were inclined to favour your views. To me you seem to be in a tolerable fair way ; but I know, in affairs of this kind, Mr. Self does not like suspense, but would willingly come to the point at once : but Mr. Faith (when he gets liberty to hold up his head) will own that, in order to make our temporal mercies wear well, and to give us a clearer sense of the hand that bestows them, a waiting and a praying time are very seasonable. Worldly people expect their schemes to run upon all-fours, as we say, and the objects of their wishes to drop into their mouths without difficulty ; and if they succeed, they of course burn incense to their own drag, and say, This was my doing : but believers meet with rubs and disappointments, which convince them, that if they obtain any thing, it is the Lord who must do it for them. For this reason I observe that He usually brings a death upon our prospects, even when it is His purpose to give us success in the issue. Thus we become more assured that we did not act in our own spirits, and have a more satisfactory view that His providence has been concerned in filling up the rivers and removing the mountains that were in our way. Then when He has given us our desire, how pleasant is it to look at it, and say, This I got not by my own sword, and my own bow, but I wrestled for it in prayer, I waited for it in faith, I put it into the Lord's hand, and from His hand I received it !

You have met with the story of one of our kings (if I

mistake not) who wanted to send a nobleman abroad as his ambassador, and he desired to be excused on account of some affairs which required his presence at home : the king answered, " Do you take care of my business, and I will take care of yours." I would have you think the Lord says thus to you. You were sent into the world for a nobler end than to be pinned to a girl's apron-string ; and yet if the Lord sees it not good for you to be alone, He will provide you a helpmeet. I say, if He sees the marriage state best for you, He has the proper person *already* in His eye ; and though she were in Peru or Nova-Zembla, He knows how to bring you together. In the mean time, go thou and preach the Gospel. Watch in all things ; endure afflictions ; do the work of an evangelist ; make full proof of your ministry ; and when other thoughts rise in your mind (for you have no door to shut them quite out), run with them to the throne of grace, and commit them to the Lord. Satan will, perhaps, try to force them upon you unseasonably and inordinately ; but if he sees they drive you to prayer, he will probably desist, rather than be the occasion of doing you so much good. Believe, likewise, that as the Lord has the appointment of the person, so He fixes the time. His time is like the time of the tide ; all the art and power of man can neither hasten nor retard it a moment : it must be waited for ; nothing can be done without it, and when it comes, nothing can resist it. It is unbelief that talks of delays : faith knows that properly there can be no such thing. The only reason why the Lord seems to delay what He afterwards grants, is that the best hour is not yet come. I know you have been enabled to commit and resign your all to His disposal. You did well. May He help you to stand to the surrender ! Sometimes He will put us to the trial, whether we mean what we say. He takes His course in a way we did not expect ; and then, alas ! how often does the trial put us to shame ! Presently there is an outcry raised in the soul against His management ; this is wrong, that unnecessary, the other has spoiled the whole plan ; in short, all these things are against us. And when we go into the pulpit, and gravely tell the people how wise and how good He is ; and preach submission to His will, not only as a duty, but a privilege ; alas ! how deceitful is the heart ! Yet, since it is and will be so, it is necessary we should know it by experience. We have reason, however, to say, He is good and wise ; for He bears with our perverseness, and in the event shows us, that if He had listened to our murmurings, and taken the methods we would have prescribed to Him, we should have been ruined indeed, and that He has been all the while doing us good in spite of ourselves.

If I judge right, you will find your way providentially opened more and more ; and yet it is possible, that when you begin to think yourself sure, something may happen to put you in a panic again. But a believer, like a sailor, is not to be surprised if the wind changes, but to learn the art of suiting himself to all winds for the time ; and though many a poor sailor is shipwrecked, the poor believer shall gain his port. O, it is good sailing with an infallible Pilot at the helm, who has the wind and weather at His command !

I have been much abroad, which of course puts things at sixes and sevens at home. If I did not love you well, I could not have spared so much of the only day I have had to myself for this fortnight past. But I was willing you should know that I think of you, and feel for you, if I cannot help you.

I have read Mr. ——'s book. Some things I think strongly argued ; in some he has laid himself open to a blow, and I doubt not but he will have it. I expect answers, replies, rejoinders, &c. &c. and say, with Leah, *Gad—a troop cometh*. How the wolf will grin to see the sheep and the shepherds biting and worrying one another ! And well he may. He knows that contentions are a surer way to weaken the spirit of love, and stop the progress of the Gospel, than his old stale method of fire and sword. Well, I trust we shall be of one heart and one mind when we get to Heaven at least.

Let who will fight, I trust neither water nor fire shall set you and me at variance. We unite in love to you. The Lord is gracious to us, &c.

I am, &c.

LETTER VIII

DEAR SIR, —— 1776.

I DO not often serve your letters so, but this last I burnt, believing you would like to have it out of danger of falling into improper hands. When I saw how eagerly the flames devoured the paper, how quickly and entirely every trace of the writing was consumed, I wished that the fire of the love of Jesus might as completely obliterate from your heart every uneasy impression which your disappointment has given you. * * * * *

  * * * * * * * * * *

Surely when He crosses our wishes, it is always in mercy, and because we short-sighted creatures often know not what we ask, nor what would be the consequences if our desires were granted.

Your pride, it seems, has received a fall, by meeting a repulse. I know Self does not like to be mortified in these affairs ; but if you are made successful in wooing souls for Christ, I hope that will console you for meeting a rebuff when only wooing for yourself. Besides, I would have you pluck up your spirits. I have two good old proverbs at your service : " There are as good fish in the sea as any that are brought out of it ; " and, " If one won't, another will, or wherefore serves the market ? " Perhaps all your difficulties have arisen from this, that you have not yet seen the right person ; if so, you have reason to be thankful that the Lord would not let you take the wrong, though you unwittingly would have done it if you could. Where the right one lies hid I know not, but upon a supposition that it will be good for you to marry, I may venture to say,

> Ubi, ubi est, diu celari non potest,

The Lord in His providence will disclose her, put her in your way, and give you to understand, This is she. Then you will find your business go forward with wheels and wings, and have cause to say, His choice and time were better than your own.

Did I not tell you formerly, that if you would take care of His business He will take care of yours ? I am of the same mind still. He will not suffer them who fear Him and depend upon Him to want anything that is truly good for them.   In the mean while, I advise you to take a lodging as near as you can to Gethsemane, and to walk daily to mount Golgotha, and borrow (which may be had for asking) that telescope which gives a prospect into the unseen world. A view of what is passing within the veil has a marvellous effect to compose our spirits, with regard to the little things that are daily passing here.   Praise the Lord, who has enabled you to fix your supreme affection upon Him, who is alone the proper and suitable object of it, and from whom you cannot meet a denial, or fear a change.   He loved you first, and He will love you for ever ; and if He be pleased to arise and smile upon you, you are in no more necessity of begging for happiness to the prettiest creature upon earth, than of the light of a candle on midsummer noon.

Upon the whole, I pray and hope the Lord will sweeten your cross, and either in kind or in kindness make you good amends.   Wait, pray, and believe, and all shall be well. A cross we must have somewhere ; and they who are favoured with health, plenty, peace, and a conscience sprinkled with the blood of Jesus, must have more causes for thankfulness than grief.   Look round you, and take notice of the very severe afflictions which many of the Lord's own people are groaning under, and your trials will appear comparatively light.   Our love to all friends.

I am, &c.

LETTER IX

DEAR SIR,   *June* 3, 1777.

It seems I must write something about the smallpox, but I know not well what : not having had it myself, I cannot judge how I should feel if I were actually exposed to it.   I am not a professed advocate for inoculation ; but if a person who fears the Lord should tell me, " I think I can do it in faith, looking upon it as a salutary expedient, which

He in His providence has discovered, and which, therefore, it appears my duty to have recourse to, so that my mind does not hesitate with respect to the lawfulness, nor am I anxious about the event ; being satisfied, that whether I live or die, I am in that path in which I can cheerfully expect His blessing,"—I do not know that I could offer a word by way of dissuasion.

If another person should say, " My times are in the Lord's hands ; I am now in health, and am not willing to bring upon myself a disorder, the consequences of which I cannot possibly foresee : If I am to have the small-pox, I believe He is the best Judge of the season and manner in which I shall be visited, so as may be most for His glory and my own good ; and therefore I choose to wait His appointment, and not to rush upon even the possibility of danger without a call. If the very hairs of my head are numbered, I have no reason to fear that, supposing I receive the small-pox in a natural way, I shall have a single pimple more than He sees expedient ; and why should I wish to have one less ? Nay, admitting, which however is not always the case, that inoculation might exempt me from some pain and inconvenience, and lessen the apparent danger, might it not likewise, upon that very account, prevent my receiving some of those sweet consolations, which I humbly hope my gracious Lord would afford me, if it were His pleasure to call me to a sharp trial ? Perhaps the chief design of this trying hour, if it comes, may be to show me more of His wisdom, power, and love, than I have ever yet experienced. If I could devise a mean to avoid the trouble, I know not how great a loser I may be in point of grace and comfort. Nor am I afraid of my face ; it is now as the Lord has made it, and it will be so after the small-pox. If it pleases Him, I hope it will please me. In short, though I do not censure others, yet, as to myself, inoculation is what I dare not venture upon. If I did venture, and the issue should not be favourable, I should blame myself for having attempted to take the management out of the Lord's hand into my own, which I never did yet in other matters without finding I am no more able than I am worthy to choose for myself. Besides, at the best, inoculation would only secure me from *one* of the innumerable natural evils the flesh is heir to ; I should still be as liable as I am at present to a putrid fever, a bilious cholic, an inflammation in the bowels or in the brain, and a thousand formidable diseases which are hovering round me, and only wait His permission to cut me off in a few days or hours : and therefore I am determined, by His grace, to resign myself to His disposal. Let me fall into the hands of the Lord (for His mercies are great) and not into the hands of men."

If a person should talk to me in this strain, most certainly I could not say, " Notwithstanding all this, your safest way is to be inoculated."

We preach and hear, and I hope we know something of faith, as enabling us to intrust the Lord with our souls : I wish we had all more faith, to intrust Him with our bodies, our health, our provision, and our temporal comforts likewise. The former should seem to require the strongest faith of the two. How strange is it, that when we think we can do the *greater*, we should be so awkward and unskilful when we aim at the *less* ! Give my love to your friend. I dare not advise ; but if she can quietly return at the usual time, and neither run intentionally into the way of the small-pox, nor run out of the way, but leave it simply with the Lord, I shall not blame her. And if you will mind your praying and preaching, and believe that the Lord can take care of her without any of your contrivances, I shall not blame you ; nay, I shall praise Him for you both. My prescription is, to read Dr. Watts, Psal. cxxi. every morning before breakfast, and pray it over till the cure is effected. *Probatum est.*

> Hast Thou not given Thy word
> To save my soul from death ?
> And I can trust my Lord,
> To keep my mortal breath.
> I'll go and come
> Nor fear to die,
> Till from on high
> Thou call me home.

Adieu. Pray for yours.

THREE LETTERS

TO

MISS TH——

LETTER I

My Dear Madam,

LET what has been said on the subject of acquaintance, &c., suffice. It was well meant on my side, and well taken on yours. You may, perhaps, see that my hints were not wholly unnecessary, and I ought to be satisfied with your apology, and am so. The circumstance of your being seen at the play-house has nothing at all mysterious in it : as you say you have not been there these six or seven years, it was neither more nor less than a mistake. I heard you had been there within these two years : I am glad to find I was misinformed. I think there is no harm in your supposing, that of the many thousands who frequent public diversions, some may in other respects be better than yourself ; but I hope your humble and charitable construction of their mistake will not lead you to extenuate the evil of those diversions in themselves. For though I am persuaded, that a few, who know better what to do with themselves, are, for want of consideration, drawn in to expose themselves in such places ; yet I am well satisfied, that if there is any practice in this land sinful, attendance on the play-house is properly and eminently so. The theatres are fountains and means of vice : I had almost said, in the same manner and degree as the ordinances of the Gospel are the means of grace ; and I can hardly think there is a Christian upon earth who would dare to be seen there, if the nature and effects of the theatre were properly set before them. Dr. Witherspoon of Scotland has written an excellent piece upon the stage,

333

or rather against it, which I wish every person who makes
the least pretence to fear God had an opportunity of perusing.
I cannot judge much more favourably of Ranelagh, Vauxhall,
and all the innumerable train of dissipations, by which the
god of this world blinds the eyes of multitudes, lest the light
of the glorious Gospel should shine in upon them.   What
an awful aspect upon the present times have such texts
as Isaiah xxii. 12—14, iii. 12 ; Amos vi. 3, 6 ; James iv. 4 !
I wish you, therefore, not to plead for any of them, but to
use your influence to make them shunned as pest-houses,
and dangerous nuisances to precious souls ; especially, if
you know any who you hope, in the main, are seriously
disposed, who yet venture themselves in those purlieus of
Satan, endeavour earnestly and faithfully to undeceive
them.

The time is short ; eternity at the door : were there
no other evil in these vain amusements than the loss of
precious time, (but, alas ! their name is Legion,) we have
not leisure in our circumstances to regard them.   And,
blessed be God ! we need them not.   The Gospel opens a
source of purer, sweeter, and more substantial pleasures :
we are invited to communion with God ; we are called
to share in the theme of angels, the songs of Heaven ; and
the wonders of redeeming love are laid open to our view.
The Lord Himself is waiting to be gracious, waiting with
promises and pardons in His hands.   Well, then, may we bid
adieu to the perishing pleasures of sin ; well may we pity
those who can find pleasure in those places and parties
where He is shut out ; where His name is only mentioned
to be profaned ; where His commandments are not only
broken, but insulted ; where sinners proclaim their shame,
as in Sodom, and attempt not to hide it ; where at best
wickedness is wrapt up in a disguise of delicacy, to make it
more insinuating ; and nothing is offensive that is not
grossly and unpolitely indecent.

I sympathise with all your complaints ; but if the Lord
is pleased to make them subservient to the increase of your
sanctification, to wean you more and more from this world,
and to draw you nearer to Himself, you will one day see
cause to be thankful for them, and to number them amongst
your choicest mercies.   A hundred years hence it will

signify little to you whether you were sick or well the day I wrote this letter.

We thank you for your kind condolence. There is a pleasure in the pity of a friend ; but the Lord alone can give true comfort. I hope He will sanctify the breach, and do us good. Mrs. ―――― exchanges forgiveness with you about your not meeting in London ; that is, you forgive her not coming to you, and she forgives your entertaining a suspicious thought of her friendship (though but for a minute) on account of what she was really unable to do.

I am, &c.

LETTER II

MY DEAR MADAM, *Sept.* 1, 1767.

I SHALL not study for expressions to tell my dear friend how much we were affected by the news that came last post. We had, however, the pleasure to hear that your family was safe. I hope this will find you recovered from the hurry of spirits you must have been thrown into, and that both you and your papa are composed under the appointment of Him who has a right to dispose of His own as He pleases ; for we know that whatever may be the second causes and occasions, nothing can happen to us but according to the will of our Heavenly Father. Since what is past cannot be recalled, my part is now to pray, that this and every dispensation you meet with may be sanctified to your soul's good ; that you may be more devoted to the God of your life, and have a clearer sense of your interest in that Kingdom which cannot be shaken, that treasure which neither thieves nor flames can touch, that better and more enduring substance which is laid up for believers, where Jesus their Head and Saviour is. With this view you may take joyfully the spoiling of your goods.

I think I can feel for my friends ; but for such as I hope have a right to that promise, that all things shall work together for their good, I soon check my solicitude, and ask myself, Do I love them better, or could I manage more wisely for them, than the Lord does ? Can I wish them to be in safer or more compassionate hands than in His ? Will He who delights in the prosperity of His servants afflict them with sickness, losses, and alarms, except He sees there is need of these things ? Such thoughts calm the emotions of my mind. I sincerely condole with you ; but the command is to rejoice always in the Lord. The visitation was accompanied with mercy. Not such a case as that of the late Lady Molesworth's, which made every one's ears to tingle that heard it. Nor is yours such a case as of some, who in almost every great fire lose their all, and, perhaps, have no knowledge of God to support them.

Though our first apprehensions were for you, we almost forgot you for a moment, when we thought of your next-door neighbour, and the circumstances she was in, so unfit to bear either a fright or a removal. We shall be in much suspense till we hear from you. God grant that you may be able to send us good news, that you are all well, at least as well as can be expected after such a distressing scene. If what has happened should give you more leisure or more inclination to spend a little time with us, I think I need not say we shall rejoice to receive you.

I am, &c.

LETTER III

My Dear Madam, *Sept.* 3, 1767.

THE vanity of all things below is confirmed to us by daily experience. Amongst other proofs, one is the precariousness of our intimacies, and what little things, or rather what nothings, will sometimes produce a coolness, or at least a strangeness, between the dearest friends. How is it that our correspondence has been dropped, and that, after having written two letters since the fire which removed you from your former residence, I should be still disappointed in my hopes of an answer ? On our parts I hope there has been no abatement of regard ; nor can I charge you with anything but remissness. Therefore, waiving the past, and all apologies on either side, let me beg you to write soon, to tell us how it is with you, and how you have been supported under the various changes you have met with since we saw you last. I doubt not but you have met with many exercises. I pray that they may have been sanctified to lead you nearer to the Lord, the Fountain of all consolation, who is the only refuge in time of trouble, and whose gracious presence is abundantly able to make up every deficiency and every loss. Perhaps the reading of this may recall to your mind our past conversations, and the subjects of the many letters we have exchanged. I know not in what manner to write after so long an interval. I would hope your silence to us has not been owing to any change of sentiments, which might make such letters as mine less welcome to you. Yet when you had a friend, who I think you believed very nearly interested himself in your welfare, it seems strange, that in a course of two years you should have nothing to communicate. I cannot suppose you have forgotten me ; I am sure I have not forgotten you ; and therefore, I long to hear from you soon, that I may know how to write : and should this likewise pass unanswered, I must sit down and mourn over my loss.

As to our affairs, I can tell you the Lord has been and is exceedingly gracious to us ; our lives are preserved, our healths continued, an abundance of mercies and blessings on every side ; but especially we have to praise Him that He is pleased to crown the means and ordinances of His grace with tokens of His presence. It is my happiness to be fixed amongst an affectionate people, who make an open profession of the truth as it is in Jesus, and are enabled in some measure to show forth its power in their lives and conversation. We walk in peace and harmony. I have reason to say the Lord Jesus is a good Master, and that the doctrine of free salvation, by faith in His name, is a doctrine according to godliness ; for through mercy I find it daily effectual to the breaking down of the strongholds of sin, and turning the hearts of sinners from dead works to serve the living God. May the Lord give my dear friend to live in the power and consolation of His precious truth !

I am, &c.

C.

SEVEN LETTERS

TO

_____

LETTER I

March 18, 1767.

I CAN truly say, that I bear you upon my heart and
in my prayers. I have rejoiced to see the beginning of a
good and gracious work in you ; and I have confidence in
the Lord Jesus, that He will carry it on and complete it ;
and that you will be amongst the number of those who shall
sing redeeming love to eternity. Therefore fear none of
the things appointed for you to suffer by the way ; but gird
up the loins of your mind, and hope to the end. Be not
impatient, but wait humbly upon the Lord. You have one
hard lesson to learn, that is, the evil of your own heart :
you know something of it, but it is needful that you should
know more ; for the more we know of ourselves, the more we
shall prize and love Jesus and His salvation. I hope what
you find in yourself by daily experience will humble you,
but not discourage you ; humble you it should, and I believe
it does. Are not you amazed sometimes that you should
have so much as a hope that, poor and needy as you are, the
Lord thinketh of you ? But let not all you feel discourage
you ; for if our Physician is almighty, our disease cannot be
desperate ; and if He casts none out that come to Him, why
should you fear ? Our sins are many, but His mercies
are more : our sins are great, but His righteousness is
greater : we are weak, but He is power. Most of our
complaints are owing to unbelief, and the remainder of a
legal spirit ; and these evils are not removed in a day. Wait
on the Lord, and He will enable you to see more and more

338

of the power and grace of our High Priest. The more you know Him, the better you will trust Him ; the more you trust Him, the better you will love Him ; the more you love Him, the better you will serve Him. This is God's way : you are not called to buy, but to beg ; not to be strong in yourself, but in the grace that is in Christ Jesus. He is teaching you these things, and I trust He will teach you to the end. Remember the growth of a believer is not like a mushroom, but like an oak, which increases slowly indeed, but surely. Many suns, showers, and frosts pass upon it before it comes to perfection ; and in winter, when it seems dead, it is gathering strength at the root. Be humble, watchful, and diligent in the means, and endeavour to look through all, and fix your eye upon Jesus, and all shall be well. I commend you to the care of the good Shepherd, and remain, for His sake,

Yours, &c.

LETTER II

May 31, 1769.

I WAS sorry I did not write as you expected, but I hope it will do now. Indeed I have not forgotten you ; you are often in my thoughts, and seldom omitted in my prayers. I hope the Lord will make what you see and hear while abroad profitable to you, to increase your knowledge, to strengthen your faith, and to make you from henceforth well satisfied with your situation. If I am not mistaken, you will be sensible, that though there are some desirable things to be met with in London preferable to any other place, yet, upon the whole, a quiet situation in the country, under one stated ministry, and in connexion with one people, has the advantage. It is pleasant now and then to have opportunity of hearing a variety of preachers, but the best and greatest of them are no more than instruments ; some can please the ear better than others ; but none can reach the heart any farther than the Lord is pleased to open it. This He showed you upon your first going up, and I doubt not but your disappointment did you more good than if you had heard with all the pleasure you expected.

The Lord was pleased to visit me with a slight illness in my late journey. I was far from well on the Tuesday, but supposed it owing to the fatigue of riding, and the heat of the weather; but the next day I was taken with a shivering, to which a fever succeeded. I was then near sixty miles from home. The Lord gave me much peace in my soul, and I was enabled to hope He would bring me safe home, in which I was not disappointed; and though I had the fever most part of the way, my journey was not unpleasant. He likewise strengthened me to preach twice on Sunday; and at night I found myself well, only very weary, and I have continued well ever since. I have reason to speak much of His goodness, and to kiss the rod, for it was sweetened with abundant mercies. I thought that had it been His pleasure I should have continued sick at Oxford, or even have died there, I had no objection. Though I had not that joy and sensible comfort which some are favoured with, yet I was quite free from pain, fear, and care, and felt myself sweetly composed to His will, whatever it might be. Thus He fulfils His promise in making our strengthen equal to our day; and every new trial gives us a new proof how happy it is to be enabled to put our trust in Him.

I hope, in the midst of all your engagements, you find a little time to read His good Word, and to wait at His mercy-seat. It is good for us to draw nigh to Him. It is an honour that He permits us to pray; and we shall surely find He is a God hearing prayer. Endeavour to be diligent in the means; yet watch and strive against a legal spirit, which is always aiming to represent Him as a hard master, watching as it were to take advantage of us. But it is far otherwise. His name is Love! He looks upon us with compassion; He knows our frame, and remembers that we are but dust; and when our infirmities prevail, He does not bid us despond, but reminds us that we have an Advocate with the Father, who is able to pity, to pardon, and to save to the uttermost. Think of the names and relations He bears. Does He not call Himself a Saviour, a Shepherd, a Friend, and a Husband? Has He not made known unto us His love, His blood, His righteousness, His promises, His power, and His grace, and all for our encouragement ? Away, then, with all doubting, unbelieving thoughts ; they will not only distress your heart, but weaken your hands. Take it for granted upon the warrant of His word, that you are His, and He is yours ; that He has loved you with an everlasting love, and therefore in loving-kindness has drawn you to Himself ; that He will surely accomplish that which He has begun, and that nothing which can be named or thought of shall ever be able to separate you from Him. This persuasion will give you strength for the battle ; this is the shield which will quench the fiery darts of Satan ; this is the helmet which the enemy cannot pierce. Whereas, if we go forth doubting and fearing, and are afraid to trust any farther than we can feel, we are weak as water, and easily overcome. Be strong, therefore, not in yourself, but in the grace that is in Christ Jesus. Pray for me, and believe me to be

Yours, &c.

LETTER III

March 14.

I THINK you would hardly expect me to write if you knew how I am forced to live at London. However, I would have you believe I am as willing to write to you as you are to receive my letters. As a proof, I try to send you a few lines now, though I am writing to you, and talking to Mrs. ——, both at once ! and this is the only season I can have to exchange a few words with her. She is a woman of a sorrowful spirit ; she talks and weeps. I believe she would think herself happy to be situated as you are, notwithstanding the many advantages she has at London. I see daily, and I hope you have likewise learned, that places and outward circumstances cannot of themselves either hinder or help us in walking with God. So far as He is pleased to be with us, and to teach us by His Spirit, wherever we are we shall get forward ; and if He does not bless us and water us every moment, the more we have of our own wishes and wills, the more uneasy we shall make ourselves.

One thing is needful; an humble, dependent spirit, to renounce our own wills, and give up ourselves to His disposal without reserve. This is the path of peace; and it is the path of safety; for He has said, the meek He will teach His way, and those who yield up themselves to Him He will guide with His eye. I hope you will fight and pray against every rising of a murmuring spirit, and be thankful for the great things which He has already done for you. It is good to be humbled for sin, but not to be discouraged : for though we are poor creatures, Jesus is a complete Saviour; and we bring more honour to God by believing in His name, and trusting His word of promise, than we could do by a thousand outward works.

I pray the Lord to shine upon your soul, and to fill you with all joy and peace in believing. Remember to pray for us, that we may be brought home to you in peace.

I am, &c.

LETTER IV

London, Aug. 19, 1775.

You see I am mindful of my promise; and glad should I be to write something that the Lord may be pleased to make a word in season. I went yesterday into the pulpit very dry and heartless. I seemed to have fixed upon a text, but when I came to the pinch, it was so shut up that I could not preach from it. I had hardly a minute to choose, and therefore was forced to snatch at that which came first upon my mind, which proved 2 Tim. i. 12. Thus I set off at a venture, having no resource but in the Lord's mercy and faithfulness; and, indeed, what other can we wish for ? Presently my subject opened; and I know not when I have been favoured with more liberty. Why do I tell you this ? Only as an instance of His goodness, to encourage you to put your strength in Him, and not to be afraid even when you feel your own weakness and insufficiency most sensibly. We are never more safe, never have more reason to expect the Lord's help, than when we are most sensible that we can do nothing without Him. This was the lesson Paul learnt, to rejoice in His own poverty and emptiness, that the power of Christ might rest upon Him. Could Paul have done anything, Jesus would not have had the honour of doing all. This way of being saved entirely by grace, from first to last, is contrary to our natural wills; it mortifies self, leaving it nothing to boast of, and through the remains of an unbelieving, legal spirit, it often seems discouraging. When we think ourselves so utterly helpless and worthless, we are too ready to fear that the Lord will therefore reject us; whereas, in truth, such a poverty of spirit is the best mark we can have of an interest in His promises and care.

How often have I longed to be an instrument of establishing you in the peace and hope of the Gospel! and I have but one way of attempting it, by telling you over and over of the power and grace of Jesus. You want nothing to make you happy, but to have the eyes of your understanding more fixed upon the Redeemer, and more enlightened by the Holy Spirit to behold His glory. O! He is a suitable Saviour! He has power, authority, and compassion, to save to the uttermost. He has given His word of promise, to engage our confidence, and He is able and faithful to make good the expectations and desires He has raised in us. Put your trust in Him; believe (as we say) through thick and thin, in defiance of all objections from within and without. For this, Abraham is recommended as a pattern to us. He overlooked all difficulties; he ventured and hoped even against hope, in a case which to appearance was desperate; because he knew that He who had promised was also able to perform.

Your sister is much upon my mind. Her illness grieves me; were it in my power, I would quickly remove it. The Lord can, and I hope will, when it has answered the end for which He sent it. I trust He has brought her to us for good, and that she is chastised by Him that she may not be condemned with the world. I hope, though she says little, she lifts up her heart to Him for a blessing. I wish you may be enabled to leave her and yourself, and all

your concerns, in His hands. He has a sovereign right to
do with us as He pleases ; and if we consider what we
are, surely we shall confess we have no reason to complain ;
and to those who seek Him, His sovereignty is exercised
in a way of grace. All shall work together for good ;
everything is needful that He sends ; nothing can be needful
that He withholds. Be content to bear the cross ; others
have borne it before you. You have need of patience ;
and if you ask, the Lord will give it : but there can be
no settled peace till our will is in a measure subdued. Hide
yourself under the shadow of His wings ; rely upon His
care and power ; look upon Him as a physician who has
graciously undertaken to heal your soul of the worst of
sicknesses, sin. Yield to His prescriptions, and fight
against every thought that would represent it as desirable
to be permitted to choose for yourself. When you cannot
see your way, be satisfied that He is your leader. When
your spirit is overwhelmed within you, He knows your
path ; He will not leave you to sink. He has appointed
seasons of refreshment, and you shall find He does not forget
you. Above all, keep close to the throne of grace. If we
seem to get no good by attempting to draw near Him
we may be sure we shall get none by keeping away from
Him.

I am, &c.

LETTER V

I PROMISED you another letter ; and now for the per-
formance. If I had said, it may be, or perhaps I will,
you would be in suspense ; but if I promise, then you
expect that I will not disappoint you unless something
should render it impossible for me to make my word good.
I thank you for your good opinion of me, and for thinking
I mean what I say ; and I pray that you may be enabled
more and more to honour the Lord by believing His promise :
for He is not like a man that should fail or change, or be
prevented by anything unforeseen from doing what He has

said. And yet we find it easier to trust to worms than to the God of truth. Is it not so with you ? And I can assure you it is often so with me. But here is the mercy, that His ways are above ours, as the heavens are higher than the earth. Though we are foolish and unbelieving, He remains faithful ; He will not deny Himself. I recommend to you especially that promise of God, which is so comprehensive that it takes in all our concernments, I mean, that all things shall work together for good. How hard is it to believe, that not only those things which are grievous to the flesh, but even those things which draw forth our corruptions, and discover to us what is in our hearts, and fill us with guilt and shame, should in the issue work for our good ! Yet the Lord has said it. All your pains and trials, all that befals you in your own person, or that affects you upon the account of others, shall in the end prove to your advantage. And your peace does not depend upon any change of circumstance which may appear desirable, but in having your will bowed to the Lord's will, and made willing to submit all to His disposal and management. Pray for this, and wait patiently for Him, and He will do it. Be not surprised to find yourself poor, helpless, and vile ; all whom He favours and teaches will find themselves so. The more grace increases, the more we shall see to abase us in our own eyes ; and this will make the Saviour and His salvation more precious to us. He takes His own wise methods to humble you, and to prove you, and I am sure He will do you good in the end.

I am, &c.

LETTER VI

September 16, 1775.

WHEN you receive this, I hope it will give you pleasure to think that, if the Lord be pleased to favour us with health, we shall all meet again in a few days. I have met with much kindness at London, and many comforts and mercies : however, I shall be glad to return home.

There my heart lives, let my body be where it will. I long
to see all my dear people, and I shall be glad to see you.
I steal a little time to write another line or two, more to
satisfy you, than for anything particular I have to say. I
thank you for your letter. I doubt not but the Lord
is bringing you forward, and that you have a good right
to say to your soul, Why art thou cast down and disquieted?
Hope thou in God; for I shall yet praise Him. An evil
heart, an evil temper, and the many crosses we meet with
in passing through an evil world, will cut us out trouble
but the Lord has provided a balm for every wound, a
cordial for every care; the fruit of all is to take away
sin, and the end of all will be eternal life in glory. Think
of these words; put them in the balance of the sanctuary;
and then throw all your trials into the opposite scale,
and you will find there is no proportion between them.
Say then, " Though He slay me, I will trust in Him ; "
for when He has fully tried me, I shall come forth like
gold. You would have liked to have been with me last
Wednesday. I preached at Westminster Bridewell. It
is a prison and house of correction. The bulk of my congre-
gation were housebreakers, highwaymen, pickpockets, and
poor unhappy women, such as infest the streets of the city,
sunk in sin and lost to shame. I had a hundred or more
of these before me. I preached from 1 Tim. i. 15, and began
with telling them my own story : this gained their attention
more than I expected. I spoke to them near an hour
and a half. I shed many tears myself, and saw some
of them shed tears likewise. Ah! had you seen their
present condition, and could you hear the history of some
of them, it would make you sing, " O to grace how great a
debtor ! " By nature they were no worse than the most
sober and modest people. And there was doubtless a time
when many of them little thought what they should live to
do and suffer. I might have been, like them, in chains,
and one of them have come to preach to me, had the Lord
so pleased.

                                        I am, &c.

LETTER VII

October 10, 1777.

I AM just come from seeing A —— N ——. The people told me she is much better than she was, but she is far from being well. She was brought to me into a parlour, which saved me the painful task of going to inquire and seek for her among the patients. My spirits always sink when I am within these mournful walls, and I think no money could prevail on me to spend an hour there every day. Yet surely no sight upon earth is more suited to teach one thankfulness and resignation. Surely I have reason, in my worst times, to be thankful that I am out of hell, out of Bedlam, out of Newgate. If my eyes were as bad as yours, and my back worse, still I hope I should set a great value upon this mercy, that my senses are preserved. I hope you will think so too. The Lord afflicts us at times; but it is always a thousand times less than we deserve, and much less than many of our fellow-creatures are suffering around us. Let us therefore pray for grace to be humble, thankful, and patient.

This day twelvemonth I was under Mr. W ——'s knife; there is another cause for thankfulness, that the Lord inclined me to submit to the operation, and brought me happily through it. In short, I have so many reasons for thankfulness, that I cannot count them. I may truly say, they are more in number than the hairs of my head. And, yet, alas! how cold, insensible, and ungrateful! I could make as many complaints as you; but I find no good by complaining, except to Him who is able to help me. It is better for you and me to be admiring the compassion and fulness of grace that is in our Saviour, than to dwell and pore too much upon our own poverty and vileness. He is able to help and save to the uttermost; there I desire to cast anchor, and wish you to do so likewise. Hope in God, for you shall yet praise Him.

I am, &c.

FIVE LETTERS

MR. C——

LETTER I

DEAR SIR, *Jan.* 16, 1775.

THE death of a near relative called me from home in
December, and a fortnight's absence threw me so far behind-
hand in my course, that I deferred acknowledging your letter
much longer than I intended. I now thank you for it. I
can sympathize with you in your troubles : yet knowing
the nature of our calling, that by an unalterable appoint-
ment the way to the Kingdom lies through many tribulations,
I ought to rejoice rather than otherwise, that to you it is
given, not only to believe, but also to suffer. If you escaped
these things, whereof all the Lord's children are partakers,
might you not question your adoption into His family ?
How could the power of grace be manifest, either to you, in
you, or by you, without afflictions ? How could the corrup-
tions and devastations of the heart be checked without a
cross ? How could you acquire a tenderness and skill in
speaking to them that are weary, without a taste of such
trials as they also meet with ? You could only be a hearsay
witness to the truth, power, and sweetness of the precious
promises, unless you have been in such a situation as to
need them, and to find their suitableness and sufficiency.
The Lord has given you a good desire to serve Him in the
Gospel, and He is now training you for that service. Many
things, yea, the most important things belonging to the
Gospel ministry, are not to be learned by books and study,
but by painful experience. You must expect a variety of
exercises : but two things He has promised you, that you

shall not be tried above what He will enable you to bear, and that all shall work together for your good. We read somewhere of a conceited orator, who declaimed upon the management of war in the presence of Hannibal, and of the contempt with which Hannibal treated his performance. He deserved it ; for how should a man who had never seen a field of battle be a competent judge of such a subject ? Just so, were we to acquire no other knowledge of the Christian warfare than what we could derive from cool and undisturbed study, instead of coming forth as able ministers of the New Testament, and competently acquainted with the τα νοηματα, with the devices, the deep-laid counsels and stratagems of Satan, we should prove but mere declaimers. But the Lord will take better care of those whom He loves and designs to honour. He will try, and permit them to be tried, in various ways. He will make them feel much in themselves, that they may know how to feel much for others ; according to that beautiful and expressive line,

> Haud ignara mali, miseris succurrere disco.

And as this previous discipline is necessary to enable us to take the field, in a public capacity, with courage, wisdom, and success, that we may lead and animate others in the fight, it is equally necessary, for our own sakes, that we may obtain and preserve the grace of humility, which I perceive with pleasure he has taught you to set a high value upon. Indeed, we cannot value it too highly ; for we can be neither comfortable, safe, nor habitually useful, without it. The root of pride lies deep in our fallen nature, and where the Lord has given natural and acquired abilities, it would grow apace, if He did not mercifully watch over us and suit His dispensations to keep it down. Therefore, I trust He will make you willing to endure hardships, as a good soldier of Jesus Christ. May He enable you to behold Him with faith, holding out the prize, and saying to you, Fear none of these things that thou shalt suffer : "Be thou faithful unto death, and I will give thee a crown of life."

We sail upon a turbulent and tumultuous sea ; but we are embarked on a good bottom, and in a good cause, and we have an infallible and almighty Pilot, who has the winds and weather at His command, and can silence the storm into a calm with a word whenever He pleases. We may be persecuted, but we shall not be forsaken ; we may be cast down, but we cannot be destroyed. Many will thrust sore at us that we may fall, but the Lord will be our stay.

I am sorry to find you are quite alone at Cambridge, for I hoped there would be a succession of serious students, to supply the place of those who are transplanted to shine as lights in the world. Yet you are not alone ; for the Lord is with you, the best Counsellor and the best Friend. There is a strange backwardness in us (at least in me) fully to improve that gracious intimacy to which He invites us. Alas ! that we so easily wander from the fountain of life, to hew out cisterns for ourselves, and that we seem more attached to a few drops of His grace in our fellow-creatures, than to the fulness of grace that is in Himself ! I think nothing gives me a more striking sense of my depravity, than my perverseness and folly in this respect ; yet He bears with me, and does me good continually.

I am, &c.

LETTER II

DEAR SIR,   *March*, 1776.

I KNOW not the length of your college terms, but hope this may come time enough to find you still resident. I shall not apologize for writing no sooner, because I leave other letters of much longer date unanswered, that I may write so soon. It gave me particular pleasure to hear that the Lord helped you through your difficulties, and succeeded your desires ; and I have sympathized with you in the complaints you make of a dark and mournful frame of spirits afterwards. But is not this, upon the whole, right and salutary, that if the Lord is pleased at one time to strengthen us remarkably in answer to prayer, He should leave us at another time, so far as to give us a real sensibility that we were supported by His power, and not our own ? Besides, as you feel a danger of being elated by the respect paid you, was it not a merciful and seasonable dispensation that made you feel your own weakness, to prevent your being exalted above measure ? The Lord, by withdrawing His smiles from you, reminded you that the smiles of men are of little value, otherwise, perhaps, you might have esteemed them too highly. Indeed, you scholars that know the Lord, are singular instances of the power of His grace ; for (like the young men in Dan. iii.) you live in the very midst of the fire. Mathematical studies, in particular, have such a tendency to engross and fix the mind to the contemplation of cold and uninteresting truth, and you are surrounded with so much intoxicating applause if you succeed in your researches, that for a soul to be kept humble and alive in such a situation, is such a proof of the Lord's presence and power, as Moses had when he saw the bush unconsumed in the midst of the flames. I believe I had naturally a turn for the mathematics myself, and dabbled in them a little way ; and though I did not go far, my head, sleeping and waking, was stuffed with diagrams and calculations. Everything I looked at, that exhibited either a right line, or a curve, set my wits a wool-gathering. What, then, must have been the case, had I proceeded to the interior *arcana*, of speculative geometry ? I bought my namesake's *Principia*, but I have reason to be thankful that I left it as I found it, a sealed book, and that the bent of my mind was drawn to something of more real importance before I understood it. I say not this to discourage you in your pursuits : they lie in your line and path of duty ; in mine they did not. As to your academies, I am glad that the Lord enables you to show those among whom you live, that the knowledge of His Gospel does not despoil you either of diligence or acumen. However, as I said, you need a double guard of grace, to preserve you from being either puffed up or deadened by those things which, considered in any other view than *quo ad hoc*, to preserve your rank and character in the University while you remain there, are, if taken in the aggregate, little better than a *splendidum nihil*. If my poor people at ———— could form the least conception of what the learned at Cambridge chiefly admire in each other, and what is the intrinsic reward of all their toil, they would say (supposing they could speak Latin), *Quam suave istis suavitatibus carere* ! How gladly would some of them, if such mathematical and metaphysical lumber could by any means get into their heads, how gladly would they drink at Lethe's stream to get it out again! How many perplexities are they freed from by their happy ignorance, which often pester those to their life's end who have had their natural proneness to vain reasoning sharpened by academical studies!

LETTER III

DEAR SIR,   *May* 18, 1776.

THOUGH I wished to hear from you sooner, I put a candid interpretation upon your silence, was somewhat apprehensive for your health, but felt no disposition to anger. Let your correspondence be free from fetters. Write when you please, and when you can : I will do the like. Apologies may be spared on both sides. I am not a very punctual correspondent myself, having so many letters to write, and therefore have no right to stand upon punctilios with you.

I sympathize with you in your sorrow for your friend's death. Such cases are very distressing. But such a case might have been our own. Let us pray for grace to be thankful for ourselves, and submit everything in humble silence to the sovereign Lord, who has a right to do as He pleases with His own. We feel what happens in our own little connexions ; but O the dreadful mischief of sin! Instances of this kind are as frequent as the hours, the minutes, perhaps the moments, of every day : and though we know but one in a million, the souls of others have an equal capacity for endless happiness or misery. In this situation the Lord has honoured us with a call to warn our fellow-sinners of their danger, and to set before them His free and sure salvation ; and if He is pleased to make us instrumental in snatching but one as a brand out of the fire, it is a service of more importance than to be the means of preserving a whole nation from temporal ruin. I congratulate you upon your admission into the ministry, and pray Him to favour you with a single eye to His glory, and a fresh anointing of His Holy Spirit, that you may come forth as a scribe well instructed in the mysteries of His Kingdom, and that His word in your mouth may abundantly prosper.

I truly pity those who rise early and take late rest, and eat the bread of carefulness with no higher prize and prospect in view than the obtaining of academical honours. Such pursuits will ere long appear (as they really are) vain as the sports of children. May the Lord impress them with a noble ambition of living to and for Him ! If these adventurers, who are labouring for pebbles under the semblance of goodly pearls, had a discovery of the pearl of great price, how quickly and gladly would they lay down their admired attainments, and become fools that they might be truly wise ! What a snare have you escaped ! You would have been poorly content with the name of a mathematician or a poet, and looked no further, had not He visited your heart, and enlightened you by His grace. Now I trust you account your former gain but loss, for the excellency of the knowledge of Jesus Christ the Lord. What you have attained in a way of literature will be useful to you if sanctified, and chiefly so by the knowledge you have of its insufficiency to any valuable purpose in the great concerns of walking with God, and winning souls.

I am pleased with your fears, lest you should not be understood in your preaching. Indeed, there is a danger of it. It is not easy for persons of quick parts duly to conceive how amazingly ignorant and slow of apprehension the bulk of our congregations generally are. When our own ideas are clear, and our expressions proper, we are ready to think we have sufficiently explained ourselves ; and yet, perhaps, nine out of ten (especially of those who are destitute of spiritual light) know little more of what we say than if we were speaking Greek. A degree of this inconvenience is always inseparable from written discourses. They cast our thoughts into a style which, though familiar to ourselves, is too remote from common conversation to be comprehended by narrow capacities ; which is one chief reason of the preference I give, *cæteris paribus*, to extempore preaching. When we read to the people, they think themselves less concerned in what is offered, than when we speak to them point blank. It seems a good rule, which I have

met with somewhere, and which perhaps I have mentioned
to you, to fix your eyes upon some one of the auditory whom
we judge of the least capacity ; if we can make him under
stand, we may hope to be understood by the rest. Let
those who seek to be admired for the exactness of their
composition, enjoy the poor reward they aim at. It is best
for Gospel preachers to speak plain language. If we thus
singly aim at the glory of our Master and the good of souls,
we may hope for the accompanying power of His Spirit,
which will give our discourses a weight and energy that
Demosthenes had no conception of.

I can give you no information of a curacy in a better situa-
tion. But either the Lord will provide you one, or I trust
He will give you usefulness and a competency of health and
spirits where you are. He who caused Daniel to thrive
upon pulse, can make you strong and cheerful even in the
Fens, if He sees that best for you. All things obey Him,
and you need not fear but He will enable you for whatever
service He has appointed you to perform.

This letter has been a week in hand ; many interruptions
from without, and indispositions within. I seem to while
away my life, and shall be glad to be saved upon the footing
of the thief upon the cross, without any hope or plea but
the power and grace of Jesus, who has said, " I will in no
wise cast out." Adieu.

Pray for yours, &c.

LETTER IV

DEAR SIR,   *Sept.* 10, 1777.

I WAS glad to hear from you at last, not being willing
to think myself forgotten. I supposed you were ill. It seems,
by your account, that you are far from well : but I hope
you are as well as you ought to be ; that is, as well as the Lord
sees it good for you to be. I say, I hope so : for I am not
sure that the length and vehemence of your sermons, which
you tell me astonish many people, may not be rather
improper and imprudent, considering the weakness of your

constitution ; at least, if this expression of yours be justly expounded by a report which has reached me, that the length of your sermons is frequently two hours, and the vehemence of your voice so great, that you may be heard far beyond the church-walls. Unwilling should I be to damp your zeal ; but I feel unwilling, likewise, that, by excessive unnecessary exertions, you should wear away at once, and preclude your own usefulness. This concern is so much upon my mind, that I begin with it, though it makes me skip over the former part of your letter ; but when I have relieved myself upon this point, I can easily skip back again. I am perhaps the more ready to credit the report, because I know the spirits of you nervous people are highly volatile. I consider you as mounted upon a fiery steed ; and provided you use due management and circumspection, you travel more pleasantly than we plodding folks upon our sober phlegmatic nags ; but then, if instead of pulling the rein you plunge in the spurs, and add wings to the wind, I cannot but be in pain for the consequences. Permit me to remind you of the Terentian adage, *Ne quid nimis*. The end of speaking is to be heard, and if the persons farthest from the preacher can hear, he speaks loud enough. Upon some occasions, a few sentences of a discourse may be enforced with a voice still more elevated ; but to be uncommonly loud from beginning to end, is hurtful to the speaker, and, I apprehend, no way useful to the hearer. It is a fault which many inadvertently give in to at first, and which many have repented of too late ; when practice has rendered it habitual, it is not easily corrected. I know some think, that preaching very loudly, and preaching with power, are synonymous expressions ; but your judgment is too good to fall in with that prejudice. If I were a good Grecian, I would send you a quotation from Homer, where he describes the eloquence of Nestor, and compares it, if I remember right, not to a thunder-storm or a hurricane, but to a fall of snow, which, though pressing, insinuating, and penetrating, is soft and gentle. You know the passage : I think the simile is beautiful and expressive.

Secondly (as we say), as to long preaching. There is still in being an old-fashioned instrument called an hour-glass, which, in days of yore, before clocks and watches abounded, used to be the measure of many a good sermon, and I think it a tolerable stint.   I cannot wind up my ends to my own satisfaction in a much shorter time, nor am I pleased with myself if I greatly exceed it.   If an angel were to preach for two hours, unless his hearers were angels likewise, I believe the greater part of them would wish he had done.   It is a shame it should be so ; but so it is, partly through the weakness, and partly through the wickedness, of the flesh ; we can seldom stretch our attention to spiritual things for two hours together, without cracking it, and hurting its spring ;   and when weariness begins, edification ends. Perhaps it is better to feed our people like chickens, a little and often, than to cram them like turkeys, till they cannot hold one gobbet more.   Besides, overlong sermons break in upon family concerns, and often call off the thoughts from the sermon to the pudding at home, which is in danger of being overboiled.   They leave likewise but little time for secret or family religion, which are both very good in their place, and are entitled to a share in the Lord's Day. Upon the preacher they must have a bad effect, and tend to wear him down before his time :   and I have known some, by overacting at first, have been constrained to sit still, and do little or nothing for months or years afterwards.   I rather recommend to you the advice of your brother Cantab, Hobson the carrier, so to set out, that you may hold out to your journey's end.

Now, if Fame, with her hundred mouths, has brought me a false report of you, and you are not guilty of preaching either too long or too loud, still I am not willing my remonstrance may stand for nothing.   I desire you will accept it, and thank me for it, as a proof of my love to you, and likewise of the sincerity of my friendship ;   for if I had wished to flatter you, I could easily have culled another subject.

I have one more report to trouble you with, because it troubles me ;   and, therefore, you must bear a part of my burden.   Assure me it is false, and I will send you one of the handsomest letters I can devise, by way of thanks.   It is reported, then (but I will not believe it till you say I must) that you stand upon your tiptoes, upon the point of being whirled out of our vortex, and hurried away, comet-like, into the regions of eccentricity :   in plain English, that you have a hankering to be an itinerant. If this be true, I will not be the first to tell it in St. John's College or to publish it on the banks of Cam, lest the mathematicians rejoice, and the poets triumph. But to be serious, for it is a serious subject, let me beg you to deliberate well, and to pray earnestly before you take this step. Be afraid of acting in your own spirit, or under a wrong impression ; however honestly you mean, you may be mistaken. The Lord has given you a little charge : be faithful in it, and in His good time He will advance you to a greater ; but let His providence evidently open the door for you, and be afraid of moving one step before the cloud and pillar. I have had my warm fits and desires of this sort in my time ; but I have reason to be thankful, that I was held in with a strong hand. I wish there were more itinerant preachers. If a man has grace and zeal, and but little funds, let him go and diffuse the substance of a dozen sermons over as many counties ; but you have natural and acquired abilities, which qualify you for the more difficult, and in my judgment, not less important, station of a parochial minister. I wish you to be a burning, shining, steady light. You may perhaps have less popularity, that is, you will be less exposed to the workings of self and the snares of Satan, if you stay with us ; but I think you may live in the full exercise of your gifts and graces, be more consistent with your voluntary engagements, and have more peace of mind, and humble intercourse with God, in watching over a flock which He has committed to you, than, by forsaking them, to wander up and down the earth without a determined scope.

Thus far I have been more attentive to the *utile* than the *dulce*. I should now return to join you in celebrating the praises of poetry, and the other subjects of your letter ; but time and paper fail together. Let me hear from you soon, or I shall fear I have displeased you, which, fond as I am of poetry, would give me more pain than I ever found pleasure in reading Alexander's Feast. Indeed I love you ; I often measure over the walks we have taken together ; and when I come to a favourite stile, or such a favourite spot upon the hill top, I am reminded of something that passed, and say, or at least think, *Hic stetit* C———.

Yours, &c.

LETTER V

DEAR SIR,

BY your flying letter from London, as well as by your more particular answer to my last, I judge that what I formerly wrote will answer no other end than to be a testimony of my fidelity and friendship. I am ready to think you were so far determined before you applied to the Bishop, as to be rather pleased than disappointed by a refusal, which seemed to afford you liberty to preach at large. As your *testimonium* was not countersigned, the consequence was no other than might have been expected ; yet I have been told (how true I know not), that the Bishop would have passed over the informality, if you had not, unasked by him, avowed yourself a Methodist. I think, if you had been unwilling to throw hindrances in your own way, the most perfect simplicity would have required no more of you than to have given a plain and honest answer to such questions as he might think proper to propose. You might have assisted Mr. ———— for a season without being in full orders ; and you may still, if you are not resolved at all events to push out. He wrote to me about you, and you may easily judge what answer I gave. I have heard from him a second time, and he laments that he cannot have you. I likewise lament that you cannot be with him. I think you would have loved him ; and I hoped his acquaintance might not have proved unuseful to you.

If you have not actually passed the Rubicon, if there be yet room for deliberation, I once more intreat you to pause and consider. In many respects I ought to be willing to learn from you ; but in one point I have a little advantage of you : I am some years older, both in life and in profession ; and in this difference of time perhaps I have learned something more of the heart, the world, and the devices of Satan than you have had opportunity for. I hope I would not damp your zeal, but I will pray the Lord to direct it into the best channel for permanent usefulness ; I say permanent ; I doubt not that you would be useful in the itinerant way ; but I more and more observe great inconveniences follow in the way. Where you make a gathering of people, others will follow you; and if they all possessed your spirit, and had your disinterested views, it might be well. But generally an able preacher only so far awakens people to a desire to hear, as exposes them to the incursions of various winds of doctrine, and the attempts of injudicious pretenders, who will resemble you in nothing but your eagerness to post from place to place. From such measures in time proceed errors, parties, contentions, offences, enthusiasm, spiritual pride, and a noisy ostentatious form of godliness, but little of that power and life of faith which shows itself by humility, meekness, and love.

A parochial minister, who lives among his people, who sees and converses with them frequently, and exemplifies his doctrine in their view by his practice, having knowledge of their states, trials, growth, and dangers, suits himself to their various occasions, and, by the blessing of God, builds them up, and brings them forward in faith and holiness. He is instrumental in forming their experience; he leads them to a solid, orderly, Scriptural knowledge of Divine things. If his name is not in so many mouths as that of the itinerant, it is upon the hearts of the people of his charge. He lives with them as a father with his children. His steady, consistent behaviour silences in some measure the clamours of his enemies; and the Lord opens him doors of occasional usefulness in many places, without provoking our superiors to discountenance other young men who are seeking Orders.

I now wish I had taken larger paper, for I have not room for all I would say. I have no end to serve. I am of no party. I wish well to irregulars and itinerants, who love and preach the Gospel. I am content that they should labour that way who have not talents nor funds to support the character and fill up the office of a parochial minister. But I think you are qualified for more important service. If you had patient faith to wait awhile for the Lord's opening, I doubt not but you might yet obtain Priest's Orders. We are hasty, like children; but God often appoints us a waiting time. Perhaps it requires as much or more grace to wait than to be active; for it is more trying to self. After all, whatever course you take, I shall love you, pray for you, and be glad to see you. I am, &c.

EIGHT LETTERS

TO

MRS. ———

LETTER I

My Dear Madam,   *July* — 1764.

THE complaints you make are inseparable from a
spiritual acquaintance with our own hearts : I would
not wish you to be less affected with a sense of indwelling
sin. It becomes us to be humbled in the dust ; yet our
grief, though it cannot be too great, may be under a wrong
direction ; and if it leads us to impatience or distrust, it
certainly is so.

Sin is the sickness of the soul, in itself mortal and incurable
as to any power in Heaven or earth, but that of the Lord
Jesus only. But He is the great, the infallible Physician.
Have we the privilege to know His name ? Have we been
enabled to put ourselves into His hand ? We have then
no more to do but to attend to His prescriptions, to be satis-
fied with His methods, and to wait His time. It is lawful
to wish we were well ; it is natural to groan, being burdened ;
but still He must and will take His own course with us ;
and, however dissatisfied with ourselves, we ought still to be
thankful that He has begun His work in us, and to believe
that He will also make an end. Therefore while we mourn,
we should likewise rejoice ; we should encourage ourselves
to expect all that He has promised ; and we should limit
our expectations by His promises. We are sure, that when
the Lord delivers us from the guilt and dominion of sin,
He could with equal ease free us entirely from sin if He
pleased. The doctrine of sinless perfection is not to be
rejected as though it were a thing simply impossible in

360

itself, for nothing is too hard for the Lord, but because it is contrary to that method which He has chosen to proceed by. He has appointed that sanctification should be effected, and sin mortified, not at once completely, but by little and little ; and doubtless He has wise reasons for it. Therefore, though we are to desire a growth in grace, we should at the same time acquiesce in His appointment, and not be discouraged or despond, because we feel that conflict which His word informs us will only terminate with our lives.

Again, some of the first prayers which the Spirit of God teaches us to put up, are for a clearer sense of the sinfulness of sin, and our vileness on account of it. Now, if the Lord is pleased to answer your prayers in this respect, though it will afford you cause enough for humiliation, yet it should be received likewise with thankfulness, as a token for good. Your heart is not worse than it was formerly, only your spiritual knowledge is increased ; and this is no small part of the growth in grace which you are thirsting after to be truly humbled, and emptied, and made little in your own eyes.

Further, the examples of the saints recorded in Scripture prove (and indeed of the saints in general), that the greater measure they have had of the grace of God in truth, the more conscientious and lively they have been ; and the more they have been favoured with assurances of the Divine favour, so much the more deep and sensible their perception of indwelling sin and infirmity has always been : so it was with Job, Isaiah, Daniel, and Paul. It is likewise common to overcharge ourselves. Indeed, we cannot think ourselves worse than we really are ; yet some things which abate the comfort and alacrity of our Christian profession, are rather impediments than properly sinful, and will not be imputed to us by Him who knows our frame, and remembers that we are but dust. Thus, to have an infirm memory, to be subject to disordered, irregular, or low spirits, are faults of the constitution, in which the *will* has no share, though they are all burdensome and oppressive, and sometimes needlessly so, by our charging ourselves with guilt on their account. The same may be observed of the unspeakable and fierce suggestions of Satan, with which some persons are pestered, but which shall be laid to him from whom they proceed, and not to them who are troubled and terrified, because they are forced to feel them. *Lastly*, it is by the experience of these evils within ourselves, and by feeling our utter insufficiency either to perform duty, or to withstand our enemies, that the Lord takes occasion to show us the suitableness, the sufficiency, the freeness, the unchangeableness, of His power and grace. This is the inference St. Paul draws from his complaints, Rom. vii. 25 ; and he learnt it upon a trying occasion from the Lord's own mouth, 2 Cor. xii. 8, 9.

Let us then, dear Madam, be thankful and cheerful, and while we take shame to ourselves, let us glorify God, by giving Jesus the honour due to His name. Though we are poor, He is rich ; though we are weak, He is strong ; though we have nothing, He possesses all things. He suffered for us ; He calls us to be conformed to Him in sufferings. He conquered in His own person, and He will make each of His members more than conquerors in due season. It is good to have one eye upon ourselves, but the other should ever be fixed on Him who stands in the relation of Saviour, Husband, Head, and Shepherd. In Him we have righteousness, peace, and powe : He can control all that we fear ; so that if our path should be through the fire or through the water, neither the flood shall drown us, nor the flame kindle upon us, and ere long He will cut short our conflicts, and say, Come up hither. " Then shall our grateful songs abound, and every tear be wiped away." Having such promises and assurances, let us lift up our banner in His name, and press on through every discouragement.

With regard to company that has not a savour of the best things, as it is not your choice, I would advise you (when necessary) to bear it as a cross : we cannot suffer by being where we ought to be, except through our own impatience ; and I have an idea, that when we are providentially called amongst such (for something is due to friends and relations, whether they walk with us or no), that the hours need not be wholly lost ; nothing can pass but may be improved ; the most trivial conversation may afford us new views of the heart, new confirmation of Scripture, and renew a sense of our obligations to distinguishing grace, which has made us in any degree to differ. I would wish, when you go among

your friends, that you do not confine your views to getting
safe away from them without loss, but entertain a hope that
you may be sent to do some of them good.   You cannot
tell what effect a word or a look may have, if the Lord is
pleased to bless it.   I think we may humbly hope, that while
we sincerely desire to please the Lord, and to be guided by
Him in all things, He will not suffer us to take a journey, or
hardly to make a short visit, which shall not answer some
good purpose to ourselves or others, or both.   While our
gay friends affect an air of raillery, the Lord may give you
a secret witness in their consciences ; and something they
observe in you, or hear from you, may set them on thinking,
perhaps after you are gone, or after the first occasion has
entirely slipped your memory, Eccles. xi. 1.   For my own
part, when I consider the power, the freedom of Divine
grace, and how sovereign the Lord is in the choice of the
instruments and means by which He is pleased to work,
I live in hopes from day to day of hearing wonders of this
sort.   I despair of nobody ; and if I sometimes am ready
to think such or such a person seems more unlikely than
others to be brought in, I relieve myself by a possibility
that that very person, and for that very reason, may be the
first instance.   The Lord's thoughts are not like ours ;
in His love and in His ways there are heights which we cannot
reach, depths which we cannot fathom, lengths and breadths
beyond the ken of our feeble sight.   Let us then simply
depend upon Him and do our little best, leaving the event
in His hand.

I cannot tell if you know anything of Mrs. ——.   In
a letter I received yesterday, she writes thus :—" I am at
present very ill with some disorder in my throat, which
seems to threaten my life ; but death or life, things present
or things to come, all things are mine, and I am Christ's,
and Christ is God's.   O glorious privilege !   precious founda-
tion of soul-rest and peace, when all things about us are most
troublous !   Soon we shall be at home with Christ, where
sin, sorrow, and death, have no place ; and, in the mean time,
our Beloved will lead us through the wilderness.   How
safe, how joyous are we, may we be, in the most evil case ! "
—If these should be some of the last notes of this swan,
I think them worth preserving.   May we not with good

reason say, who would not be a Christian ? The Lord grant that you and I, Madam, and yours and mine, may be happy in the same assurance, when we shall have death and eternity near in view.

I am, &c.

LETTER II

My Dear Madam,   *Sept.*, 1764.

YOUR welfare I rejoice in ; your warfare I understand something of.   St. Paul describes his own case in few words : " Without were fightings, within were fears." Does not this comprehend all you would say ?   And how are you to know experimentally, either your own weakness, or the power, wisdom, and grace of God, seasonably and sufficiently afforded but by frequent and various trials ?   How are the graces of patience, resignation, meekness, and faith, to be discovered and increased, but by exercise ?   The Lord has chosen, called, and armed us for the fight ; and shall we wish to be excused ?   Shall not we rather rejoice that we have the honour to appear in such a cause, under such a Captain, such a banner, and in such a company ?   A complete suit of armour is provided, weapons not to be resisted, and precious balm to heal us, if haply we receive a wound, and precious ointment to revive us when we are in danger of fainting.   Further, we are assured of the victory beforehand ; and O what a crown is prepared for every conqueror, which Jesus the righteous Judge, the gracious Saviour, shall place upon every faithful head with His own hand !   Then let us not be weary and faint, for in due season we shall reap.   The time is short ; yet a little while, and the struggle of indwelling sin, and the contradiction of surrounding sinners, shall be known no more.   You are blessed, because you hunger and thirst after righteousness ; He whose name is *Amen* has said you shall be filled. To claim the promise, is to make it our own ; yet it is becoming us to practise submission and patience, not in temporals only, but also in spirituals.   We should be

ashamed and grieved at our slow progress, so far as it is
properly chargeable to our remissness and miscarriage ;
yet we must not expect to receive everything at once, but
wait for a gradual increase ; nor should we forget to be
thankful for what we may account a little, in comparison
of the much we suppose others have received. A little grace,
a spark of true love to God, a grain of living faith, though
small as mustard seed, is worth a thousand worlds. One
draught of the water of life gives interest in and earnest of
the whole fountain. It becometh the Lord's people to be
thankful ; and to acknowledge His goodness in what we
have received, is the surest as well as the pleasantest method
of obtaining more. Nor should the grief arising from what
we know and feel of our own hearts, rob us of the honour,
comfort, and joy, which the word of God designs us, in
what is there recorded of the person, offices and grace of
Jesus, and the relations He is pleased to stand in to His
people, Psalm xxiii. 1 ; Isa. liv. 5 ; Cant. v. 16 ; John xv.
15 ; 1 John ii. 1 ; John xv. 1 ; Jer. xxiii. 5 ; 1 Cor. 1. 30 ;
Matt. i. 21-23. Give me leave to recommend to your con-
sideration Psa. lxxxix. 15-18. These verses may be called
the Believers' Triumph : though they are nothing in them-
selves, yet having all in Jesus, they may rejoice in His
name all the day. The Lord enable us so to do ! The joy
of the Lord is the strength of His people ; whereas unbelief
makes our hands hang down, and our knees feeble, dispirits
ourselves, and discourages others ; and though it steals
upon us under a semblance of humility, it is indeed the very
essence of pride. By inward and outward exercises the
Lord is promoting the best desire of your heart, and answer-
ing your daily prayers. Would you have assurance ? The
true solid assurance is to be obtained no other way. When
young Christians are greatly comforted with the Lord's
love and presence, their doubts and fears are for that season
at an end. But this is not assurance ; so soon as the Lord
hides His face, they are troubled, and ready to question the
very foundation of hope. Assurance grows by repeated
conflict, by our repeated experimental proof of the Lord's
power and goodness to save ; when we have been brought
very low and helped, sorely wounded and healed, cast down
and raised again, have given up all hope, and been suddenly

snatched from danger, and placed in safety ; and when these things have been repeated to us and in us a thousand times over, we begin to learn to trust simply to the word and power of God, beyond and against appearances ; and this trust, when habitual and strong, bears the name of assurance ;—for even assurance has degrees.

You have good reason, Madam, to suppose, that the love of the best Christians to an unseen Saviour is far short of what' it ought to be. If your heart be like mine, and you examine your love to Christ by the warmth and frequency of your emotions towards Him, you will often be in a sad suspense, whether or no you love Him at all. The best mark to judge, and which He has given us for that purpose, is to inquire if His word and will have a prevailing, governing influence upon our lives and temper. If we love Him, we do endeavour to keep His commandments ; and it will hold the other way ; if we have a desire to please Him, we undoubtedly love Him. Obedience is the best test ; and when amidst all our imperfections, we can humbly appeal concerning the sincerity of our views, this is a mercy for which we ought to be greatly thankful. He that has brought us to will, will likewise enable us to do according to His good pleasure. I doubt not but the Lord whom you love, and on whom you depend, will lead you in a sure way, and establish and strengthen and settle you in His love and grace. Indeed He has done great things for you already. The Lord is your Shepherd ;—a comprehensive word ! The sheep can do nothing for themselves ; the Shepherd must guide, guard, feed, heal, recover. Well for us that our Shepherd is the Lord Almighty. If His power, care, compassion, fulness, were not infinite, the poor sheep would be forsaken, starved and worried. But we have a Shepherd full of care, full of kindness, full of power, who has said, I will seek that which was lost, and bind up that which was broken, and bring again that which was driven away, and will strengthen that which was sick. How tender are these expressions, and how well fulfilled ! His sheep fed in the midst of wolves, yet are preserved safe ; for though they see Him not, His eyes and His heart are upon them. Do we wonder that Daniel was preserved in the lions' den ? Why it is a common case. Which of God's children have not cause to say, " My

soul is among lions " ?   But the angel of the covenant stops
their mouths, or only permits them to gape and roar, to
show their teeth, and what they would do, if they might ;
but they may not, they shall not bite and tear us at their
own will.   Let us trust Him, and all shall be well.

As to daily occurrences, it is best to believe that a daily
portion of comforts and crosses, each one the most suitable
to our case, is adjusted and appointed by the Hand which
was once nailed to the cross for us ; that where the path of
duty and prudence leads, there is the best situation we could
possibly be in at that juncture.   We are not required to
afflict ourselves immoderately for what it is not in our power
to prevent, nor should anything that affords occasions for
mortifying the spirit of self be accounted unnecessary.

I am, &c.

LETTER III

1768.

I HAVE been some time hoping to hear from you, but
Mr. —— was here last Saturday, and informed me that you
were ill, or had been so very lately.   This intelligence
prompted me to write as soon as I could find leisure.   I think
the Lord has seen fit to visit you with much indisposition of
late ; I say *He* has seen fit, for all our trials are under His
immediate direction, and we are never in heaviness without
a *need-be*.   I trust He does and will give you strength equal
to your day, and sweeten what would be otherwise bitter,
with the essence of His precious love.   I hope soon to hear
that you are restored to health, and that you have found
cause to praise Him for the rod.

How happy is the state of a believer, to have a sure
promise that all shall work together for good in the end,
and in the mean time a sure refuge where to find present
relief, support, and protection !   How comfortable it is,
when trouble is near, to know that the Lord is near likewise,
and to commit ourselves and all our cares simply to Him,
believing that His eye is upon us, and His ear open to our

prayers. Under the conduct of such a Shepherd we need
not fear; though we are called to pass through fire and
water, through the valley of the shadow of death, He will
be with us, and will show Himself mighty on our behalf.
It seems almost needless to say, that we were very happy in
the company of —— : the only inconvenience was, that it
renewed the pain it always gives me to part with them.
Though the visit was full as long as I could possibly expect,
it seemed very short. This must be the case while we are
here : our pleasures are short, interrupted, and mixed with
troubles : this is not, cannot be our rest. But it will not be
always the case ; we are travelling to a better world, where
every evil and imperfection shall cease ; then we shall be
for ever with the Lord, and with each other. May the
prospect of this blessed hope set before us, revive our fainting
spirits, and make us willing to endure hardships as good
soldiers of Jesus Christ! Here we must often sow in tears,
but there we shall reap in joy, and all tears shall be wiped
from our eyes for ever. I hope the conversation of friends
whom I so greatly love and honour, afforded me not only
pleasure but profit ; it left a savour upon my mind, and
stirred up my languid desires after the Lord. I wish I
could say the good effect has remained with me to this
hour : but, alas! I am a poor creature, and have had many
causes of humiliation since. But, blessed be God! amidst
all my changes I find the foundation stands sure, and I am
seldom or never left to doubt either of the Lord's love to
me, or the *reality* of the desires He has given me towards
Himself ; though when I measure my love by the degrees
of its exercise, or the fruits it produceth, I have reason
to sit down ashamed, as the chief of sinners, and the least of
all saints. But in Him I have righteousness and peace, and
in Him I must and will rejoice.

I would willingly fill up my sheet, but feel a straitness in
my spirit, and know not what further to say. O for a ray
of Divine light to set me at liberty, that I might write a few
lines worth reading, something that might warm my heart
and comfort *yours*! Then the subject must be Jesus ;
but of Him what can I say that you do not know? Well,
though you know Him, you are glad to hear of Him again
and again. Come, then, magnify the Lord with me, and

let us exalt His name together. Let us adore Him for His love, that love which has a height, and depth, and length, and breadth, beyond the grasp of our poor conceptions ; a love that moved Him to empty Himself, to take on Him the form of a servant, and to be obedient unto death, even the death of the cross ; a love that pitied us in our lost estate, that found us when we sought Him not, that spoke peace to our souls in the day of our distress ; a love that bears with all our present weakness, mistakes, backslidings, and shortcomings ; a love that is always watchful, always ready to guide, to comfort, and to heal ; a love that will not be wearied, cannot be conquered, and is incapable of changes ; a love that will in the end prevail over all opposition, will perfect that which concerns us, and will not leave us till it has brought us perfect in holiness and happiness, to rejoice in His presence in glory. The love of Christ ! it is the wonder, the joy, the song of angels ; and the sense of it shed abroad in our hearts makes life pleasant, and death welcome. Alas ! what a heart have I, that I love Him no better ! But I hope He has given me a desire to make Him my all in all, and to account everything loss and dross that dares to stand in competition with Him.

I am, &c.

LETTER IV

1769.

I FOUND this morning among my unanswered letters one from you, but I hope I left it among them by mistake. I am willing, however, to be on the sure side, and would rather write twice than be too long silent. I heard of your being laid on the bed of affliction, and of the Lord's goodness to you there, and of His raising you up again. Blessed be His name ! He is all-sufficient and faithful ; and though He cause grief, He is sure to show compassion in supporting and delivering. Ah ! the evil of our nature is deeply rooted and very powerful, or such repeated, continual corrections and chastisements would not be necessary ; and were they not necessary, we should not have them. But such we are, and therefore such must be our treatment ; for though the Lord loves us with a tenderness beyond what the mother feels for her sucking child, yet it is a tenderness directed by Infinite Wisdom, and very different from that weak indulgence which in parents we call fondness, which leads them to comply with their children's desires and inclinations, rather than to act with a steady view to their true welfare. The Lord loves His children, and is very indulgent to them, so far as they can safely bear it, but He will not spoil them. Their sin-sickness requires medicines, some of which are very unpalatable ; but when the case calls for such, no short-sighted entreaties of ours can excuse us from taking what He prepares for our good. But every dose is prepared by His own hand, and not one is administered in vain, nor is repeated any oftener than is needful to answer the purposed end. Till then, no other hand can remove what He lays upon us ; but when His merciful design is answered, He will relieve us Himself, and in the meantime He will so moderate the operation, or increase our ability to bear, that we shall not be overpowered. It is true, without a single exception, that all His paths are mercy and truth to them that fear Him.. His love is the same when He wounds as when He heals, when He takes away, as when He gives : we have reason to thank Him for *all*, but *most for the severe.*

I received a letter from you, which mentions dear Mrs. ——'s case, a very trying one ; but in this likewise we see the Lord's faithfulness. Our own experience, and all that we observe of His dealings with others, may convince us that we need not be afraid to entrust ourselves and our dearest concerns in His hands ; for He can and will make everything work for good.

How little does the world know of that intercourse which is carried on between Heaven and earth, what petitions are daily presented, and what answers are received, at the throne of grace ! O the blessed privilege of prayer ! O the wonderful love, care, attention, and power of our great Shepherd ! His eye is always upon us ; when our spirits are almost overwhelmed within us, He knoweth our path. His ear is always open to us ; let who will overlook and disappoint us, He will not. When means and hope fail, when

everything looks dark upon us, when we seem shut up on
every side, when we are brought to the lowest ebb, still our
help is in the name of the Lord who made Heaven and earth.
To Him all things are possible ; and before the exertion of
His power, when He is pleased to arise and work, all hin-
drances give way and vanish like a mist before the sun.   And
He can so manifest Himself to the soul, and cause His good-
ness to pass before it, that the hour of affliction shall be
the golden hour of the greatest consolation.   He is the
fountain of life, strength, grace, and comfort, and of His
fulness His children receive according to their occasions :
but this is all hidden from the world : they have no guide
in prosperity, but hurry on as they are instigated by their
blinded passions, and are perpetually multiplying mischiefs
and miseries to themselves ;   and in adversity they have
no resource, but must feel all the evil of affliction, without
inward support, and without deriving any advantage from it.
We have therefore cause for continual praise.   The Lord has
given us to know His name, as a resting-place and a hiding-
place, a sun and a shield.   Circumstances and creatures may
change ; but He will be an unchangeable Friend.   The way
is rough, but He trod it before us, and is now with us in every
step we take ;   and every step brings us nearer to our
Heavenly Home.   Our inheritance is surely reserved for us,
and we shall be kept for it by His power through faith.
Our present strength is small, and without a fresh supply
would be quickly exhausted ;   but He has engaged to renew
it from day to day ;   and He will soon appear to wipe all
tears from our eyes ;   and then we shall appear with Him in
glory.

I am very sorry if our friend Mr. —— appears to be aiming
to reconcile things that are incompatible.   I am, indeed,
afraid that he has been for some time under a decline ;
and, as you justly observe, we meet with too many instances
to teach us, that they who express the warmest zeal at their
first setting out, do not always prove the most steady and
thriving afterwards ;   yet I am willing to hope in this case
that he will revive and flourish again.   Sometimes the
Lord permits those whom He loves to wander from Him
for a season ;   and when His time comes to heal their back-
slidings, they walk more humbly, thankfully and fruitfully

afterwards, from a sense of His abounding mercy, and the knowledge they have by experience acquired of the deceitfulness and ingratitude of their hearts. I hope and pray it will be so with him. However, these things for the present are grievous ; and usually before the Lord heals such breaches, He makes His people sensible, that it is an evil and bitter thing to forsake Him when He led them by the way.

Indeed London is a dangerous and ensnaring place to professors. I account myself happy that my lot is cast at a distance from it. It appears to me like a sea, wherein most are tossed by storms, and many suffer shipwreck. In this retired situation, I seem to stand upon a cliff ; and while I pity those whom I cannot help, I hug myself in the thoughts of being safe upon the shore. Not that we are without our trials here ; the evil of our own hearts, and the devices of Satan, cut us out work enough : but we are happily screened from many things which must be either burdensome or hurtful to those who live in the way of them ; such as political disputes, winds of doctrine, scandals of false professors, parties for and against particular ministers, and fashionable amusements, in some measure countenanced by the presence of persons in other respects exemplary. In this view, I often think of our dear friend's expression, upon a certain occasion, of the difference between London and country grace. I hold it in a twofold sense. By London grace, when genuine, I understand grace in a very advanced degree. The favoured few who are kept alive to God, simple-hearted, and spiritually-minded (I mean especially in genteel life), in the midst of such snares and temptations, appear to me to be the first-rate Christians of the land : I adore the power of the Lord in them, and compare them to the young men who walked unhurt in the midst of the fire. In another sense, the phrase *London grace* conveys no great idea to me. I think there is no place in the kingdom where a person may set up for a professor upon a smaller stock. If people can abstain from open immoralities, if they will fly to all parts of the town to hear sermons, if they can talk about the doctrines of the Gospel, if they have something to say upon that useless question, Who is the best preacher ? if they can attain to a speaking acquaintance with some of an acknowledged character, then they expect to pass muster. I am afraid there are many who, upon no better evidences than these, deceive both themselves and others for a course of years. Though I feel not in a writing cut to-day, I have almost filled the sheet somehow ; and if a line or a word may be a means of suggesting a seasonable and comfortable thought to you, I have my end. Through mercy we are all pretty well. My soul is kept alive, as it were, by miracle. I feel much inward warfare ; the enemy thrusts sore at me, that I may fall ; and I have abundant experience of the evil and deceitfulness of my heart ; but the Lord is gracious, and, in the midst of all conflicts, I have a peace springing from the knowledge of His power and grace, and the consideration that I have been helped to commit myself to Him.

I am, &c.

LETTER V

1769.

WE are much obliged to you for your late visit ; and I am glad to find that the Lord is pleased to give you some tokens of His presence when you are with us, because I hope it will encourage you to come again. I ought to be very thankful that our Christian friends, in general, are not wholly disappointed of a blessing when they visit us.

I hope the Lord will give me an humble sense of what I am, and that broken and contrite frame of heart in which He delights. This is to me the chief thing. I had rather have more of the mind that was in Christ, more of a meek, quiet, resigned, peaceful, and loving disposition, than to enjoy the greatest measure of sensible comforts, if the consequence should be (as perhaps it would) spiritual pride, self-sufficiency, and a want of that tenderness to others which becomes one who has reason to style himself the chief of sinners. I know, indeed, that the *proper* tendency of sensible consolations is to humble ; but I can see that, through the depravity of human nature, they have not always that effect. And I have been sometimes disgusted with an apparent want of humility, an air of self-will and self-importance, in persons of whose sincerity I could not at all doubt. It has kept me from envying them those pleasant frames with which they have sometimes been favoured ; for I believe Satan is never nearer us than at some times when we think ourselves nearest the Lord.

What reason have we to charge our souls in David's words, " My soul, wait thou *only* upon God " ! A great stress should be laid upon that word *only*. We dare not entirely shut Him out of our regards, but we are too apt to suffer something to share with Him. This evil disposition is deeply fixed in our hearts ; and the Lord orders all His dispensations towards us with a view to rooting it out ; that, being wearied with repeated disappointments, we may at length be compelled to betake ourselves to Him alone. Why else do we experience so many changes and crosses ? Why are we so often in heaviness ? We know that He delights in the pleasure and prosperity of His servants ; that He does not willingly afflict or grieve His children ; but there is a necessity on our parts, in order to teach us that we have no stability in ourselves, and that no creature can do us good but by His appointment. While the people of Israel depended upon Him for food, they gathered up the manna every morning in the field ; but when they would hoard it up in their houses, that they might have a stock within themselves, they had it without His blessing, and it proved good for nothing ; it soon bred worms, and grew offensive. We may often observe something like this occur, both in our temporal and spiritual concerns. The Lord gives us a dear friend to our comfort ; but ere long we forget that the friend is only the channel of conveyance, and that all the comfort is from Himself. To remind us of this, the stream is dried up, the friend torn away by death, or removed far from us, or perhaps the friendship ceases, and a coolness insensibly takes place, we know not *how* or *why* : the true reason is, that when we rejoiced amiss in our gourd, the Lord for our good sent a worm to the root of it. Instances of this kind are innumerable ; and the great inference from them all, Cease from man, cease from creatures, for wherein are they to be accounted of ? My soul, wait thou *only*, *only* upon the Lord, who is (according to the expressive phrase Heb. iv. 13) He with whom we have to do for soul and body, for time and eternity. What thanks do we owe, that though we have not yet attained perfectly this great lesson, yet we are admitted into that school where alone it can be learnt, and though we are poor, slow scholars, the great and effectual Teacher to whom we have been encouraged and enabled to apply, can and will bring us forward ! He communicates, not only instructions, but capacities and powers. There is none like Him : He can make the blind to see, the deaf to hear, and the dumb to speak ; and how great is His condescension and patience ! How does He accommodate Himself to our weakness, and teach us as we are able to bear ! Though all are very dunces when He first receives them, not one was ever turned out as *incapable*, for He makes them what He would have them to be. O that we may set Him always before us, and consider every dispensation, person, thing, we meet in the course of every day, as messengers from Him, each bringing us some *line of instruction* for us to copy into that day's experience ! Whatever passes within us or around us, may be improved (when He teaches us how) as a perpetual commentary upon His good Word. If we converse and observe with this view, we may learn something every moment, wherever the path of duty leads us, in the streets as well as in the closet, and from the conversation of those who know not God (when we cannot avoid being present at it), as well as from those who do.

Separation of dear friends is, as you observed, hard to flesh and blood ; but grace can make it tolerable. I have an abiding persuasion, that the Lord can easily give more than ever He will take away. Which part of the alternative must be my lot, or when, He only knows ; but, in general, I can rely on Him to appoint the time, the manner ; and I trust His promise of strength suited to the day, shall be made good. Therefore, I can for the most part rejoice, that all things are in the hand and under the direction of Him who knows our frame, and has Himself borne our griefs, and carried our sorrows in His own body. A time of weeping must come, but the morning of joy will make amends for all. Who can expound the meaning of that

one expression, " an exceeding and eternal weight of glory " ?
The case of unconverted friends is still more burdensome
to think of; but we have encouragement and warrant to
pray and to hope.   He who called *us*, can easily call others :
and He seldom lays a desire of this sort very closely and
warmly upon the hearts of His people, but when it is His
gracious design, sooner or later, to give an answer of peace.
However, it becomes us to be thankful for ourselves, and
to bow our anxieties and reasonings before His sovereign
will, who doth as He pleases with His own.

Methinks winter is your summer.   You have been, like
the bee, collecting from many flowers ; I hope you will
carry good store of honey home with you.   May you find
the Lord there, and He can easily supply the failure of means
and creatures !   We cannot be in any place to so much
advantage as where the call of duty leads.   What we cannot
avoid, may we cheerfully submit to, and not indulge a vain
thought that we should choose a better situation for our-
selves (all things considered) than He has chosen for us.

When we have opportunity of enjoying many ordinances,
it is a mercy to be able to prize and improve them ; but
when He cuts us short for a season, if we wait upon Him
we shall do well without them.   Secret prayer, and the
good Word, are the chief *wells* from whence we draw the
water of salvation.   These will keep the soul alive when
creature streams are cut off; but the richest variety of
public means, and the closest attendance upon them, will
leave us lean and pining in the midst of plenty, if we are
remiss and formal in the other two.   I think David never
appears in a more lively frame of mind than when he wrote
the 42nd, 63rd, and 84th Psalms, which were all penned in
a dry land, and at a distance from the public ordinances.

I am, &c.

LETTER VI

1772.

I HAD been wishing to hear from you, that I might know where to write. I hope I can assure you of a friendly sympathy with you in your trials. I can, in some measure, guess at what you feel, from what I have seen and felt myself in cases where I have been nearly concerned. But my compassion, though sincere, is ineffectual: if I can pity, I cannot relieve. All I can do is, as the Lord enables me, to remember you both before Him. But there is One whose compassion is infinite. The love and tenderness of ten thousand earthly friends, of ten thousand mothers towards their sucklings, if compared with His, are less than a drop of water to the ocean; and His power is infinite too. Why, then, do our sufferings continue, when He is so compassionate, and could remove them with a word? Surely, if we cannot give the particular reasons (which yet He will acquaint us with hereafter, John xiii. 7), the general reason is at hand; He afflicts not for His own pleasure, but for our profit; to make us partakers of His holiness; and because He loves us.

> Judge not the Lord by feeble sense,
>   But trust Him for His grace;
> Behind a frowning providence
>   He hides a smiling face.

I wish you much comfort from David's thought, Psa. cxlii. 3: "When my spirit was overwhelmed within me, Thou knewest my path." The Lord is not withdrawn to a great distance, but His eye is upon you, and He sees you not with the indifference of a mere spectator, but He observes with attention: He knows, He considers your path; yea, He appoints it, and every circumstance about it is under His direction. Your trouble began at the hour He saw best; it could not come before, and He has marked the degree of it to a hair's breadth, and the duration to a minute. He knows likewise how your spirit is affected; and such supplies of grace and strength, and in such seasons as He sees needful, He will afford. So that when things appear darkest, you

shall still be able to say, " Though chastened, not killed."
Therefore hope in God, for you shall yet praise Him.

I shall pray that the Bath waters may be beneficial ;
and that the waters of the sanctuary there may be healing
and enlivening to you all. Our all-sufficient God can give
seasons of refreshment in the darkest hours, and break
through the thickest clouds of outward affliction or distress.
To you it is given, not only to believe in Jesus, but to suffer
for His sake : for so we do, not only when we are called to
follow Him to imprisonment or death, but when He enables
us to bear afflictive dispensations with due submission and
patience. Then He is glorified ; then His grace and power
are manifested in us. The world, so far as they know our
case, have a proof before them, that our religion is not
merely notional, but that there is a power and reality in it.
And the Lord's people are encouraged by what they see of
His faithfulness to ourselves. And there are more eyes
upon us still. We are a spectacle, to the universe, to angels
as well as to men. Cheer up : the Lord hath put you in
your present trying situation, that you may have the fairer
opportunity of adorning your profession of the Gospel ;
and though you suffer much, He is able to make you abuud-
ant amends. Nor need I remind you, that He has suffered
unspeakably more for you : He drank for your sake a cup of
unmixed wrath, and only puts in your hand a cup of affliction
mixed with many mercies.

The account you gave of the poor man detained in the
inn was very affecting. Such scenes are or should be
instructive, to teach us resignation under the trials we must
meet with every day. For not only are we visited less than
our iniquities have deserved, but much less than many of
our fellow-creatures' daily experience. We need not look
about far or long to find others in a worse situation than
ourselves. If a fit of the gout or cholic is so grievous and
so hard to bear, what do we owe to Him who delivered
us from that place of unutterable torment, where there is
weeping, wailing, and gnashing of teeth for ever, without
hope or respite ! And if we cannot help interesting ourselves
in the groans of a stranger, how ought the groans of Jesus
to be, as it were, continually sounding in our ears ! What
are all other sufferings compared to His ? And yet He

endured them freely. He needed not to have borne them if He would have left us to perish ; but such was His love, He died that we might live, and endured the fiercest agonies, that He might open to us the gate of everlasting peace and happiness. How amazingly perverse is my heart, that I can be more affected with a melancholy story in a newspaper, concerning persons I never saw, than with all that I read of His bitter passion in the garden and on the cross, though I profess to believe He endured it all for me. O ! if we could always behold Him by faith, as evidently crucified before our eyes, how would it compose our spirits as to all the sweets and bitters of this poor life ! What a banner would it prove against all the snares and temptations whereby Satan would draw us into evil : and what a firm ground of confidence would it afford us amidst the conflicts we sustain from the working of unbelief and indwelling sin ! I long for more of that faith which is the substance of things hoped for, and the evidence of things not seen, that I may be preserved humble, thankful, watchful, and dependent. To behold the glory and the love of Jesus, is the only effectual way to participate in His image.

We are to set out to-night from the Interpreter's house towards the hill *Difficulty*, and hope to be favoured with a sight of the cross by the way. To stand at the foot of it with a softened heart and melting eyes ; to forget our sins, sorrows, and burdens, while we are wholly swallowed up in the contemplation of Him who bore our sins in His own body upon the tree, is certainly the most desirable situation on this side the grave. To speak of it, and to see it by the light of the Spirit, are widely different things ; and though we cannot always enjoy this view, yet the remembrance of what we have been, is an excellent means of encouragement to mount the hill and face the lions.

I believe I shall hardly find leisure to fill my paper this time. It is now Saturday evening, and growing late. I am just returned from a serious walk, which is my usual manner of closing the week when the weather is fine. I endeavour to join in heart with the Lord's ministers and people, who are seeking a blessing on to-morrow's ordinances. At such times I especially remember those friends with whom I have gone to the House of the Lord in company, consequently you are not forgot. I can venture to assure you, that if you have a value for our prayers you have a frequent share in them ; yea, are loved and remembered by many here : but as we are forgetful creatures, I hope you will always refresh our memory, and quicken our prayers by a yearly visit. In the morning I shall think of you again. What a multitude of eyes and hearts will be directed to our Redeemer to-morrow ! He has a numerous and necessitous family ; but He is rich enough to supply them all, and His tender compassion extends to the meanest and most unworthy. Like the sun, He can cheer and enlighten thousands and millions at once, and give to each one as bountifully as if there were no more to partake of His favour. His best blessings are not diminished by being shared among many. The greatest earthly monarch would soon be poor if he was to give a little (though but a little) to all his subjects : but Jesus has unsearchable, inexhaustible riches of grace to bestow. The innumerable assembly before the throne have been all supplied from His fulness, and yet there is enough and to spare for us also, and for all that shall come after us. May He give us an eager appetite, an hunger and thirst that will not be put off with anything short of the bread of life ; and then we may confidently open our mouths wide, for He has promised to fill them.

I am, &c.

LETTER VII

1773.

SINCE I wrote last, the Lord has been gracious to us here. He crowned the last year with His goodness, and renews His benefits to us every day. He has been pleased to bless the preaching of His Gospel amongst us, both to consolation and conviction ; and several are, I hope, earnestly seeking Him, who were lately dead in trespasses and sins. Dear Mr. ———— was released from all his complaints the 25th of November. A few days before his death, he was enabled to speak more intelligibly than usual for about a quarter of an hour, and expressed a comfortable hope, which was a great satisfaction to us ; for though we had not the least doubt of his being built upon the Rock, it was to us an answer to prayer that he could again speak the language of faith ; and much prayer had been made on this account, especially that very evening. After that night he spoke little, and hardly took any notice, but continued chiefly drowsy till he died. I preached his funeral sermon, from Lam. iii. 31, 32, 33. Mrs. L——'s complaint grows worse and worse : she suffers much in her body, and has much more perhaps to suffer ; but her consolations in the Lord abound. He enables her to maintain faith, patience, and submission, in an exemplary manner, and shows us in His dealings with her, that He is all-sufficient and faithful to those who put their trust in Him. I am glad to hear that you had comfortable seasons while at Bath. It is indeed a great mercy that God's ordinances are established in that place of dissipation ; and I hope many who go there with no higher view than to drink the Bath waters, will be brought to draw with joy the waters of life from the wells of salvation. He does nothing in vain, and when He affords the means, we may confidently hope He will bestow the blessing. The dissipation of spirit you complain of when you are in a strange place is, I suppose, felt by most, if not by all, who can be satisfied in no place without some token of the Lord's presence. I consider it rather as an infirmity than a sin, strictly speaking ; though all our infirmities are sinful, being the effects of a depraved nature. In our present circumstances, new things excite new ideas ; and when our usual course of life is broken in upon, it disjoints and unsettles our thoughts. It is a proof of our weakness ; it may and ought to be lamented ; but I believe we shall not get the better of it, till we leave the mortal body to moulder into dust. Perhaps few suffer more inconvenience from this article than myself, which is one reason why I love home, and seldom leave it without some reluctance ; and it is one reason why we should love Heaven, and long for the hour when, at liberty from all incumbrance, we shall see the Lord without a veil, and serve Him without distraction. The Lord, by His providence, seconds and confirms the declarations of His word and ministry. Much we read, and much

we hear, concerning the emptiness, vanity, and uncertainty
of the present state.   When our minds are enlightened by
His Holy Spirit, we receive and acknowledge what His word
declares to be truth ; yet if we remain long without changes,
and our path is very smooth, we are for the most part but
faintly affected with what we profess to believe.   But when
some of our dearest friends are taken from us, the lives of
others threatened, and we ourselves are brought low with
pain and sickness, then we not only *say*, but *feel*, that this
must not, cannot be our rest.   You have had several
exercises of this kind of late in your family, and I trust you
will be able to set your seal to that gracious word, that
though afflictions in themselves are not joyous, but grievous,
yet in due season they yield the peaceable fruits of right-
eousness.   Various and blessed are the fruits they produce.
By affliction, prayer is quickened ; for our prayers are very
apt to grow languid and formal in a time of ease.   Affliction
greatly helps us to understand the Scriptures, especially
the promises, most of which being made to times of trouble,
we cannot so well know their fulness, sweetness, and cer-
tainty, as when we have been in the situation to which they
are suited, have been enabled to trust and plead them, and
have found them fulfilled in our own case.   We are usually
indebted to affliction as the means or occasion of the most
signal discoveries we are favoured with, of the wisdom,
power, and faithfulness of the Lord.   These are best
observed by the evident proofs we have that He is near to
support us under trouble, and that He can and does deliver
us out of it.   Israel would not have seen so much of the
Lord's arm outstretched in their behalf, had not Pharaoh
oppressed, opposed, and pursued them.   Afflictions are
designed likewise for the manifestation of our sincerity,
to ourselves and to others.   When faith endures the fire, we
know it to be of the right kind ; and others who see we are
brought safe out, and lose nothing but the dross, will confess
that God is with us of a truth (Dan. iii. 27, 28).   Surely this
thought should reconcile us to suffer, not only with patience,
but with cheerfulness, if God may be glorified in us.   This
made the apostle rejoice in tribulation, that the power of
Christ might be noticed, as resting upon him, and working
mightily in him.   Many of our graces, likewise, cannot thrive

or show themselves to advantage without trials, such as resignation, patience, meekness, long-suffering. I observe some of the London porters do not appear to be very strong men ; yet they will trudge along under a burden which some stouter people could not carry so well ; the reason is, that they are accustomed to carry burdens, and by continual exercise their shoulders acquire a strength suited to their work. It is so in the Christian life ; activity and strength of grace is not ordinarily acquired by those who sit still and live at ease, but by those who frequently meet with something which requires a full exertion of what power the Lord has given them. So, again, it is by our own sufferings we learn to pity and sympathize with others in their sufferings ; such a compassionate disposition, which excites our feelings for the afflicted, is an eminent branch of the mind which was in Christ. But these feelings would be very faint if we did not in our experience know what sorrows and temptations mean. Afflictions do us good likewise, as they make us more acquainted with what is in our own hearts, and thereby promote humiliation and self-abasement. There are abominations which, like nests of vipers, lie so quietly within, that we hardly suspect they are there till the rod of affliction rouses them ; then they hiss and show their venom. This discovery is indeed very distressing ; yet, till it is made, we are prone to think ourselves much less vile than we really are, and cannot so heartily abhor ourselves, and repent in dust and ashes.

But I must write a sermon rather than a letter, if I would enumerate all the good fruits which, by the power of sanctifying grace, are produced from this bitter tree. May we, under our several trials, find them all revealed in ourselves, that we may not complain of having suffered in vain ! While we have such a depraved nature, and live in such a polluted world ; while the roots of pride, vanity, self-dependence, self-seeking, are so strong within us, we need a variety of sharp dispensations to keep us from forgetting ourselves, and from cleaving to the dust.

LETTER VIII

1774.

‑THE very painful illness which Mrs. ——— so long
endured, had doubtless not only prepared you to expect the
news of her dismission, but made you more willing to resign
her. You are bereaved of a valuable friend; but life,
in her circumstances, was burdensome: and who can be
sorry to consider her now as freed from all suffering, and
possessed of all happiness? But besides this, I trust the
Lord has favoured you with an habitual sense of the wisdom
and propriety of all his appointments; so that, when His
will is manifested by the event, you are enabled to say,
" All is well." " I was dumb, and opened not my mouth,
because Thou didst it." She is gone a little before you;
and after a few more changes, you will meet her again to
unspeakable advantage, and rejoice together before the
throne for ever. There every tear will be wiped away,
and you shall weep no more. The Lord could have prevented
the cause of her great sufferings; but I doubt not He
afflicted her in wisdom and mercy: He could easily have
restored her to health; but the time was hastening when
He purposed to have her with Him where He is, that she
might behold His glory, and have all the desires He put into
her heart abundantly satisfied. Precious in His sight is the
death of His saints, and every circumstance is under the
direction of infinite wisdom. His sovereignty forbids us
to say, Why hast Thou done this? And His love assures
us that He does all things well. I have lost a friend likewise;
I believe I may say, few persons not immediately related to
her could value her more highly than myself: and though
of late years I could not have the pleasure of her company,
it was a constant satisfaction to me to know I had such a
friend.

Mr. T. ———'s sickness and death followed immediately
upon this stroke. I doubt not but you have been much
affected with this dispensation likewise. But here again we
have the same stronghold to retreat to: the Lord has done
it. What a pleasing prospect of increasing usefulness is
now interrupted! How many will mourn his loss! Yet we

are sure the work which the Lord had appointed him was finished. They who loved his ministry, and were profited by it, are left apparently destitute ; but Jesus, the good Shepherd, is able to take care of His own, and will fulfil His promise to them all. He has said, Verily they shall be fed.

We have had trying and dying times here ; half my time almost has been taken up with visiting the sick. I have seen death in a variety of forms, and have had frequent occasion of observing how insignificant many things, which are now capable of giving us pain or pleasure, will appear, when the soul is brought near to the borders of eternity. All the concerns which relate solely to this life will then be found as trivial as the traces of a dream from which we are awakened. Nothing will then comfort us but the knowledge of Jesus and His love ; nothing grieve us but the remembrance of our unfaithful carriage to Him, and what poor returns we made to His abundant goodness. The Lord forbid that this thought should break our peace ! No, faith in His name may forbid our fear, though we shall see and confess we have been unprofitable servants. There shall be no condemnation to them that are in Him ; but surely shame and humiliation will accompany us to the very threshold of Heaven, and ought to do so. I surely shall then be more affected than I am now, with the coolness of my love, the faintness of my zeal, the vanity of my heart, and my undue attachment to the things of time. O these clogs, fetters, vales, and mountains, which obstruct my course, darken my views, slacken my pace, and disable me in service ! Well it is for me that I am not under the law, but under grace.

To-morrow is the Sabbath. I am usually glad when it returns, though it seldom finds me in that frame of mind which I would desire. But it is my happiness to live amongst many who count the hours from one ordinance to another. I know they pray that I may be a messenger of peace, and an instrument of good to their souls ; and I have cause to hope their prayers are in a measure answered. For their sakes, as much as my own, I am glad to go up to the house of the Lord. O that in watering others, I may be also watered myself ! I have been praying that to-morrow may be a day of power with you and with us, and with all that love Jesus in sincerity ; that we may see His glory, and taste His love in the sanctuary. When it is thus the Sabbath is a blessed day indeed, an earnest of Heaven. There they keep an everlasting Sabbath, and cease not night or day admiring the riches of redeeming love, and adoring Him who washed His people from their sins in His own blood. To have such imperfect communion with them as is in this state attainable in this pleasing exercise, is what alone can make life worth the name. For this I sigh and long, and cry to the Lord to rend the veil of unbelief, scatter the clouds of ignorance, and break down the walls which sin is daily building up to hide Him from my eyes. I hope I can say, My soul is athirst for God, and nothing less than the light of His countenance can satisfy me. Blessed be His name for the desire ; it is His own gift, and He never gives it in vain. He will afford us a taste of the water of life by the way ; and ere long we shall drink abundantly at the fountain-head, and have done with the complaint for ever. May we be thankful for what we receive, and still earnestly desirous of more !

I am, &c.

FIVE LETTERS

TO

MISS D——

LETTER I

My Dear Miss,   *Aug.* — 1772.

THE Lord brought us home in peace.   My visit to ——
was agreeable, and I shall often think of it with pleasure ;
though the deadness and dryness of my own spirit, a good
part of the time I was there, proved a considerable abate-
ment.   I am eager enough to converse with the Lord's
people, when at the same time I am backward and indisposed
to communion with the Lord Himself.   The two evils
charged upon Israel of old, a proneness to forsake the
fountain of living waters, and to trust to broken cisterns
(which can do me no good unless He supplies them), run
through the whole of my experience abroad and at home.
A few drops of grace in my fellow-worms endear them to me
exceedingly.   If I expect to see any Christian friends, I
count the hours till we meet ;   I promise myself great
benefit ;   but if the Lord withdraws His influence, the best
of them prove to me but clouds without water.   It was not,
however, wholly so with me all the time I stayed with my
friends ;   but I suffer much in learning to depend upon the
Lord alone :   I have been at this lesson many a long year ;
but am so poor and dull a scholar, that I have not yet made
any tolerable progress in it.   I think I received some
instruction and advantage, where I little expected it ;
I mean at Mr. Cox's museum.   The efforts of his ingenuity
amazed me, while, at the same time, I was struck with their
insignificance.   His fine things were beyond all I had any idea

of ; and yet, what are they better than toys and amuse-
ments suited to the taste of children ! And notwith-
standing the variety of their motions, they were all destitute
of life. There is unspeakably more wisdom and contrivance
in the mechanism of a butterfly or a bee that flies unnoticed
in the fields, than in all his apparatus put together. But the
works of God are disregarded, while the feeble imitations of
them which men can produce gain universal applause.

If you and I could make self-moving dragons and elephants
what would it profit us ? Blessed be God, that He has
given us some glimpse of his wisdom and love ! by which our
hearts, more hard and lifeless by nature than the stones in
the street, are constrained and enabled to move upwards,
and to seek after the Lord. He has given us in His Word
a greater treasure than all that we ever beheld with our eyes,
and a hope which shall flourish when the earth and all its
works shall be burnt up. What will all the fine things of
men's device be worth in that day !

I think the passage you refer to in Mr. —— justly
exceptionable. His intention is good, and the mistake
he would censure very dangerous ; but he might have
explained himself more clearly. I apprehend he and you
do not mean the same thing by being in the dark. It is not
an uncomfortable, but a careless, frame which he would
censure. They who walk in darkness and see no light, and
yet are exhorted to stay themselves upon God (Isa. l. 10),
are said to hearken to the voice of His servant. Though
they cannot see the Lord, they are seeking and mourning
after Him, and waiting in the use of means, and warring
against sin. Mr. —— had another set of people in view,
who trust in the notion of Gospel-truth, or some past
convictions and comforts ; though at present they give
no evidence of spiritual desires, but are worldly in their
spirit and conversation ; talk of trusting in the Lord ;
account it a weakness to doubt of their state, and think all
is well because they profess to believe the doctrines of grace.
In a word, it is the darkness of sin and sloth, against which
his observation is pointed. Or if, indeed, he meant more
than this, we are not obliged to believe him. Remember
your privilege ; you have the Bible in your hands, and are
not bound to follow books or preachers any farther than

what they deliver agrees with the oracles of truth. We have great reason to be thankful for the instructions and writings of spiritual men, but they are all fallible even as ourselves. One is our Master, even Christ ; what He says, we are to receive implicitly ; but we do not owe implicit subjection to the best of our fellow-creatures. The Bereans were commended that they would not take even the apostle Paul upon trust, but searched the Scriptures to see whether these things were so. May the Lord give us a spirit of humility and discernment in all things !

I am, &c.

LETTER II

May 4, 1773.

METHINKS it is high time to ask how you do, to thank you for your last letter, and to let you know, that though necessity makes me slack in writing, yet I can and do often think of you. My silence has sometimes been owing to want of leisure ; and sometimes, when I could have found leisure, my harp has been out of tune, and I had no heart to write. Perhaps you are ready to infer, by my sitting down to write at last, that my harp is now well tuned, and I have something extraordinary to offer ; beware of thinking so, lest you should be sadly disappointed. Should I make myself the subject, I could give you at present but a mournful ditty. I suppose you have heard I have been ill ; through mercy I am now well. But, indeed, I must farther tell you, that when I was sick I was well : and since the Lord has removed my illness I have been much worse. My illness was far from violent in itself, and was greatly sweetened by a calm submissive frame the Lord gave me under it. My heart seemed more alive to Him then than it has done since my cough, fever, and deafness have been removed. Shall I give you another bit of a riddle, that notwithstanding the many changes I pass through, I am always the same ? This is the very truth : " In me, that is, in my flesh, dwelleth no good thing " ; so that, if sometimes my spirit is in a measure humble, lively, and dependent, it is not that I am grown better than I was, but that the Lord is pleased to put forth His gracious power in my weakness : and when my heart is dry and stupid, when I can find no pleasure in waiting upon God, it is not because I am worse than I was before, but only the Lord sees it best that I should feel as well as say what a poor creature I am. My heart was once like a dungeon, out of the reach of day, and always dark ; the Lord, by His grace, has been pleased to make this dungeon a room, by putting windows in it ; but I need not tell you, that though windows will transmit the daylight into a room, they cannot supply the want of it. When the day is gone, windows are of little use ; when the day returns, the room is enlightened by them again. Thus, unless the Lord shines, I cannot retain to-day the light I had yesterday ; and though His presence makes a delightful difference, I have no more to boast of in myself at one time than another ; yet when it is dark, I am warranted to expect the return of light again. When He is with me, all goes on pleasantly ; when He withdraws, I find I can do nothing without Him. I need not wonder that I find it so, for it must be so, of course, if I am what I confess myself to be, a poor, helpless, sinful creature in myself. Nor need I be overmuch discouraged, since the Lord has promised to help those who can do nothing without Him, not those who can make a tolerable shift to help themselves. Through mercy He does not so totally withdraw, as to leave me without any power or will to cry for His return. I hope He maintains in me at all times a desire of His presence ; yet it becomes me to wait for Him with patience, and to live upon His faithfulness, when I can feel nothing but evil in myself.

In your letter, after having complained of your inability, you say, you converse with many who find it otherwise, who can go whenever they will to the Father of mercies with a child-like confidence, and never return without an answer —an answer of peace. If they only mean that they are favoured with an established faith, and can see that the Lord is always the same, and that their right to the blessings of the covenant is not at all affected by their unworthiness, I wish you and I had more experience of the same privilege. In general, the Lord helps me to aim at it, though I find it sometimes difficult to hold fast my confidence. But if they speak absolutely with respect to their frames, that they not only have something to support them under their changes, but meet with no changes that require such support, I must say it is well that they do not live here ; if they did, they would not know how to pity us, and we should not know how to understand them. We have an enemy at —— that fights against our peace, and I know not one amongst us but often groans under the warfare. I advise you not to be troubled by what you hear of other folks' experience, but keep close to the written word, where you will meet with much to encourage you, though you often feel yourself weary and heavy laden. For my own part, I like that path best which is well beaten by the footsteps of the flock, though it is not always pleasant and strewed with flowers. In our way, we find some hills, from whence we can cheerfully look about us ; but we meet with deep valleys likewise, and seldom travel long upon even ground.

I am, &c.

LETTER III

1775.

I AM satisfied with your answer to my question : we are not proper judges of each other's circumstances, and I am in some measure weaned from judging hastily, that what would not be convenient for me must therefore necessarily be wrong for another. However, my solicitude for your welfare made me venture to drop a hint, as I was persuaded you would take it in good part. Indeed, all situations and circumstances (supposing them not sinful in themselves, and that we are lawfully placed in them) are nearly alike. In London I am in a crowd, in the country I am sure there is a crowd in me. To what purpose do I boast of retirement, when I am pestered by a legion in every place ? How often, when I am what I call alone, may my mind be compared to a puppet-show, a fair, a Newgate, or any of those scenes where folly, noise, and wickedness most abound ! On the contrary, sometimes I have enjoyed sweet recollection and composure where I could have hardly expected it. But still, though the power be all of the Lord, and we of ourselves can do nothing, it is both our duty and our wisdom to be attentive to the use of appointed means on the one hand, and on the other, watchful against those things which we find by experience have a tendency to damp our fervour or to dissipate our spirits. A comfortable intimacy with a fellow-worm cannot be maintained without a certain delicacy and ,circumspection, a studiousness in improving oppor tunities of pleasing, and in avoiding what is known to be offensive. For though love will make large allowances for involuntary mistakes, it cannot easily brook a slight. We act thus as it were by instinct towards those whom we dearly love, and to whom we feel ourselves greatly obliged : and happy are they who are most influenced by this sentiment in their walk before the Lord. But, alas ! here we are chargeable with such inconsistencies as we should be greatly ashamed of in a common life. And well it is for us that the Lord's thoughts and ways are above ours, and that He is infinite in mercy as well as in power ; for surely our dearest friends would have been weary of us, and have renounced us long ago, had we behaved to them as we have too often done to Him. He is God, and not man, and therefore He still waits to be gracious, though we have so often trifled with Him. Surely we may well say with the prophet, " Who is a God like unto Thee, that pardoneth iniquity ? " His tenderness and forbearance towards His own people (whose sins being committed against love, and light, and experience, are more aggravated than others) is astonishing indeed. But, oh ! may the times past suffice to have grieved His Spirit, and may we be enabled from henceforth to serve Him with a single eye and a simple heart, to be faithful to every intimation of His will, and to make Him our all in all !

Mr. —— has been here, and I have been with him at —— since his return. We seem glad to be together when we can. When I am with him I feel quite at home and at ease, and can tell him (so far as I dare tell a creature) all that is in my heart : a plain proof that union of spirit depends no more upon an exact uniformity of sentiment than on a uniformity of prayers ; for in some points of doctrine we differ considerably ; but I trust I agree with him in the views I have of the excellency, suitableness, and sufficiency of the Saviour, and of His right to reign without a rival in the hearts of His redeemed people. An experimental knowledge of Jesus as the deliverer from *sin* and *wrath*, and the author of eternal life and salvation to all who are enabled to believe, is sufficient ground for a union of heart ; in this point all who are taught of God are of one mind. But an eager fighting for or against those points which are usually made the subjects of controversy, tends to nourish pride and evil tempers in ourselves, and to alienate our hearts from those we hope to spend an eternity with. In Heaven we shall neither be Dissenters, Moravians, nor Methodists; neither Calvinists nor Arminians ; but followers of the Lamb, and children of the kingdom. There we shall hear the voice of war no more.

We are still favoured with health and many temporal blessings. My spiritual walk is not so smooth as my outward path ; in public I am mercifully supported, in secret I most sensibly feel my own vileness and weakness ; but through all the Lord is gracious.

I am, &c.

LETTER IV

Jan. 10, 1775.

THERE is hardly anything in which the Lord permits me to meet with more disappointment than in the advantage I am ready to promise myself from creature converse. When I expect to meet any of my Christian friends, my thoughts usually travel much faster than my body. I anticipate the hour of meeting, and my imagination is warmed with expectation of what I shall say and what I shall hear : and sometimes I have had seasons for which I ought to be more thankful than I am. It is pleasant indeed when the Lord favours us with a happy hour, and is pleased to cause our hearts to burn within us while we are speaking of His goodness. But often it is far otherwise with me : I carry with me a dissipation of spirit, and find that I can neither impart nor receive. Something from within or from without crosses my schemes ; and when I retire, I seem to have gained nothing but a fresh conviction, that we can neither help nor be helped, unless the Lord Himself is pleased to help us. With His presence in our hearts we might be comfortable and happy if shut up in one of the cells of *Newgate* ; without it, the most select company, the most desirable opportunities, prove but clouds without water.

I have sometimes thought of asking you whether you find that difference between being abroad and at home that I do ? But I take it for granted that you do not ; your connexions and intimacies are, I believe, chiefly with those who are highly favoured of the Lord, and if you can break through or be upon your guard against the inconveniences which attend frequent changes and much company, you must be very happy in them. But, I believe, considering my weakness, the Lord has chosen wisely and well for me, in placing me in a state of retirement, and not putting it in my power were it ever so much my inclination, to be often abroad. As I stir so seldom, I believe when I do, it is not upon the whole to my disadvantage ; for I meet with more or less upon which my reflections afterwards may, by His blessing, be useful to me, though at the time my visits most frequently convince me how little wisdom or skill I have in improving time and opportunities. But were I to live in London, I know not what might be the consequence. Indeed, I need not puzzle myself about it, as my call does not lie there ; but I pity and pray for those who do live there, and I admire such of them as, in those circumstances which appear so formidable to me, are enabled to walk simply, humbly, and closely with the Lord. They remind me of Daniel, unhurt in the midst of lions, or of the bush which Moses saw, surrounded with flames, yet not consumed, because the Lord was there. Some such I do know, and I hope you are one of the number.

This is certain, that if the light of God's countenance, and communion with Him in love, afford the greatest happiness we are capable of, then whatever tends to indispose us for this pursuit, or to draw a veil between Him and our souls, must be our great loss. If we walk with Him, it must be in the path of duty, which lies plain before us when our eye is single, and we are waiting with attention upon His word, Spirit, and providence. Now, wherever the path of duty leads we are safe ; and it often does lead and place us in such circumstances as no other consideration would make us choose. We were not designed to be mere recluses, but have all a part to act in life. Now, if I find myself in the midst of things disagreeable enough in themselves to the spiritual life ; yet if, when the question occurs, "What dost thou here?" my heart can answer, "I am here by the will of God ; I believe it to be, all things considered, my duty to be here at this time rather than elsewhere " : If I say I am tolerably satisfied of this, then I would not burden and grieve myself about what I cannot avoid or alter, but endeavour to take all such things up with cheerfulness, as a part of my daily cross ; since I am called, not only to do the will of God, but to suffer it : but if I am doing my own will rather than His, then I have reason to fear, lest I should meet with either a snare or a sting at every step. May the Lord Jesus be with you !

I am, &c.

LETTER V

DEAR MADAM, *April* 13, 1776.

I AM rather of the latest to present my congratulations to you and Mr. —— on your marriage, but I have not been unmindful of you. My heart has repeatedly wished you all that my pen can express, that the new relation in which the providence of God has placed you, may be blessed to you in every respect, may afford you much temporal comfort, promote your spiritual progress, and enlarge your sphere of usefulness in the world and in the Church.

By this time I suppose visits and ceremonies are pretty well over, and you are beginning to be settled in your new situation. What an important period is a wedding-day !

What an entire change of circumstances does it produce!
What an influence it has upon every day of future life!
How many cares, inquietudes, and trials, does it expose us to,
which we might otherwise have avoided! But they who
love the Lord, and are guided by His Word and providence,
have nothing to fear; for in every state, relation, and
circumstance in life, He will be with them, and will surely
do them good. His grace, which is needful in a single, is
sufficient for a married life. I sincerely wish Mr. —— and
you much happiness together; that you may be mutually
helpmeets, and assist each other in walking as fellow heirs
of the hope of eternal life. Your cares and trials, I know,
must be increased; may your comforts be increased
proportionally! They will be so, if you are enabled heartily
and simply to entreat the Lord to keep your heart fixed near
to Himself. All the temporal blessings and accommodations
He provides to sweeten life, and make our passage through
this wilderness more agreeable, will fail and disappoint us,
and produce us more thorns than roses, unless we can keep
sight of His hand in bestowing them, and hold and use the
gifts in some due subserviency to what we owe to the Giver.
But, alas! we are poor creatures, prone to wander, prone
to admire our gourds, cleave to our cisterns, and think of
building tabernacles, and taking our rest in this polluted
world. Hence the Lord often sees it necessary, in mercy to
His children, to embitter their sweets, to break their cisterns,
send a worm to their gourds, and draw a dark cloud over their
pleasing prospects. His Word tells us, that all here is vanity
compared with the light of His countenance; and if we
cannot or will not believe it upon the authority of His Word,
we must learn it by experience. May He enable you to
settle it in your hearts, that creature-comforts are precarious,
insufficient, and ensnaring; that all good comes from His
hand, and that nothing can do us good, but so far as He is
pleased to make it the instrument of communicating, as
a stream, that goodness which is in Him as a fountain!
Even the bread which we eat, without the influence of His
promise and blessing, would no more support us than a
stone; but His blessing makes every thing good, gives a
tenfold value to our comforts, and greatly diminishes the
weight of every cross. The ring upon your finger is of some

value as gold, but this is not much ; what makes it chiefly valuable to you is, that you consider it as a pledge and token of the relation you bear to him who gave it you. I know no fitter emblem of the light in which we should consider all those good things which the Lord gives us richly to enjoy. When everything we receive from Him is received and prized as a fruit and pledge of His covenant-love, then His bounties, instead of being set up as rivals and idols to draw our heart from Him, awaken us to fresh exercises of gratitude, and furnish us with fresh motives of cheerful obedience every hour.

Time is short, and we live in a dark and cloudy day. When iniquity abounds, the love of many waxes cold : and we have reason to fear the Lord's hand is lifted up in displeasure at our provocations. May He help us to sit loose to all below, and to be found watching unto prayer, for grace to keep our garments undefiled, and to be faithful witnesses for Him in our places ! O ! it is my desire for myself and for all my dear friends, that whilst too many seem content with a half profession, a name to live, an outward attachment to ordinances, and sentiments, and parties, we may be ambitious to experience what the glorious Gospel is capable of effecting, both as to sanctification and consolation, in this state of infirmity ; that we may have our loins girded up, our lamps burning, and, by our simplicity and spirituality, constrain those who know us, to acknowledge that we have been with Jesus, have sat at His feet, and drunk of His Spirit.

I am, &c.

THREE LETTERS

MRS. H——

LETTER I

LONG and often I have thought of writing to you ; now the time is come. May the Lord help me to send a word in season ! I know not how it may be with you, but *He* does, and to Him I look to direct my thoughts accordingly. I suppose you are still in the school of the cross, learning the happy art of extracting *real* good out of *seeming* evil, and to grow tall by stooping. The *flesh* is a sad untoward dunce in this school ; but grace makes the spirit willing to learn by suffering ; yea, it cares not what it endures, so sin may be mortified, and a conformity to the image of Jesus be increased. Surely, when we see the most and the best of the Lord's children so often in heaviness, and when we consider how much He loves them, and what He has done and prepared for them, we may take it for granted that there is a need-be for their sufferings. For it would be easy to His power, and not a thousandth part of what His love intends to do for them, should He make their whole life here, from the hour of their conversion to their death, a continued course of satisfaction and comfort, without anything to distress them from within or without. But were it so, should we not miss many advantages ? In the first place, we should not then be very conformable to our Head, nor be able to say, " As He was, so are we in this world." Methinks a believer would be ashamed to be so utterly unlike his Lord. What ! the master *always* a man of sorrow and acquainted with grief, and the servant *always* happy and full of comfort ! Jesus despised, reproached, neglected, opposed, and betrayed, and His people admired and caressed ; *He* living in the want of all things, and *they* filled with abundance ; *He* sweating blood for anguish, and *they* strangers to distress ! How unsuitable would these things be ! How much better to be called to the honour of experiencing a measure of His sufferings l A cup was put into His hand on our account, and His love engaged Him to drink it for us. The wrath which it contained He drank wholly Himself ; but He left us a little affliction to taste, that we might pledge Him, and remember how He loved us, and how much more He endured for us than He will ever call us to endure for Him. Again, how could we, without sufferings, manifest the nature and truth of Gospel-grace ! What place should we then have for patience, submission, meekness, forbearance, and a readiness to forgive, if we had nothing to try us, either from the hand of the Lord, or from the hand of men ! A Christian without trials would be like a mill without wind or water ; the contrivance and design of the wheel-work within-side would be unnoticed and unknown, without something to put it in motion from without. *N*or would our graces grow, unless they were called out to exercise ; the difficulties we meet with not only prove, but strengthen, the graces of the spirit. If a person were always to sit still, without making use of legs or arms, he would probably wholly lose the power of moving his limbs at last ; but by walking and working he becomes strong and active. So, in a long course of ease, the powers of the new man would certainly languish ; the soul would grow soft, indolent, cowardly, and faint ; and therefore the Lord appoints His children such dispensations as make them strive and struggle, and pant ; they must press through a crowd, swim against a stream, endure hardships, run, wrestle, and fight ; and thus their strength grows in the using.

By these things, likewise, they are made more willing to leave the present world, to which we are prone to cleave too closely in our hearts when our path is very smooth. Had Israel enjoyed their former peace and prosperity in Egypt, when Moses came to invite them to Canaan, I think they would hardly have listened to him. But the Lord suffered them to be brought into great trouble and bondage, and then the news of deliverance was more welcome; yet still they were but half willing, and they carried a love to the flesh-pots of Egypt with them into the wilderness. We are like them : though we say this world is vain and sinful, we are too fond of it ; and though we hope for true happiness only in Heaven, we are often well content to stay longer here. But the Lord sends afflictions one after another to quicken our desires, and to convince us that this cannot be our rest. Sometimes if you drive a bird from one branch of a tree he will hop to another a little higher, and from thence to a third ; but if you continue to disturb him, he will at last take wing, and fly quite away. Thus we, when forced from one creature-comfort, perch upon another, and so on ; but the Lord mercifully follows us with trials, and will not let us rest upon any ; by degrees our desires take a nobler flight, and can be satisfied with nothing short of Himself ; and we say, " To depart and be with Jesus is best of all ! "

I trust you find the name and grace of Jesus more and more precious to you ; His promises more sweet, and your hope in them more abiding ; your sense of your own weakness and unworthiness daily increasing ; your persuasion of his all-sufficiency, to guide, support, and comfort you, more confirmed. You owe your growth in these respects in a great measure to His blessing upon those afflictions which He has prepared for you, and sanctified to you. May you praise Him for all that is past, and trust Him for all that is to come !

                                              I am, &c.

LETTER II

THOUGH I have the pleasure of hearing of you, and sending a remembrance from time to time, I am willing, by this opportunity, to direct a few lines to you, as a more express testimony of my sincere regard.

I think your experience is generally of the fearful doubting cast. Such souls, however, the Lord has given particular charge to his ministers to comfort. He knows our infirmities, and what temptations mean, and as a good Shepherd He expresses a peculiar care and tenderness for the weak of the flock (Isa. xl. 4). But how must I attempt your comfort? Surely not by strengthening a mistake to which we are all too liable, by leading you to look into your own heart for (what you will never find there) something in yourself whereon to ground your hopes, if not wholly, yet at least in part. Rather let me endeavour to lead you out of yourself; let me invite you to look unto Jesus. Should we look for light in our own eyes, or in the sun? Is it indwelling sin distresses you? Then I can tell you (though you know it) that Jesus died for sin and sinners. I can tell you that His blood and righteousness are of infinite value; that His arm is almighty and His compassions infinite; yea, you yourself read His promises every day, and why should you doubt their being fulfilled? If you say you do not question their truth, or that they are accomplished to many, but that you can hardly believe they belong to you, I would ask, what evidence you would require? A voice or an angel from Heaven you do not expect. Consider, if many of the promises are not expressly directed to those to whom they belong. When you read your name on the superscription of this letter you make no scruple to open it : why, then, do you hesitate at embracing the promises of the Gospel, where you read that they are addressed to those who mourn, who hunger and thirst after righteousness, who are poor in spirit, &c., and cannot but be sensible that a gracious God has begun to work these dispositions in your heart? If you say, that though you do at times mourn, hunger, &c., you are afraid you do it not enough, or not aright, consider that this sort of reasoning is very far from the spirit and language of the Gospel; for it is grounded on a secret supposition, that in the forgiveness of sin God has a respect to something more than the atonement and mediation of Jesus; namely, to some previous good qualifications in a sinner's heart, which are to share with the blood of Christ in the honour of salvation. The enemy deceives us in this matter the more easily, because a propensity to the covenant of works is a part of our natural depravity. Depend upon it you will never have a suitable and sufficient sense of

C.   2 C the evil of sin, and of your share in it, so long as you have any sin remaining in you. We must see Jesus as He is before our apprehension of any spiritual truth will be complete. But if we know that we must perish without Christ, and that He is able to save to the uttermost, we know enough to warrant us to cast our souls upon Him, and we dishonour Him by fearing that when we do so He will disappoint our hope. But if you are still perplexed about the high points of election, &c., I would advise you to leave the disposal of others to the great Judge ; and as to yourself, I think I need not say much to persuade you, that if ever you are saved at all, it must be in a way of free and absolute grace. Leave disputes to others ; wait upon the Lord, and He will teach you all things in such degree and time as He sees best. Perhaps you have suffered for taking things too much upon trust from men. Cease from man, whose breath is in his nostrils. One is your master, even Christ. Study and pray over the Bible ; and you may take it as a sure rule, that whatever sentiment makes any part of the Word of God unwelcome to you, is justly to be suspected. Aim at a cheerful spirit. The more you trust God, the better you will serve Him. While you indulge unbelief and suspicion, you weaken your own hands, and discourage others. Be thankful for what He has shown you, and wait upon Him for more : you shall find He has not said, " Seek ye My face " in vain. I heartily commend you to His grace and care,

And am, &c.

LETTER III

At length, and without farther apology for my silence, I sit down to ask you how you fare.´ Afflictions I hear have been your lot ; and if I had not heard so, I should have taken it for granted : for I believe the Lord loves you ; and as many as He loves He chastens. I think you can say, afflictions have been good for you, and I doubt not but you have found strength according to your day ; so that, though you may have been sharply tried, you have not been overpowered. For the Lord has engaged His faithfulness for this to all His children, that He will support them in all their trials : so that the fire shall not consume them, nor the floods drown them (1 Cor. x. 13 ; Isa. xliii. 2).

If you can say thus much, cannot you go a little further, and add, in the apostle's words, " None of these things move me, neither count I my life dear. I rather glory in my infirmities, that the power of Christ may rest upon me : yea, doubtless, I count all things loss and of no regard, for the excellency of the knowledge of Christ Jesus my Lord ; for when I am weak, then am I strong " ? Methinks I hear you say, " God, who comforteth those who are cast down, has comforted my soul ; and as my troubles have abounded, my consolations in Christ have abounded also. He has delivered, He does deliver, and in Him I trust that He will yet deliver me." Surely you can set your seal to these words. The Lord help you then to live more and more a life of faith, to feed upon the promises, and to rejoice in the assurance that all things are yours, and shall surely work for your good.

If I guess right at what passes in your heart, the name of Jesus is precious to you, and this is a sure token of salvation, and that of God. You could not have loved Him, if He had not loved you first. He spoke to you, and said, " Seek My face," before your heart cried to Him, " Thy face, O Lord, will I seek." But you complain, " Alas ! I love Him so little." That very complaint proves that you love Him a great deal ; for if you loved Him but a little, you would think you loved Him enough. A mother loves her child a great deal, yet does not complain for not loving it more ; nay, perhaps she hardly thinks it possible. But such an infinite object is Jesus, that they who love Him better than parents or child, or any earthly relation or comfort, will still think they hardly love Him at all ; because they see such a vast disproportion between the utmost they can give Him, and what in Himself He deserves from them. But I can give you good advice and good news : love Him as well as you can now, and ere long you shall love Him better. O when you see Him as He is, then I am sure you will love Him indeed ! If you want to love Him better now while you are here, I believe I can tell you the secret how this is to be attained : *Trust Him.* The more you trust Him, the better you will love Him. If you ask, farther, How shall I do to trust Him ? I answer, *Try Him :* the more you make trial of Him, the more your trust in Him will be strengthened. Venture upon His promises ; carry them to Him, and see if He will not be as good as His word. But, alas ! Satan and unbelief work the contrary way. We are unwilling to try Him, and therefore unable to trust Him ; and what wonder, then, that our love is faint, for who can love at uncertainties ?

If you are in some measure thankful for what you have received, and hungering and thirsting for more, you are in the frame I would wish for myself ; and I desire to praise the Lord on your behalf. Pray for us. We join in love to you.

I am, &c.

TWO LETTERS

MISS P——

LETTER I

August 17, 1767.

IT is indeed natural to us to wish and to plan, and it is merciful in the Lord to disappoint our plans, and to cross our wishes. For we cannot be safe, much less happy, but in proportion as we are weaned from our own wills, and made simply desirous of being directed by His guidance. This truth (when we are enlightened by His Word) is sufficiently familiar to the judgment ; but we seldom learn to reduce it to practice, without being trained awhile in the school of disappointment. The schemes we form look so plausible and convenient, that when they are broken, we are ready to say, What a pity ! We try again, and with no better success ; we are grieved, and perhaps angry, and plan out another, and so on ; at length, in a course of time, experience and observation begin to convince us, that we are not more able than we are worthy to choose aright for ourselves. Then the Lord's invitation to cast our cares upon Him, and His promise to take care of us, appear valuable ; and when *we* have done planning, *His* plan in our favour gradually opens, and he does more and better for us than we either ask or think. I can hardly recollect a single plan of mine, of which I have not since seen reason to be satisfied, that had it taken place in season and circumstance just as I proposed, it would, humanly speaking, have proved my ruin ; or at least it would have deprived me of the greater good the Lord had designed for me. We judge of things by their present appearances, but the Lord sees them in their consequences; if we could do so likewise, we should be perfectly of His mind; but as we cannot, it is an unspeakable mercy that He will manage for us, whether we are pleased with His management or not; and it is spoken of as one of his heaviest judgments, when He gives any person or people up to the way of their own hearts, and to walk after their own counsels.

Indeed we may admire His patience towards us. If we were blind, and reduced to desire a person to lead us, and should yet pretend to dispute with him, and direct him at every step, we should probably soon weary him, and provoke him to leave us to find the way by ourselves if we could. But our gracious Lord is long-suffering and full of compassion; He bears with our forwardness, yet He will take methods to both shame and to humble us, and to bring us to a confession that He is wiser than we. The great and unexpected benefits He intends us, by all the discipline we meet with, is to tread down our wills, and bring them into subjection to His. So far as we attain to this, we are out of the reach of disappointment; for when the will of God can please us, we shall be pleased every day, and from morning to night; I mean with respect to His dispensations. O the happiness of such a life! I have an idea of it; I hope I am aiming at it, but surely I have not attained it. Self is active in my heart, if it does not absolutely reign there. I profess to believe that one thing is needful and sufficient, and yet my thoughts are prone to wander after a hundred more. If it be true that the light of His countenance is better than life, why am I solicitous about anything else? If He be all-sufficient, and gives me liberty to call Him mine, why do I go a-begging to creatures for help? If He be about my path and bed; if the smallest, as well as the greatest, events in which I am concerned, are under His immediate direction; if the very hairs of my head are numbered; then my care (any farther than a care to walk in the paths of His precepts, and to follow the openings of His providence) must be useless and needless, yea, indeed, sinful and heathenish, burdensome to myself, and dishonourable to my profession. Let us cast down the load we are unable to carry, and if the Lord be our Shepherd, refer all and trust all to Him. Let us endeavour to live to Him and for Him to-day, and be glad that to-morrow, with all that is behind it, is in His hands.

It is storied of Pompey, that when his friends would have dissuaded him from putting to sea in a storm, he answered, It is necessary for me to sail, but it is not necessary for me to live. A pompous speech, in Pompey's sense! He was full of the idea of his own importance, and would rather have died than have taken a step beneath his supposed dignity. But it may be accommodated with propriety to a believer's case. It becomes us to say, It is not necessary for me to be rich, or what the world accounts wise; to be healthy, or admired by my fellow-worms; to pass through life in a state of prosperity and outward comfort;—these things may be, or they may be otherwise, as the Lord in His wisdom shall appoint;—but it is necessary for me to be humble and spiritual, to seek communion with God, to adorn my profession of the Gospel, and to yield submissively to His disposal, in whatever way, whether of service or suffering, He shall be pleased to call me to glorify Him in the world. It is not necessary for me to live long, but highly expedient that whilst I do live I should live to Him. Here, then, I would bound my desires; and here, having His word both for my rule and my warrant, I am secured from asking amiss. Let me have His presence and His Spirit, wisdom to know my calling, and opportunities and faithfulness to improve them; and as to the rest, Lord, help me to say, " What Thou wilt, when Thou wilt, and how Thou wilt."

I am, &c.

LETTER II

Dear Madam,

What a poor, uncertain, dying world is this! What a wilderness in itself! How dark, how desolate, without the light of the Gospel and the knowledge of Jesus! It does not appear so to us in a state of nature, because we are then in a state of enchantment, the magical lantern blinding us with a splendid delusion.

Thus in the desert's dreary waste,
By magic power produc'd in haste,
   As old romances say,
Castles and groves, and music sweet,
   The senses of the trav'ller cheat,
   And stop him in his way.

But while he gazes with surprise,
The charm dissolves, the vision dies ;
   'Twas but enchanted ground ;
Thus, if the Lord our spirit touch,
The world, which promis'd us so much,
   A wilderness is found.

It is a great mercy to be undeceived in time ; and though our gay dreams are at an end, and we awake to everything that is disgustful and dismaying, yet we see a highway through the wilderness ;] a powerful guard, an infallible Guide at hand to conduct us through ; and we can discern, beyond the limits of the wilderness, a better land, where we shall be at rest and at home. What will the difficulties we meet by the way then signify ? The remembrance of them will only remain to heighten our sense of the love, care, and power of our Saviour and Leader. O how shall we then admire, adore, and praise Him, when He shall condescend to unfold to us the beauty, propriety, and harmony of the whole train of His dispensations towards us, and give us a clear retrospect of all the way, and all the turns of our pilgrimage !

In the mean while, the best method of adorning our profession, and of enjoying peace in our souls, is simply to trust Him, and absolutely to commit ourselves and our all to His management. By casting our burdens upon Him, our spirits become light and cheerful ; we are freed from a thousand anxieties and inquietudes, which are wearisome to our minds, and which, with respect to events, are *needless* for us, yea *useless*. But though it may be easy to speak of this trust, and it appears to our judgment perfectly right and reasonable, the actual attainment is a great thing ; and especially so, to trust the Lord, not by fits and starts, surrendering one day and retracting the next, but to abide by our surrender, and go habitually trusting through all the changes we meet, knowing that His love, purpose,

and promise are unchangeable. Some little faintings, per-
haps, none are freed from ; but I believe a power of trusting
the Lord in good measure at all times, and living quietly
under the shadow of His wing, is what the promise warrants
us to expect, if we seek it by diligent prayer ; if not all at
once, yet by a gradual increase. May it be your experience
and mine !

I am, &c.

FOURTEEN LETTERS

TO THE

REV. MR. B——

LETTER I

DEAR AND REV. SIR   *Jan. 27, 1778.*

I CALL you *dear* because I love you, and I shall continue
to style you *Reverend* as long as you dignify me with that title.
It is indeed a pretty sounding epithet, and forms a striking
contrast in the usual application.   The inhabitants of the
moon (if there be any) have perhaps no idea how many
Reverend, Right Reverend, and Most Reverend sinners
we have in Europe.   And yet you are reverend, and I revere
you, because I believe the Lord liveth in you, and has
chosen you to be a temple of His presence, and an instru-
ment of His grace.

I hope the two sermons you preached in London were
made useful to others, and the medicines you took there
were useful to yourself.   I am glad to hear you are safe at
home, and something better.   Cheerful spring is approaching,
then I hope the barometer of your spirits will rise.   But the
presence of the Lord can bring a pleasanter spring than
April, and even in the depth of winter.

At present it is January with me, both within and without.
The outward sun shines and locks pleasant, but his beams
are faint, and too feeble to dissolve the frost.   So is it in
my heart !   I have many bright and pleasant beams of truth
in my view, but cold predominates in my frost-bound spirit,
and they have but little power to warm me.   I could tell a
stranger something about Jesus that would perhaps astonish
him ; such a glorious Person ! such wonderful love ! such
humiliation ! such a death ! and then what He is now

in Himself, and what He is to His people. What a sun! What a shield! What a root! What a life! What a Friend! My tongue can run on upon these subjects sometimes; and could my heart keep pace with it, I should be the happiest fellow in the country. Stupid creature! to know these things so well, and yet be no more affected with them! Indeed I have reason to be upon ill terms with myself. It is strange that pride should ever find anything in my experience to feed upon; but this completes my character for folly, vileness, and inconsistence, that I am not only poor, but proud; and though I am convinced I am a very wretch, a nothing before the Lord, I am prone to go forth among my fellow-creatures as though I were wise and good.

You wonder what I am doing; and well you may; I am sure you would, if you lived with me. Too much of my time passes in busy idleness, too much in waking dreams. I aim at something; but hindrances from within and without make it difficult for me to accomplish anything. I dare not say I am absolutely idle, or that I wilfully waste much of my time. I have seldom one hour free from interruption. Letters come that must be answered, visitants that must be received, business that must be attended to. I have a good many sheep and lambs to look after, sick and afflicted souls dear to the Lord; and, therefore, whatever stands still, these must not be neglected. Amongst these various avocations, night comes before I am ready for noon; and the week closes, when, according to the state of my business, it should not be more than Tuesday. O precious, irrecoverable time! O that I had more wisdom in redeeming and improving thee! Pray for me, that the Lord may teach me to serve Him better.   I am, &c.

LETTER II

DEAR SIR,   *April* 28, 1778.

I was not much disappointed at not meeting you at home. I knew how difficult it is to get away from ———, if you are seen in the street after breakfast. The horse-leech has three daughters, saying, Give, give : the cry there is, Preach, preach. When you have told them all, you must tell them more, or tell it them over again. Whoever will find tongue, they will engage to find ears. Yet I do not blame this importunity ; I wish you were teased more with it in your own town : for though, undoubtedly, there are too many both at N——— and here, whose religion lies too much in hearing, yet in many it proceeds from a love to the truth, and to the ministers, who dispense it. And I generally observe, that they who are not willing to hear a stranger (if his character is known) are indifferent enough about hearing their own minister.

I beg you to pray for me. I am a poor creature full of wants. I seem to need the wisdom of Solomon, the meekness of Moses, and the zeal of Paul to enable me to make full proof of my ministry. But, alas ! you may guess the rest.

Send me " The Way to Christ." I am willing to be a debtor to the wise and unwise, to doctors and shoemakers, if I can get a hint, or a *nota bene*, from any one, without respect to parties. When a house is on fire, Churchmen, Dissenters, Methodists, Papists, Moravians, and Mystics, are all welcome to bring water. At such times nobody asks, Pray, friend, whom do hear ? or, What do you think of the five points ? &c., &c.

                                                                I am, &c.

LETTER III

My Dear Friend,   *July* 17, 1778.

I know not that I have anything to say worth postage, though, perhaps, had I seen you before you set off, something might have occurred which will not be found in my letter. Yet I write a line because you bid me, and are now in a far, foreign country. You will find Mr. ——— a man to your tooth, but he is in Mr. W———'s connexion. So I remember Venerable Bede, after giving a high character of some contemporary, kicks his full pail of milk down, and reduces him almost to nothing, by adding, in the close, to this purpose : " But, unhappy man, he did not keep Easter our way ! " A fig for all connexions, say I, and say you, but that which is formed by the bands, joints, and ligaments, the apostle speaks of, Eph. iv. 16, *et alibi*. Therefore I venture to repeat it, that Mr. ———, though he often sees and hears Mr. W———, and I believe loves him well, is a good man ; and you will see the invisible mark upon his forehead, if you examine him with your spiritual spectacles.

Now, methinks, I do pity you : I see you melted with heat, stifled with smoke, stunned with noise. Ah ! what a change from the brooks, and bushes, and birds, and green fields, to which you had lately access ! Of old they used to retire into the deserts for mortification. If I were to set myself a moderate penance, it might be to spend a fortnight in London in the height of summer. But I forget myself : I hope the Lord is with you, and then all places are alike. He makes the dungeon and the stocks comfortable, Acts xvi. ; yea, a fiery furnace and a lion's den. A child of God in London seems to be in all these trying situations : but Jesus can preserve His own. I honour the grace of God in those few (comparatively few, I fear) who preserve their garments undefiled in that Sardis. The air is filled with infection, and it is by special power and miraculous preservation they enjoy spiritual health, when so many sicken and fall around them on the right hand and on the left. May the Lord preserve you from the various epidemical soul-diseases which abound where you are, and be your comfort and defence from day to day !

Last week we had a lion in town. I went to see him. He was wonderfully tame ; as familiar with his keeper, as docile and obedient as a spaniel. Yet the man told me he had his surly fits, when they durst not touch him. No looking-glass could express my face more justly than this lion did my heart. I could trace every feature, as wild and fierce by nature, yea, much more so, but grace has in some measure tamed me, I know and love my Keeper, and sometimes watch His looks that I may learn His will. But, oh ! I have my surly fits too ; seasons when I relapse into the savage again, as though I had forgotten all.

I am, &c.

LETTER IV

My Dear Friend,   *July* 13, 1778.

As we are so soon to meet, and as I have nothing very important to communicate, and many things occur which might demand my time, I have no other plea to offer, either to you or myself, for writing again, but because I love you.

I' pity the unknown considerable minister, with whom you smoked your morning pipe. But we must take men and things as we find them ; and when we fall in company with those from whom we can get little other good, it is likely we shall at least find occasion for the exercise of patience and charity towards them, and of thankfulness to Him who hath made us to differ. And these are good things, though perhaps the occasion may not be pleasant. Indeed, a Christian, if in a right spirit, is alway in his Lord's school, and may learn either a new lesson, or how to practise an old one, by everything he sees or hears, provided he does not wilfully tread upon forbidden ground. If he were constrained to spend a day with the poor creatures in the common side of Newgate, though he could not talk with them of what God has done for his soul, he might be more sensible of His mercy by the contrast he would observe around him. He might rejoice for himself, and mourn over them, and thus perhaps get as much benefit as from the best sermon he ever heard.

It is necessary, all things taken together, to have connection more or less with narrow-minded people. If they are, notwithstanding their prejudices, civil to us, they have a right to some civility from us. We may love them though we cannot admire them ; and pick something good from them, notwithstanding we see much to blame. It is perhaps the highest triumph we can obtain over bigotry, when we are able to bear with bigots themselves. For they are a set of troublesome folks, whom Mr. Self is often very forward to exclude from the comprehensive candour and tenderness which he professes to exercise towards those who differ from him.

I am glad your present home (a believer should be always

at home) is pleasant ; the rooms large and airy ; your host and hostess kind and spiritual ; and, upon the whole, all things as well as you could expect to find them, considering where you are. I could give you much such an account of my usual head-quarters in the city ; but still London is London. I do not wish you to live there, for my own sake as well as yours ; but if the Lord should so appoint, I believe He can make you easy there, and enable me to make a tolerable shift without you. Yet I certainly should miss you ; for I have no person in this neighbourhood with whom my heart so thoroughly unites in spirituals, though there are many whom I love. But conversation with most Christians is something like going to court ; where, except you are dressed exactly according to a prescribed standard, you will either not be admitted, or must expect to be heartily stared at. But you and I can meet and converse, *sans contrainte*, in an undress, without fear of offending, or being accounted offenders, for a word out of place, and not exactly in the pink of the mode.

I know not how it is : I think my sentiments and experience are as orthodox and Calvinistical as need be ; and yet I am a sort of speckled bird among my Calvinist brethren. I am a mighty good Churchman, but pass amongst such as a Dissenter in prunello. On the other hand, the Dissenters (many of them I mean) think me defective, either in understanding or in conscience, for staying where I am. Well, there is a middle party called Methodist, but neither do my dimensions exactly fit with them. I am somehow disqualified for claiming a full brotherhood with any party. But there are a few among all parties who bear with me and love me, and with this I must be content at present. But so far as they love the Lord Jesus, I desire, and by His grace I determine (with or without their leave) to love them all. Party-walls, though stronger than the wall of Babylon, must come down in the general ruin, when the earth and all its works shall be burnt up, if not sooner.

I am, &c.

LETTER V

My Dear Sir, *July*, 1778.

I was glad to hear that you were again within a few miles of me ; and I would praise the Lord, who led you out and brought you home in safety, and preserved all in peace while you were abroad, so that you find nothing very painful to embitter your return. Many go abroad well, but return no more. The affectionate wife, the prattling children listen for the well-known sound of papa's foot at the door ; but they listen in vain : a fall or a fever has intercepted him, and he is gone far, far away. Some leave all well when they go from home ; but how changed, how trying the scene, when they come back ! In their absence the Lord has taken away the desire of their eyes with a stroke ; or, perhaps, ruffians have plundered and murdered their family in the dead of the night, or the fire has devoured their habitation.

Ah ! how large and various is the list of evils and calamities with which sin has filled the world ! You and I and ours escape them ; we stand, though in a field of battle where thousands fall around us, because the Lord is pleased to keep us. May He have the praise, and may we only live to love and serve Him !

Mrs. —— has been very ill, and my heart often much pained while you have been absent. But the Lord has removed His hand ; she is much better, and I hope she will be seen in His house to-morrow. I have few trials in my own person ; but when the Lord afflicts her, I feel it. It is a mercy that He has made us *one*; but it exposes us to many a pain, which we might have missed if we cared but little for each other. Alas ! there is usually an ounce of the golden calf of idolatry and dependence, in all the warm regard we bear to creatures. *Hinc illæ lacrymæ !* For this reason, our sharpest trials usually spring from our most valued comforts.

I cannot come to you, therefore you must come hither speedily. Be sure to bring Mr. B—— with you. I shall be very glad to see him ; and I long to thank him for clothing my book. It looks well on the outside, and I hope to find it sound and savoury. I love the author, and that is a step

towards liking the book. For where we love, we are gener-
ally tender, and favourably take everything by the best
handle, and are vastly full of candour : but if we are pre-
judiced against the man, the poor book is half condemned
before we open it. It had need be written well, for it will
be read with a suspicious eye, as if we wished to find treason
in every page. I am glad I diverted and profited you by
calling myself a speckled bird. I can tell you, such a bird
in this day, that wears the full colour of no sect or party, is
rara avis ; if not quite so scarce as the phœnix, yet to be met
with but here and there. It is impossible I should be all of
a colour, when I have been a debtor to all sorts ; and, like
the jay in the fable, have been beholden to most of the
birds in the air for a feather or two. Church and Meeting,
Methodist and Moravian, may all perceive something in
my coat taken from them. None of them are angry with
me for borrowing from *them* ; but then, why could I not be
content with *their* colour, without going amongst other
flocks and coveys, to make myself such a motley figure ?
Let them be angry : if I have culled the best feathers from
all, then surely I am finer than any.

I am, &c.

LETTER VI

DEAR SIR, *Aug.,* 1778.

IF the Lord affords health ; if the weather be tolerable ;
if no unforeseen change takes place ; if no company comes
in upon me to-night (which sometimes unexpectedly hap-
pens) ; with these provisos, Mr. S.—— and I have engaged to
travel to —— on Monday next, and hope to be with you by
or before eleven o'clock.

In such a precarious world, it is needful to form our
plans at two days' distance, with precaution and exceptions
(James iv. 13.) However, if it be the Lord's will to bring us
together, and if the proposed interview be for His glory and
our good, then I am sure nothing shall prevent it. And who
in his right wits would wish either to visit or be visited upon

C. 2 D

any other terms ?　O ! if we could but be pleased with His
will, we might be pleased from morning to night, and every
day in the year !

Pray for a blessing upon our coming together.　It would
be a͏̆ pity to walk ten miles to pick straws, or to come with
our empty vessels upon our heads, saying, " We have found
no water."

I am, &c.

LETTER VII

YOUR letters are always welcome ;　the last doubly so,
for being unexpected.　If you never heard before of a line
of yours being useful, I will tell you for once, that I get some
pleasure and instruction whenever you write to me.　And I
see not but your call to letter-writing is as clear as mine,
at least when you are able to put pen to paper.

I must say something to your queries about 2 Sam.
xiv.　I do not approve of the scholastic distinctions about
inspiration, which seem to have a tendency to explain away
the authority and certainty of one-half of the Bible at least.
Though the penmen of Scripture were ever so well informed
of some facts, they would, as you observe, need express, full,
and infallible inspiration, to teach them which the Lord
would have selected and recorded for the use of the Church,
amongst many others which to themselves might appear
equally important.

However, with respect to historical passages, I dare not
pronounce positively that any of them are, even in the literal
sense, unworthy of the wisdom of the Holy Ghost, and the
dignity of inspiration.　Some, yea, many of them, have often
appeared trivial to me ; but I check the thought, and charge it
to my own ignorance and temerity.　It must have some
importance, because I read it in God's Book.　On the other
hand, though I will not deny that they may all have a
spiritual and mystical sense (for I am no more qualified to
judge of the deep things of the Spirit, than to tell you what

is passing this morning at the bottom of the sea), yet if, with my present modicum of light, I should undertake to expound many passages in a mystical sense, I fear such a judge as you would think my interpretations fanciful and not well supported. I suppose I should have thought the Bible complete, though it had not informed me of the death of Rebekah's nurse, or where she was buried. But some tell me that Deborah is the law, and that by the oak I am to understand the cross of Christ : and I remember to have heard of a preacher who discovered a type of Christ crucified in Absalom hanging by the hair on another oak. I am quite a mole when compared with these eagle-eyed divines ; and must often content myself with plodding upon the lower ground of *accommodation* and *allusion* ; except when the New Testament writers assure me what the mind of the Holy Ghost was. I can find the Gospel with more confidence in the history of Sarah and Hagar, than in that of Leah and Rachael ; though without Paul's help, I should have considered them both as family-squabbles, recorded chiefly to illustrate the general truth, that vanity and vexation of spirit are incident to the best men, in the most favoured situations. And I think there is no part of Old Testament history from which I could not (the Lord helping me) draw observations, that might be suitable to the pulpit, and profitable to His people : so I might perhaps from Livy or Tacitus. But then, with the Bible in my hands, I go upon sure grounds : I am certain of the facts I speak from, that they really did happen. I may likewise depend upon the springs and motives of actions, and not amuse myself and my hearers with speeches which were never spoken, and motives which were never thought of, till the historian rummaged his pericranium for something to embellish his work. I doubt not but were you to consider Joab's courtly conduct only in a literal sense, how it tallied with David's desire, and how gravely and graciously he granted himself a favour, while he professed to oblige Joab ; I say, in this view you would be able to illustrate many important scriptural doctrines, and to show that the *passage* is important to those who are engaged in studying the anatomy of the human heart.

I am, &c.

LETTER VIII

My Dear Friend,   *Oct.* 27, 1778.

I have been witness to a great and important revolution this morning, which took place while the greatest part of the world was asleep. Like many state-revolutions, its first beginnings were almost undiscernible ; but the progress, though gradual, was steady, and the event decisive. A while ago darkness reigned. Had a man then dropped, for the first time, into our world, he might have thought himself banished into a hopeless dungeon. How could he expect light to rise out of such a state ? And when he saw the first glimmering of dawn in the east, how could he promise himself that it was the forerunner of such a glorious sun as has since arisen ? With what wonder would such a newcomer observe the bounds of his view enlarging, and the distinctness of objects increasing, from one minute to another ; and how well content would he be to part with the twinklings of the stars, when he had the broad day all around him in exchange ! I cannot say this revolution is extraordinary, because it happens every morning ; but surely it is astonishing, or rather it would be so, if man was not astonishingly stupid.

Such strangers once were we. Darkness, gross darkness, covered us. How confined were our views ! And even the things which were within our reach we could not distinguish. Little did we then think what a glorious day we were appointed to see ; what an unbounded prospect would ere long open before us ! We knew not that there was a Sun of Righteousness, and that He would dawn, and rise, and shine upon our hearts. And as the idea of what we see now was then hidden from us, so at present we are almost equally at a loss how to form any conception of the stronger light and brighter prospects which we wait and hope for. Comparatively we are in the dark still ; at the most, we have but a dim twilight, and see nothing clearly ; but it is the dawn of immortality, and a sure presage and earnest of glory.

Thus, at times, it seems, a darkness that may be felt broods over your natural spirits ; but when the Day-star rises upon your heart, you see and rejoice in His light.

You have days as well as nights; and after a few more vicissitudes, you will take your flight to the regions of everlasting light, where your sun will go down no more. Happy you, and happy I, if I shall meet you there, as I trust I shall. How shall we love, and sing, and wonder, and praise the Saviour's name!

Last Sunday a young man died here of extreme old age, at twenty-five. He laboured hard to ruin a good constitution, and unhappily succeeded; yet amused himself with the hopes of recovery almost to the last. We have a sad knot of such poor creatures in this place, who labour to stifle each other's convictions, and to ruin themselves and associates, soul and body. How industriously is Satan served! I was formerly one of his most active under-tempters. Not content with running the broad way myself, I was indefatigable in enticing others; and had my influence been equal to my wishes, I would have carried all the human race with me. And doubtless some have perished, to whose destruction I was greatly instrumental, by tempting them to sin, and by poisoning and hardening them with principles of infidelity; and yet I was spared. When I think of the most with whom I spent my unhappy days of ignorance, I am ready to say, " I only am escaped alive to tell thee." Surely I have not half the activity and zeal in the service of Him who snatched me as a brand out of the burning, as I had in the service of His enemy. Then the whole stream of my endeavours and affections went one way; now my best desires are continually crossed, counter-acted, and spoiled, by the sin which dwelleth in me: then the tide of a corrupt nature bore me along; now I have to strive and swim against it. The Lord cut me short of opportunities, and placed me where I could do but little mischief; had my abilities and occasions been equal to my heart, I should have been a Voltaire and a Tiberius in one character, a monster of profaneness and licentiousness. " O to grace how great a debtor!" A common drunkard or profligate is a petty sinner to what I was. I had the ambition of a Cæsar or an Alexander, and wanted to rank in wickedness among the foremost of the human race. When you have read this, praise the Lord for His mercy to the chief of sinners, and pray that I may have grace to be faithful. But

I have rambled. I meant to tell you, that on Sunday afternoon I preached from *Why will ye die ?* Ezek. xxxiii. 10, 11. I endeavoured to show poor sinners, that if they died, it was because they *would*, and if they *would*, they *must*. I was much affected for a time : I could hardly speak for weeping, and some wept with me. From some, alas! I can no more draw a tear or a relenting thought, than from a millstone.

I am, &c.

LETTER IX

My Dear Friend,   *Nov.* 27. 1778.

You are a better expositor of Scripture than of my speeches, if you really inferred from my last that I think you shall die soon. I cannot say positively you will not die soon, because life at all times is uncertain ; however, according to the doctrine of probabilities, I think, and always thought, you bid fair enough to outlive me. The gloomy tinge of your weak spirits led you to consider yourself much worse in point of health than you appear to me to be.

In the other point I dare be more positive, that, die when you will, you will die in the Lord. Of this I have not the least doubt ; and I believe you doubt of it less, if possible, than I, except in those darker moments when the atrabilious humour prevails.

I heartily sympathize with you in your complaints ; but I see you in safe hands. The Lord loves you, and will take care of you. He who raises the dead, can revive your spirits when you are cast down. He who sets bounds to the sea, and says, " Hitherto shalt thou come and no further," can limit and moderate that gloom which sometimes distresses you. He knows why He permits you to be thus exercised. I cannot assign the reasons, but I am sure they are worthy of His wisdom and love, and that you will hereafter see, and say, He has done all things well. If I were as wise as your philosopher, I might say a great deal about a melancholy complexion ; but I love not to puzzle myself with second causes, while the first cause is at hand, which sufficiently accounts for every phenomenon in a believer's experience. Your constitution, your situation, your temper, your distemper, all that is either comfortable or painful in your lot, is of His appointment. The hairs of your head are all numbered : the same power which produced the planet Jupiter is necessary to the production of a single hair, nor can one of them fall to the ground without His notice, any more than the stars can fall from their orbits. In providence, no less than in creation, He is *Maximus in minimis.* Therefore fear not ; only believe. Our sea may sometimes be stormy, but we have an infallible Pilot, and shall infallibly gain our port.

I am, &c.

LETTER X

MY DEAR FRIEND, *Feb. 23, 1779.*

ON Saturday, and not before, I heard you had been ill. Had the news reached me sooner, I should have sent you a line sooner. I hope you will be able to inform me that you are now better, and that the Lord continues to do you good by every dispensation He allots you. Healing and wounding are equally from His hand, and equally tokens of His love and care over us. I have but little affliction in my own person, but I have been often chastened of late by proxy. The Lord, for His people's sake, is still pleased to give me health and strength for public service ; but when I need the rod, He lays it upon Mrs. ——. In this way I have felt much without being disabled or laid aside. But He has heard prayer for her likewise, and for more than a fortnight past she has been comfortably well. I lay at least one half of her sickness to my own account. She suffers for me, and I through her. It is, indeed, touching me in a tender part. Perhaps, if I could be more wise, watchful, and humble, it might contribute more to the re-establishment of her health, than all the medicines she takes.

I somehow neglected to confer with you about the business of the fast-day. The last of my three sermons, when I had, as I expected, the largest congregation, was a sort of historical discourse from Deut. xxxii. 15, in which, running over the leading national events from the time of Wickliff, I endeavoured to trace the steps and turns by which the Lord has made us a fat and thriving people, and in the event blessed us beyond His favourite Jeshurun of old, with civil and religious liberty, peace, honour, and prosperity, and Gospel privileges. How fat we were when the war terminated in the year 1763, and how we have kicked and forsaken the Rock of our salvation of late years! Then followed a sketch of our present state and spirit as a people, both in a religious and political view. I started at the picture while I drew it, though it was a very inadequate representation. We seemed willing to afflict our souls for one day, as Dr. Lowth reads Isa. lviii. 5. But the next day things returned into their former channel ; the fast and the occasion seemed presently forgotten, except by a few simple souls, who are despised and hated by the rest for their preciseness, because they think sin ought to be lamented every day in the year.

Who would envy Cassandra her gift of prophecy upon the terms she had it, that her declarations, however true, should meet with no belief or regard ? It is the lot of Gospel ministers, with respect to the bulk of their hearers. But blessed be the grace which makes a few exceptions ! Here and there, one will hear, believe, and be saved. Every one of these is worth a world ; and our success with a few should console us for all our trials.

Come and see us as soon as you can, only not to-morrow, for I am then to go to T——. My Lord, the Great Shepherd, has one sheep there, related to the fold under my care. I can seldom see her, and she is very ill : I expect she will be soon removed to the pasture above. Our love to Mrs. B——.

Believe me yours, &c.

LETTER XI

MY DEAR FRIEND,   *April* 23, 1779.

MAY I not style myself a friend, when I remember you
after the interval of several weeks since I saw you, and
through a distance of three-score miles ? But the truth is,
you have been neither absent nor distant from my heart
a day. Your idea has travelled with me ; you are a kind
of familiar, very often before the eye of my mind. This,
I hope, may be admitted as a proof of friendship.

I know the Lord loves you, and you know it likewise :
every affliction affords you a fresh proof of it. How wise
His management in our trials ! How wisely adjusted in
season, weight, continuance, to answer His gracious purposes
in sending them ! How unspeakably better to be at His
disposal than at your own ! So you say ; so you think ;
so you find. You trust in Him, and shall not be disappointed.
Help me with your prayers, that I may trust Him too, and
be at length enabled to say without reserve, " What Thou
wilt, when Thou wilt, how Thou wilt." I had rather speak
these three sentences from my heart, in my mother-tongue,
than be master of all the languages in Europe.

I am, &c.

LETTER XII

MY DEAR FRIEND,   *Aug.* 19, 1779.

AMONG the rest of temporal mercies, I would be thank-
ful for pen, ink, and paper, and the convenience of the
post, by which means we can waft a thought to a friend
when we cannot get at him. My will has been good to see
you ; but you must accept the will for the deed. The Lord
has not permitted me.

I have been troubled of late with the rheumatism in my
left arm. Mine is a sinful, vile body, and it is a mercy that
any part of it is free from pain. It is virtually the seat and
subject of all diseases ; but the Lord holds them like wild

beasts in a chain, under a strong restraint; were that restraint taken off, they would rush upon their prey from every quarter, and seize upon every limb, member, joint, and nerve, at once. Yet, though I am a sinner, and though my whole texture is so frail and exposed, I have enjoyed for a number of years an almost perfect exemption both from pain and sickness. This is wonderful indeed, even in my own eyes.

But my soul is far from being in a healthy state. There I have laboured, and still labour, under a complication of diseases; and, but for the care and skill of an infallible Physician, I must have died the death long ago. At this very moment my soul is feverish, dropsical, paralytic. I feel a loss of appetite, a disinclination both to food and to medicine: so that I am alive by miracle; yet I trust I shall not die, but live, and declare the works of the Lord. When I faint He revives me again. I am sure He is able, and I trust He has promised, to heal me; but how inveterate must my disease be, that is not yet subdued, even under His management!

Well, my friend, there is a land where the inhabitants shall no more say, "I am sick." Then my eyes will not be dim, nor my ear heavy, nor my heart hard.

> One sight of Jesus as he is
> Will strike all sin for ever dead.

Blessed be His name for this glorious hope! May it cheer us under all our present uneasy feelings, and reconcile us to every cross! The way must be right, however rough, that leads to such a glorious end.

O for more of that gracious influence, which in a moment can make the wilderness-soul rejoice and blossom like the rose! I want something which neither critics nor commentators can help me to. The Scripture itself, whether I read it in Hebrew, Greek, French, or English, is a sealed book in all languages unless the Spirit of the Lord is present to expound and apply. Pray for me. No prayer seems more suitable to me than that of the Psalmist: "Bring my soul out of prison, that I may praise Thy name."

I am, &c.

LETTER XIII

MY DEAR FRIEND,   *August* 28, 1779.

I WANT to hear how you are. I hope your complaint is not worse than when I saw you. I hope you are easier, and will soon find yourself able to move about again. I should be sorry, if to the symptoms of the stone you should have the gout superadded in your right hand ; for then you will not be able to write to me.

We go on much as usual ; sometimes very poorly, sometimes a little better ; the latter is the case to-day. My rheumatism continues ; but it is very moderate and tolerable. The Lord deals gently with us, and gives us many proofs that He does not afflict willingly.

The days speed away apace ; each one bears away its own burden with it, to return no more. Both pleasures and pains that are past are gone for ever. What is yet future will likewise be soon past. The end is coming. O to realize the thought, and to judge of things now in some measure suitable to the judgment we shall form of them, when we are about to leave them all ! Many things which now either elate or depress us, will then appear to be trifles light as air.

One thing is needful : to have our hearts united to the Lord in humble faith ; to set Him always before us ; to rejoice in Him as our Shepherd and our portion ; to submit to all His appointments, not of necessity, because He is stronger than we, but with a cheerful acquiescence, because He is wise and good, and loves us better than we do our-selves ; to feed upon His truth ; to have our understandings, wills, affections, imaginations, memory, all filled and impressed with the great mysteries of redeeming love ; to do all for Him, to receive all from Him, to find all in Him. I have mentioned many things, but they are all comprised in one, a life of faith in the Son of God. We are empty vessels in ourselves, but we cannot remain empty. Except Jesus dwells in our hearts, and fills them with His power and presence, they will be filled with folly, vanity, and vexation.

I am, &c.

LETTER XIV

My Dear Friend,   *October* 26, 1779.

BEING to go out of town to-day, I started up before light to write to you, and hoped to have sent you a long letter ; when, behold ! I could not get at any paper. I am now waiting for a peep at Mr. B—— at his lodgings, who came to town last night ; and I shall write as fast as I can till I see him.

I feel for you a little in the same way as you feel for yourself. I bear a friendly sympathy in your late sharp and sudden trial. I mourn with that part of you which mourns : but, at the same time, I rejoice in the proof you have, and which you give, that the Lord is with you of a truth. I rejoice on your account, to see you supported and comforted, and enabled to say, " He has done all things well." I rejoice on my own account. Such instances of His faithfulness and all-sufficiency are very encouraging. We must all expect hours of trouble in our turn. We must all feel in our concernments the vanity and uncertainty of creature-comforts. What a mercy is it to know from our own past experience, and to have it confirmed to us by the experience of others, that the Lord is good, a strong hold in the day of trouble, and that He knoweth them that trust in Him ! Creatures are like candles, they waste while they afford us a little light, and we see them extinguished in their sockets one after another. But the light of the sun makes amends for them all. The Lord is so rich that He easily can, so good that He certainly will, give His children more than He ever will take away. When His gracious voice reaches the heart, " It is I, be not afraid ; be still, and know that I am God ; " when He gives us an impression of His wisdom, power, love, and care, then the storm which attempts to rise in our natural passions is hushed into a calm ; the flesh continues to feel, but the spirit is made willing. And something more than submission takes place, —a sweet resignation and acquiescence, and even a joy that we have anything which we value, to surrender to His call.

Yours, &c.

MORGAN AND SCOTT, LD., LONDON, ENGLAND

From Morgan & Scott's List.

REVIVALS OF RELIGION.

By CHARLES G. FINNEY. With the Author's Revisions and Corrections. Edited, with Introductory and Original Notes, by W. H. HARDING. Printed in bold, readable type. Cloth, 2s. 6d.

OLD-WORLD STORIES:

Retold for To-day. By GEORGE E. MORGAN, M.A. Vivid and practical studies, calculated to stimulate interest in somewhat less familiar portions of the Old Testament. Beautifully Illustrated. 3s. 6d.

WHILE WE'RE YOUNG:

Talks with Young People. By the same Author. Written in a friendly and sympathetic style, it readily wins the confidence of boys and girls. 1s. 6d. net.

GLIMPSES OF FOUR CONTINENTS:

The Travels of R. C. Morgan, Founder of "The Christian." By MRS. R. C. MORGAN. With Four Photogravures and Sixteen Half-Tone Illustrations. Cloth, 2s. 6d. net.

OVERWEIGHTS OF JOY:

Mission Work in Southern India. By AMY WILSON-CARMICHAEL, Keswick Missionary, C.E.Z.M.S., Author of " Things as They Are," Preface by Rev. T. WALKER, C.M.S. Thirty-four beautiful Illustrations. Cloth Boards, 2s. 6d. net (*post free*, 2/10).

THINGS AS THEY ARE:

Mission Work in Southern India. By AMY WILSON-CARMICHAEL. (Companion Volume to " Overweights of Joy.") With Preface by Dr. EUGENE STOCK. Admirably Illustrated. Ninth Edition. Paper, 1s. 6d. net (*post free*, 1/9) ; Cloth Boards, 2s. 6d. net (*post free*, 2/10).

MORGAN & SCOTT LD., 12, PATERNOSTER BUILDINGS, LONDON, E.C.

THE PUBLICATIONS OF
MORGAN & SCOTT Lᴅ.

Comprise—

BIBLES in various sizes and styles of Binding.

SACRED SONGS AND SOLOS, By Ira D. Sankey.

THE SONG COMPANION TO THE SCRIPTURES, Compiled by Dr. Campbell Morgan.

HELPS FOR CHRISTIAN WORKERS.

AIDS TO BIBLE STUDY.

WORKS ON CHRISTIAN EVIDENCES.

MY COUNSELLOR : Daily Readings for Morning and Evening.

BIBLE CHARACTERS AND EXPOSITIONS.

DEVOTIONAL VOLUMES.

BOOKS ON MISSIONARY ENTERPRISE.

CHRISTIAN BIOGRAPHIES.

HYMN AND TUNE BOOKS.

FINE ART PUBLICATIONS :
Scripture Text Cards, Wall Mottoes, Sunday School Reward Sheets, etc. New and Artistic Designs, Specially Selected Texts and Verses.

₊ A Complete List of the Publications of MORGAN AND SCOTT LD. will be sent post free to any address on application to 12, Paternoster Buildings, London, E.C.

43519769R00242

Made in the USA
Middletown, DE
11 May 2017